Advance Praise for THE POSTZIO

"THE POSTZIONISM DEBATES is one of the most important books on Israeli culture that will be published in the next few years. It documents for the first time in English major shifts in Israeli culture, as well as peripherally in Jewish political culture outside of Israel. A Foucauldian study of the discourse of post-Zionism in its varied forms, as a shift from the unqualified knee-jerk Zionism endemic only fifteen or so years ago, Silberstein's book prepares the way for a rethinking of Jewish politics at the end of the 20th century."
—**Daniel Boyarin,** author of *Unheroic Conduct: The Rise of Heterosexuality and the Invention of the Jewish Man*

"In the past decade a younger generation of Israeli scholars began opening a window on the power implications of the conventional Zionist discourse. In **THE POSTZIONISM DEBATES,** Laurence Silberstein has accomplished a formidable task by providing a sensitive and insightful account of these academic debates and literary works, the ways in which they problematized conventional academic discourse, and the means they propose for integrating marginalized or excluded groups into a broader Israeli cultural identity. This is **one of the best scholarly books on contemporary Israel.**"
—**Gershon Shafir,** author of *Land, Labor, and the Origins of the Israeli-Palestinian Conflict, 1882–1914*

"This is **a wonderfully systematic, clear, and passionate exploration** of recent (and heated) Israeli debates about the very nature of Israel and 'the political discursive contexts in which they thrive.' It clearly seeks to broaden the pool of readers who find Israel interesting, even compelling. But it also offers something else to those not especially taken with Israeli debates—namely, the chance to see how politically involved intellectuals using poststructuralist or postmodernist thinking re-imagine the society in which they live and about which they care deeply. Seemingly abstract theories will never look the same again!"
—**Virginia R. Dominguez,** author of *People as Subject, People as Object: Selfhood & Peoplehood in Contemporary Israel*

"Laurence Silberstein's new book takes us deep inside the cultural and political meanings of the current turmoil in Israel. Deftly deploying his remarkable knowledge of relevant theoretical debates, in history, philosophy, and cultural studies, **he provides a sophisticated guide to the complexities of the 'post-Zionist moment,'** and shows how the seemingly ironclad structures of national identity are being painfully unlocked. Anyone interested in the relationship of history and theory, and the instabilities of national identity, as well as Israeli history, politics, and culture, will want to read this book."
—**Geoff Eley,** co-editor of *Becoming National*

THE POSTZIONISM DEBATES

Knowledge and Power in Israeli Culture

LAURENCE J. SILBERSTEIN

Routledge
New York and London

Published in 1999 by
Routledge
29 West 35th Street
New York, NY 10001

Published in Great Britain by
Routledge
11 New Fetter Lane
London EC4P 4EE

Copyright © 1999 by Routledge
Printed in the United States of America on acid-free paper.

Library of Congress Cataloging-in-Publication Data

Silberstein, Laurence J.
     The Postzionism debates: knowledge and power in Israeli
culture / Laurence J. Silberstein.
          p. cm.
     Includes bibliographical references (p.241) and index.
     ISBN 0-415-91315-2.—ISBN 0-415-91316-0 (pbk. : alk. paper)
     1. Zionism—Philosophy. 2. Zionism. 3. Post-Zionism.
     4. Israel—Politics and government.   I. Title.
     DS149.S5257   1998   98-39895
     320.54'095694—dc21   CIP

To my children and grandchildren

*Don't stop after beating the swords
into ploughshares, don't stop! Continue beating them
into musical instruments.*

*Whoever wishes to wage war again
will first have to turn them back into tools.* *

*   *"An Appendix to the Vision of Peace,"
by Yehuda Amichai, from Shalvah Gedolah: Sheelot uTeshuvot
Schocken Publishing House, Tel Aviv, Israel*

CONTENTS

ACKNOWLEDGMENTS

Since I first began to think about the issues addressed in this book in 1988, many colleagues and friends have contributed valuable suggestions, comments, and criticisms. Among those who have read and commented on various parts of the manuscript I want to thank the following: Hannan Hever, who was a constant source of important information on the history and culture of zionism and the state of Israel and, in particular, the writings of Anton Shammas and Emile Habiby; and Adi Ophir, who provided me with important background information concerning the establishment of *Theory and Criticism*. This book owes much to the friendship and constant encouragement of these two colleagues. Roni Kuzar helped me to better understand the Canaanites and Mazpen, while James Diamond, in numerous conversations, helped me to clarify my thinking on postzionism in general. Diamond's 1990 review of Boaz Evron's book both introduced me to this important thinker and stimulated my earliest reflections on postzionism. Laura Levitt, in numerous conversations, has helped me to clarify the way in which I have framed my interpretation and the style in which I have framed my arguments. Phyllis Cohen Albert provided important comments and criticisms to the Introduction.

Earlier versions of chapters 1 and 4 were presented at various meetings of the colloquium on Judaism & Postmodern Culture that has been meeting annually at Lehigh University since 1994. I thank the members of the group who shared their comments and criticisms with me. In addition to Hannan Hever, Adi Ophir, and Laura Levitt, these include Gordon Bearn, Daniel Boyarin, Jonathan Boyarin, Michelle Friedman, Elliot Ginsburg, Tresa Grauer, Steven Kepnes, Anita Norich, Peter Ochs, Miriam Peskowitz, Ruth Setton, Susan Shapiro, and Chava Weissler.

An earlier version of chapter 5 was presented at the University of Michigan at Ann Arbor. I thank Elliot Ginsburg and The Frankel Center for Jewish Studies for hosting me, and Anton Shammas for his gracious and insightful comments. Menahem Friedman invited me to share my preliminary thinking on postzionist scholarship with his seminar at the Institute for Advanced Studies in Jerusalem. I thank Steven Goldman for sharing with me his observations and comments on that encounter.

Yaacov Serrousi, who served as my research assistant in Israel, provided valuable assistance without which I could not have conducted the research for this book. In addition to locating, photocopying, and carefully annotating sources, he showed great initiative in finding new materials previously unknown to me. I also thank my Israeli colleagues Gerald Cromer and Zvi Ganin for providing me with sources that were unavailable in the United States.

Maud Lavin, who served as content editor, provided guidance that far exceeded her editorial responsibilities. A meticulous and insightful reader, she repeatedly urged me to present my ideas in a clearer and more effective manner than I otherwise might have done, and to convey to my readers what I take to be the stakes involved in the postzionism debates.

At various points in the writing of the book I benefited from extended conversations with Ilai Alon, Mordecai Bar On, Gordon Bearn, Amos Elon, Ted Friedgut, Gad Gilbar, Edwin Kay, Tami Katz-Freiman, Rajan Menon, Ilan Peleg, Michael Raposa, Ruth Setton, and Eric Zakim.

During the winter of 1995–96 I conducted interviews in Israel with Boaz Evron, Shlomo Fisher, Hannan Hever, Baruch Kimmerling, Orly Lubin, Ilan Pappe, Yoav Peled, Uri Ram, Adi Ophir, and Amnon Raz-Krokotzkin. These interviews were of inestimable value in helping me to clarify the conceptual issues surrounding postzionism.

I thank Carolyn Hudacek for her exceptional assistance in preparing the manuscript and Shirley Ratushny for her valuable editorial advice. I also thank both of them for willingly assuming additional responsibilities at the Phillip and Muriel Berman Center for Jewish Studies so that I could more freely devote my efforts to the writing of this book.

Bill Germano, Gayatri Patnaik, Brian Phillips, and Anthony Mancini of Routledge provided valuable assistance in bringing the book to press. Marlie Wasserman, while she was at Routledge, provided the initial encouragement that led me to formulate my interest in postzionism into a book project.

I am grateful to the Philip and Muriel Berman Chair in Jewish Studies and the Philip and Muriel Berman Center for Jewish Studies for proving generous financial support throughout the writing of this book. I particularly thank Muriel Berman and the late Philip Berman, whose friendship and continuing support provided conditions that enabled me to complete the research and writing of this book. I also thank the Office of Research and Sponsored Programs at Lehigh University for providing me with several research grants to assist in the writing and editing of the book.

Without my wife Mimi's continuous encouragement, patience, and willingness to do without my companionship on occasions too numerous to count, this book would never have been written.

As Israel prepared to celebrate the fiftieth anniversary of the establishment of the state, the fissures and breaks in the internal fabric of the nation became increasingly evident. In the press, in academic forums, and in everyday conversations, there was evidence of open conflict over the meaning and purpose of both the state and Israeli national identity. In the state that, according to zionist discourse, was to solve once and for all the identity problems of Jews throughout the world, conflicts over these issues continue to erupt daily.

Such a conflict occurred recently in the wake of a television series, entitled "Tekuma" (Hebrew for "renewal" or "rebirth"), which covered the history of the state. In an angry response reported in the *New York Times,* Israel's Minister of Communications, Limor Livnat, forbade her fourteen-year-old son to view the series. Denouncing the series, Livnat claimed that it "depicts the Palestinian side sympathetically, systematically distorts the great zionist deeds and causes severe and probably irreparable damage to our image.... To my understanding, the Israeli public broadcasting channel is not supposed to show the propagandistic position of the Palestinians while pushing aside our myths."[1] Ariel Sharon, a cabinet minister known for his hawkish views, protested in a letter to the Education Minister that the film "distorts the history of the rebirth and undermines any moral basis for the establishment of the state of Israel and its continued existence."[2] Referring to the series as "postzionist," Livnat demanded that it be taken off the air. Sharon urged the Education Minister "to ban the series from schools."

Responding to these and other critics, Gidon Drori, the executive director and editor of the series, quoted in the Israeli daily *Haaretz,* denied that the series shattered any myths: "We didn't choose to shatter myths. The myths were already shattered."[3] According to Drori, the controversy provoked by the series is a clear indication that Israelis "are still in the process of forming our identity."[4] In the course of their struggle to formulate a clearer understanding of who they are as a nation, Israelis, according to one woman interviewed in the series, are experiencing "the end of a loss of innocence."

According to a writer in *Haaretz:* "The anger at 'Tekuma' is because we don't want to know and we can't bear the sense of guilt. The establishment of the State of Israel was justice for the Jews, but it was accompanied by a terrible injustice for the Palestinians."[5]

As these comments suggest, the public controversy precipitated by "Tekuma" is part of a larger conflict over Israeli collective memory, collective identity, and collective meaning. The counternarrative in "Tekuma" of Israel's beginnings, by presenting an alternative to the dominant Israeli historical narratives, translates the results of scholarship produced by a select group of Israeli scholars in the 1980s into a popular medium. These scholars, who came to be known as "new historians," produced alternatives to the dominant academic accounts of the history of the state and zionism, the national movement that was instrumental in bringing it into being. Like "Tekuma," these scholarly writings had also precipitated heated controversies. Although originating in the scholarly community, these controversies soon spilled over onto the pages of the Israeli press, where they became the subject of a broad public debate. With the showing of "Tekuma," these debates were extended into the realm of Israeli popular culture. At the heart of these broader debates is what proponents and opponents have come to refer to as "postzionism."

In a general sense, postzionism is a term applied to a current set of critical positions that problematize zionist discourse, and the historical narratives and social and cultural representations that it produced. Like the term zionism, postzionism encompasses a variety of positions. The growing use of the term postzionism is indicative of an increasing sense among many Israelis that the maps of meaning provided by zionism are simply no longer adequate. To critics and detractors, postzionism presents a challenge to the basic principles and values of zionism. To its advocates, the postzionist critique is a necessary prerequisite to Israel's emergence as a fully democratic society.

As the controversy over "Tekuma" indicates, the conflict over postzionism is, among other things, a conflict over national memory. However, such conflicts are less about the past than about "how the past affects the present" (Sturken 1997, 2). For Israelis, as for all national groups, the narratives of their nation's past provide a framework through which to interpret the events of the present. In calling into question prevailing Israeli historical narratives, the new historians, together with a group known as critical sociologists, render problematic the very foundations on which Israeli group identity has been based. In the words of one scholar closely identified with the postzionist position, the scholarly debate

> reflects not only an academic dispute, but also an identity crisis of a society that stands on the threshold of a period of peace, in which the national consensus, previously built upon threats to survival and security problems, clears a space for a debate across the society and its culture. (Pappe 1995a, 45)

Accordingly, the struggles over postzionism are struggles for the control of cultural space, that is, the space within which the meanings of Israeli collective identity are constructed, produced, and circulated.[6] At stake in these struggles are such questions as: Who is included in or excluded from Israeli cultural space? Whose voice will be granted a hearing? Who will be allowed to speak?

Zionist critics of postzionism, committed to protecting zionism's dominant position, seek to defend Israeli cultural space from alien incursions. As they see it, any threat to the zionist hegemony threatens Israel's ideological foundations and calls into question its raison d'être as a state. Their use of the term postzionism is part of a broader strategic effort to discredit and delegitimate tendencies in Israeli culture that subvert the power and efficacy of zionist discourse. Policing the borders of Israeli cultural spaces, these defenders of zionism often identify postzionism with antizionism. Considering zionism as the only valid Jewish discourse, many of these defenders go so far as to link postzionism to anti-Semitism.[7]

Those who pronounce themselves to be postzionists sharply reject the claim of some zionist critics that postzionism is but another form of antizionism and anti-Israelism, refusing to accept the premise that loyalty to the state is synonymous with loyalty to zionism.[8] While disagreeing with specific Israeli policies and military actions, they remain committed to the survival of the state and willingly serve in the military to defend the country whenever it is threatened.[9] Insofar as they problematize dominant historical narratives and representations of Israeli identity, postzionists challenge zionism's claim to control Israeli culture exclusively.

Those who embrace the designation postzionist and those who sympathize with this position regard conventional Israeli scholarship as conscripted to the service of zionist ideology. The knowledge produced and disseminated by Israeli academicians, including historical narratives, is seen by postzionists to be grounded in zionist "truths" or doxa. Disseminated through schools, universities, scholarly texts, the military, the media, state documents, laws, geographical sites, memorials, and the official calendar, this knowledge serves to ground the prevailing conception of Israeli national identity and culture.[10]

British cultural critic Paul Gilroy has argued that all efforts to construct a group identity—notions of who we are and how we differ from others—entail acts of power. In the course of constructing its identity, a group excludes or closes itself off from certain discourses and narratives. This is particularly evident in the ways in which we designate as "other" those individuals and groups whose discourse and narratives we reject as alien to "us."[11] A recurring theme in the writings of postzionists is the need to open spaces for the voices of those who have been designated as the Other in Israeli society, including diaspora Jews, Jews of Middle Eastern origin,

Palestinian Arabs, and women. Thus, postzionists may be said to be engaged in a "space clearing gesture," (Appiah 1992, 145) clearing space both for previously silenced voices and for alternatives to the dominant zionist discourse.

In addition to the struggle for discursive or cultural space, the postzionist debates clearly relate to the struggle for physical space. This is evident from the key role played by the Israeli–Palestinian conflict in the conflict between postzionists and their critics. The postzionist academicians, born either shortly before or after the establishment of the state, were shaped by conditions significantly different from those that had shaped previous Israeli generations. Having survived numerous wars, they came to regard the Palestinian conflict as the defining one in the life and history of the nation. Troubled by Israel's continued occupation and oppression of Palestinians in the West Bank and Gaza and disturbed by the disparities between Israel's actions and its claim to be a democratic society, many reached the conclusion that the source of the problem is zionism. In the words of Benny Morris, a seminal representative of the new historiography who eschews the label postzionist, the scholarly debate "is as much about the nature of Zionism as it is about what exactly happened in 1948" (Morris 1988, 99).

To postzionists, the problems that beset Israel, particularly the conflict with the Palestinians, will only be settled when viable alternatives are found to the dominant zionist discourse. Zionism, emerging at the end of the nineteenth century, challenged the basic assumptions of a European Jewry that understood its collective identity in religious terms by creating the possibility of a secular Jewish identity.[12] Eschewing an identity derived from religious beliefs and practices, zionism produced an alternative construct of Jewish identity grounded in a secular definition of Jewish peoplehood and reinforced by secularized narratives of the Jewish past. In contrast to other formulations of Jewish identity, zionism's notion of identity was rooted neither in genetics nor in religious beliefs and practices but, rather, in one's relation to the Jewish past and to cultural values and practices that were designated as "Jewish."

Within zionist discourse, the entity known as "the Jewish people" or "the Jewish nation" was imagined to possess basic unchanging characteristics and a continuous historical existence. A central premise of zionism is the indisputable claim of the Jewish people to the land of Israel. This premise, informing virtually all contemporary writings on Jewish identity and Jewish history, is represented concisely in the official Proclamation of the State of Israel:

> The Land of Israel was the birthplace of the Jewish people. Here their spiritual, religious and national identity was formed. Here they achieved independence and created a culture of national and universal significance.... Exiled

from Israel, the Jewish people remained faithful to it in all countries of their dispersion.[13]

In the pre-state era and in the early decades of Israel's relatively brief life, zionism provided the dominant language through which Israelis made sense of and rendered meaningful their collective history and identity. In recent decades, responding to far-reaching historical and cultural changes, a growing number of Israelis found zionism's effectiveness in mapping everyday events to be waning. For the generations growing to maturity in the period after the establishment of the state, everyday realities increasingly revealed zionism's inadequacies. Unable to affirm the certainties that grounded the previous generation's sense of Israeli history and identity, many Israelis have felt a growing skepticism concerning the historical narratives produced by zionism.[14] Consequently, Israeli intellectuals, including but not limited to those designated as postzionists, have been struggling to formulate persuasive alternatives to zionism.

As I read them, at the heart of the controversies over postzionism are issues of knowledge and power. As Foucault (1979) has persuasively argued:

> Power and knowledge directly imply one another; there is no power relation without the correlative constitution of a field of knowledge, nor any knowledge that does not presuppose or constitute at the same time power relations. (p. 27)

Power, for Foucault, is the basic form of relation that shapes social and cultural processes.[15] Power operates both positively and negatively, that is, it functions both constructively and creatively, or repressively. Positively,

> Power invents, power creates, power produces. It produces more than the law that forbids desire—it produces desire itself, power induces and produces desire, it gives desire its objects, power, indeed, is desirable. Power not only produces desire...power produces the very form of the subject; it produces what makes up the subject. The form that the subject takes is, precisely, determined by power. (Foucault 1996, 158)

Negatively, power relates to the imposition of limits on what people can do and say.

According to Foucault (1983), the ubiquity of power relations within society is not a cause for despair. Far from being rendered immobile and helpless by such revelations, we are, instead, confronted with a different kind of political task, that is, to bring to the surface the relationship between and functioning of discourse, knowledge, power, and social relations:

> For us to say that there cannot be a society without power relations is not to say that those which are established are necessary or, in any case, that power

constitutes a fatality at the heart of societies, such that it cannot be under-mined. Instead, I would say that the analysis, elaboration, and bringing into question of power relations and the "agonism" between power relations and intransivity of freedom is a permanent political task inherent in all social rela-tions. (p. 223)

Central to the analysis of power relations is the concept of discourse. In my usage, based on Foucault, discourse refers to the practices, linguistic and nonlinguistic, through which we produce what we take to be knowledge. What we know, we only know because of the discourse through which we formulate it. Discourse provides us with the ways in which we produce the meanings that we ascribe to the people and things we encounter. As explained by Stuart Hall (1997), a key figure in the field of cultural studies, discourse:

defines and produces the objects of our knowledge. It governs the way that a topic can be meaningfully talked about and reasoned about. It also influences how ideas are put into practice and used to regulate the conduct of others. Just as a discourse "rules in" certain ways of talking about a topic, defining an acceptable and intelligible way to talk, write, or conduct oneself, so also, by definition, it "rules out," limits and restricts other ways of talking. (p. 44)

No one talks or thinks in a vacuum. Instead, we talk and think by means of discursive systems. To speak of discursive systems is to say that words do not acquire their meaning in isolation. Instead, they derive their meaning through their connection to other words, through the context in which we use them, and through their relationship to practices. What we know, we know through discourse. Discourse determines the limits of what can be said in particular situations.

As postzionists succeed in their efforts to open new spaces within Israeli culture in which alternative discourses can flourish, it becomes increasing-ly clear that, in the words of Hall (1996b), "some other, related but as yet 'emergent' new configurations of power-knowledge relations are beginning to exert their distinctive and specific effects" (p. 254).

Conventional studies of zionism (and postzionism), particularly those written by Israelis, tend to neglect or minimize power relations. Focusing on individual motives and actions, these studies tend to obscure the multiple ways in which power is imbricated in and actualized through zionist prac-tice.[16] A clear indication of the limitations of this approach is its neglect or minimizing of the disempowering effects of zionism on groups such as Palestinians, diaspora Jews, Jews of Middle Eastern origin, women, and nonzionist Jewish religious groups.[17] To the extent that they address issues of power, conventional Israeli scholarly studies limit themselves to discussing zionism's empowering effects on Jews, the power struggles among zionists, or the struggles between zionists and their opponents.[18]

The neglect of these areas in the study of zionism prevent us from grasping the processes that have contributed to the current crisis in Israeli culture, and in the Middle East in general. As long as scholars continue to conceal the power relations that are embedded in and legitimated by zionism, they will have great difficulty breaking out of an ethnocentric, unreflective framework of interpretation. Similarly, until Israelis in general understand the effects of zionism on others, they will not understand the urgent need to break free of the limitations it imposes on the complex situation both within Israel and in Israel's relations with other peoples and states.

As with any "ism," including zionism, postzionism incorporates diverse and conflicting positions. Just as there is no essential zionism, a claim that I argue in chapter 1, there is no essential postzionism. Given the absence both of a consensus and of universally accepted criteria that could be applied to establish postzionism's "true" meaning, it is not surprising that postzionism is currently being used in numerous ways.[19] While some writers use it to refer to a type of scholarly inquiry, others see it as also referring to a political position. The matter is further complicated by the reluctance of some who are positioned by others within the postzionist camp to accept the label. Nevertheless, even those who are hesitant to embrace the label are skeptical of the dominant historical narratives and social and cultural representations shaped within the spaces of zionist discourse.

Moreover, in their efforts to create alternative representations of Israeli history, society, and culture, postzionists employ differing approaches and differing theoretical frameworks. In one instance, as I discuss in chapter 4, those associated with the new historiography focus their critique on historical narratives produced by zionism. In another, the "critical sociologists" question the dominant representations of Israeli society and culture formulated by leading Israeli social scientists in the first three decades of the state.

Another group of writers, whom I discuss in chapter 6, carry the critique of zionism beyond the point to which it had been brought by the new historians and critical sociologists. Grounded in such recent critical practices as poststructuralism, feminism, and postcolonialism, this group of postzionists regard as problematic the discursive practices by means of which historical narratives and sociological representations are constructed. In an effort to free themselves from the limits imposed by historical and social science discourses, they seek alternative ways to engage the past and represent the present.

Some who embrace the postzionist label take it to indicate that the era of zionist hegemony is over and that a new—postzionist—era has begun.

Others argue that postzionist discourse ignores and conceals the continuing power effects of zionist discourse in shaping the basic mechanisms and structures of Israeli society, politics, and culture. In the latter view, to assert that the era of zionism is past encourages a disengagement from the urgent political and cultural problems it produced.

While not comprising an organized political group, postzionists generally agree that Israel should be a democratic state of all of its citizens. They thus reject the zionist principle, inscribed in Israel's Declaration of Independence, that Israel is the state of the Jewish people, a Jewish state. In contrast to zionists, postzionists wish Israel to become a state that belongs to all who live within it, including Palestinian Arab citizens.

There is no consensus among postzionists as to how to bring about the desired democratization, nor do all who advocate further democratization of Israel identify as postzionists.[20] While some advocate repealing the Law of Return, which virtually grants immediate citizenship to all Jews desiring it, others, although advocating full and equal rights for the Palestinian minority, continue to see the need for this law. Thus, Ilan Pappe, a Haifa University historian, who prefers to describe himself as nonzionist or azionist, advocates revoking the Law of Return as a necessary step to a genuine Western-style democracy (Pappe 1993c). Baruch Kimmerling, a sociologist who, although frequently identified as a postzionist, eschews the designation, has not, to my knowledge, advocated the repeal of the law.[21]

The current usages of the term postzionism are by no means the first. Prior to the 1990s, one encounters scattered uses of the term. For the most part, it served to indicate that zionism, having established a refuge for the Jewish people and effecting a renewal of a Hebrew national culture, had fulfilled its goal of normalizing the existence of the nation. Insofar as zionism had attained two of its basic goals, the establishment of a Jewish state and the normalization of Jewish life, zionist institutions were no longer necessary.

Now, postzionism means something very different. In its current usage, postzionism is the product of a crisis in Israeli life. To its proponents, postzionism is an outcome of "a genuine need, the need to overcome a crisis of understanding produced by the inability of the old categories to account for the world" (Dirlik 1997, 520).

Recent discussions of another post, "postmodernism," help to shed light on postzionism and its relationship to zionism. Like postmodernism, postzionism arises out of a sense that "complex transformations, questions, and problems deemed to be constitutive of the present are not adequately articulated in prevailing…forms of theory and analysis" (Smart 1992, 182). The increasing use of the term postzionist in Israeli public discourse is indicative of a growing sense that the complex transformations, questions, and problems that characterize Israeli culture cannot be adequately addressed by zionism. Like postmodernism, postzionism suggests the need to move beyond the prevailing (zionist) discourse in search of more adequate ways to talk about Israeli culture, identity, and history. At the same time, postmodernism, by positioning itself in relation to modernism, serves to perpetuate and highlight the concept. In a similar way, postzionism, focusing on the problematics of zionist discourse, helps to preserve the central position of the concept in Israeli discourse.

The significance of the debates over postzionism is by no means limited to Jews living in Israel. For Israelis, these debates involve issues of national identity, national memory, and national boundaries. Although these issues have no apparently urgent connection to Jews living in countries other than Israel, they nonetheless have significant implications for such Jews. Since the latter part of the eighteenth century, Jews have been engaged in an ongoing struggle to preserve and legitimate a distinct group identity. For many Jews, zionism appeared, particularly after the establishment of the state, to provide many of the components necessary to that goal. Thus, by the late 1960s, zionism and the state that it helped to produce had become major factors in shaping the ways in which Jews in the United States and other countries position themselves as Jews.[22] Basic zionist concepts such as the Jewish people, nation, and homeland were appropriated and came to play a major role in the identity construction of such Jews. Throughout the world, Jews came to view the connection to Israel as one of the foundations of their Jewish identity.

Accordingly, the Israeli debates over postzionism and the conflicts over Israeli national memory and national identity have profound implications for American Jewish identity.[23] For many American Jews, loyalty to Israel and zionism has replaced religious faith and practice as the test—or heretical lack—of Jewish loyalty. As the life and future of world Jewry was increasingly perceived to be intertwined with the life and future of Israel, American Jewish institutions refrained from public criticism of Israel. In American Jewish communal institutions and public forums, to question zionism or the policies and actions of the state of Israel is considered tantamount to questioning the foundations of Jewish identity. Israeli intellectuals, speaking before American Jewish audiences, often found themselves in the position of defending their right to enunciate criticisms that they had no hesitation expressing in Israel.

The debates over postzionism are important on a number of levels. First of all, they concern relations of power that affect the lives of Israelis, Palestinians, and all others affected by events in the Middle East. In addition, they pertain to the unfolding character of the state and the place of democracy in it.[24] Finally, the problems raised in these debates touch upon core issues of Israeli identity in particular, and Jewish identity in general. How these problems are resolved will have much to do with the ways in which these identities are understood and lived in the future.

STRUCTURE OF THIS BOOK

All efforts to establish a fixed definition of an "ism" such as postzionism are futile.[25] As a dynamic process, postzionism's meaning undergoes constant change depending upon who is using it, where, and to what end. Rather than focus on what postzionism means, I prefer to examine the ways in which it functions.

I read postzionism, as I do zionism, as a dynamic process incorporating conjunctural and antagonistic forces, lines, and vectors. Thus, this study should not be read as a "history" of postzionism. Rather than trace continuities and influences, my concern is to map postzionism by positioning it within Israeli culture and connecting it to other cultural sites at which critiques of zionism have been produced. I thus seek to provide the reader with a map that will enable him or her to make sense of the debates over postzionism and grasp their significance for Israeli culture in particular and Jewish culture in general. Following French philosophers Giles Deleuze and Felix Guattari, I regard mapping as an imaginative process wherein one seeks to establish lines and connections that historical discourse tends to occlude.

In the discussion of zionism in chapter 1, I emphasize the spatial dimension of zionism. Framing Jewish history in spatial terms, zionism places space and territory at the center of Jewish discourse. Insofar as it maps territories and imbues spaces with transcendent meanings, zionism produces boundaries, establishing what and who is included and excluded. Moreover, the zionist mapping relates not only to physical space, but also to imaginative and symbolic space. Viewed in this light, zionism represents one of the most far-reaching efforts to remap the (Jewish) world. One may thus speak of zionism as a mapping machine that inscribes boundaries around the ways in which we speak of Jewish history, culture, identity, and space. In representations, images, and symbols, zionism produced a new map of the (Jewish) world, thereby redrawing the boundaries of (Jewish) material, spatial, and cultural life.[26] Thus, the debates over zionism and postzionism are struggles over cartography, representation, and mapping.

In chapter 1, I point out some of the power effects of zionism that are overlooked or neutralized in most studies of zionism. Critically analyzing the taken-for-granted axioms of the knowledge produced and disseminated by zionism, I discuss the subject positions that zionism produced and the new concept of Jewish identity and history that it presumed.

At the same time, I show that, from its inception, zionism was a site of ongoing controversy and conflict. Critics, including those who identified as zionists and those who did not, repeatedly sought to reveal the basic contradictions and problems within zionist discourse. This is clearly evident in early debates among three significant shapers of that discourse, Ahad Haam, Yosef Haim Brenner, and Mikhah Yosef Berdiczewski (Bin Gurion), Russian Jewish writers in the late nineteenth and early twentieth centuries who were instrumental in shaping that discourse. These debates clearly demonstrate zionism's inherently contingent, essentially contested character. Notwithstanding zionism's effort to fix the meaning of key terms such as homeland, exile, and redemption, these debates reveal their nomadic character, their tendency to assume alternative meanings as they articulate with other discourses.

Thus, within the spaces of zionism, there were ongoing conflicts over such questions as: What is the authentic character of "Judaism"? What are the criteria of Jewish identity? What are the characteristics of the new subject that zionism strives to produce? What is the nature of Jewish history? What is the relationship of zionism to Judaism? What are the central characteristics of Jewish exilic existence? What is the nature of life in the homeland that will provide the cure for the evils of exile? What are the limits of zionist discourse? What is the relationship between the individual Jew, the collective, and tradition?

In chapters 2 and 3, I map out several critiques that either preceded the debates over postzionism or, although contemporary, have not been identified with that rubric. Although these critiques were deflected or neutralized by the dominant zionist discourse, many of the problems that they raise resurface in the debates over postzionism. Accordingly, a discussion of them is important to any mapping of postzionism. In chapter 2, I discuss a series of critiques that emerged within zionism. Some, like those of Mordecai Bar On, Amos Oz, and the late Martin Buber—who openly profess zionism—point out basic flaws, contradictions, or anachronisms that, to them, require repair. Others, like those of Amos Elon and Meron Benvenisti—who shy away from openly professing loyalty to zionism—stop short of cutting the ties. Both groups severely criticize what they see as zionism's shortcomings and failures.

In chapter 3, I discuss several groups and individuals who advocate displacing zionism with alternative discourses. While none of them succeeded in this effort, they did succeed in raising problems that continue to be debated today. The Canaanites, who emerged on the cultural scene in the 1950s, had a significant impact on Israeli literature, painting, and sculpture. While unsuccessful in displacing zionism, the Canaanites raised fundamental problems about the nature of Israeli collective identity, particularly the relationship of Israeliness to Judaism and Israelis to Jews. Mazpen, a left-wing socialist antizionist group that emerged in the 1960s, made the relationship with Palestinians a key issue. Critical of what they regarded as Israel's oppressive and imperialistic practices, Mazpen advocated positions that at the time were regarded as extreme, but appear far less so in the current context.

Boaz Evron, whose writings I discuss at length, has produced what to this day is the most comprehensive and thoughtful critique of zionism. Through a combination of historical argument and ideology critique, Evron challenges zionism's basic foundations and argues for the need for a viable alternative. Thus far, zionists in Israel have refrained from giving his critique the attention it deserves. Although Evron's book has recently been translated into English, few in the United States seem aware of it. Although many postzionists are aware of Evron's work and often cite it, his relationship to postzionism is complex. Although raising many of the same issues as the postzionists do, Evron's distinctive form of analysis differs from the postzionist critiques that I discuss in chapters 4–6.

In chapter 4, I turn to the early debates over postzionism that were precipitated by the scholarly writings of the new historians and critical sociologists. Responding to writings by such scholars as historians Benny Morris and Ilan Pappe and sociologists Uri Ram and Baruch Kimmerling, critics first began to circulate the term "postzionist" in its contemporary usage. The responses by these historians and sociologists, and the ensuing debates comprise the first wave of postzionism. The new historians, claiming that the boundaries of the dominant zionist/Israeli narratives were far too narrow, sought to broaden them. The critical sociologists sought to redefine the boundaries of Israeli society and culture to include marginalized and excluded minorities, thereby problematizing the dominant zionist mappings.

Other scholars, like social scientists Baruch Kimmerling and Gershon Shafir, carried the critique of zionism in another direction. Focusing on the practices of the earliest zionist settlers, Kimmerling and Shafir undertook to demonstrate that zionism was, as many external critics had argued, a colonial enterprise. Shafir based his argument on a comparison of zionist practices and the formal characteristics of zionist settlement with those of other settler societies generally recognized to be colonialist.

Notwithstanding the efforts of Kimmerling and Shafir to uncover the colonialist effects of zionist settlement on the native Palestinian population, they, like their colleagues, speak in the voice of the hegemonic Jewish Israeli group. As a result, they can only convey an insider's sense of zionism's power effects. In contrast, Anton Shammas and Emile Habiby, whose writings I discuss in chapter 5, speak in the voices of the Palestinian minority. Their writings, I argue, have produced some of the most cogent critiques of zionist discourse.

Their marginal positions aside, both Shammas and Habiby have succeeded in attaining an important place within Israeli cultural space. Attempting to remap Israeli physical and cultural space, they problematize hegemonic Jewish Israeli mappings and undo the forgetting on which those mappings are based.

Shammas, uncovering the power effects produced by Jewish Israeli discourse in the realm of culture, problematizes the position of Israeli liberals. Whereas Israeli liberals advocate reforms, Shammas represents a condition of cultural hegemony that cannot be adequately addressed through such reforms. Insofar as zionism produces and prolongs the oppressive conditions in which Palestinians live, only a far-reaching structural transformation of the state will succeed in bringing about the necessary changes.

Writing in Hebrew and publishing widely in Israeli journals and newspapers, Shammas represents one of the few Palestinian voices that has gained a wide hearing within Israeli culture. In addition to discussing the important role of his novel *Arabesques* (1988a), one of the few novels written in Hebrew by a Palestinian, I also focus on his nonfiction writings of cultural and social critique.

Habiby, a leader of Israel's communist party and a long-time member of the Knesset (parliament), was the author of several novels and many short stories. Although originally composed in Arabic, Habiby's writings have been made available to Jewish Israeli readers through Hebrew translations. Like Shammas, Habiby enjoyed a unique place in Israeli culture; in Habiby's case, he was the only Arab to have received the Israel Prize for Literature. In his novels, Habiby deftly employed a variety of discursive strategies to effectively subvert the dominant zionist mapping of the physical and social spaces of the Israeli landscape.

As the writings of Shammas and Habiby make clear, the ability of the Jewish Israeli scholars to represent the complex and multiple power effects of zionism on the Palestinian minority was limited. However, even as the historical and sociological critiques were being produced, another, more theoretical critique of zionism emerged. In contrast to the historians and sociologists, those who formulate this critique use the discourses of postmodernism and postcolonialism to represent the complexities of zionism's power effects in new ways.

The key site of this form of postzionism is the journal *Theory and Criticism,* first published in 1991 under the sponsorship of the Van Leer Institute in Jerusalem. This journal, which I analyze in chapter 6, occupies a unique space within Israeli culture. Seeking to combat the hegemony of zionism, *Theory and Criticism* introduces new theoretical considerations into Israeli cultural and political life. At the same time, it applies the postzionist critique to areas not analyzed by the historians and social scientists.

While not all of its writers would describe themselves as either postzionists or postmodernists, *Theory and Criticism* is the only journal in Israel to ground the critique of zionism in postmodern, poststructuralist, postcolonial, and feminist theory. As a result, it problematizes zionist discourse in a different way than do the historians and sociologists. Focusing on processes of representation and discursive practices, many writers, clearly indebted to Foucault, among others, reveal aspects of zionism's power effects that the writings of the historians and sociologists could not. It is this critique, I would argue, that poses the greatest challenge to those who undertake to defend zionism and preserve its hegemonic role in Israeli culture.

As indicated earlier, I regard postzionism as a space-clearing enterprise. Postzionists strive to free Israeli public discourse from the limits imposed by zionism and to clear space in which to talk about Israeli history, culture, and identity in new and exciting ways. In so doing, they strive to participate in producing a society that is democratic, creative, and humane.[27]

CHAPTER 1

MAPPING ZIONISM/ ZIONIST MAPPING

The development of a given into a question, this transformation of a group of difficulties and obstacles into problems to which the diverse solutions will attempt to produce a response, this is what constitutes the point of problematization and the specific work of thought.... It is a question of critical analysis in which one tries to see how the different solutions to a problem have been constructed; but also how these different solutions result from a specific form of problematization. (Foucault 1984a, 389)

A living civilization is a drama of struggle between interpretations, outside influences, and emphases, an unrelenting struggle over what is the wheat and what is the chaff, rebellion for the sake of innovation, dismantling for the purpose of reassembling differently, and even putting things in storage to clear the stage for experiment and new creativity. And it is permissible to seek inspiration from and be fertilized by other civilizations as well. This implies a realization that struggle and pluralism are not just an eclipse or a temporary aberration but, rather, the natural climate for a living culture. And the rebel, the dismantler, is not necessarily perverted or trying to assimilate. And the heretic and the prober are, sometimes, the harbingers of the creator and the innovator. (Oz 1984, 137)

To write about postzionism, it is useful to first write about zionism, the object of the postzionist critique. However, as Nietzsche, among others, has taught us, there simply are no innocent readings. To write about zionism is to step into an already flowing stream of diverse, often conflicting representations. To paraphrase Deleuze and Guattari (1989), we begin "in the middle." My discussion of zionism begins in the middle, that is, in the middle of a critical debate over how best to represent zionism. In this debate, as I show in chapters 4–6, the ways in which zionism is usually discussed and analyzed have been rendered problematic, and alternative ways have been developed.

My goal in this chapter is not to add to an existing body of knowledge about zionism, which presumes a conception of knowledge that I find problematic. Instead, I wish to reframe the discourse through which zionism is discussed. Thus, my analysis is already a "post" analysis, that is, I already take for granted many of the problems and criticisms raised by discourses such as postmodernism, postcolonialism, and postzionism.

Most historical studies seek to locate the origins of zionism, trace its development, describe the various forms it assumed, and detail its realization in the establishment of the nation state of Israel. Such studies, while acknowledging the conflicts that emerged within the zionist movement, usually regard zionism as a coherent, logically consistent, rational system of ideas and values or sociopolitical movement.[1] With few exceptions, historical representations of zionism take for granted zionist representations of space, time, and subjectivity. Although using tools of historical criticism, Israeli scholars rarely, if ever, problematize zionist discourse. Taking basic zionist claims at face value, they pay little attention to the contested social and cultural processes by means of which zionist discourse is produced and disseminated. We learn little from these studies about the cultural processes that create the politically charged norms of zionism—for example, the processes whereby spaces such as the homeland and exile or concepts such as "Jewish state" or "ingathering of the exiles" are produced and imbued with particular meanings.

Historians tend to accept uncritically such zionist assumptions as (1) the Jews are first and foremost a national body; (2) the normal location for that nation is its own homeland; (3) the spaces outside the land are inimical to Jewish life and culture; and (4) the Jewish claim to that land is legitimate, and all other claims are not. Moreover, many historical studies of zionism assume that the "return" of the nation to its homeland and the subsequent establishment of a state were the natural culmination of Jewish historical development. These studies tend to confirm Eric Hobsbawm's (1990) claim that "no serious historian of nations and nationalism can be a committed political nationalist. . . . Nationalism requires too much belief in what is patently not so" (p. 12).

When viewed from the perspective of current critical theory, these representations do not do justice to the multiple layers and planes subsumed under the concept of zionism. For example, zionism is used to refer alternately to individuals, collectivities, places, institutions, narratives, actions, events, and subjectivities. It includes what can be seen, what can be read, what can be thought about, and what can be imagined.

In recent years, writers such as Foucault, Deleuze, and Guattari have sought to address these issues by formulating alternative discourses to those conventionally used by historians and social scientists. It is not at all unusual for one encountering their writings for the first time to find them confusing, disorientating, and disconcerting. Nevertheless, I would argue, the rewards are worth the effort. They, more than most other writers, have succeeded in revealing or bringing to the surface the complex, multidimensional, heterogeneous, conflicted, dynamic character of social and cultural processes.[2]

Accordingly, in approaching zionism I find such terms as discourse, apparatus, assemblage, and subjectivities to be extremely useful. To speak of zionism as a discourse is to emphasize the dynamic processes and mechanisms through which zionism produced and disseminated contested representations of Jewish history, Jewish culture, Jewish community, and Jewish subjectivity or identity. As explained by British cultural critic Stuart Hall (1997):

> The discursive approach is more concerned with the effects and consequences of representation—its "politics." It examines not only how language and representation produce meaning, but how the knowledge which a particular discourse produces connects with power, regulates conduct, makes up or constructs identities and subjectivities, and defines the way certain things are represented, thought about, practiced, and studied. (p. 6)

As a discourse, zionism involves both language and practice, what one says and what one does. Zionist discourse is produced and disseminated through an apparatus, that is, an assemblage of institutions, spatial arrangements, laws, administrative organizations, and philanthropic activities.[3] Zionism also produces particular kinds of subjectivities or subject positions that position people who identify with it as well as those who resist it. Accordingly, zionism generates and legitimates specific power relations.

Most studies of zionism, while acknowledging that the early zionists faced opposition within the Jewish community, convey a sense that zionism's success was a seemingly natural historical outcome, the result of inner historical forces. In light of this, it is important to note that zionism has not always dominated modern Jewish discourse on identity and that it was, and still is, but one of several options available to Jews in their quest for self-definition. In its efforts to impose particular mappings of Jewish space, history, culture, and identity, zionism conflicted with a number of competing Jewish discourses. These included liberal political discourse, religious discourse (traditional as well as liberal), socialist discourse, nonterritorial Jewish nationalist discourses, and *haskalah*, the secular humanistic discourse of the Eastern European Enlightenment. In the late nineteenth century, these discourses struggled with one another to position Jews through conflicting conceptual frameworks grounded in differing conceptions of community, history, culture, and identity.

In its struggle for hegemony, zionism sought to position Jews to identify with and attach themselves to its representations of Judaism, Jewish history, and Jewish identity. In the process, zionism, like all nationalist discourses, struggled to impose unity in place of multiplicity, consensus in place of conflict, and homogeneity in place of heterogeneity.[4]

At different points, zionist discourse came into contact with numerous other discourses. Among these were European liberalism, Marxist and non-Marxist socialism; a Tolstoyan ideology of labor as spiritual and redemptive (Gordon); Nietzschean philosophy; organic social evolutionism; romantic nationalism; and religious messianism. Within the space of zionist discourse, these articulations with other discourses produced sites in which key zionist concepts acquired different, often conflicting meanings. At such sites, conflicting representations of Jewish culture, Jewish identity, and Jewish history were produced. Thus, zionism has been marked by ongoing "internal" conflicts over the meaning and significance of its foundational concepts.[5]

One of the ways that power operates positively is to produce, through discursive practices, knowledge. For Foucault, to speak of discourse and knowledge is to speak simultaneously of power.[6] Imposing a new direction in Jewish life and thought, zionist discourse produced a new knowledge of Jewish history, Jewish culture, and Jewish identity. This, in turn, entailed new hierarchies of power and new subject positions. Zionist discourse represented this knowledge as true, natural, and commonsensical. The subject positions produced by zionism, a function of efforts to position Jews so that they would identify with this knowledge and these power relations, were represented in terms of fixed, essential identities.

Zionism defined its basic subject positions in opposition to those of Jews living in exile. At different points, the new subjects were referred to as new Hebrews, new Jews, pioneers [*halutzim*], *sabras*, or Israelis. Although most studies of zionism discuss these types, they pay little, if any, attention to the discursive practices and power relations that produced and sustain them.

Despite efforts by scholars to represent an essential, fixed, constant core of zionist teachings, discourses such as zionism are inherently conflicted and heterogeneous. As with any discourse, zionism is in constant flux, marked by ongoing, often conflicting efforts to apply its concepts to a range of questions and problems. Notwithstanding the efforts of scholars to represent zionism as an essential body of ideas and values, I find it more useful to treat it as "diverse sets of conjoint positions in contention with each other at a variety of sites" (Grossberg 1993, 30–31). Recognizing the dynamic, contingent, contested character of zionism and the identities and power relations that it has produced allows us to see possibilities of change and multiplicity that conventional approaches tend to conceal.

ZIONISM'S REGIME OF TRUTH

Like other discourses, zionism produces what Foucault calls a "regime of truth," a set of codes, practices, apparatuses, and discursive processes that have the effect of rendering the knowledge that it produces true. Through its regime of truth, zionism seeks to govern the ways about which reality is talked and reasoned. It thus attempts to regulate what can and cannot be said about these topics. This entails imposing limits so as to control the ways in which Jewish history, the relationship of the Jewish homeland and exile, Jewish culture, and Jewish identity are represented and discussed. Moreover, zionist discourse seeks to position subjects so that they accept these representations as "natural" or "commonsensical."[7]

In the modernist discourse used in most studies of zionism, its concepts are taken as describing or mirroring actual preexisting political, social, cultural objects and conditions. Accordingly, concepts such as homeland and exile are taken to reflect ontological realities. In contrast, I regard "homeland" and "exile," together with zionism's other categories, as products of discursive processes. Far from simply describing or reflecting objective conditions, these categories participate in the construction of these conditions. While undoubtedly there are actual physical spaces to which these representations are applied, the grids and categories used to produce the meanings of such spaces are the product of human imagination and presuppose specific relations or hierarchies of power.[8]

One way to reveal the power effects of zionist discourse is to view it not in terms of meaning, but in terms of its functions and effects. Rather than ask "What do the terms mean?" one asks "How do they function?" and "What do they do?" (cf. Deleuze 1995, 21–22). From this perspective, basic terms of zionist discourse are seen as "order words" [*mots d'ordre*] that codify, direct, order, prescribe, and limit. Thus, terms such as *galut* [exile], *moledet* [homeland], *aliyah* [ascent to the land], *yeridah* [descent from the land], and *kibbush haaretz* [conquest of the land] are used not only to describe or represent reality, but also to prescribe particular sets of practices and relations. For example, while on one level terms such as *aliyah* and *yeridah* refer to processes of immigration/emigration, they also imbue these processes with specific meaning and value, privileging immigration and those who immigrate, while deprivileging emigration and those who emigrate. In zionist discourse, the act of immigrating to Israel is viewed positively, a sign of loyalty to the Jewish people. On the other hand, the act of emigrating from Israel is regarded as an act of betrayal, and the one who emigrates is viewed as a traitor.[9]

These and other such concepts form part of a body of knowledge produced and disseminated by zionism. Basic to this knowledge are such "subjects/objects" as the Jewish people, the land of Israel as the Jewish homeland, and exile.[10] Those whom zionist discourse effectively positions regard them not as cultural constructs, but as taken-for-granted givens. This, in turn, conceals or occludes their culturally constructed character.

The binarism of homeland/exile is central to zionism. Zionists imagine a homeland in which the Jewish people can find security, both physical and psychic. Freed from the trials of living as aliens in exile, Jews, according to zionism, will find rest and fulfillment in their true home. Through common endeavors, common values, and shared practices, they will come to experience genuine community. Space and territory thus form an essential part of the fantasies, desires, dreams, yearnings, and aesthetic practices produced by zionism.

The fulfillment of the zionist dream depends upon acts of deterritorialization and reterritorialization. On one hand, Jews and Jewish culture must be deterritorialized from diaspora spaces and reterritorialized in the spaces of the homeland. Thus, beyond imposing grids and boundaries on symbolic and imaginative spaces, zionism also imposes them on physical spaces. Zionist mappings of physical spaces produced concrete effects on Jews and Palestinian Arabs alike. Although not anticipated by early zionists, these effects included the deterritorializing and reterritorializing of large numbers of Palestinian Arabs, particularly during the 1948 War.[11] Holding the historical and moral right of Jews to settle the contested territory and inscribe its own culture on it to be unquestionable, zionism silenced the voices of the existing population and delegitimated the historical narratives that it produced. As we shall see, a basic postzionist concern is to problematize zionist historical narratives, thereby bringing to light the effects of zionist discourse on the Palestinians.

Among Jews, zionism set up distinct hierarchies of power and grids of inclusion and exclusion that privilege the space of the homeland over all other spaces and Jews living in the "homeland" over Jews living outside of it. In its efforts to concentrate decisionmaking power of the Jewish nation in the hands of Jews living in the homeland, zionism disempowered Jews living outside the homeland. For the most part, zionist discourse valued diaspora Jews primarily for their contribution, actual and potential, to the process of building the homeland. Moreover, in privileging the culture of European Jews and making it the dominant Israeli culture, zionism marginalized Jews from Middle Eastern countries as well as their cultures.[12]

ZIONIST DISCOURSE AND ITS
BINARY FOUNDATIONS

While most scholars and zionist spokespeople represent zionism as a coherent discourse resting upon essential axioms, it is neither closed, fixed, nor unified. Within zionist discourse, however, the prevailing tendency is to gloss over conflicting positions, minimize their significance, or subsume these differences under an overall sense of cohesion.[13] In contrast, I focus on

> the multiplicity and diversity of its possible meanings, its incompleteness, the omissions which it displays but cannot describe...and the collisions between its divergent meanings. (Belsey 1980, 107)

Although zionist discourse is essentially contested, it is possible to identify within its spaces shared premises that all who identify with it accept. Like all nationalist discourse, zionism takes as a given that humanity is divided into natural social and cultural units called nations. These nations are held to be distinguished from one another by such factors as origins, history, language, culture, and ethnic kinship, or a combination thereof. Zionism also takes for granted a preexisting Jewish nation with an essential identity that differentiates it from all other nations. Jewish history, as represented in zionist discourse, then becomes the story of the origins and development of the nation.

Zionists, like all nationalists, presume a natural, isomorphic relationship between the nation, its culture, and the space it represents as its homeland. Only in the homeland do conditions exist that are necessary for the growth and flourishing of the nation and its culture. Conversely, spaces outside the homeland, referred to as "exile," are represented as inimical to such growth and dangerous to the health of the nation. Thus, zionist discourse positions its subjects to accept as true the claim that the "return" of the nation to its homeland is essential to the survival of the nation and the renewal of its culture.

Included in the discourse of homeland/exile are such concepts as exile/redemption. In zionist discourse, the departure of a sizable part of the Jewish community from the land of Israel, voluntarily or coerced, is represented as the nation going into exile. On the other hand, the migration of a significant part of the nation to the land, such as occurred in the twentieth century, is represented as a return, a redemptive process.

Basic to all zionist discourse is the premise that there exists a universal "Jewish problem" that defines the overall Jewish condition. Informing this perspective is the fantasy that the basic lack in the nation's life—that is, the lack of wholeness and fulfillment—can be resolved and the nation made healthy and whole through a return to its homeland. In contrast to the multiplicity of complex problems affecting different Jewish communities in different locations, zionism focuses on "the" universal Jewish problem.

Yet, within zionist discourse, there are diverse, often conflicting representations of "the Jewish problem" linked to conflicting solutions, strategies, and goals. While some zionist representations depict the Jewish problem and its solution in political terms, others depict it in socioeconomic or cultural terms. Thus, within zionist discourse, the Jewish problem has been alternatively represented in terms of anti-Semitism and persecution, social fragmentation, cultural assimilation, cultural deterioration, suppression of individual creativity, absence of opportunities for productive labor, alienation from the land, and existential alienation. Accordingly, proposed solutions to be effected through a return to the homeland include safety and physical security, the unification of the nation, protection from external cultural influences, the renewal of Jewish culture, individual creativity, agricultural labor, and spiritual renewal. Informing all of the solutions is the sense that a return to the homeland would bring both individual and collective wholeness and unity.

These representations of the Jewish problem and its solution form part of the "knowledge" that zionist discourse produced and disseminated through a network of practices and institutions including schools, family, media, regulations, laws, administrative measures, scholarly interpretations, philosophical propositions, and philanthropical enterprises. This knowledge also incorporated historical narratives and other scholarly representations of Israeli society and culture.

Basic to this knowledge is a series of binaries, including homeland/exile, Hebrew/Jew, Jews/Judaism, (Jews created Judaism/not vice versa), nation/religious community, secular culture/religion, national feeling/religious belief, collective/individual, continuity/discontinuity, evolution/rupture, creativity/stagnation, unity/fragmentation, order/chaos, and, in the case of socialist zionism, workers/bourgeoisie.[14]

Zionist discourse takes it as a given that the land of Israel, also known as Palestine, is the legitimate home of the group represented as the Jewish people. It further assumes that there is a qualitative, essential difference between the space within that land and the spaces outside of it. For those who are positioned by zionist discourse, this knowledge legitimates the Jewish claim to the land while delegitimating the claims of others.

The binary structure of homeland/exile is extended in a series of other oppositions. These include homeland as source of security, stability, refuge, nurturing, safety/exile as site of danger, insecurity, instability, threat, anxiety; *heimlich/unheimlich*; homeland is good/exile is bad; homeland is productive/exile is parasitic; homeland is conducive/exile is not conducive to redemption through labor; homeland is welcoming/exile is hostile; homeland is life-giving/exile is life-threatening; homeland is creative/exile is stultifying; homeland is nurturing to Jewish national culture/exile is destructive; homeland is unifying/exile is fragmenting.

The distinction between the land and its Other, that is, exile, is represented through a rhetoric of travel or movement. Zionist discourse represents travel to the land for purposes of settlement as *aliya* [ascent] and emigration from the land as *yeridah* [descent]. Moreover, one who immigrates to the land is referred to by the privileged term *oleh* [one who ascends], while one who emigrates is called a *yored,* a term of approbation. Similarly, while privileging the subject position formed within the land, referred to as the new Hebrew, zionist discourse deprivileged and disparaged the subject position of the exilic "Jew." In the same way, all activity devoted to the settlement and development of the homeland was privileged, while activity devoted to the building of communities outside of the homeland was either regarded negatively or, at the most, tolerated as necessary in zionist discourse.

Embedded in these binaries are hierarchies of power that privilege Jews over Palestinian Arabs and Hebrews or Israelis over diaspora Jews. Insofar as zionist discourse takes for granted the legitimacy of the Jewish nation's claim to the land, it denies the Palestinian Arab claim. It is only recently that it became possible within some forms of zionist discourse to speak about an existing Palestinian people. As remarkable as this may seem, the first time that an Israeli leader did this publicly and officially was in 1993 in Yitzhak Rabin's remarks on the White House lawn marking the signing of the Declaration of Principles between Israel and the Palestinians.[15]

Zionism's effort to produce a new Jewish subject in the "homeland" entailed a new form of Jewish identity or belonging. In zionist discourse this subject position was represented as the "new Hebrew" or "new Jew." In contrast to the subject position of exile, referred to disparagingly as the "Jew," the "new Hebrew" is represented positively. The Jew, a product of exile, is thus represented as inauthentic, obsolete, and unproductive. The "new Hebrew," on the other hand, a product and producer of the renewed national life in the homeland, is represented as authentic, modern, and productive.[16]

In addition to producing new individual subject positions, zionist discourse also produced new representations of the Jewish collective. The knowledge produced by (secular) zionist discourse takes it for granted that Jews, comprising diverse populations dispersed in different geographical, political, and cultural settings, are a nation in the modern sense of the word. This premise is built upon the distinction within zionist discourse between nation/religious community and national culture/religion.

For zionists, representing the Jews as a worldwide national group posed unique problems. As one of the leading contemporary theorists of nationalism, Benedict Anderson, has argued, creative imagination forms a basic part in the production of any nation. Insofar as its members do not live in physical proximity or maintain regular physical contact with one another, a nation, in Anderson's widely appropriated term, is an "imagined community." Jews, however, lacking both recognized sovereignty over a homeland and a substantial community in that land, faced additional difficulties in representing themselves as a nation.

One of the strategies employed by zionists in their effort to represent Jews as a nation was the construction of a national narrative. In place of the previously dominant religious-theological narrative of Jewish history, zionism constructed a secular national narrative. In contrast to the religious representation of the community's origins as deriving from a covenant with God, zionism represented these origins in terms of shared events and common memories.

Zionist discourse represented the culture originally produced by Jews in their homeland as a secular national culture. In exile, faced with the danger of extinction, the nation produced religious forms that helped ensure its survival. Thus, according to the zionist narrative, what was originally a national secular culture was transformed, under the conditions of exile, into religion.[17]

The return to the homeland under zionism created conditions for the renewal of secular national culture rooted in a revived Hebrew language. This, in turn, made it possible for turn-of-the-century Hebrew writers like Ahad Haam, Mikhah Yosef Berdiczewski, and Yosef Haim Brenner, whom I discuss shortly, to discard, or at the very least minimize the role of religion in Jewish national life. Through what in zionist discourse is represented as a process of normalization, Jewish national culture would once again resume its original secular form.[18]

As mentioned earlier, the binaries of homeland/exile and exile/redemption are foundational to the zionist historical narrative. Jewish history is framed through the dialectic of exile/homeland and exile/return.[19] In this narrative, the Jewish nation is represented as having come into existence in the homeland, where it produced a Jewish national culture. A national catastrophe, dated either in 70 CE or 132–135 CE, forcibly displaced the nation from its natural habitat and forced it to live in "exile," where its culture languished.

Although privileging the homeland and its culture over exile, zionism produced differing views of what is positive and creative about the homeland and what is negative and destructive about exile.[20] Moreover, the meaning of the foundational concepts of zionist discourse were neither univocal nor static. Sustaining multiple, often conflicting interpretations, they are also nomadic, assuming or discarding different meanings as they articulate with or disengage from other concepts or clusters of concepts.

Ahad Haam and His Critics: Power and Knowledge in Early Zionist Discourse

As has been stressed thus far, zionist discourse entails conflicting representations of the Jewish problem, exile/homeland, Hebrew/Jew, culture/religion. We thus encounter conflicting representations of individual and group identity and conflicting historical narratives. At the same time, as with any discourse, zionism is also marked by recurring efforts to impose strict boundaries or limits on this discourse so as to eliminate conflict and produce unity and, to a certain degree, homogeneity.

These conflicted processes are already evident in the early struggles of zionist discourse. One of the most important sites of this struggle is a corpus of Hebrew writings produced primarily in Eastern Europe in the decades just prior to and immediately following the turn of the century. These writings form part of a public controversy over the character of zionism, Judaism, Jewish history, Jewish culture, and Jewish identity. This controversy was precipitated by the writings of one of the major shapers of zionist discourse, the Russian Hebrew writer Asher Ginsburg (1856–1927). Known by his pen name Ahad Haam (meaning "one of the people"), his representations of Judaism, Jewish history, Jewish subject, and Jewish knowledge—disseminated through Hebrew journals, particularly *HaShiloah*—were among the most comprehensive and influential among Eastern European Jews in the late nineteenth and early twentieth century. At the same time, his representations were vehemently contested by other zionist writers. The ensuing controversy clearly demonstrates the inherently conflicted character of zionist discourse and early efforts to impose strict limits on it.[21]

Notwithstanding the significant contribution of individual writers such as Ahad Haam, zionist discourse exceeds the writings of individual authors.[22] The writings of individuals are socially and culturally effective only insofar as they are inscribed in discourses and practices. Most discussions of this period of zionism focus on Ahad Haam, the individual creator, originator, and producer of a coherent system of ideas. In contrast, I am concerned with the ways in which Ahad Haam's concepts and categories were appropriated by zionist discourse and served as the basis of internal debates. Viewed in this way, Ahad Haam's writings and those of his interlocutors were part of a wider zionist discourse into which they were selectively incorporated, integrated, and inscribed.

Nevertheless, Ahad Haam can also be considered as what Foucault terms a founder/initiator of discursivity, that is, one who plays a major role in producing/shaping a discourse. Like any contributor to the formation of a nationalist discourse, Ahad Haam's representation of the nation, its culture, and its history was a product of imagination.[23] Positioned within modernist discourse, Ahad Haam saw himself engaged in providing true representations of the essence of the Hebrew nation and national culture, their origins and development over time. Based on these representations, he formulated a view of the problems confronting the nation and their solutions.[24]

Ahad Haam, drawing from discourses of European Romantic nationalism and social evolution, privileged spiritual and cultural factors over material factors. Representing nations as organic wholes that derive from a primordial national unity, Ahad Haam described the Jewish problem alternately in terms of cultural stagnation and social fragmentation. In his narrative, the preexisting unified organic entity known as the Jewish nation first emerged in the land of Israel where it produced a culture known as Judaism. It was the homeland, for Ahad Haam, that provided the "natural" environment necessary to the nation's health. Upon being exiled from its homeland, the nation was forced to live in conditions of exile. This resulted in the erosion or atrophying of Jewish culture, the spiritual essence of the nation. The creative, mutually fructifying relationship between the collective and its culture became, in the conditions of exile, rigid and oppressive. Having become reified, Jewish culture was no longer able to function as an authentic expression of the nation's spiritual yearnings and creativity. This, in turn, resulted in the nation's growing alienation from its culture. What, to Ahad Haam, was once a creative "literary people" [*am sifruti*] became, in exile, a "people of the book" [*am hasefer*], enslaved to the literal meaning of the printed page:

> It has surrendered its soul to the written word. The book ceases to be what it should be, a source of renewed inspiration and moral strength; quite the opposite, its function in life is to weaken and finally crush all spontaneous action and emotion. People have grown to be so wholly dependent on the written word, that they are incapable of responding to any natural stimulus without its permission and approval. (Hertzberg 1970, 252 modified)

In addition to the discourse of cultural atrophy and alienation, Ahad Haam also represented the Jewish problem through the language of social fragmentation. As a consequence of the growing acceptance of modern Jews as citizens of the nation-states within which they lived, Jews were increasingly assuming the social and cultural characteristics of those nations. Thus, the once organically integrated, cohesive group united around its religion was, under the impact of modern social and cultural processes, becoming increasingly fragmented:

> When it [Judaism] leaves the ghetto walls, it is in danger of losing its essential being or—at the very least—its national unity; it is in danger of being divided

into many kinds of Judaism as there are countries of the diaspora, each with a different character and life. (Hertzberg 1970, 267 modified)[25]

The problems that Ahad Haam and his contemporaries represented and struggled to address were also, of course, visible in the lives of many other groups. Throughout Europe, long-standing representations of culture, community, and identity were being called into question. Along with many other groups, Jews were being challenged to find alternative ways to effectively talk about and represent their communities, their history, their culture, and their identity.[26] While the physical violence, persecution, and economic deprivation suffered by Jews was undoubtedly real, the causes and "meaning" attributed to that suffering were functions of the discourse used to represent it. Rather than one underlying problem with many ways of representing it, there were multiple problems that were differently represented by conflicting discourses.[27]

Although zionists generally represented these changes and their effects on the Jews in terms of one universal Jewish problem, there was no consistent agreement as to the nature of this problem. To some, such as the early Russian zionist writer Leo Pinsker, and Theodor Herzl, the Viennese journalist who formulated the idea of political zionism, the problem was best represented in terms of the ubiquitous perception of Jews as aliens, a perception encapsulated in the term anti-Semitism. Yet even those defining the basic problem in terms of anti-Semitism disagreed as to its causes and essential character. To some (Pinsker), the problem was embedded in the psyche of non-Jews and could never be eradicated. To others (Herzl and Borochov), it was the product of socioeconomic conditions that could be overcome. To still others (Kaufmann), it was the product of Jewish religious beliefs and practices, ethnic distinctions, and the rise of modern nationalism.

Similarly, in the debates surrounding Ahad Haam's writings we encounter multiple, conflicting representations of the Jewish problem. Moreover, these conflicting representations of the solution of the Jewish problem appear along with conflicting representations of zionism's goals. Ahad Haam's representations, like those of other zionist writers, are produced through the articulation of multiple discourses, Jewish and non-Jewish alike.

In Ahad Haam's writings, we find evidence of the discourses of biblical and rabbinic Judaism, the nineteenth-century Eastern European Jewish Enlightenment [*haskalah*], eighteenth-century European Enlightenment philosophy (e.g., Kant), nineteenth-century European romantic nationalism, and nineteenth-century social thought. Each of these discourses, themselves products of multiple other discourses, produced its own knowledge and its own subject positions. Accordingly, Ahad Haam's discourse, like all zionist discourse and all other Jewish discourse, was a multiplicity.

Representing the Jewish Collective

Ahad Haam's representation of the Jewish problem ultimately depended on his representation of the Jews as a group. As explained earlier, religious Jews tended to represent Jews as a covenantal people whose existence was grounded in a unique relationship to God. However, Ahad Haam, drawing from nineteenth-century nationalist discourse, depicted Jews as a nation in the modern sense of the term. Rather than represent the nation as a covenantal community whose significance derived from its ongoing inter-action with God, Ahad Haam described the nation's development in terms of social laws interpreted through the discourse of social evolutionism.

Ahad Haam's discourse on nation and culture was grounded in the basic binary opposition of spirit/matter. At the heart of any nation was its essential spirit, which was expressed in its culture. As organic entities or organisms moved by their innate will to survive, nations evolved gradual-ly, adapting to changing sociocultural conditions. The external forms of the nation may change, as they did in the case of the Jewish nation in exile. However, the basic "spirit" or essence of the nation remains constant.

Ahad Haam's representation of Judaism privileged the national over the religious. The core or essence of Judaism was the nation's essential spir-it, rather than divine revelation. While acknowledging the role of religious ideas and practices in preserving the nation, he nevertheless represented Judaism in secular national rather than religious terms.

Besides representing the nation and its culture, Ahad Haam formulated an outline for the nation's historical narrative, an essential component of any theory of nationalism. Again drawing on nineteenth-century organistic evolutionist discourse, Ahad Haam represented the history of the nation as a gradual evolutionary process. Its essential national spirit [*ruah haleumi*], driven by the nation's will to survive [*hefetz hakiyyum haleumi*] and inter-acting with other national cultures, assumed and discarded a variety of forms and shapes. The major form, the one that served to preserve the nation throughout its long sojourn amidst the hostile conditions of galut, was religion (Hertzberg 1970, 262).

Representing Homeland/Exile

Like all zionists, Ahad Haam presumed a natural isomorphic relation between the nation, its national culture, and the space represented as the national homeland. Just as vegetation/plants have sites that are more or less conducive to their growth, each nation has one natural place that is most conducive to its healthy growth, the place represented as the homeland.

Using terms drawn from nineteenth-century social and cultural theory, Ahad Haam represented Jewish national culture as being fully nurtured and actualized only in the land of Israel. In conditions of exile, that culture languished. Accordingly, the only solution was its renewal in its natural habitat:

> [There] it will be able to live a life developing in a natural way, to bring its powers into play in every department of human culture, to broaden and perfect those national possessions which it has acquired up to now...only the creation in its native land of conditions favorable to its development; a good sized settlement of Jews working without hindrance in every branch of civilization, from agriculture to handicrafts to science and literature. (Hertzberg 1970, 267)

Here we see a clear example of the difference between Ahad Haam's representation of the Jewish problem and its solution and that of Herzl and his followers. To Herzl, the author of the seminal zionist text *The Jewish State [Der Judenstaat]*, published in 1895, the Jewish problem was the result of the abnormal social and economic conditions of exile. Consequently, only an independent Jewish state would solve the problem. For Ahad Haam, who framed the Jewish problem in cultural-spiritual terms, an independent state was neither a prerequisite for national renewal nor a solution to the Jewish problem. While not explaining how the nation could attain conditions necessary to its cultural and social growth without political sovereignty, he refused to make that cultural renewal dependent on the achievement of elusive political goals.

To Ahad Haam, a zionist program based solely on political and diplomatic activities was wholly inadequate. For the nation to undertake the necessary political activities, it had to be sufficiently motivated. Insofar as that motivation depended on a renewed national spirit, any collective return to the "homeland" had to be preceded by a cultural-spiritual renewal. This renewal could only be initiated in the lands of the diaspora.

As we saw earlier, the meaning attached in zionist discourse to the homeland depends upon the meaning assigned to its binary opposite, exile. Exile, in zionist discourse, represented the sickness that had to be cured, the problem that had to be solved. The solution, in turn, depended on how the sickness was represented. Similarly, whatever negative qualities or lack were attributed to exile, the homeland was represented as the opposite. Whereas exile was described as lacking the conditions necessary to the nation's health, the homeland was represented as possessing these qualities/conditions.

Thus, a central concept within early zionist discourse is that of the "negation of the diaspora" [*shelilat hagalut*]. Once again, whereas all of zionist discourse, then and now, has shared this negative attitude, there has been no agreement on what constituted the negative core of life in exile.

Within zionist discourse, one finds diverse, often conflicting representations of exile. While some represent the negative characteristics in terms of material deprivation and physical persecution, others represent it in terms of spiritual deprivation and cultural atrophy.

Similarly, within zionist discourse there have been differing conflicting positions regarding the viability of Jewish life in exile and the possibilities of mass emigration. Whereas Herzl was persuaded that eventually all diaspora Jews who did not completely assimilate would immigrate to Palestine, Ahad Haam was skeptical.[28] Insofar as Ahad Haam's definition of the Jewish problem presumed a cultural renewal, he could not write off Jewish culture in the diaspora.

Nevertheless, Ahad Haam disagreed with nonzionist diaspora nationalists such as his contemporary Simon Dubnow (1860–1941), a Russian Jewish historian who believed that a viable Jewish culture could exist in the diaspora.[29] For a diaspora Jewish culture to survive, a viable national Jewish center in the homeland was necessary. Only such a center could inspire diaspora Jewish communities "with new life and to preserve the overall unity of our people" (Hertzberg 1970, 267).

Representing Jewish Identity/Subjectivity

Zionist discourse produced a new form of Jewish subjectivity, a new mode of cultural identity. Positioned by the hegemonic Jewish religious discourse as members of a covenantal community, Jews were obligated to fulfill the divine will by following a set of religious norms and practices. In this religious discourse, to be a Jew was to believe in the God of Israel and observe the commandments, which were inscribed in sacred texts such as the Bible and the Talmud.

Critics of the religious position, who framed their interpretation of Jewish culture and history through the discourse of secular Enlightenment, sought to translate Jewish society and culture into universalistic categories. Through Hebrew language periodicals and books, they disseminated among Eastern European Jews a modern, secularized alternative to the dominant religious discourse. Other groups, using Yiddish as their linguistic vehicle, framed a conception of Judaism grounded in the life of the worker.

Western European proponents of the Jewish Enlightenment advocated a form of Jewish social and cultural life into which European social and cultural values were fully integrated. Advocating a universalistic discourse, they sought to eliminate all barriers preventing Jews from being a full part of humanity in general. Their views also filtered into Western European Jewish religious discourse, liberal as well as traditional, in which being Jewish was represented as fully compatible with being a citizen of a

European nation-state. In constructing their identities, Western European Jews sought to combine Jewish religious discourse with the cultural discourse of the nations in which they lived.

Ahad Haam sharply criticized all of these representations of Jewish culture and identity. Rejecting liberal, socialist, and traditional religious representations of Jewish identity, Ahad Haam formulated a radically new model of Jewish subjectivity. In his discourse, the Jew was first and foremost a member of a nation, the Jewish nation. Accordingly, the norms and values of that nation shaped the core of a Jew's identity. To seek to integrate the norms and values of diverse national cultures could only have negative effects.

One gains a clear indication of Ahad Haam's representation of Jewish belonging and Judaism as a form of life in the following response he wrote to an open letter written by an anonymous correspondent and published in the Hebrew journal *HaShiloah* in 1898:

> What do we call a Jew who loves his people, its literature and its cultural heritage, and who yearns for its renewal; but who at the same time is a free thinker in the fullest sense of the term? While he believes in nature and natural law, he does not believe in a creator God, or the providential God (who watches over His people) and who is the Giver of the Torah.... Is such a person a Jew or isn't he [*Halanu hu o'lezarenu*]? (Ahad Haam 1947, 291)

The conditions in which this Jew found himself reflected those confronting large numbers of Eastern European Jews whose sense of identity had been disrupted by cultural and social changes. No longer able to effectively position themselves through Jewish religious narratives, they nevertheless continued to identify with the Jewish community and its culture. Having moved beyond the limits of traditional Jewish religious discourse and the legitimations that it provided, they were, nevertheless, seeking a way to maintain a positive connection to Jewish history and culture.[30]

Ahad Haam was fully aware of the far-reaching changes affecting the lives of young Jews. In previous generations, he argued, Jews living within the parameters of Jewish religious discourse would never question their Jewish identity: "It never occurred to them to ask: 'Why am I a Jew?' Such questions would have not only been considered blasphemy but would have been seen as the highest level of stupidity" (Ahad Haam 1947, 150). To put it differently, Ahad Haam was saying that previous Jewish discourses did not allow for the kind of questioning that was becoming common among younger Jews.

As a result of massive social, cultural, and political changes, many Jews were now experiencing pervasive doubt. Insofar as the inherited Jewish discourse no longer provided them with an effective way of representing their Jewish identity, they had little recourse. As he wrote in the journal *HaShiloah* in 1898,

> In the last few generations, this condition has changed. The new Jew, entering into the mainstream of Western culture, no longer sees himself as superior, as a member of a unique group, distinct from the rest of humanity. On the contrary, he does all that is in his power not to be different.... It is no wonder, therefore, that one hears him uttering the powerful question: Of what advantage is my Jewishness to me? Why should I continue to suffer for it? Why should I continue to cherish it? (Ahad Haam 1947, 150)

Ahad Haam represented these Jews as needing a discourse that would enable them to continue to identify as Jews, position themselves within the Jewish community, and participate in its culture. As he formulated it, this could only occur if the discourse grounded in religious faith was replaced by one grounded in national feeling. Whereas previously Jews expressed their Jewishness through the language of religious faith ("I believe"), the new Jews would express their Jewishness through the language of feeling ("I feel") (Ahad Haam 1947, 308). This Jew, designated by his contemporary Mikhah Yosef Berdiczewski (Bin Gurion) (1865–1921) as the "new Hebrew," "loved his people and its literature and its entire cultural heritage." Seeing from within the creative power of the nation's spirit, he "willingly chooses to embrace his national culture;...willingly identifies with the national history" (Ahad Haam 1947, 292).

Not only, in Ahad Haam's view, was such a person Jewish, but this form of Jewishness, insofar as it was freely chosen rather than divinely imposed, was on a higher plane than that of the religious Jew. No longer obligated to accept the theological assumptions that legitimated prior forms of Jewish identity, the new Jew identified with the Jewish people and their cultural heritage.

Importing into Jewish nationalist discourse a dichotomy borrowed from Kantian philosophy, Ahad Haam opened the way for a new discourse of secular Jewish identity. In contrast to the "old" Jewish subject who was "chosen" to fulfill God's will through adherence to specific beliefs and a regimen of practices, the identity of the "new" Jew, or the new Hebrew, was grounded in nationalist feelings and attitudes.

As a part of the new language for talking about the Jewish group and its distinctive identity, Ahad Haam produced a new way of conceptualizing Judaism. What had previously been represented as a body of divinely ordained norms and practices was transformed, in the discourse of secular Jewish nationalism, into a secular culture produced by the nation:

Judaism was created not only for the Jews, but by the Jews themselves. They devoted their best energies for thousands of years to Judaism's creation and preservation. (Ahad Haam 1947, vi)

Insofar as Jews, according to the new discourse, constitute a nation in the modern sense, norms and practices formerly represented as sacred were now represented as the natural norms and practices of a nation.

Thus, secular national discourse as formulated by Ahad Haam produced a new knowledge of Judaism, Jewish history, and Jewish identity. In the religious discourse, the principles for analyzing and interpreting knowledge of Judaism were considered to be divinely produced. To understand the life and history of the community, one applied religious principles of interpretation.

The new discourse of secular nationalism, which in Foucault's terms we would describe as a regime of truth, entailed new forms of inquiry and evaluation based on lawful patterns common to all human groups:

Each subject should be understood in terms of general causes that are rooted in human nature. Judaism should no longer be seen as an upside-down universe grounded in miracles, independent of the general laws of life. (Ahad Haam 1947, 106)

When this form of inquiry was applied to the Jewish group, according to Ahad Haam, it could be seen, like any nation, as a living organism driven by an innate will to survive.[31] Thus, Ahad Haam mapped the path of Jewish history as a progressive, evolutionary process in which the nation assumed or discarded different forms in accordance with its will to survive.

The national-secular representations of Jewish culture, history, and identity produced by Ahad Haam and his contemporaries were widely disseminated among Jews in Eastern and Western Europe. Within a few years, there emerged a network of newspapers, journals, books, pamphlets, annual zionist congresses, and schools established by zionist organizations. As described by cultural historian Michael Berkowitz (1993):

Ideals and images of Zionist culture were available...in cafes, university and Jewish community reading rooms, Zionist society reading rooms and social groups, and through literary or journalistic subscriptions. They were conveyed in many forms through participation in the Zionist congresses and local meetings, through verbatim reports of such events in the Zionist press and in bound volumes; and through periodicals, newspapers, books, pictures, postcards, and materials produced or expressly endorsed by the Zionist organizations. (p. 6)[32]

In addition, scholars produced articles and books through which a nationalist interpretation of Jewish history was disseminated. Eventually,

Jewish history was retold in secular-national terms rather than in religious terms.

Ahad Haam considered being a Jew and living Jewishly to be thoroughly consistent with intellectual freedom. Thus, he considered the question occupying Western European Jews—"Why be Jewish?"—to be meaningless. All efforts to provide external legitimations for one's Jewishness were not only unnecessary, but were also signs of spiritual servitude: "I am my own person; my beliefs, feelings, are my own and no one can force me to contradict or deny them" (Ahad Haam 1947, 69). No longer were Jews limited by the boundaries imposed by the religious authorities. Instead, they were free to discard outmoded ideas and practices inherited from the past, while adopting new ideas that were compatible with the modern science outlook. Thus, the national Jew was free to embrace any new scientific ideas, even those of Darwin, while remaining within the boundaries of Jewish culture or collective identity (Ahad Haam 1947, 69).[33]

To Ahad Haam, this intellectual freedom distinguished the new nationalist Jew from traditional religious Jews, liberal religious Jews, and universalistic "enlightened" Western European Jews. The latter two groups, in their zeal to integrate themselves into European society and culture, discarded the trappings of national identity such as the Hebrew language or the link to the land of Israel. Nevertheless, many of them wanted to retain some form of reformed Jewish religious faith and practice. However, Ahad Haam was contemptuous of those Jews who, abandoning their Jewish national identity, nevertheless sought to provide a transcendental legitimation for their Jewish identity:

> I, at least, have no need to exalt my people to Heaven, to trumpet its superiority above all other nations, in order to justify my existence. I, at least, know "why I remain a Jew"—or rather, I find no meaning in such a question any more than I would in the question why I remain my father's [sic] son. (Ahad Haam 1947, 194)

Yet it soon became clear that in Ahad Haam's discourse, there were limits to intellectual freedom. For one thing, he represented Western Jews who, in adopting the discourses of Enlightenment and emancipation, produced a new form of Jewish subjectivity, as having transgressed those limits. Such Jews, in return for acceptance into European culture, had betrayed their Jewish national origins and jettisoned their national heritage. Embracing life in the diaspora as a positive value, they had transgressed the limits of what Ahad Haam represented as "authentic" or "true" Jewish discourse. To Ahad Haam, these Jews, suffering from a basic insecurity, lived in a state of spiritual servitude. Their need to provide transcendent legitimations for their Jewish identity was a clear indication of this insecurity.[34]

Ahad Haam's new secular nationalist discourse of Judaism sought to answer a variety of questions such as: What is it to be Jewish? What is the essence and structure of Jewish culture? What is Jewishness? What are the essential teachings, values, and ideals of Judaism? How did Judaism emerge, develop, and grow? In the process, it produced new representations of Judaism/Jewish culture, Jewish history, and Jewish identity. In his representation of Jewish culture, Ahad Haam drew upon the romantic nationalist discourse that had been produced in Germany in the early part of the nineteenth century and that had been widely disseminated across Europe over the next few decades. This discourse privileged unity over diversity, the collective over the individual, and the realm of the spiritual/cultural over that of material practices.

What Ahad Haam had not anticipated, however, was that his act of displacing the long-accepted theological grounding of Judaism and Jewish identity opened the way for multiple, conflicting representations. Thus, whereas Ahad Haam proclaimed the compatibility of Judaism with intellectual freedom, other, more radical voices arose to expand the limits of Jewish culture and Jewish identity in a way that transgressed what he regarded as acceptable limits. Ensuing debates in Hebrew journals between Ahad Haam and his critics Mikhah Yosef Berdiczewski and Yosef Haim Brenner provide clear examples of the essentially contested, heterogeneous character of zionist discourse.

Ahad Haam and His Interlocutors

Like Ahad Haam, Mikhah Yosef Berdiczewski and Yosef Haim Brenner also privileged the nation over the religious community, secular culture over religious teachings and practices, and national identity over religious faith. Rebelling against the religious interpretation, they, too, sought to displace the teachings and practices of rabbinic Judaism with secular national ones. Moreover, like Ahad Haam, they both argued for a territorial solution to the "Jewish problem."

However, their representations of Judaism, the Jewish subject, and Jewish history clearly diverged from those of Ahad Haam. In contrast to Ahad Haam's biological, organic, collectivistic discourse, Berdiczewski, and to a lesser extent Brenner, imported into the debates over Jewish nationalism a modified Nietzschean interpretation. Whereas Ahad Haam emphasized social and cultural continuity and evolution, Berdiczewski and Brenner stressed conflict, upheaval, and discontinuity. While Ahad Haam emphasized the national collective and its culture, Berdiczewski and Brenner both emphasized individual imagination and creativity.

Berdiczewski, like Ahad Haam, defined the Jewish problem in terms of cultural atrophy and alienation. However, his conception of the problem was far more radical. Drawing a sharp dichotomy between past and present, inherited culture and individual experience, and the religious and the secular, Berdiczewski's language was inflammatory and provocative:

> Our young people were made to believe that spiritual attachment to the Jewish people necessarily meant faith in a fixed and parochial outlook, so they turned away and left us, for their souls sought another way.

> We are torn to shreds: at one extreme, some leave the House of Israel to venture among foreign peoples, devoting to them the service of their hearts and spirits and offering their strength to strangers; while, at the other extreme, the pious sit in their gloomy caverns, obeying and preserving what God had commanded them. And the enlightened, standing between, are men of two faces; half Western—in their daily life and thoughts; and half Jews—in their synagogues. Our vital forces disperse while the nation crumbles. (Hertzberg 1970, 294)

Berdiczewski and Brenner both found Ahad Haam's historical narrative, grounded as it was in evolutionary theory and emphasizing preservation and evolution, to be much too conservative. Although Ahad Haam had painted Judaism as a secular culture, his representation was, nevertheless, marked by religious concepts. For example, although by no means advocating a return to traditional religious practices, Ahad Haam nevertheless emphasized their important historical function in preserving the nation. Accordingly, he took issue with all who sought to exclude Jewish law, Hebrew scriptures, and the Sabbath from the new Jewish national culture.[35] Although neither personally adhering to traditional Jewish religious practices nor prescribing that other Jews do so, he nevertheless sought to impose limits. Thus, he considered Jews who openly rejected Jewish law, particularly the Sabbath, and disavowed any connection to Hebrew scriptures as having transgressed the boundaries of authentic national Judaism.[36]

In contrast to Ahad Haam's organic, developmental discourse, Berdiczewski embraced a historical narrative that emphasized discontinuity, rebellion, and flight from centralized authority. Privileging discontinuity over continuity and the individual over the collective, he represented conflict as the driving force of Jewish historical and cultural development. Over and against continuity, he highlighted historical struggles and schisms. He thus drew a sharp dichotomy between Hebrew and Jew, the individual and the nation, and the needs of the present generation and inherited traditions.

Whereas Ahad Haam advocated a policy of gradual change and evolution, Berdiczewski espoused radical upheaval and rebellion. He also depicted inherited Jewish culture as exercising a stranglehold on the present. Moreover, in contrast to Ahad Haam, Berdiczewski opposed setting limits or boundaries to Jewish culture.

In contrast to Ahad Haam's preference for the positive over the negative, Berdiczewski favored the negative:

> The negative precedes the positive, and destruction precedes construction. The new positives will be born after the old ones have been destroyed. The advocates of the new should not wonder at "the slander" that "they have come to move the boundary of the old." For even before they come to build the new, the old had already been destroyed in a thunderous storm. (Berdiczewski 1960, 36)

Berdiczewski sharply criticized Ahad Haam for avoiding open conflict, for refusing to acknowledge the incompatibility of the past and the present, and for striving to integrate them. To Berdiczewski, such efforts were ultimately destructive to the life of the community:

> We are the slaves of our memories, of our heritage; we are embalmed in the transmitted, delimited thoughts. But we are exhausted from returning to teach that which has already been thought and said. New needs have arisen within us that yearn for new values. We want to be a people that knows its place and its emotional needs. (Berdiczewski 1960, 36)

In the final analysis, Jewish tradition was oppressive:

> Among us, man is crushed, living by traditional customs, laws, doctrines, and judgments—for many things were bequeathed us by our ancestors that deaden the soul and deny it freedom. (Hertzberg 1970, 299)

In contrast to Ahad Haam's depiction of Jewish culture as homogeneous and organically cohesive, Berdiczewski depicted it as heterogeneous and conflicted. Denying the existence of a unified Jewish culture, Berdiczewski defended a vision of a community continually arguing over the meaning of that culture. In response to Ahad Haam's efforts to represent a "national morality" as the core of the Jewish national spirit, Berdiczewski denied that any such morality exists. In traditional sources, he argued, one can find conflicting moral views. Which one, he asked, is authentically "Jewish" (Berdiczewski 1960, 37–38)?

To Berdiczewski, Jewish culture included everything that individual Jews had created over time. To Ahad Haam's objection that such an approach subverted the unity of that culture, Berdiczewski denied that there had ever been a unified, continuous, coherent Judaism. The very question of what Judaism is had been an ongoing subject of conflict: "But that's the question: What is Judaism? What is the common and eternal Judaism?" (1960, 38).

Berdiczewski viewed Ahad Haam's Judaism as abstract and remote from the lives of individual Jews. To him, Judaism was "an actual event, not an abstract world view." As a living event, or process, it must be open to diverse positions:

> An abstract Judaism cannot serve as a candle, as this or that Judaism. We are Hebrews, and we will serve our own hearts. We want to make a place among us for those with all kinds of beliefs and opinions; we shall worship or not worship all kinds of gods. (Berdiczewski 1960, 38)

He thus opposed the individual "Hebrew" to the collective tradition: "We are simply Hebrews, Hebrews in all of the views that we adapt and all the thoughts that we think" (1960, 38).

Nevertheless, Berdiczewski was convinced that alongside the forces that deadened the soul and crushed the individual, Jewish culture also contained energizing forces, "paeans to life and its bounty," such as the *Song of Songs* (Hertzberg 1970, 299). What was needed was a process of transvaluation whereby those life-giving aspects of Hebrew culture that had been subordinated or buried could be restored to a privileged place. In this process of transvaluation, a concept that he borrowed from Nietzsche, the sword, a symbol of the material dimension of life, would be privileged over the book, and nature and the realm of the aesthetic would be priviledged over the study of sacred texts to which it had been subordinated:

> I recall from a teaching of the sages: Whoever walks by the way and interrupts his study to remark, How fine is that tree, how fine is that field, forfeits his life! But I assert that then alone will Judah and Israel be saved, when another teaching is given to us, namely: Whoever walks by the way and sees a fine tree and a fine field and a fine sky and leaves them to think on other thoughts that man is like one who forfeits his life. (Hertzberg 1970, 297)

Berdiczewski concluded with the plea: "Give us back our fine trees and fine fields! Give us back our universe" (Hertzberg 1970, 297).

Berdiczewski thus took issue with Ahad Haam's representation of the "Jewish problem." Whereas Ahad Haam stressed the collective's alienation from traditional Hebrew literary culture, Berdiczewski emphasized the individual. Incapable of nourishing the soul of the individual Jew, Jewish culture could no longer sustain individual creative drives or provide artists and builders with raw material:

> The individual finds in his Jewish nationality a power hostile to what is in his heart. Every one of us feels the opposition the moment he begins to improve himself and seek for culture. (Hertzberg 1970, 298)

In Berdiczewski's view, Ahad Haam's claim to espouse intellectual freedom was clearly contradicted by his ongoing efforts to set boundaries and limits to Jewish culture and thought:

If I [as Ahad Haam had written] can evaluate the beliefs and knowledge that
our ancestors transmitted to us, can I not also judge their values and even completely negate them, without cutting myself off from my people? (Berdiczewski
1960, 38)

While agreeing with Ahad Haam that exile was the major factor imped-
ing Jewish creativity, he rejected Ahad Haam's gradualist solution. Instead,
he advocated a form of cultural revolution:

Our hearts, ardent for life, sense that the resurrection of Israel depends on a
revolution—the Jews must come first, before Judaism—the living man, before
the legacy of his ancestors. (Hertzberg 1970, 294)

Whereas Ahad Haam desired to conserve values inherited from the past,
Berdiczewski, drawing upon Nietzsche, called for "fundamental transvalu-
ations in the whole course of our life, in our thoughts, in our very souls":

We can no longer solve the riddles of life in the old ways, or live and act as our
ancestors did. We are the sons [*sic*], and sons of sons, of older generations, but
not their living monuments. (Hertzberg 1970, 294–295)

Berdiczewski's representation of the Hebrew subject was also more radical than that of Ahad Haam. While Ahad Haam represented the new
Hebrew subject as integrating past and present, inherited values and modern attitudes, Berdiczewski's subject was more fragmented and rebellious.
Far from being a passive recipient of that which he received from previous
generations, the new Hebrew was an initiator and a creator:

We must cease to be tablets on which books are transcribed and thoughts handed down to us—always handed down.

Through a basic revision of the very foundations of Israel's inner and outer life,
our whole consciousness, our predispositions, thoughts, feelings, desires, and
will and aim will be transformed. (Hertzberg 1970, 295)

In Nietzsche's terms, the new Hebrew subject must cease to be reactive and
become active. Rather than "satisfy the national conscience that lived in
their hearts by preserving what had been handed down from their ancestors" (Hertzberg 1970, 295), the new Hebrew had to make a decisive
choice: "To be the last Jews or the first Hebrews" (Hertzberg 1970, 293),
to be "the last Jews—or the first of a new nation" (Hertzberg 1970, 295).
    The contrast between Ahad Haam and Berdiczewski is clearly evident
in the different binaries used to represent Jewish nationhood and identity.
Whereas Ahad Haam's binaries, as we have seen, were drawn from an
organic, evolutionary model in which apparent contradictions would ulti-

mately be resolved or transcended, Berdiczewski spoke in terms of irreconcilable conflict: last Jews/first Hebrews, Jews/Judaism, living person/legacy of ancestors, monuments/sons, abstract Judaism/living Judaism, Israel/Torah, book/sword, beauty/*mizvot*, transvaluations/reforms.

Berdiczewski seemed to resist all culturally imposed hierarchies, codifications, and limits. In contrast to Ahad Haam, he wanted to free the individual from the constraints imposed by the narratives of past and all codified discourses and structures. To Ahad Haam, Berdiczewski's approach was a threat to the order, stability, and continuity of Jewish life. Although committed to intellectual freedom, he nevertheless spoke in terms of the essentials of Jewish life, and his conception of knowledge, society, and culture was objectivistic rather than perspectival. Berdiczewski, on the other hand, rejected the hierarchies of power that were inscribed in objectivistic thinking, advocating an adventurous experimentation in their place.

Yet, for all of his apparent radicalism, Berdiczewski, no less than Ahad Haam, remained positioned by nationalist discourse. On the one hand, Berdiczewski sought to bring the commitment to intellectual freedom to fruition. Intellectual freedom did not mean simply breaking free of the limits imposed by transcendental religious discourse as Ahad Haam seemed to be saying. To be truly free, one had to be able to transgress all limits, including the ones that Ahad Haam sought to impose.

However, although espousing rebellion and discontinuity, Berdiczewski, positioned within the discourse of nationalism, nevertheless imposed collective limits on individual creativity. While advocating a seemingly unlimited creative freedom, he asserted the individual's dependence on the culture of the nation:

> What the individual cannot achieve for himself, he can acquire when he attaches himself to the group, and when his ear is attuned to the still voice of the whole.... The individual is not simply impoverished when he participates in the group, he may also be enriched through the enduring wealth of the community. (Hertzberg 1970, 300)

In opposition to Ahad Haam, Berdiczewski insisted that subordinating individual creativity to the group's culture meant that "it is we, and our sons, and the sons of our sons who are conquered" (Hertzberg 1970, 301).[37] Yet, when all was said and done, he, too, like Ahad Haam, made individual creativity conditional on Jewish national culture.

Thus, notwithstanding the seemingly radical character of Berdiczewski's critique, in the final analysis, he, too, set distinct limits. While criticizing the oppressive effects of inherited culture, he nonetheless insisted that the creative life of the individual is dependent on national culture. Berdiczewski, however, was not unaware of his paradoxical position. In despair, he proclaimed that inherited Jewish culture, simultaneously inspiring and suffocating, is "elixir and poison in one and the same substance" (Hertzberg 1970, 301).

Although Berdiczewski's rhetoric was more extreme than that of Ahad Haam, privileging the individual over hierarchical structures and present over past, in the final analysis, he remained tied to narratives of the past. Insofar as the individual was shaped in significant ways by inherited culture and depended on it for his or her full actualization, Jews had to continue struggling with that culture.[38] "Who," he lamented, "will show us the way? Who will clear us a path?" (Hertzberg 1970, 301).

Yosef Haim Brenner

As radical as Berdiczewski's critique was perceived to be by Ahad Haam and others, he was not, by any means, the most radical of Ahad Haam's critics. For all of his rebelliousness, Berdiczewski, unwilling to sever all ties, continued to engage Jewish cultural tradition. Far more radical was the position of Yosef Haim Brenner, who advocated the removal of all cultural boundaries. In contrast to Berdiczewski, Brenner insisted that the new Hebrew could sever all ties with traditional Jewish cultural forms and values while nonetheless remaining a Jew. It was possible, he argued, to identify with the Hebrew nation without reproducing its cultural forms.[39] The new Hebrew's only obligation to the nation was to act in behalf of the nation's survival. Rejecting all attempts to impose any other limitation on beliefs and practices, he declared:

> We, the living Jews, whether or not we fast on Yom Kippur, whether or not we eat meat with milk, whether or not we embrace the morality of the old Testament, whether or not we are faithful disciples of the Epicurean world-view—we do not cease to feel ourselves as Jews, to speak in the Jewish language, to derive our spiritual nourishment from our [Hebrew] literature, to stand up for our free national culture, to defend our national honor and fight openly for our national survival in any form that struggle takes. (Brenner 1985, vol. III, 487)

For Brenner, living as a Jew was neither a religious nor a cultural matter:

> The new Jews...have nothing to do with Judaism. Nevertheless, we are still a part of the community no less than those who put on phylacteries or wear fringed garments [*magdilei hazizit*]. (Brenner 1985, vol. III, 493)

Whereas Berdiczewski emphasized both cultural and material aspects of national life, Brenner did not hesitate to break the connection:

> Jewish nationalism does not obligate its free-thinking sons to embrace a specifically Jewish worldview. The enlightened Jew, as long as he lives in the midst of

his people, speaks their language, and participates in their life, even if he denies the entire Torah of Moses and thinks about the Bible (and the Koran, and the Veda, and all sacred scriptures)—whatever he thinks, is not excluded because of these ideas. (Brenner 1985, vol. III, 488)

Thus, going beyond both Ahad Haam and Berdiczewski, Brenner pictured the new subjectivity as entailing only an active identification with and participation in the life of the nation:

We are members of the Hebrew nation true to ourselves. We live among our people and cannot imagine a life outside of it, regardless of whether our nation is good or evil. (Brenner 1985, vol. III, 493)

In defining the Jewish problem, Brenner once again broke with his contemporaries. Criticizing Ahad Haam for describing the Jewish problem in terms of the survival of Judaism, Brenner declared: "We must extirpate this hybrid [*raayon hataarovet*] idea":

We, Ahad Haam's free-thinking Jewish comrades, have nothing to do with Judaism. Nevertheless, we are a part of the community no less than those who put on *tefillin* [phylacteries] or wear *tzitzit* [fringed garments]. We say: our life question is the question of a place for productive labor for Jews. (Brenner 1985, vol. III, 487)

To Brenner, the Jewish problem was solely a material one. Unlike Herzl, he did not see anti-Semitism or persecution as the basic issue. The basic problem confronting the Jews was neither that they were persecuted nor that they lacked conditions conducive to the development of their national culture. The basic dilemma was that the conditions of exile did not afford them the opportunity to engage in productive labor:

Our life question is that of a place of productive labor for us Jews. We Jews are strangers in every land, bent Jews without land, without language, etc.... The environment of the Christian majority does not allow us to be complete Jews in the way that our free Russian or Polish comrades etc...are complete Russians and Poles. The environment of the majority confuses us, devours us, distorts our form, injects confusion into our lives everywhere—but we are far from assimilation, very far, and the issue of conversion is neither madness nor a joke. Our people is exilic, sick, stumbling, repeatedly falling and rising. We must raise it up. The restorative power of its will—we must strengthen it. (Brenner 1985, vol. III, 487)

Brenner developed the full implications of his radical position in an essay published in the journal *HaPoel HaZair* in 1910. Rejecting any and all cultural limits to Jewish identity, Brenner argued contra Ahad Haam that the new Hebrew could even discard the Hebrew Bible without cutting his or her ties to the nation. In one of the most radical statements to emerge within zionist discourse, Brenner insisted that even a Jew who embraced the Christian scriptures did not, in so doing, place himself or herself beyond the boundaries of Jewish national life:

> For me, the "old Testament" does not have the same value that it has for all those who call it "Sacred Scriptures," "The Book of Books," "the Eternal book":...I have long since been liberated from the hypnotic spell of the twenty-four books of the Bible. Many secular books from the last generations are dearer to me and strike me as greater and more profound. I consider the Hebrew Bible to be an important source of distant memories and the embodiment of our national spirit, and that of humanity in general, over the generations and ages. But I also find and acknowledge this significance [*hashivut*] in the books of the New Testament (I am not addressing their literary power). The New Testament is also our book, an essential part of us. (Brenner 1985, vol. III, 482–483)

From the perspective of Ahad Haam and his disciples, Brenner had transgressed the acceptable limits of Jewish nationalist discourse. Accordingly, in an outstanding example of the power-knowledge nexus in zionist discourse, Ahad Haam took steps to ensure that Brenner's views would no longer have access to a public hearing. Thus, Ahad Haam wrote to a leading member of the Hovevei Zion Society of Odessa that provided financial support to the Hebrew zionist journal *HaPoel HaZair*, where Brenner's article had been published. In that letter, Ahad Haam insisted that responsibility for allowing such articles to appear fell on the members of the board that provided financial support. As a member of the board, Ahad Haam protested the society's support for such writings. Ahad Haam insisted that Brenner, having transgressed the acceptable limits of zionist discourse, must be deprived of any opportunity to repeat this transgression. The society acceded to Ahad Haam's wishes and imposed the restriction on the journal.[40]

Ahad Haam's efforts to restrict Brenner's ability to disseminate his ideas can be best understood in light of his effort to formulate and prescribe the limits of Jewish nationalist discourse. In his most comprehensive statement on this issue, a 1911 article entitled "Torah from Zion" [*Torah Mezion*] published in *HaShiloah* and written largely as a response to Brenner, Ahad Haam sought to clarify those limits. He had earlier argued that as long as a Jew loved the people, their literature, and their history, he/she was a loyal son/daughter of the Jewish people. Now, however, challenged by Brenner, he sought to clarify his position (Ahad Haam 1947, 407–9).

Ahad Haam, pushed to the limit by his younger critics, sought to make it clear that however much of a departure from the past Jewish nationalist discourse represented, there were, nevertheless, limits as to how far one could go without breaking the bonds. These limits included not so much religious belief, but rather a positive attitude and relation to the Bible and to the Hebrew concept of God. Given the central role played by the God idea in the history of the nation, one who says "I have no bond with the God of Israel, with that historical force which infused the People with life and which shaped its spiritual qualities and life path for two millennia" transgressed the acceptable limits of Jewish national culture.

The same argument applied to the Hebrew Bible. Unlike the religious believer who accepts the Hebrew scriptures as divinely revealed, unique among literary creations, and immune to literary criticism, the nonbeliever's link is both literary and national. Whereas from a literary perspective he acknowledged Brenner's right to regard other books as greater and more profound, from a national perspective it was simply unacceptable. There is, he insisted, "a feeling of special closeness enwrapped in national sanctity" that links one by a thousand threads to past generations.[41]

It is clear that Ahad Haam, like most other Jewish nationalists, operated with an essentialistic and totalistic notion of nation, national culture, national identity, and national history. He thus endeavored to uncover, excavate, and bring to light the "essence" of Jewish culture by studying the Jewish past and its cultural productions and extrapolating from them the "essential" characteristics/qualities of Judaism. What he was not able to understand is that his selection was a highly arbitrary attempt to impose fixed boundaries, to arrest what was a dynamic, flowing, interactive, often conflictual process of culture formation.

Berdiczewski, as we have seen, in rejecting this holistic way of thinking, sought to uncover lines of flight within Jewish culture. Brenner, however, went even further. To him, there were no limits to Jewish cultural discourse. Nevertheless, for all of his radicalness, Brenner, too, remained positioned within the parameters of Jewish nationalist discourse. He thus accepted as a given that nations, divided on the basis of land and language, constituted natural units. Similarly, while representing exile differently than many of his contemporaries, he nonetheless accepted zionism's homeland/exile binary and its representation of exile as a site of national sickness and weakness.

The debates among Ahad Haam, Mikhah Yosef Berdiczewski, and Yosef Haim Brenner and their dissemination through the Hebrew press clearly reveal the inherently conflicted character of zionist discourse. This, in turn, renders problematic all efforts to extract its essence. Far from having a unified, continuous essence, zionist discourse, as stated earlier, is heterogeneous and inherently conflicted. Numerous other sites of controversy support this claim, including the controversy at the 1903 Zionist Congress concerning the establishment of a temporary homeland in Uganda, the conflict over the validity and desirability of cultural activities in the diaspora, the conflict between revisionists and "general" or centrist zionists over the goals and tactics of zionism, the debates between Haim Weizmann and Louis Brandeis over the character of the zionist movement, and the debates of Brith Shalom and the labor zionist leadership over the relationship of the Jewish nation to the Arabs. The debates between Canaanites and zionists over the nature of Jewish nationalism and, more recently, the conflicts between secular-humanist zionists and Gush Emunim also deal with the character of zionism. Each of these controversies reflects the inherently conflicted character of zionist discourse.

Scholars positioned within zionist discourse have sought to frame the debates between Ahad Haam and his critics in terms of freedom of speech or conflicting interpretations of Judaism.[42] However, in the reading suggested here, the controversy relates to issues of power and knowledge. More than a controversy over an abstract principle, the debate provoked by Brenner's article and Ahad Haam's response revolves around efforts to impose distinct boundaries or limits on Jewish/zionist discourse. While insisting on his own right to disseminate a secularized discourse that Jewish religious leaders regarded as heretical, Ahad Haam denied to Brenner the same power. While rejecting the power of the rabbis to set limits on Jewish public discourse, Ahad Haam himself was prepared to do exactly that. In the process, Ahad Haam sought to appropriate the power mechanisms related to the dissemination of Jewish national discourse. The result was a prolonged and heated public debate among the Russian Jewish intellectual community as to what could and could not be said within the spaces of Jewish public discourse.

CHAPTER 2

CRITIQUE OF ZIONISM: CRITICS FROM WITHIN

Throughout its history, zionism has been criticized from within and from without. As I discuss in chapters 4–6, postzionist critiques of zionism differ significantly from previous critiques. Yet, many problems raised by postzionists first emerged in previous critiques. In this chapter and the next, to help set the stage for the discussion of postzionism, I discuss a select group of earlier critics. Implicit in all of the critiques of zionism are questions such as: What are the boundaries of legitimate zionist discourse? Who has the authority to define such boundaries? By what means could these boundaries be enforced? Despite repeated efforts to circumscribe the space of zionist discourse through the establishment of borders separating "authentic" from "inauthentic" zionists and zionists from nonzionists or antizionists, there are not, nor could there be, universally agreed upon procedures for either determining or enforcing such borders.

As we saw in the previous chapter, there were ongoing, significant disagreements among theorists of zionism such as Ahad Haam, Berdiczewski, and Brenner, among others. Notwithstanding the diversity of positions that emerged, critics who positioned themselves within zionist discourse took it for granted that zionism was the authentic form of Jewish life and that there was only one true representation of zionism, Jewish history, Jewish culture, and Jewish identity. To such critics, necessary changes could be achieved through the reform of zionist discourse and practices. Critics from within, whom I discuss in this chapter—including Martin Buber (1878–1965), Mordecai Bar On (b. 1928), Amos Elon (b. 1926), Amos Oz (b. 1939), and Meron Benvenisti (b. 1934)—continued to insist on zionism's viability. Writing after the establishment of the state, they rejected the calls of critics outside zionism for the dismantling of the zionist apparatus.

MARTIN BUBER: A STATE FOR TWO NATIONS

Among zionists, there were very few who placed the relation between Jews and Arabs at the center of their concerns. One group, established in 1925 as Brith Shalom [Covenant of Peace], which eventually evolved in the 1940s into Ichud [Unity], stands out for their efforts on behalf of Arab–Jewish rapprochement.[1] One of the most prolific and articulate representatives of the group was the German-born Jewish philosopher and Hebrew University professor Martin Buber. Although never questioning the Jews' claim to their homeland, Buber also acknowledged the validity of the Palestinian Arabs' claim as well. Buber insisted that zionism reject any approach to settlement of the land that suppressed or dominated the Arab population.[2] This put him in a very small minority among zionists.

Buber continually pressed for Jewish recognition of the validity of the Arab claim. Until 1948, Buber and his colleagues in Brith Shalom advocated a binational state based upon the "absolute political equality of two culturally autonomous peoples" (Buber 1983, 74):

> A bi-national social-political entity, with its areas of settlement defined and limited as clearly as possible, and with, in addition, economic cooperation to the greatest possible extent; with complete equality of rights between the two partners, disregarding the changing numerical relationship between them; and with joint sovereignty founded upon these principles—such an entity would provide both peoples with all that they truly need. (p. 199)

In Buber's view, such a state would eventually become incorporated into a federation of Middle Eastern states.

However, Buber never denied the Jewish people's claim to the land of Israel, a claim that was legitimated by historical ties to the land, the reclamation activities of Jewish settlers, and the Jewish people's right to live as a nation.[3] In a letter to the Indian leader Mahatma Gandhi, Buber (1983) wrote:

> We considered it a fundamental point that in this case two vital claims are opposed to each other, two claims of a different nature and origin, which cannot be pitted one against the other and between which no objective decision can be made as to which is just or unjust. We considered and still consider it our duty to understand and honor the claim which is opposed to ours and to endeavor to reconcile both claims. (p. 120)[4]

Buber was critical of the way in which the question of Arab–Jewish relations had become politicized by zionist leaders. Rather than confirm the basic humanity of the Arabs and recognize the validity of their aspirations to national autonomy, they had dehumanized them through political slogans. Buber, however, opposed granting politicians the power to set the conditions for the fulfillment of zionism. In public and private debates, he vigorously tried to persuade the nation's leaders that they were pursuing a path that would end in disaster.[5]

If the Arab–Jewish conflict was to be justly resolved, it was necessary to shift the focus from power politics to human relationships. This required of Jews that they discard their stereotypical views of the Arabs and recognize their basic humanity. Moreover, he insisted that Jews try to view the situation from the perspective of the Arabs.

To the overwhelming majority of Jews living in Palestine, Buber and his colleagues were naive idealists who ignored social, political, and military realities. As they saw it, the Arabs were guilty of perpetrating violence against a guiltless Jewish minority who wanted nothing more than to live in peace. Arab violence, most zionists believed, resulted from ignorance of the authentic humane zionist aspirations and the violent, uncivilized Arab character.

Buber and his colleagues framed the situation differently. Jews had to bear much of the responsibility for Arab violence. Arab attacks on Jews had to be understood against the background of the zionists' failure to establish a relationship of "genuine togetherness [*Miteinanderleben*] with the Arabs" (Buber 1983, 93).

When, in 1929, Arabs attacked and killed Jews, Buber argued that the Jews were not blameless. In words that to most Jews appeared treasonous, Buber insisted that "perhaps we ourselves provided the motive for the religious fanaticism of the [Arab] masses" (Buber 1983, 94). Moreover, he criticized the Jewish community for using violence. In his view, the means adopted by the Jews had a profound influence on the ends achieved:

> If the people justifies the murder, identifies with the perpetrators, and thus accepts responsibility for the sin as its own, we will bequeath to our children not a free and pure land but a thieves' den to live in and raise our children in. (Buber 1983, 133)

Instead of violence, Buber, like many Jewish leaders, advocated a policy of *havlagah* [restraint].

Even in 1948, in the midst of the battle, Buber continued to publicly assert Jewish responsibility. In his view, the Jewish claim that their settlement of the land had been peaceful was a distortion of history:

> The truth of the matter is that, when we started our infiltration into the country, we began an attack "by peaceful means." We did so because we were forced to, in order that we might reestablish an independent productive and dignified life for our people. (Buber 1983, 227)[6]

Buber's metaphor of peaceful invasion was based on several assumptions: first, the Jews never attempted to reach an agreement with the Arabs regarding the terms of ongoing Jewish settlement; second, they had failed to convince the Arabs of their common interests through mutually beneficial economic activity; third, purchasing land from wealthy land owners, the zionist settlers assumed a dominant economic position at the expense of the Arabs; and fourth, the Jews insisted on establishing a Jewish state.[7] These factors, according to Buber, generated and fortified among Palestinian Arabs the perception that the Jews were invaders bent upon dispossessing the Arab masses.

Following the establishment of the state in 1948, Buber and his colleagues, having failed in their efforts to achieve a binational state, reluctantly embraced the new Jewish state. For Buber, the destruction of six million Jews in Europe and the resulting need for a home for masses of Jewish refugees created pressures that were virtually impossible to resist. Acknowledging that "our historical re-entry into our land took place through a false gateway" (Buber 1983, 291), he nonetheless accepted the state as his own (Buber 1983, 292–93).

But Buber did not cease to campaign on behalf of the Palestinian Arabs. In a series of debates with prime minister David Ben Gurion, he criticized the politicization of zionism and the elevation of the state to a supreme value.[8] Buber and his colleagues in Ichud (the successor to Brith Shalom) also campaigned for the repatriation of Arab refugees who had fled in 1948, and demanded the abolition of the military government that deprived Israeli Arabs of their civil rights (Buber 1983, 284). On several occasions, when Israeli soldiers killed Arab civilians, Buber spoke out publicly.[9] He also criticized the government for confiscating Arab lands to build a Jewish development town (Buber 1983, 301).

To Ben Gurion's argument that Israeli Arabs enjoyed economic, social, and educational benefits, Buber insisted that such benefits did not justify the inequities and indignities that they were made to suffer. While acknowledging that a state could not avoid committing unjust acts, he nevertheless insisted that it was obligated to limit such acts to the minimum necessary for its survival. Daily, he argued, the Jews must confront their responsibility to redraw the line of demarcation between just and unjust acts. In such instances, political slogans were totally inadequate.

Buber placed moral and religious concerns over and against the dominant zionist view that framed Israel's survival solely in physical and military terms:

> There can be no peace between Jews and Arabs that is merely a cessation of war; there can only be a peace of genuine cooperation. Today, under circumstances so manifoldly aggravated, the command of the spirit is to pave the way for the cooperation of peoples. (Ben Ezer 1974, 120)

LIBERAL ZIONIST CRITIQUES:
MORDECAI BAR ON'S POSTREVOLUTIONARY ZIONISM

Many critics operating within the borders of zionism acknowledged that there was a clear need, in the light of changing conditions, to reassess the basic concepts of zionism. One such internal critic who enunciated this position was Mordecai Bar On, a former high-ranking military officer, a historian, and a leader of Peace Now, Israel's largest Israeli peace movement.[10] Although affirming his commitment to zionism, Bar On (1983) nonetheless has insisted on "the need to repair and refurbish the run-down Zionist edifice" (p. 6). Notwithstanding the problems that he has uncovered within zionism, Bar On defends its viability. While acknowledging that the time may come when zionism is no longer necessary, Bar On insists that present realities demand not the replacement of zionism, but its repair. In contrast to postzionists, whose position he has repeatedly criticized, Bar On has insisted that zionism remains a discourse capable of defining and addressing the problems of contemporary Israeli life.

According to Bar On (1983),

> Zionism, in its essence, was a revolution that attempted to revive the nationhood of the Jewish people out of the assessment that the religious framework of Judaism was disintegrating and could never again serve as a unifying principle. (p. 6)

Discarding the religious aspects of Judaism, zionism "broke the chain of Jewish continuity as well" (p. 6).

Bar On's essentialistic approach to zionism is evident in the distinction that he, like many liberal zionists, draws between its authentic core and the "distortions and aberrations" that subsequently beset it.[11] The essential core of zionism was actualized in zionism's program of immigration, the creation of "a territorial and economic infrastructure to support the Jewish collective then taking root in the land," and the achievement of "Jewish sovereignty in a Jewish state" (1983, 2).

In the case of immigration, Bar On readily acknowledges that the zionist program attracted only a small minority of Jews. Of the four million Jews who immigrated from European nations between 1880 and 1920, only 100,000 came to the land of Israel. In its efforts to create a territorial and economic infrastructure, zionism advocated agriculture and rural settlement over urban development. At the same time, zionism relinquished the original goal of gaining sovereignty "over the territories of the biblical land of Israel, which included the East, as well as the West Bank of the Jordan" (Bar On 1983, 2). The establishment of the state of Israel in 1948 was the culmination of the struggle for Jewish territorial sovereignty. Bar On insists, however, that "this sovereignty is flawed" and incomplete and will remain so until Israel is accepted by her neighbors and a substantial part of the international community.[12]

According to Bar On, one can distinguish between two types of zionism, which in Israel are represented by "two polar camps" (Bar On 1983, 4). The first type, which he refers to as maximalist, maintains a belief in revolutionary zionism and utilizes a militant discourse to mobilize the nation. This group adheres to such nineteenth-century nationalist values as "absolute unity, unquestioned loyalty, and the exclusive priority of nationalist considerations" (1983, 4).

The second camp, the moderate zionists, "has been forced to admit that the expansionist phase of Zionism is over" (1983, 4). Basically accepting the 1948 borders of the state, it adopts a strategy of compromise and coexistence with neighboring Arab countries.

Speaking of the "important implications" of these divisions, Bar On renders problematic the very principles that he identifies as basic and essential to zionism. Thus, he argues, "settlement is no longer able to serve as a central motive and focus of zionist activity" (Bar On 1983, 4). Neither, he argues, is agricultural activity: "Whoever puts his faith in agricultural settlement, will find himself cultivating a tree whose branches will never again bear new fruits" (Bar On 1983, 4). Another "cornerstone of classical zionist thought" that he considers to be no longer tenable is the ingathering of the exiles. This, according to Bar On, is linked in zionist discourse to a negative attitude toward and rejection of the diaspora.

According to Bar On, an examination of immigration facts and statistics reveals that the original Herzlian belief in the mass immigration of diaspora Jews to Israel is simply unrealistic. This new reality had been recognized by David Ben Gurion (the first Prime Minister of Israel) in the 1950s, when he spoke of Israel as the home of the majority, rather than all, of world Jewry. Bar On accepts the more recent zionist argument that defines the primary danger confronting diaspora Jewry in terms of assimilation rather than physical persecution.

Bar On (1983) also argues against the classical zionist view of negation of the diaspora. It is clear that the majority of diaspora Jewry will not choose to emigrate. Therefore, to continue to negate Jewish life in the diaspora is to maintain a hope "again unintentional, for the gradual disappearance of the Jewish people in the Diaspora" (p. 5), a position that Bar On rejects. While not going so far as to advocate the necessity of the Golah, Bar On argues that zionists must accept it as a reality and abandon the core idea of negation of the diaspora. In its place, zionists must seek to foster dialogue for the purpose of "aiding Golah Jews in their struggle against assimilation" (1983, 5).

Bar On brings to the surface several of the basic problems/contradictions that beset zionist discourse. Notwithstanding the fact that many zionists would consider his position "heretical," Bar On (1983) nonetheless proclaims: "I unequivocally assert that I am a loyal Zionist" (p. 5). To differentiate his views from those who continue to adhere to a revolutionary, militant zionism, Bar On refers to his position as *post*revolutionary zionism. The goal of postrevolutionary zionism, he argues, is "in this final phase of her functioning, [to] straighten the lines which have become crooked, clear away the bridges which have become blocked and mend the fences which have become breached" (p. 6).[13]

Thus, in contrast to postzionist critics who believe that zionism's contradictions are inherent, thereby rendering it untenable, Bar On speaks of distortions and aberrations that must be eliminated or corrected. Although acknowledging that several original key zionist tenets are no longer tenable, he speaks of the need for zionism to undergo a new stage in its development.

AMOS ELON

Amos Elon's *The Israelis: Founders and Sons,* published in 1971, represents an early and incisive attempt to reveal the unintended outcomes and inconsistencies of zionist discourse and practice. While praising the accomplishments of zionism, Elon, a highly respected writer, journalist, and social critic, does not hesitate to reveal its shortcomings as well. Thus, while criticizing various antizionist and nonzionist positions, he also asserts that "wrong were those Zionists who thought that there was no future and no safety anywhere for Jews as Jews except in their own state" (Elon 1971, 32).

In contrast to most historians of zionism, Elon did not hesitate to criticize the zionists for what he considered to be their mistakes. At the same time that he acknowledged zionism's accomplishments, he also highlighted its blind spots. Basic to his critique of zionism is his explication of its failure to anticipate and justly resolve the conflict with the indigenous Arab population. To Elon, zionism's failure to consider Arab nationalist aspirations was one of its most dangerous blind spots. In their zeal to create a normal national existence, the early zionists failed to recognize the prior presence of the Arab population or to calculate the conflicts that would ensue. Thus, from the outset, the zionist dream of "normalization" seemed to contain the seeds of its own subversion:

> The early zionists proclaimed their hope to "normalize" Jewish life. They wanted to take a holiday from Judaism as it had existed throughout two millennia. But as the Arab-Israeli conflict intensified, with little if any hope of reconciliation, it became evident that even in Israel, there was to be no holiday. (Elon 1971, 24)

Elon rejects the argument of those who argue that in the early years of zionism, there was little evidence of Arab nationalism to which zionists could respond. The same, he argues, could be said about Jewish national-ism in its early stages.[14] Yet, while insisting that others recognize Jewish nationalism and treat the Jews as a nation, early zionists refused to do the same for the Arabs.

To Elon, the blindness of the zionists to the Arabs remains a mystery:

> We reach here one of the strangest most baffling aspects of our theme. The zionists were fervently, and at great human sacrifice, pursuing a national and social renaissance in their ancient homeland. They were blind to the possibility that the Arabs of Palestine might entertain similar hopes for themselves. More responsive than most people of their time to the compelling force of ideas, they ignored the power of related ideas on their adversaries. (Elon 1971, 152)

Although acknowledging the terrible effects of the zionist revolution on the Palestinian Arabs, Elon speaks of the uncontrollable forces of fate that brought about the displacement of the Arabs of Palestine:

> Every revolution has its price, of course, and the Zionist revolution was no exception. By a brutal twist of fate, unexpected, undesired, unconsidered by the early pioneers, this price was paid partly by the Arab inhabitants of Palestine. The Arabs bore no responsibility for the centuries-long suffering of Jews in Europe, yet, in the end, the Arabs were punished because of it. The price exact-ed was heavy, it is impossible to measure it in terms of human bitterness and suffering. Whatever their subsequent follies and outrages may be, the punish-ment of the Arabs for the sins of Europe must burden the conscience of Israelis for a long time to come. (Elon 1971, 23)

Elon (1971) describes the zionist leaders as frightened men whose "eyes were hung with monumental blinkers" (p. 156). He also speaks of them as egocentric revivalists "moving in a strange twilight zone, seeing the Arabs and at the same time not seeing them":

> Their attitude was a combination of blind spots and naivete, of wishful think-ing, paternalistic benevolence, and that ignorance which is often a factor in international events, and sometimes their cause. (p. 157)

Attributing much of their blindness to "the spirit of the time" (p. 158), Elon even insists that given their liberal, humanistic values, had zionist leaders, even as late as 1931, realized that "their success might contribute to bring-ing about a tragedy for the Arabs, they might have revised their scheme, or even have withdrawn from action in good time" (p. 158).

Like many other Israeli liberals, Elon describes the Israeli–Palestinian conflict as a tragedy.[15] While acknowledging that the zionist policy and practices of Hebrew labor [*avodah ivrit*], which advocated employing only Jews, were clearly exclusionary, he represents this as "a deep and tragic irony." While, as he characterizes it, the goal of separating the communities was to avoid conflict, it actually exacerbated it insofar as it "compounded the future tragedy by causing the deliberate exclusion of the natives from the New Society" (Elon 1971, 171).[16]

At the same time, Elon seeks to balance his critique by focusing on the good intentions of the early settlers, a practice common to the writings of liberal scholars. Rejecting the position of those who characterize zionist settlement as colonialist, Elon insists that while often guilty of cultural arrogance, zionist settlers were never motivated by colonialist motives. The settlers' sense of moral superiority over colonialists was, in his words, "deeply felt and totally sincere" (Elon 1971, 170).

Like many liberal Israelis, Elon speaks of the fate of "the roughly 600,000 Arab refugees displaced by the 1948 War which followed the declaration of Israel's statehood, as a tragedy, one of the most excruciatingly bitter prices exacted by zionism" (p. 23). Insisting on the validity of both Jewish and Arab claims to the land, Elon (1971) represents the protagonists as trapped in circumstances beyond their control:

> The clash in Palestine was not between natives and colonialists in the ordinary sense, but between two nationalist movements. Both were, in their own way, "right" and "natural." The fault, if there was one, lay less with the men directly involved on both sides than with the new world of ferociously hostile nation-states in which they lived. If men had higher aims there would have been no Palestine conflict, nor, probably, "Jews" and "Arabs." (p. 26)

The ultimate fault, therefore, lies neither with nationalism in general nor with zionism in particular, but rather with "the new world of ferociously hostile nation states" (p. 26).

Ironically, while seeking to eradicate, or at the very least contain the conditions that nurture anti-Semitism, zionism actually contributed to them. Zionists hoped to eliminate the causes of persecution and anti-Semitism by removing the Jews from the conditions that fostered it and establishing them in a safe and secure homeland. However, far from eliminating anti-Semitism, the ensuing conflict with the Arab population actually exacerbated it, creating, in the process, a new form of it:

> The Arab–Israeli conflict was producing a species of anti-Semitism never before seen. This newly generated anti-Semitism was making it almost impossible for Jews to continue to live in Arab countries. Even Moslem countries which were not Arab, or geographically so remote that they had never been involved in the Palestine conflict, were affected.... The Arab–Israeli conflict forced almost a

million Jews to leave the Islamic countries. Of them, about two-thirds, mainly the poor, have found their way to Israel. (Elon 1971, 24)

While pointing to the "tragic" contradictions inherent in zionism, Elon refrains from placing the blame on zionist discourse or suggesting that it be altered. Implicit in his writing is the premise, or the hope, that a liberalization of the Israeli stance would bring about a solution. Elon does, however, bring to the surface effects of zionism on the Palestinian population that have been ignored by most other Israeli writers. Like Bar On, he believes that were the system reformed from within, the problems that it has generated, particularly the Palestinian conflict, could be resolved.[17]

AMOS OZ: ZIONISM AS ESSENTIALLY CONFLICTED AND CREATIVE

Yet another example of a liberal critique of zionism is found in the writings of Amos Oz, one of Israel's leading novelists and social critics. Particularly in his nonfiction writings *In the Land of Israel, Under This Blazing Light,* (in Hebrew, 1979), and *Slopes of Lebanon,* Oz tends to problematize such concepts as zionism, Jewish peoplehood, Jewish culture, and Jewish identity.[18] In *In the Land of Israel,* Oz, rejecting essentialistic notions of zionism and Judaism, graphically portrays countervailing voices within zionism and within present-day Israel.

In Oz's view, conflict was inherent in the very foundations of zionism. He thus speaks of zionism as "a querulous family and its trends and nuances, the panoply of love–hate relationships, the competitiveness, the use of covert influence, and the overt rivalry between its various components" (Oz 1989, 73). Zionism, as represented by Oz, is an essentially contested discourse. We have seen examples of this in the previous chapter in our discussion of the disputes among Ahad Haam, Berdiczewski, and Brenner. In addition, there were ongoing conflicts in the early years of zionism between the followers of Theodore Herzl and Ahad Haam over zionism's character, goals, and strategies.

In *In the Land of Israel,* Oz, an active participant in the Israeli peace movement, graphically depicts the fault lines within Israeli society. He thus represents the conflicts between Jews and Palestinian Arabs, doves and hawks, religious believers and secularists, secular humanists and antihumanists, and Ashkenazim and Sephardim. As represented by Oz, Israeli culture and society are sharply divided.[19] However, rather than decry this ongoing conflict, Oz sees it as ripe with creative possibilities.

According to Oz, conflict is necessary to a creative culture. He thus depicts the zionist movement, and Israeli culture in general, as a drama of ongoing struggle among competing interpretations, outside influences, and differing emphases. In Oz's (1984) words, it is "an unrelenting struggle over what is the wheat and what is the chaff, rebellion for the sake of innovation, dismantling for the purpose of reassembling differently, and even putting things in storage to clear the stage for experiment and new creativity" (p. 137).

The questions that divide Israelis are, for the most part, the same questions that plagued the zionist movement and the pre-state Yishuv. These include such questions as: Do Israeli society and culture represent continuity or discontinuity with the Jewish historical past formed in the diaspora? Do Jews constitute a national-ethnic group or a religious community? What is the relationship between zionism and Judaism? between Israeli culture and traditional Jewish culture? between Israeli identity and Jewish identity? between the state of Israel and diaspora Jewry? Is Israel a Jewish state or a pluralistic, democratic, secular state?

To Oz, the struggle over zionism in contemporary Israel is a struggle over Jewish culture and Jewish identity.[20] In *The Slopes of Lebanon* (1989), a volume of social and political criticism, he argues that the real dispute within Israeli society is not about territories, security, or borders, but about "differing concepts of Judaism—some of them humanitarian, others tribal and primitive, and still others midway between" (p. 205). Largely as a consequence of the wars of 1967, 1973, and 1982, Israelis have been experiencing a severe identity crisis, continually confronted with such questions as "who we are, what we want to be, and what our source of authority should be" (p. 75).

Oz's confrontation with proponents of Gush Emunim reveals one of the fundamental splits within Israeli culture. To the citizens of the West Bank settlement of Ofrah, authentic zionism, grounded in Jewish religious sources, has been contaminated by ideas and values derived from Western humanism. In their eyes, the basic division within Israel today is between those whom they designate as Israelis—who, like Oz, identify with the humanistic values of the West—and Jews such as themselves, who ground themselves in the teachings of the Bible and other Jewish sources (Oz 1984, 103–53).

Arguing against critics from the right, Oz, now a professor at Ben Gurion University, eloquently represents the position of a secular, Western-oriented, humanistic zionism. His graphic representation of Israeli society and culture seems to challenge all claims of a unified Jewish people, a unified zionism, or a unified Israeli culture. However, like Bar On and Elon, Oz believes that the resolution of such disputes is possible within the framework of zionist discourse. In the end, Oz positions himself within that discourse, arguing against the religious, expansionist discourse of Gush Emunim in favor of a humanistic, Western-oriented zionism.

MERON BENVENISTI: ZIONISM, DISCOURSE, AND POWER

One of the most powerful and distinctive critiques of zionist discourse to have emerged from within the labor zionist establishment is that of Meron Benvenisti (b. 1934). While not going so far as to position himself outside of the boundaries of zionism, Benvenisti reveals many of its problems, particularly its power effects. While denying that zionism prior to 1967 could be legitimately regarded as colonialist, he acknowledges that post-1967 zionism might merit that designation. Regardless of his categorization, Benvenisti, highlighting the power effects of zionist discourse and practice, comes closer than any other zionist critic to revealing the colonialist character of zionist settlement.

A former youth leader in the labor zionist movement, Benvenisti initiated large numbers of Israeli youth into the discourse and practices of labor zionism:

> When I turned eighteen, I became a high priest in the cult of *moledet* [homeland], complete with the romantic attire that went with it. (Benvenisti 1986, 31)

As a leader, Benvenisti was responsible for taking large numbers of Israeli youth on hikes and trips and for imbuing in them the values of labor zionism.

However, like others of his generation, he became disillusioned by what he regarded as Israel's militant and paternalistic stance toward the Palestinians in the wake of the 1967 War. Serving from 1974 to 1978 as Deputy Mayor of Jerusalem under Teddy Kollek, he antagonized many fellow Israelis by empathizing with the plight of the Palestinians and acknowledging the validity of many of their claims. As director of a research project tracking Israeli policies and practices in the West Bank, he published a number of important reports and maps that highlighted the contradictions between Israel's professed humanistic, democratic values and the oppressive results of their actions.

Benvenisti draws a clear connection between the discourse and practices of labor zionism and the discourse of early zionism. The classical zionist concept of "negation of the diaspora" was the starting point of the education of his generation. This concept instilled in zionist youth "a deep sense of shame and reflection of the wretched life of our ancestors in the shtetl before the Holocaust" (Benvenisti 1986, 12). The discourse of labor zionism was also woven from many other concepts drawn from nationalism and socialism, including: homeland [*moledet*], knowing the homeland intimately [*yediat haaretz*], conquest of the homeland [*kibbush haaretz*], and conquest of labor [*kibbush haavodah*]. Each term, in turn, was linked to the concept of redeeming the homeland [*geulat haaretz*].[21] A basic term of labor zionist discourse, the concept of *moledet* "became the pivot around which the entire Israeli educational system would revolve" (p. 21).

Benvenisti clearly shows that, notwithstanding their linguistic meaning, these concepts functioned as practices of power. This can be clearly seen in a concept such as *moledet,* which generates and legitimates practices of dispossession and possession. On the one hand, *moledet* conveyed a notion of zionism as "a radical and revolutionary transformation of the situation of the Jewish people by transporting it to its own soil" (Benvenisti 1986, 28). At the same time, *moledet* embodied the act of possessing and, by extension, dispossessing:

> But moledet is more than a cultural and character forming experience. It is a positive act. When you hike in the desert you actively possess its wadis and rocky promontories. The circuitous mountain roads skirting dense pine forests become Jewish when you drive along them. Sighting gazelles, identifying wild plants, excavating archaeological sites are all symbolic acts of possession. Caring about the homeland proves ownership. (p. 23)[22]

Similarly, the related concept of *yediat haaretz,* seemingly a benign educational value, was also an act of possessing:

> Yediat Haaretz is not a passive acceptance of the landscape, but is rather a dynamic concept of molding it to a new form—modern, productive, progressive, and efficient. (p. 25)

Central to the process through which labor zionism produced and disseminated a distinctive knowledge was what Foucault has called an apparatus, a network of practices and institutions. As described by Benvenisti, this apparatus included seemingly benign institutions, among them formal and informal educational systems through which labor zionist discourse was disseminated; a Society for the Protection of Nature; ceremonies for planting trees to redeem the land; and the publication of pamphlets and books. All of these served as vehicles for the dissemination of this discourse. Even the garb worn by the leaders, whom Benvenisti labels "the priest[s] of the cult of moledet," which consisted of "a black embroidered 'rubashka' [Russian blouse], a kaffiyeh [Arab headdress], army boots, and a map case" (p. 31), were a means of dispersing power.

Benvenisti (1986) speaks of this apparatus as comprising part of a highly ritualized "cult of the homeland" [*moledet*], a cult that pursues "development and greening of the landscape" (p. 25). Through this cult, Israeli youth were initiated into the discourse and practices of labor zionism, framed in terms of the sacred zionist project of redeeming the land.

The apparatus for disseminating labor zionism also included physical sites. A major site, the meaning of which was a product of the labor zionist discourse, was the fortress of Masada, the desert fortress overlooking the Dead Sea. Masada was one of the primary objectives of the organized hikes that served to instill in the youth a love of the land. There, the discourse of homeland and negation of the diaspora is concretized and materialized. At Masada, writes Benvenisti (1986),

> moledet is brought to its final destination.... Our attempt to eradicate the painful memories of our exile and diaspora had given license to destroy what others did in this land in our absence, to chase the gentiles away and restore the temple cult. Our boundless preoccupation with the physical landscape and our perception of the Arabs as objects in that landscape unwittingly contributed to the loss of humanitarian values. (p. 45)

In addition to producing this discourse, labor zionism sought to imbue it with a transcendental meaning. Within labor zionism, Enlightenment values of equality, social justice, and the brotherhood of humanity struggled for ascendancy with the value of *moledet*. The privileging of the latter opened the way to chauvinism and xenophobia:

> With our adulation of development, our habit of attaching transcendental values to human creations in concrete and steel, to every grove of trees planted, we paved the way to a new form of Jewish paganism, and for an exotic growth of believers in the End of the Days. Our obsession with instilling moledet, together with our negligence of equally cherished values such as the brotherhood of man, social justice, and civil equality to all, had lead inexorably to chauvinism and xenophobia. (Benvenisti 1986, 45)

Benvenisti (1986) also reveals the ways in which "forgetting" the actual pre-state conditions that fostered the conflict between Jews and Palestinians was inscribed into the Israeli collective memory following the establishment of the state:

> We wanted to forget that phase because it reminded us that there was a Palestinian community with which we shared our cities and our land, a community that bitterly fought for what it believed had been its national objectives but which had been utterly defeated. Their total collapse, and the exodus of hundreds of thousands from the areas under our control made us an ethnically homogeneous society. The "Palestinian question" we felt, had been eliminated by the disappearance of the Palestinians from our midst. Conceptual exclusion became a reality....The Palestinians became "refugees" or "infiltrators" and the conflict became an Israeli–Arab conflict, a conflict between sovereign states. The opaque glass wall separating Rehavia from Katamon was replaced by barbed wire and minefields along the armistice line. (p. 90)[23]

This forgetting also affected the ways in which the Israelis viewed the Palestinians who remained within the borders of Israel and became citizens of the state. Within zionist discourse, this population was framed as the internal alien and excluded other, "a nonassimilating and nonassimilable alien group at best, a 'fifth column' at worst" (p. 91). Excluded from Israeli society, the Palestinians were designated a secondary extraneous element in a homogeneous Jewish nation-state, a mere symptom of the overall conflict (p. 91). This exclusion also made it possible to legitimate acts of discrimination and land expropriation.

Zionists, like other nationalist settler groups, also sought to erase all Arabic names and replace them with Hebrew names:

> We have done more than create a paper empire. We have actually transformed the physical reality, built cities, drained marshes, made the desert bloom. We not only eradicated Arab place names, we actually destroyed the places as well. (p. 196)[24]

Another basic component in the apparatus for producing and disseminating the knowledge of labor zionism was a coterie of "experts" whose representations, wrapped in the language of scholarship, were held to be true. In the case of zionism and the state of Israel, these representations were produced by Middle East experts, referred to as Orientalists, stationed at universities or in government agencies. Echoing Edward Said's postcolonial critique of Orientalism, Benvenisti (1986) describes how the knowledge that these experts produced served as the basis for Israeli policies in relation to the minority Palestinian population:

> "Arab affairs" were entrusted to the capable and professional hands of "Arabists," experts for Arab affairs. Governors, advisers, correspondents, and Oriental scholars had monopolized the treatment of internal and external "Arab matters." Only they could interpret and represent them because they were acquainted with the "Arab mentality." Arab attitudes, sociology, even demography were not subjects that could be studied through "normal" behavioral sciences or by the "uninitiated." (p. 91)[25]

Benvenisti is one of the few Israeli writers to recognize the power effects of mapping in the zionist enterprise. Mapping, according to Benvenisti, is a "natural impulse of people coming to a new place; the people who have lived in the country for centuries rarely need it themselves" (p. 193). Rather than a somewhat passive representation of existing space, map drawing "is an act of possession, of creating a new reality" (p. 192). Imposing a grid on free-flowing spaces through their maps, the zionists came to believe that they "have 're-created' the country and gained symbolic ownership" (p. 192). Fixing spaces by imposing names upon them, zionist mapmakers con-

cealed their dynamic character. Rather than seeing these maps as representations, they saw them as reflections of the real.²⁶

The knowledge of the land produced and disseminated through these
and other practices of labor zionism was the result not of acts of interpreting, but of positive acts of power, "a dynamic concept of molding it into a
new form—modern productive, progressive, and efficient" (p. 25). The
study of the land together with the agricultural practices connected to it
instilled in the young zionists "a primary and enduring bond with the land"
(p. 25).

The new Hebrew subject represented in the discourse of labor zionism
differed from the one that had been imagined by early zionist theorists. The
new subject position produced and disseminated by labor zionism was
based upon the physical and emotional bond to the homeland and was
imbricated in the knowledge and practices that it generated. To be a
Hebrew, to be a zionist, meant to physically live and work on the land. This
Hebrew subject was represented by the *halutz,* the pioneer, who, sacrificing
comfort and safety, devoted himself/herself to the physical redemption of
the land. Related to this subject position were new models of social relationships based upon the ideals of socialism.

Yet, argues Benvenisti (1986), labor zionism's efforts to create a new
kind of Jew and produce new forms of social relationships failed:

> We made a magnificent attempt to create new social frameworks for nurturing
> new and wholesome human relationships, but in the final analysis we have to
> admit that it achieved very little. People essentially stayed the same. And it is
> not even so demonstrable that an Israeli Jew is necessarily an improvement on
> his Diaspora counterpart. (p. 60)

Following the establishment of the state, the dual social, cultural, and economic systems for Jews and Arabs established by labor zionism in the pre-
state era were perpetuated and institutionalized into a discriminatory system:

> The establishment of a sovereign state did not alter the concept of the dual soci-
> ety. Zionist policies of separate development continued, resulting in a system-
> atic discrimination of the Israeli Arab minority. However, the altered circum-
> stances of the old concept under new circumstances was revealed in full after
> 1967 in the occupied territories; instead of equally ranked ethnic-social sys-
> tems, a status hierarchy of superior-subordinate groups was institutionalized. A
> separate but unequal principle is employed in all sectors enforced by the instru-
> ments of coercion of the state. (Benvenisti 1986, 78)

Benvenisti is unique among zionist critics for revealing the intricate
ways in which zionist discourse and practices are connected to the dis-

placement and marginalization of Palestinian Arabs. Insofar as these practices helped to bring about the Jews' possession of the land, it had the effect of deterritorializing Palestinian Arabs. His analysis of the effects of labor zionist discourse and practices provides graphic support of Foucault's arguments concerning the discourse/knowledge/power nexus. Benvenisti, more than any other zionist critic, brings to the surface the power effects of zionist discourse and the inexorable connection between power and knowledge in Israeli culture.

Benvenisti's description of the disillusionment shared by many of his generation of labor zionists provides a telling representation of the extent to which they had been positioned by labor zionist discourse. Notwithstanding the similarities between his representations and those of Foucault to which we referred earlier, it is clear that his discourse, unlike Foucault's, remains tied to the socialist concept of ideology.

Notwithstanding his scathing critique of zionist discourse and its effects, Benvenisti (1986) stops short of calling for the dismantling of zionism. Instead, he reverts to the liberal discourse of intentions gone astray, representing the problem in terms of a conflict between "primary intentions and the objective realities" (p. 75).

Benvenisti and his peers, the inheritors of labor zionism, had been imbued with a sense that labor zionism was transcendentally legitimated. Consequently, they were unable to treat it pragmatically. Imbued with the idea that labor zionism was "a comprehensive theory," they did not have a sense of its flexibility in responding to changing circumstances. Consequently, when circumstances caught them unaware, they, in a state of cognitive dissonance, lost the initiative to other forces, who "never shared our parents' hope for a reconciliation of humanism and nationalism, Judaism and universalism" (p. 75).

Like Oz and other labor zionists, Benvenisti objects to the ways in which zionist discourse has been preempted by the militant, expansionist Gush Emunim. Far from accepting the group's self-representation as an authentic manifestation of zionism, Benvenisti insists that they had actually reversed the old values of labor zionism. Turning the values of labor zionism upside down, they had replaced the socialist ideals with intense fundamentalist religious ideology: "Our nationalism was a secular, rational concept, 'New Zionism' is messianic deliverance" (pp. 69–70).

The discourse of labor zionism, which had, in different circumstances, been "honorable and moral," has, in the new circumstances, been transformed into legitimations of what Benvenisti (1986) sees as "repugnant policies and immoral actions":

> We watch in despair how our parents' sense of mission, their deed, even their pragmatic tactics are usurped and twisted. The fossilized shell of the pioneer-

ing ideology, while keeping its brilliant exterior and attractive contours, is totally empty within and used to justify repugnant policies and immoral actions. Basic concepts which under different circumstances were honorable and moral have turned out to be sinister and reactionary.

All lofty social ideals are double-edged swords. (p. 75)

At the same time, Benvenisti recognizes points of convergence between these very different forms of zionism:

The content is totally different, but the form and appearance are not so different.... In listening to Gush Emunim members, I detected the same sense of elitism, the same contempt for the petit-bourgeois flavor of urban life and the ravages of a consumer society that we felt. (pp. 69–70)

While regarding Israeli practices and policies following the 1967 War as colonialist, Benvenisti refuses to apply the colonialist label to zionism prior to that time. Yet his critique of the practices of deterritorialization and reterritorialization, of land expropriation and population displacement, has much in common with the postcolonial critique developed by Said and others. Although providing important insights into unanticipated and frequently ignored power effects of zionism, Benvenisti, in the final analysis, stops short of designating zionism as colonialist.[27]

What postcolonial theory would regard as an inconsistency or contradiction in Benvenisti's writing can be explained, at least in part, by his structural model of colonialism. In his view, colonialism requires an external colonial power in whose military, political, and economic interests a space is colonized. It further requires a group of settlers acting on behalf of the colonial regime, who "form a superior class, control a disproportionate part of the economy, and exploit the local population through their monopoly on political and military power" (p. 159). Insofar as the zionists were not citizens of an external country and did not undertake their enterprise to serve the interests of that country, zionism cannot, according to Benvenisti, be designated as colonialist.

Benvenisti (1986) also justifies the pre-state policy of *avodah ivrit,* a policy designated by other scholars as indicative of colonialism. As he argues, this policy was

essential at the time to prevent the rise of a colonial society consisting of Jewish masters and Arab peons. Labor leaders in the thirties waged an uncompromising and aggressive struggle against Jewish orange grove owners who used cheap Arab labor, and they fought the Arab laborers themselves. (p. 149)

Yet, Benvenisti acknowledges that *avodah ivrit* provided a belief system that insulated the zionists from objective reality. In the eyes of labor zionists, this policy was a legitimate part of their effort to create a homogenous Jewish state where they would be free "from the Palestinian presence in their midst" (Benvenisti 1986, 150). This had the effect of exacerbating discriminatory attitudes and legitimating inequities.

Arguing that not every case in which one nation rules another is colonialism, Benvenisti prefers to frame the conflict between Israel and the Palestinians as intercommunal. In his view, the refusal or inability of Israelis to understand the intercommunal character of the Israeli–Palestinian conflict prevents them from grasping the true character of the conflict.

Benvenisti does acknowledge that following the 1967 War, labor politicians "created almost absentmindedly a system that conforms to classic colonial models." But Benvenisti attributes this to institutional neglect rather than an official policy of state. Thus, he concludes that the colonial model does not really fit Israel's occupation of the territories conquered in the 1967 War:

> I began to wonder if the model is appropriate. The colonial model implies a distinct "mother country" whose seat of power, symbolized by the capital, is situated outside of the colony.... Colonial situations are externally generated, but who are the external powers. One is Israel, but is it external? (p. 161)[28]

In the final analysis, unlike postzionists, Benvenisti locates the source of the problem not in zionist discourse itself, but rather in the younger generation's failure to grasp the ways in which that discourse was being distorted. Thus, Benvenisti talks in terms of good intentions, legitimate goals, and changing circumstances:

> Our zionist, liberal socialist philosophy did not escape the fate of other great liberating ideologies. Its failure to adjust to changing realities enabled dark forces to usurp its revered symbols, now fossilized and anachronistic, and turn enlightened, moral, and progressive ideas into reactionary beliefs and immoral deeds. (p. 78)

CONCLUSION

As this chapter shows, numerous critiques of zionist discourse emerged in the pre-state Yishuv and in the state of Israel which succeeded it. Taken together, they touch upon virtually all of the basic components of zionist discourse and practice. Each of the critics discussed in this chapter framed their critiques in different ways and focused on different issues. However, a problem shared by most of these critics is the ongoing conflict between Israel and the Palestinians. In the wake of the 1967 War, critics on the zionist left became increasingly aware that a normal national life would not be possible unless the conflict was resolved in a just way. While Benvenisti feared that the conflict had gone too far to be reversed, Buber, Elon, Bar On, and Oz continued to insist that zionism has the capacity to bring about the changes and reforms needed to end the conflict.

More than other critics who position themselves within zionism, Benvenisti effectively uncovers the power effects of zionist discourse, and of the diverse practices, sites, and institutions that comprise the zionist apparatus. In this respect, he anticipates a number of arguments presented by the postmodern postzionists whom I shall discuss below in chapter 6. However, the postmodern postzionists frame their critique within the context of postmodern and postcolonial theory. In addition, many of those postzionist critics, unlike Benvenisti, identify zionism with forms of colonialism.

Sharing the frustrations of many of his peers, Benvenisti asks: "Are we entitled to make a choice—are we not compelled to formulate a new national agenda to replace the century-old Zionist program?" (Benvenisti 1986, ix). Nonetheless, like the other liberal critics discussed here, Benvenisti never actually disassociates himself from zionism. Notwithstanding the force of his critique, he continues to position himself within zionist discourse while seeking to rid it of what he considers to be its perversion. In contrast, those critics to whom I now turn reject the zionist label and position themselves outside the spaces of zionist discourse.

CHAPTER 3

CRITIQUE OF ZIONISM: CRITICS FROM WITHOUT

THE CANAANITE CRITIQUE

While the critiques of zionism considered thus far are all positioned within zionist discourse, efforts have also been undertaken to create alternative spaces outside of that purview for nonzionist and antizionist views of Israeli culture identity. One of the major attempts to produce a nonzionist discourse of Israeli cultural identity was undertaken by the group known as the Canaanites. Emerging in the late 1940s and early 1950s, the small group of intellectuals, so labeled by their critics, sought to formulate an alternative secular nationalist discourse to zionism. To this day, their critique, although marginalized in Israeli culture, represents one of the few significant efforts to challenge the zionist mapping of the Jewish national entity.

Canaanite discourse was basically the creation of the poet and ideologue Jonathan Ratosh (1909–1981), who first articulated its basic tenets as an alternative to zionism. The Canaanites' starting point was that the revolution that the zionists sought to enact was never realized. Although zionism was grounded in the rejection of diaspora life, it never succeeded in separating itself from Judaism, the product of that life. Consequently, the new subject produced by zionism was still linked to the very history and culture from which zionism had sought to free it.

Over and against zionism's new Hebrew, the Canaanites, through the writings of Ratosh, produced an alternative concept of the new Hebrew subject. Severing all ties with Judaism and Jewish history, this new subject, a native of Palestine, defined his or her identity through ties to the land and its history.[1] By Hebrews, the Canaanites meant a national group united through territory and language.[2] It was the new Hebrew who had effected the revolution of which the zionists spoke.

Carrying the "negation of the diaspora" to an extreme, the Canaanites argued that in order to normalize national life, all links with diaspora Jewry had to be dissolved. The zionist concept of a worldwide Jewish people or nation was an oxymoron. The real nation was built around the territory, the Hebrew language, and the culture that it produced. In place of the zionist mapping of the land of Israel as the homeland of the Jewish people, the Canaanites envisioned the land as the center of a regional entity dominated by a hegemonic Hebrew culture. Instead of relating to the land of Israel as the Jewish holy land, the Canaanites defined it as a natural spatial, territorial site.

The Canaanites also rejected the zionist historical narrative that represents Jews as a nation that, emerging in the ancient Near East, survived almost two millennia of exile, and, in 1948, reestablished a Jewish state in the land of Israel. Rejecting the zionist representation of the biblical Israelites as a distinct and separate group, the Canaanites argued that the Hebrew nation originated as part of a larger Near Eastern civilization that included Philistines, Edomites, Moabites, and Canaanites. This original character of the Hebrew nation was drastically altered when Ezra the Priest, in the fifth century BCE, succeeded in imposing a separatist, particularistic, religious discourse on the nation. In the new discourse disseminated by Ezra and his followers, Judaism was treated as a universalistic faith no longer dependent on a specific territory.

Emerging at a time in which faith in the national-secular vision of Israel was beginning to fade, Canaanism was embraced by only a small intellectual minority. Transformed in the early years of the state "from a potential avant-garde to a rearguard" (Shavit 1987, 20), its influence was decidedly lessened in the years following 1967 owing to a strengthening of Israel's bonds with diaspora Jewry.[3] Nevertheless, although never succeeding in displacing zionism, the Canaanites had a decisive effect on Israeli cultural discourse. Numerous artists and writers drew upon Canaanite motifs and integrated them in their work. Notwithstanding the small number who openly identified themselves with Canaanite discourse, the group generated significant controversy within Israeli culture. While rejected by the zionist establishment, it was seen by a number of critics as posing a serious challenge to Israeli culture.[4]

While the Canaanites never established themselves as a political presence on the Israeli scene, they did, in 1951, establish a public group, The Center for Young Hebrews. According to one scholar, "the Center was to be the closest Ratosh would ever come to translating his vision into political action" (Diamond 1986, 44–45). The Center's program, published in a twenty-four-point declaration, never actually entered the political debate. However, the fact that it set forth ideas that later were enunciated in the discourse of postzionism makes it relevant to our discussion.

The document called for a state that was based on the self-definition "of all the inhabitants of the State of Israel, regardless of religion, faith-community or origin." It further called for the "official granting of full political, civil, and social rights and obligations to all citizens of the state, regardless of religion, faith community, or origin, on the basis of a recognition of the fundamental freedoms and civil rights of all residents of the land" (Diamond 1986, 65). While mentioning nothing of the recently passed Law of Return, the program advocated a citizenship law that "would make the conferral of citizenship conditional upon permanent residency in the country, knowledge of its language, and observance of its laws" (Diamond 1986, 67).

BOAZ EVRON'S NATIONAL RECKONING: A POST-CANAANITE POSTZIONIST CRITIQUE

The Canaanite critique of zionism, along with its alternative representation of the new Hebrew identity, was based primarily on the replacement of one essentialistic vision of Jewish nationalism with another. Rather than undertake a comprehensive critique of the premises of zionism, the Canaanites, through programmatic statements, pronounced the errors of zionism and put in its place their alternative vision. However, a comprehensive critique of zionism has been formulated by a Boaz Evron, a journalist and critic for two Israeli daily newspapers, *Yediot Aharonot* and *Haaretz*, who was, for a time, a follower of the Canaanites. His book, *A National Reckoning* (in Hebrew, 1988; in English, 1995), represents one of the, if not the most, comprehensive attempts to formulate a nonzionist interpretation of Israeli history, culture, and national identity.

Evron (1995) regarded Canaanite discourse as "the most systematic and audacious attempt to cut through the tangle of contradictions" that informed zionism. Carrying the zionist representations of a secular nation, secular-national culture, and national territory to their logical conclusion, the Canaanites sought to complete the zionist process (pp. 2–7). In contrast to those who see Canaanism as a heresy, Evron sees it as a logical extension of zionism. Zionism had failed to realize its original goal of replacing the ethnic-communal form of Jewish life with a national one by grounding national identity solely on territory and language. This, according to Evron, opened the way for the alternative Canaanite vision:

> This ideology was important [evidence] of a tremendous intellectual hunger of which we were not even conscious. It defined for us why we rejected zionism, why we felt that we, children and products of this land, were intrinsically different from Jews in the diaspora, whose thought processes and sensibility

seemed qualitatively foreign. (Evron, "The Event—and Its Academic Reflection," cited in Diamond 1986, p. 80)

However, Evron finds several problems in the Canaanite effort. First, although the Canaanites offered important political insights concerning the future of the state of Israel, Evron characterizes their effort to separate the new Hebrew culture from historical Judaism as naive. In claiming that "a Hebrew cannot be a Jew and a Jew cannot be a Hebrew," Ratosh ignored the fact that the ancient Hebrew civilization only survived in and through Judaism and therefore was inextricably bound up with Jewish culture. One simply cannot, insists Evron, skip over 2,500 years of history. In addition, Evron rejected the political implications of the Canaanite plan. Even if the peoples of the region agreed to participate in a regional political framework, a highly unlikely prospect, they would certainly resist any "attempt to impose on them foreign cultural and spiritual forms and contents" (Evron 1995, 211).[5]

At the same time, Evron (1995) considers the Canaanites to be right on several counts. First of all, they "brought to full logical development and conclusion the basic theses of secular political zionism, which aspired to a normalization of the Jewish people" (p. 221). Second, the distinction that they draw between Hebrews and Jews, is, argues Evron (1995), necessary for the "creation of an Israeli nation" (p. 221). Moreover, the Canaanites were correct in recognizing the need for a broad, regional political framework.

Like the Canaanites, Evron rejects the zionist assumption that the Jews are and have always been a nation. Characterizing such classical zionist concepts as "national will" and "the Jewish people" as mystical, Evron insists that they have no historical basis. Like Ratosh, he distinguishes between the autochthonous Hebrew nation and the worldwide Jewish religious community that emerged at the time of Ezra. However, unlike Ratosh, Evron seeks to ground his counterhistory of Hebrew origins in contemporary scholarship.

Judaism, according to Evron, is the product of discontinuity rather than continuity. Highlighting the dialectic of religion and political power, he, like Ratosh, represents Judaism as an outgrowth of Ezra and Nehemiah's successful efforts, with the support of Persian rulers, to establish a priestly hegemony.

Evron bases his critique of zionism's nationalist assumptions on its contingent, time-bound character. Zionism, in his view, is based upon assumptions deriving from nineteenth-century Eastern European political realities. With the passing of those realities, zionism became obsolete. Whereas zionism constructed a historical narrative based upon the projection of the peculiar conditions of nineteenth-century Eastern European Jewish life back into Jewish history, Evron argues for a historical analysis that pays careful attention to the specific characteristics of different historical communities. Thus, he rejects the zionist view of anti-Semitism as a metahistorical phenomenon transcending time and place. To Evron, any manifestations of anti-Jewish attitudes and behavior can only be understood it terms of specific social and political contexts.

A highly original thinker, Evron engages in what I would call *ideology critique*. His synthetic approach, while grounded in historical research, differs from that which postzionist historians and social scientists were just beginning to formulate. The latter, as we shall see, concentrated on producing alternative historical narratives and sociological representations. Evron, on the other hand, was primarily concerned with revealing the contradictions and inconsistencies in zionist discourse. Although recasting the zionist accounts of Jewish history beginning with the biblical era, this was, for Evron, a strategy to provide support for his theoretical critique. Unlike the theory-oriented postzionists I discuss in chapter 6, Evron makes no use of postmodern, poststructuralist, and feminist theories. Nevertheless, as we shall see, he succeeded in articulating many criticisms of zionism that were reiterated by postzionists.

Taking up each of the premises of zionist discourse, Evron seeks to reveal the fallacies on which they rest. He thus problematizes such fundamental zionist axioms as: (1) Jews constitute a nation and have done so since their historical beginnings; (2) Jewish history is best represented as the history of a nation; (3) there is a natural relationship between that nation and the land of Israel; (4) there is a universal Jewish problem, defined by political zionists in terms of anti-Semitism and by cultural zionists in terms of assimilation and cultural atrophy; (5) these problems can be solved by the return of the Jewish "nation" to the homeland; (6) in the Jewish homeland, the life of the nation will be normalized; (7) Jewish life in the diaspora is, and always has been, destructive; (8) in the homeland, a new Jewish subject has emerged that is clearly different from the Jewish subject produced in diaspora; (9) zionism has always been and continues to be fully committed to the rescue of the Jewish people; (10) in the Jewish state, the Jewish people will be unified; (11) a Jewish state, the state of Israel, is the best and most effective solution to the problems facing world Jewry today.

Jews as a Nation: A Critique

According to Evron, all efforts to provide universally objective criteria to determine nationhood have proven to be problematic. Besides these general definitional problems, the specific zionist claim that Jews constitute a nation in the modern sense simply cannot withstand criticism:

The inner contradiction in Zionism derived from the assumption that all the Jews in the world constitute a single entity, an exiled territorial nation. Religion was conceived as a manifestation of this essential national trait, not as the very essence [*sic*] of Jewishness. But any attempt to discover extrareligious traits typical of the Jews as a whole, as Jews, has failed.... The very attempt to go beyond religion, for all Jews, was trapped again in religion. The general formula defeated itself. (Evron 1995, 62)

Evron acknowledges that it was appropriate to apply a national model to Jewish life in Eastern Europe in the late nineteenth and early twentieth centuries. However, this national model did not accurately represent the condition of the rest of world Jewry, either at the time of zionism's emergence or in the present. Thus, one of zionism's fundamental mistakes was to have universalized a local condition applicable to specific Jewish communities and make this a foundational premise of zionist discourse:

[T]he difference between East European Jewry (where the earliest rumblings of zionist discourse emerged) and the rest of the Jews in the world lies not in the fact that the other Jews were "less Jewish," a preposterous proposition, but that East European Jewry had demographic, geographical, and sociological traits that enabled it to develop a national consciousness. (Evron 1995, 58)

Given that the Jews, as a whole, did not comprise a nation, zionism's state goal of reviving a previously existing nation and renewing its national culture cannot be sustained. Whereas zionists represented their goal as reviving an original national ethos that had been weakened or lost and restoring an original national social body that had been fragmented as a result of exile, Evron saw the zionist enterprise as one not of reawakening or renewal, but of creating and constructing. Drawing conclusions that conform with those expressed in many recent scholarly studies of modern nationalism, Evron insists that rather than rebuilding an existing nation, zionism was faced with the task of constructing a national consciousness and building a national group where none previously existed.

Evron acknowledges the validity of the zionist claim of having precipitated a revolution in Jewish life. However, whereas the zionists represented that revolution as a part of the ongoing course of Jewish history, Evron insists that it was discontinuous with the Jewish past:

In order for Jewish national potential to be realized, a complete dissociation from the old Jewish framework was required.... This dissociation had to be territorial, cultural-linguistic, and psychological. It was necessary to create a new mentality the mentality of a territorial nation. (Evron 1995, 102)

Reading zionist sources against the grain, Evron (1995) argues that far from effecting the renewal of the nation, zionism constructed a new Jewish nation and a new nationalist mythos. Included in the "new nationalist myth" was a "myth of an 'exiled, territorial nation,'" "a myth of restoration," and a "myth of ancestral soil" (p. 102).

Problematizing the Jewish Problem

As we saw in chapter 2, zionists spoke of the "Jewish problem," the universal problem that zionism came into being to solve. Political zionists like Herzl framed this problem in terms of inherent, continuous anti-Semitism, which he regarded as a product of socionational conditions. Ahad Haam and cultural zionists, on the other hand, represented the Jewish problem as one of cultural atrophy and social fragmentation. Evron, however, finds each of these representations to be faulty.

Evron criticizes zionism's ahistorical approach to anti-Semitism. Anti-Semitism, like all aspects of Jewish life, cannot be understood apart from specific political, social, economic, and cultural conditions. There is no "essential," indigenous anti-Semitism that remains constant throughout history, in all times and all places. Instead, specific conditions produce particular attitudes concerning Jews. Insofar as the Jews are not a nation, the assumption of theorists like Yehezkel Kaufmann (1889–1963) that anti-Semitism is a result of national or ethnic conflict cannot be sustained.

Since discrimination against diaspora Jewry is one of the main factors motivating Jews to immigrate to the homeland, there remains a vested interest in continuing to foster the view that anti-Semitism is all-pervasive and continuous. This ironically forms "an objective community of interests" between anti-Semitism and zionism (Evron 1995, 154).

Evron also finds Ahad Haam's claim that Israel can be the site of renewal of a Hebrew national culture to be highly problematic. First of all, among Eastern European Jewry, which was the only Jewish community that could rightfully be designated a "national" body, Yiddish, rather than Hebrew, was the language of everyday life. This undermines the zionist premise that the cultural renewal of the nation depends upon a renewal of the Hebrew language. Second, the Hebrew culture that did emerge in Israel was mainly comprised of Hebrew-speaking secular nationalists who denied all connection to diaspora Jews. These nationalists, and the culture that they created, estranged as they were from diaspora Jewish culture and identity, could not function as the model for world Jewry, as Ahad Haam had hoped.

Evron sees yet another contradiction in the ascendancy of the labor movement to a position of hegemony within the zionist movement and in the Yishuv. Espousing and disseminating a policy of "Hebrew labor" based on a sharp separation of the Hebrew and Arab economic sectors, the Yishuv found itself increasingly dependent economically on diaspora Jewry. As a result of this dependence,

The existence of the Yishuv and of the state that followed necessitated the non-realization of zionism, if zionism means the concentration of all Jews in their country, as well as making the Jewish people in its country economically and politically independent, like other nations. (Evron 1995, 130)

Far from leading to a normal state economy in which all citizens, Jewish and Arab alike, would be equal participants, the labor zionist hegemony, with its ideology of "Hebrew labor," prevented this from occurring. Moreover, since control of the funds collected from abroad, particularly from the United States government and from world Jewry, remained in the hands of the dominant political parties, "the power elite has a vested, inherent interest in the continued dependence of the country on foreign financial resources, in the thwarting and postponement of economic independence" (Evron 1995, 132). Ironically, zionism perpetuated the very conditions that it was committed to end. This, in turn, precluded the possibility of normalizing the Jewish people and transforming them into an independent territorial nation functioning as an equal member of the family of nations.

According to Evron (1995), the goal of normalization depended on creating a new Hebrew nation in the land of Israel. This, in turn, entailed "either the immigration of all Jews to Eretz Israel or the dissociation of the Eretz Israel nation from the Jewish diaspora and its becoming a separate, distinct national group" (p. 184). Yet the state of Israel viewed itself as what Evron refers to as "a Vatican of a national diaspora." Consequently, insofar as it maintained dependency on the human and financial resources of the diaspora, Israel could never be a nation like all other nations.

Shelilat Hagalut

Evron also finds the zionist axiom of *shelilat hagalut,* the negation of the diaspora, to be highly problematic. Here, too, historical inquiry reveals the difficulties in the zionist position. First of all, Evron considers it invalid to describe the condition of diaspora Jews in nationalist terms. For example, Jews in Europe, Great Britain, and the United States simply do not feel that they are a nation living in exile. In contrast to the situation of Eastern European Jewry at the time that zionism emerged, anti-Semitism does not play a decisive role in the public discourse or the political practices of these democratic countries.

Whereas zionism represents diaspora life as inherently unsuitable to Jewish productivity, this cannot be historically supported:

Contrary to zionist theory, Jews could become productive within advanced host societies and…this need not have any national significance. Indeed, throughout their history, except for brief interludes such as the mass impoverishment of East European Jews during the nineteenth century, the Jews fulfilled vital functions for their hosts. They were productive. (Evron 1995, 101)

In addition, Evron finds an ambivalent attitude within zionist discourse regarding the religious core of diasporic Jewish culture. Notwithstanding the commitment to creating a life in the homeland that differed from the religious culture of the diaspora, the leaders of the state, led by Ben Gurion, created a structure that prolonged religion's effects in Israeli life. This is clearly reflected in the so-called "status quo agreement" of 1948, which relegated to religious authorities control over personal matters such as marriage and divorce, while mandating Sabbath and dietary restrictions in government institutions and the public realm. This agreement, an attempt by government leaders to avoid a conflict with religious authorities, empowered those authorities by inscribing religious categories and practices in the official and legal life of the state.[6]

Thus, the movement that proclaimed its rebellion against traditional religious authority actually perpetuated the power of that authority. Were Israel a secular society as zionism had intended, membership in the national community would be determined by the individual's self-perception, rather than by religious criteria. Moreover, were Israel a normal nation, as zionists had hoped, the national community would be defined according to one's membership in the Israeli rather than the Jewish nation. Yet the Israeli supreme court, ruling in the 1960s that identification with the Jewish religious community was a criteria for membership in the Jewish people, perpetuated a religiously based concept of identity (Evron 1995, 191–93).

Another glaring example of the continuing influence of diaspora religion on Israeli life and culture is the recurring parliamentary debate over "who is a Jew." The fact that this issue, raised by the Orthodox parties, continues to preoccupy Israeli political leaders, contradicts the zionist claim that in a secular Jewish state, the values of the diaspora will be replaced with the values of secular Jewish nationalism:

> Zionist ideology...has always striven for the broadest possible definition of the term Jew. Acceptance of the Orthodox approach is, therefore, a betrayal of the principles of zionism....The betrayal of the [secular] definition of Jewishness and the passing of it into the hands of the Orthodox meant the abdication and demise of the zionist conception. (Evron 1995, 196)

Zionism and the *Shoah*

The discourse of "negation of the diaspora" helped bring about what Evron, following an increasingly common usage, calls "cruel zionism." This cruel zionism privileged the building of the homeland over all else, includ-

ing the well-being of Jews throughout the world. It emerged as a consequence of the controversy in the first decade of the century surrounding the
possibility of establishing a Jewish national homeland in Uganda.[7]
According to Evron, by deciding against this option, zionists indicated that
their primary concern was not the rescue of Jews, but rather the attaining
of a specific site as a national home. Thus, argues Evron (1995), "Zionism
ceased being a territorial movement aimed at the solution of the problems
of the Jewish people, and as a matter of fact ceased being zionist in the
Herzlian sense of the word" (p. 155). A significant consequence of this shift
was a growing indifference to the rescue of Jews when it did not further the
zionist enterprise:

> Diaspora Jews came to be regarded more and more as raw material for the
> needs of Zionism, whether as potential immigrants or as supporters of Zionism
> by financial or political activity. Zionism was not interested in them for their
> own sake. (Evron 1995, 157)

Evron finds the most chilling example of the shift in zionist priorities in
attitudes and behavior of zionist leaders in Palestine toward the victims of
Nazism. As represented in the Israeli Declaration of Independence, the
Shoah was one of the major primary legitimations of a Jewish state.[8] To
zionists, the destruction of millions of Jews in Europe, most of whom per-
ished without offering any resistance, was the ultimate confirmation of
zionism's negative view of the diaspora. According to zionist leaders, only
a Jewish state could protect Jewish lives, and only in a Jewish state could
Jews be safe.

However, citing recent studies of the problematic behavior of zionist
leaders during the period of the *Shoah,* Evron sees it as evidence against the
view of zionism as the protector of the Jewish people. Quoting from the
controversial 1977 book by Shabtai Beit Zvi, the first to criticize the behavior of zionist leaders during the *Shoah,* Evron describes the transformation
of zionism from a movement devoted to saving the Jewish people to "just
another organization with a specific aim to build a national home for the
Jewish people in Eretz Yisrael" (quoted in Evron 1995, 159).[9] According to
Beit Zvi, an interpretation basically confirmed by later studies, zionist leaders resisted initiating diplomatic initiatives on behalf of European Jews.
Moreover, these leaders refused to invest significant resources in rescue
operations on behalf of European Jews if they did not result in strengthening the Yishuv. Clearly contradicting zionism's self-definition as a movement concerned with the well-being of world Jewry, this behavior clearly
reveals that zionism is but one among many Jewish movements struggling
for hegemony within the Jewish world.

Citing the widely acclaimed research of Tel Aviv University professor
Dina Porat (1990), Evron (1995) acknowledges that the resources available

to the Yishuv leadership to combat Nazism "were insufficient in any case for exerting a significant influence on the fate of European Jews," and such efforts could have significantly undermined the Yishuv's ability to fortify itself (p. 162). Yet Evron rejects the argument that no rescue efforts by the zionists during the *Shoah* would have made a significant difference. Since no such efforts were attempted, it is simply impossible to know how effective they would have been.

Consequently, Evron (1995) attacks "the self-righteous posture of the zionist movement, its readiness to accuse all and sundry of indifference toward the fate of Europe's Jews and its determination to extract all possible material advantage, in cash and political support, from the Western sense of guilt about this indifference—a guilt which the zionists largely shared" (p. 172).

Although certainly not a sufficient cause, Evron (1995) argues that the ideology of *shelilat hagalut* played a major role in shaping the attitudes and motivating the behavior of the zionist leaders during the *Shoah:*

> In assessing the material, it is hard to overcome the suspicion that in addition to those reasons, the zionists' aversion to Galut Jewry, from which they sought to entangle themselves, was so deeply ingrained that they found it difficult to identify with it in its most difficult hour. (pp. 162–163)[10]

To Evron, their "total rejection of Jewish galut existence" and their psychological aversion to the life of exile created in zionist leaders "a psychological barrier between them and the Jewish disaster" (p. 171). Evron, unlike Porat, author of a major study on zionist leadership and the *Shoah* (1990), concludes that the zionist leadership was guilty of "amazing and horrifying apathy to the catastrophe that overwhelmed Europe's Jews" (p. 171).

Evron finds further evidence of zionist antipathy and insensitivity toward the fate of diaspora Jews in the attitudes of zionist leaders toward Jews of Middle Eastern origins. Notwithstanding zionist representations of the messianic fervor that permeated these communities, the major motivating factor for Jewish emigration from Arab countries was the growing anti-Jewish sentiment, a product of the Israeli–Arab conflict. Citing Tom Segev's study of the first year of Israel's existence as a state (1986), Evron accuses the zionists of complicity in fomenting this anti-Jewish sentiment through propaganda, economic subterfuge, and other disturbances. Moreover, the negative attitude toward diaspora Jewry, buttressed by a Eurocentric, Orientalist mentality, created the conditions for a "stratified class society" in which the Jews from Middle Eastern countries occupied the lowest rung (Evron 1995, 167). Although persuaded that they were working for the betterment and eventual rescue of the Jewish populations in Islamic countries, the zionist leaders, argues Evron, were driven primarily by a will to power.

Further indication of the insensitivity of zionist leaders to the needs and concerns of diaspora Jews is the position taken by the Israeli government toward Jews seeking to flee the Soviet Union. In the 1980s, the Israeli government pressured the Joint Distribution Committee and the Hebrew Sheltering and Immigrant Aid Society "to cease helping Soviet Jewish immigrants in Europe in order to force them to emigrate to Israel" (p. 160). In addition, they brought pressure on the German government to refuse refugee status to Jews fleeing Russia. Thus, decades after the *Shoah,* Israeli leaders, making the needs of the state their primary concern, continued to demonstrate a callousness toward the plight and the desires of diaspora Jews.

The New Hebrew Subject

Notwithstanding the behavior and attitude of zionist leaders just discussed, the dominant zionist narrative proclaimed that the return to the homeland would restore Jews to their true national selves, removing the dross with which Jewish identity in exile has been covered. Taking issue with this narrative, Evron argues that the identities of the early settlers had been largely shaped prior to their coming to the land. Even the most zealous advocates of the return to the soil, such as the Russian Jewish philosopher of the redemptive power of labor, Aharon David Gordon (1856–1922), immediately encountered problems. Rather than experience an immediate, natural bond with the land, they instead felt the same sense of alienation that had estranged them from the lands of exile (Evron 1995, 103–05).

Notwithstanding zionism's attempt to represent the new Hebrew and the new culture as the recovery or renewal of an essential national identity, it was, argues Evron, actually a new construct. The new Jewish subject, the new Hebrew, was a mental transformation of a society that was diametrically opposed to the concepts and values of the diaspora Jewish life. Evron understood the process as one of cultural construction, rather than a natural process in which the encounter with the homeland produced a new kind of Jew and a new Jewish national culture. Thus, the effort to create the new Hebrew had to be understood in relation to the desire to counter the effects of their earlier diaspora life. Similarly, the effort to create a new Hebrew culture can only be understood in terms of the desire to counter the effects of the moribund culture of the diaspora.

Even the labor zionist ideology promulgated by leaders like Ben Gurion was not, contrary to the zionist narrative, a product of the "homeland." The idealistic pioneering elite that had come from Germany between 1905 and 1914 with only the vaguest notion of Judaism, "simply translated their identification with the German people and the German land into an identification with Eretz Yisrael, both with the people and the land—sans any Jewish spiritual content" (Evron 1995, 107).

Thus, claims Evron, only a minority of the early settlers actually underwent a transformation. Nevertheless, acknowledges Evron, they succeeded in constructing an apparatus of "institutional and attitudinal patterns that...had a decisive influence on the psychology of succeeding generations" (p. 106). Under the impact of the discourse of *shelilat hagalut,* they came to feel themselves far removed from "Jewish historical consciousness" and alienated "from Jewish historical suffering" (p. 109). Depicting diaspora Jewish life in terms that mirrored the anti-Semitic discourse, zionist writers, struggling to transform themselves into a new Hebrew nation, sought to liberate themselves from what Israeli novelist and cultural critic A. B. Yehoshua has described as the neurosis of exilic existence.

Evron also challenges the zionist premise that the land of Israel constituted a viable site for the renewal of Jewish national culture. While a national secular culture built around the Hebrew language clearly did emerge in Israel, this culture "lacks any distinguishing Jewish mark" (p. 66). Consequently, it cannot function, as Ahad Haam had hoped, as the Jewish national culture. Evron sees evidence of this in the sense of estrangement felt by Israeli Jews from Jews in other countries. Ironically, the community that Ahad Haam had expected to serve as the center for world Jewry was incapable of providing a viable social or cultural model for diaspora Jews. Despite their best efforts, Ahad Haam and his successors could not establish in Israel a distinct Hebrew culture separate from the Jewish culture of exile. Neither did they succeed in constructing a national narrative to displace the religious narratives of diaspora Jews. Even in its Declaration of Independence, Israel is proclaimed as the state of the Jewish people—a Jewish state.

Evron (1995) is fully aware that many diaspora Jews have turned to Israelis as role models of dynamic, creative Jewish life. However, in contrast to the zionist position that encourages such a move and even includes it as part of its self-legitimation, Evron considers it to be detrimental to diaspora Jews and Israelis alike. The uncritical identification with Israel, the vicarious identity that forms a part of the core of the identity of many diaspora Jews, is simply untenable: "This potential Israeli identity," which is expected to function as the basis of the new Jewish identity,

> is utterly imaginary; there is no such thing. A person is what he is, not what he is not. The Israeli, required to act out a role for which he is paid and to adopt affinities which are foreign to his nature, is also unable to realize his true identity whatever it is. (p. 131)

Citing the slogan widely disseminated by Jewish fundraisers and Israeli politicians, "We are all one people," Evron brands it as "a cliche that hides from both sides their problems of identity. It also creates a state of collective, if one may be permitted to use such a term in a work with a sociopolitical bent" (p. 131).

The Current Crisis in Israeli Life

Pointing out the contradictions inherent in zionist discourse, Evron wishes to reveal the conditions that make possible the current crisis in Israeli life. That crisis, he believes, revolves, to a large extent, around the Jewish/Israeli–Palestinian conflict. In his view, as in the view of the postzionists, zionist discourse, and the practices connected to it, preclude a peaceful resolution of that conflict.

Evron offers an alternative, nonnationalist narrative of Jewish history, as well as a nonzionist analysis of the current problems confronting Israel as a state and the Jews as a people. Zionist leaders, accusing those who criticize Israeli policies and actions of being anti-Semites, have distorted the nature of the conflict. Rather than recognize the specific historical circumstances that have produced the Palestinian claims and enmity, Israeli leaders like Menachem Begin (prime minister from 1977 to 1983) and his successor Yitzhak Shamir (prime minister from 1983 to 1992) lump Palestinians together with all the anti-Semites who have ever sought to destroy the Jewish people, including Hitler and the Nazis. Such an interpretation, besides distorting history, has the effect of masking the national character of the Israeli–Palestinian conflict. Instead of defining the conflict as one between two nations, each seeking control over what it regards as its "natural" homeland, zionist discourse represents it as a continuation of thousands of years of hatred and persecution of Jews. Such a representation of the conflict precludes a peaceful resolution. In the worst-case scenario, it can lead to the destruction of the state. At the very least, it makes it impossible to attain the zionist dream of a normal national existence.

Evron's transnational critique of zionism considers nationalistic discourse to be obsolete and harmful. According to Evron, since World War II, the world has increasingly moved into a postnationalist era. Events throughout the world, particularly in Europe, together with the increased compression of distance and time produced by rapidly changing technology, have produced a situation in which the political and economic survival of nations depends on their ability to form regional cooperative enterprises. This is evident in the expansion of supranational confederations and common markets; the formation of regional, supranational alliances; the rapid growth of multinational corporations; and the emergence of a new capital structure. Such changing political and economic conditions, calling for transnational approaches, have helped to render nationalistic discourses such as zionism obsolete.[11] Thus, concludes Evron (1995), "neither the inner conditions in the present-day Jewish people nor the historical conditions under which Jews live are capable of generating a national consciousness or a desire to solve a problem which today is largely non-existent Zionism has largely lost its raison d'être" (pp. 96–97).

Zionist/Israeli leaders are not unaware of these changed conditions. This is evident in their increasing retreat from traditional arguments concerning the impending physical destruction of diaspora Jews, even in Eastern Europe. In place of these arguments, we find an emphasis on such problems as cultural, national, and religious assimilation. To Evron, however, this reveals yet another inner contradiction of zionist discourse, which represents Israel as a safe haven conducive to the construction of a strong Jewish identity. Since the establishment of the state, despite the efforts of zionist leaders to disseminate a greater consciousness of Jewishness and Jewish history and thereby create a link to diaspora Jewry among young Israelis, the gulf separating the culture of Israel and the culture of Judaism has been growing larger. In this sense, the critics of secularism, including followers of Gush Emunim, are correct.

Whereas zionist discourse represented the Jewish homeland and the Jewish state as the vehicle for unifying the Jewish people, the result of establishing the state has been quite different. The state of Israel, by concentrating Jews of diverse religious and ethnic groups in one place, has had the effect of sharpening the differences among them. The Jewish population in the state of Israel has been increasingly fragmented by the growing conflict between religious and secular groups over the nature of "Jewish" identity. In addition, ethnic divisions among Jews have been sharpened. The multiethnic character of the state has precluded the realization of the zionist vision of a unified national culture. Contrary to Ahad Haam's representation of a unified Jewish secular culture, the actual materialization of that culture in the state has revealed the fallacy of that thinking:

> It thus became clear that the various Jewish communities had no common ethnic culture except the religious one. No general national content was found, while that content that was upheld, like secular political movements, press, a secular national ideology, etc., was always that of East European Jewry, its West European and American branches, and a thin scattering from the more developed Arab counties such as Egypt and Iraq. For the Zionist leadership, this East European Jewish culture was the national Jewish culture per se, while other Jewish cultures, all religious-communal, were conceived as having a folkloristic communal character distinct from the dominant national culture. (Evron 1995, 198)

As has been increasingly acknowledged in recent years, zionist discourse has been marked by a blindness toward the native Arab population in Palestine. From the outset, as recent research has made clear, zionist leaders, with few exceptions, have neglected the national concerns of the

Palestinians. Thus, zionism represented the land as empty and awaiting restoration. When zionists could no longer ignore the presence of Palestinian Arabs, they argued that the building of the land would benefit them economically as well.

According to Evron (1995), the definition of Israel as the state of the Jewish people, as described in the Declaration of Independence, produces yet another internal contradiction. Insofar as Israel is not defined as the state of its citizens, then one group, the Jewish group, is privileged over the others.[12] Despite the statement contained in the Declaration of Independence guaranteeing equal rights for all minorities, the inscription of Judaism in the structure of the state makes this impossible. The policy of gathering as many Jews as possible to the state, a policy that derives from the discourse of "ingathering of the exiles," serves to intensify the nationalistic feelings of the primary minority group, thereby contributing to a heightening of internal conflict. Moreover, the rhetoric of the land as belonging to the Jewish people produced massive expropriation practices, in 1948 and after. According to Evron, the concessions made to the religious groups, as well as the expropriation of Arab lands, militates against drafting a constitution and precludes the possibility of Israel becoming a pluralistic democracy in the Western sense of the term:

> A constitution would have enabled non-Jewish citizens of Israel to demand, and the Supreme Court necessarily would have upheld this demand, that the state refrain from extending any preferential treatment to an ethnic group whose members are not citizens, and definitely not at the expense of citizens. (p. 188)[13]

Consequently, while proclaiming Israel to be a nation like all other nations, zionists, in Evron's view, seemed to exclude pluralistic democracies.

Further Contradictions in Zionist Discourse

One of the outcomes of the contradictions within zionism, according to Evron, has been the emergence of Gush Emunim. The power of this group is indicative of zionism's inability to fulfill the desires of the nation. Committed to Jewish territorial expansion and the conquest of the "greater land of Israel" and rejecting the zionist goals of normalization, secular culture, and Western-style humanism, Gush Emunim views itself as the legitimate heir of the "original" authentic zionism. The success of this "essentially anti-Zionist ideology," which clothes itself in zionist discourse and utilizes traditional zionist practices indicates that zionism has lost its ability to provide the Israeli public with a frame of meaning that can explain reality (Evron 1995, 225). Gush Emunim, with its discourse of religious faith combined with colonialization, seeks to fill this vacuum. A large segment of the Israeli public and leadership, under the spell of zionism, was drawn to Gush Emunim's rhetoric of pioneering spirit and its practices of establishing settlements and redeeming territory. In the wake of the decline of labor zionism and the loss of the spiritual values embodied in the kibbutz movement, Gush Emunim fulfilled a strong need.

Evron rejects Gush Emunim's claims to be the legitimate heirs of zionism. Although engaged in a pursuit of and accumulation of power consistent with the practices of the militant wing of the zionist movement, Gush Emunim, in his view, is a decidedly *post-zionist* phenomenon that contradicts classical zionist assumptions. Evron thus sharply rebukes Ratosh and other Canaanites for supporting Gush Emunim's expansionist program in the belief that the annexation of the occupied territories would somehow precipitate the emergence of a secular Hebrew state. To Evron, this ultranationalism constitutes "the greatest danger to the existence of Israel" (p. 375).

In contrast to the Canaanite solution of a regional framework under a dominant Hebrew culture, Evron's vision is drawn from Western democratic premises. He thus envisions a pluralistic state "of the West European or North American type, which allows for cultural and ethnic pluralism within the framework of a shared and neutral citizenship" (p. 221). Such a framework must, as the Canaanites recognized, be a supranational, regional structure. Like many postzionists, Evron (1995) advocates a Hebrew state based upon "equality before the law of all citizens living within Israeli territory, irrespective of ethnic origins, race, religion, or sex" (p. 243).

Together with the shift from a Jewish nation based on ethnicity or religion to one based on territoriality, Evron advocates redefining the connection of that nation to the Jewish people outside of the land. Instead of being connected to the state politically, Jews would be connected culturally and economically. While the state would maintain a "political preference for Jews...such as the readiness to grant asylum to any Jews who are persecuted for their Jewishness," it would no longer grant them automatic citizenship. Advocating a position that, as we see in the next chapter, accords with that of the Palestinian writer Anton Shammas, Evron argues that like all citizens of the new state, Jewish refugees would have to pass the "ordinary tests of citizenship" (p. 244).

Evron, whose critique of zionism was thorough and incisive, distinguished his position from that of the antizionists. Acknowledging in a 1970 interview his dialectical relationship with zionism, he argued:

> Israeli criticism must understand that it is dialectically linked to the Israeli reality. Along with opposition there is an identification at the deepest level [*hizdahut broved haamuk beyoter*]. Suddenly you see that your criticism concerns things that are changing, not essential. For example, when in Russia they attack

zionism as the mother of all sin, when they say that the zionists are guilty of the slaughter at Babi Yar, when the criminal band announces things like this—then I cannot announce myself today as antizionist. That is treason. If I, myself, say things like that, I become a partner to the Russians. Therefore now, for the sake of [out of the exigencies of] the war, I am a zionist. I must acknowledge that I am a product [*zeza*] of zionism. (quoted in Ben Ezer 1986, 187)

While Evron's name is rarely mentioned in the debates over postzionism, I find that his critique of zionism's inherent contradictions and fallacies voices many, if not most of, the criticisms soon to be associated with postzionism.[14] It is not surprising, therefore, that in 1996, in the midst of the debates over postzionism, he identified himself as a postzionist. However, his usage of the term differed, as we shall see, from many of those at the center of the controversy:

This writer is not an academician and his approach is more theoretical, insofar as he problematizes the basic premises of zionist history and historiography. He defines himself as a postzionist in the sense that, in his opinion, zionism has fulfilled its historic function, the creation of a Hebrew nation in the land of Israel. The continuation of zionism at a time when there is no serious danger to world Jewry is nothing but the exploitation of zionist ideology in order to discriminate against non-Jews in Israel, and to prevent the establishment of a state of its citizens that is not the state of the Jewish people, a most confusing concept, living in the diaspora. (Evron 1996, 20)

MAZPEN: THE DISCOURSE OF ANTIZIONIST RADICAL SOCIALISM

A radical critique of zionism that differed significantly from Evron's was advocated by the radical Israeli socialist group Mazpen, the Israel Socialist Organization (ISO). Mazpen sought to replace zionist discourse with an alternative essentialistic Marxist discourse. Emerging in the 1960s among students at the Hebrew University, Mazpen called for the dezionization of Israeli society and culture. In contrast to the cultural and aesthetic concerns broached by the Canaanites, Mazpen focused its critique almost exclusively on political and socioeconomic issues.

Mazpen repeatedly advocated the need for an alternative social, cultural, and political discourse in Israel. Key issues in its critique of zionism included Israel's aggressive role in the Israeli–Palestinian conflict, Israel's colonialist attitudes and practices toward Palestinian Arabs within and without its borders, and the oppression of Jews of Middle Eastern origin and women. Mazpen was one the few groups within Israeli culture that sought to position the marginalized or excluded Others at the center of Israeli public discourse.

Mazpen's critique of zionism was formulated from a Marxist-socialist perspective. To Mazpen's proponents, zionism, as an oppressive, colonializing movement, was counterrevolutionary:

> The Israeli Jews constitute a society of settler colonialists, and the Zionist state is the instrument that procures benefits for them based on the denial of these benefits to the Palestinians. (Bober 1972, 192)

Israel, according to Mazpen, is a client state of American imperialism, and Israeli-Jewish society represents a bourgeois "counterrevolutionary, military outpost of imperialism" (Bober 1972, 193).

Mazpen linked the oppression of the Palestinians directly to zionist discourse, a position, as discussed earlier, subsequently taken by Benvenisti. Through such basic concepts of "conquest of labor," "conquest of the land," and "produce of the land," zionism has oppressed and exploited the Palestinian Arabs:

> We, therefore, hold that a solution of the problem necessitates the dezionization of Israel. The state of Israel must undergo a deep revolutionary change which will transform it from a zionist state (i.e., a state of the Jews all over the world) into a socialist state that represents the interest of all the masses who live in it. (Bober 1972, 210)[15]

Toward this end, Mazpen argued for an end to the Law of Return, a position that has been reiterated by postzionists. Moreover, Mazpen advocated extending the right of return to all Palestinians who fled from the state in 1947–1948. Finally, Mazpen called for the end to all oppressive measures against Palestinian Arabs, including the expropriation of lands belonging to Palestinians and all discriminatory legislation.

Unlike Arab antizionists, Mazpen did not call for the dissolution of the state of Israel:

> The argument that this nation has been formed artificially and at the expense of the indigenous Arab population does not change the fact that the Hebrew nation now exists. It would be a disastrous error to ignore this fact. (Bober 1972, 211)

Rejecting all Arab calls for *a jihad* to liberate Palestine from Jewish control, Mazpen insisted on the right of a Hebrew nation, as well as a Palestinian nation, to self-determination. However, rather than a two-state solution, Mazpen urged the integration of Israel into a political and economic union of Middle Eastern nations based on socialism (Bober 1972, 212).[16]

Proponents of Mazpen also rejected the zionist principle of negation of the diaspora. Against zionism's representation of anti-Semitism as a natural structural characteristic of exile, Mazpen argued that anti-Semitism is a historical phenomenon that grew out of specific socioeconomic conditions. Accordingly, Mazpen rejects the zionist solution of deterritorializing world Jewry and reterritorializing them in the homeland. Instead, like other socialist groups, Mazpen supported the political struggle against anti-Semitism wherever it arises.[17]

Mazpen was also critical of zionism for abandoning the cause of the safety of diaspora Jews and subordinating it to the building of the homeland. Thus, it criticized the Israeli government for only being interested in those Soviet Jews who were prepared to emigrate to Israel. Citing the recently published work of Shabtai Beit Zvi, Mazpen denounced what has been labeled cruel zionism:

> The leaders of Zionism reacted with indifference and even hostility towards the emigration of Jews from the endangered countries to places other than Palestine. Zionism clearly showed that in principle it is not interested in saving the Jews themselves, but only in saving them by emigration to Palestine. (Machover and Offenberg 1978, 43)[18]

The proponents of Mazpen also took up the cause of other groups that they considered to be marginalized, including Jews of Middle Eastern origins and women. In analyzing the position of these groups, Mazpen again went beyond the liberal call for reform. Instead, they argued that there was a link between zionist discourse and practice and the oppressed conditions of these groups. To Mazpen, dezionization of the state was the only viable solution.

As a result of the Ashkenazic hegemony within the zionist movement and the subsequent state institutions, zionism adopted a Eurocentric or Orientalist perspective on Middle Eastern Jewry. To the Ashkenazi zionists, Jews from Middle Eastern countries were uncultivated and primitive. Nevertheless, driven by the need for manual laborers and immigrants, zionists undertook to encourage, even cajole, Jews from Middle Eastern countries to emigrate to Israel. In some instances, "zionist agents went so far as to employ methods of provocation and terrorism" (Shapiro 1978, 16).

Even though, by the 1960s Jews from Middle Eastern countries comprised the majority of the Jewish population in Israel, they were still regarded by the Ashkenazi leadership as a minority. In contrast to zionists who argued that political reform and progressive developments will bring about an end to this situation, Mazpen insisted that the situation will not change as long as Israel is a zionist state. Only the dezionization of Israel would open the way for conditions in which the discriminatory practices of the Ashkenazi hegemony could be significantly altered.

Another example of the oppression produced by zionism, according to Mazpen, is the position of women in Israel. As they see it, the condition of women in Israel is a product of secular zionist parties' ongoing need for support from religious parties. To acquire this support, secular zionist parties are willing to compromise on a number of issues relating to women, such as abortion, marriage, and divorce laws. However, according to Mazpen, as long as these laws are controlled by the religious parties, women in Israel will remain subordinate and oppressed.[19]

Mazpen further argued that the inequality of women in the Israeli economy is a direct product of the zionist program. According to this argument, the place of women in Israeli society

> cannot be discussed in isolation from the zionist characteristics of society. The colonialization process, its requirements, its constraints, its internal contradictions and the political conflicts to which it gave birth are reflected in every aspect of life of Israeli society—including the position of women. (Ehrlich 1980, 88)

While agreeing with many of the criticisms voiced by liberal feminists in Israel, Mazpen criticized them for their failure to understand that the status of women in Israel could not be significantly changed without changing the zionist framework. As long as zionist values favoring colonization, a Jewish majority, and Hebrew labor continue, the condition of women cannot be substantially changed.

CONCLUSION

As the discussion in chapters 2 and 3 has shown, a small, but significant number of Israeli critics related the basic problems of that society to the discourse and practices of zionism. Those problems include: the Israeli-Palestinian conflict, the continuing Israeli occupation of the West Bank and Gaza; and the marginalization and exclusion of Palestinian citizens of Israel, Jews of Middle-Eastern origin, and women. As will become clear in the following chapters, many of these criticisms recur in writings of postzionists. This is particularly true of the writings of Mazpen and Boaz Evron which may be seen as important sites for what subsequently becomes known as postzionism.

For the Canaanites, Mazpen, and Evron, any solution to the fundamental problems of the Israeli society and culture necessitates a move beyond the limits of zionist discourse. Each of them called for a regional solution to these problems grounded in a restructuring of Middle Eastern society. Whereas the Canaanite critique focused on cultural issues, that of Mazpen was oriented toward socioeconomic inequities and political oppression. Evron, while concerned with these issues, framed his analysis of them within the context of a thorough, systematic critique of zionist discourse.

In contrast to these critics of zionism, the postzionist historians and sociologists whom I discuss in chapter 4 do not engage in a systematic critique of zionism's ideological premises. Instead, they focus their critique on the dominant Israeli historical narratives and sociological representations. In contrast to those who call for a transnational, pluralistic, democratic entity in the Middle East, postzionists tend to speak of a pluralistic, democratic Israeli state of all of its citizens. Finally, although the postzionists whom I discuss in chapter 6 reiterate several of the points made by Mazpen and Evron, they, unlike Mazpen and Evron, ground their critique in postmodern and postcolonial theory.

Although several postzionists refer to Evron, there is no clear indication that his writings played a significant role in shaping their views. Whereas Evron has much to say about the current situation in Israel, his critique was shaped in the context of Israeli cultural debates of the 1940s and 1950s. In contrast, as we shall see in the next chapter, the postzionist critique emerged in the context of more recent conditions. Thus, while many positions advocated by postzionists converge with those advocated by Mazpen and Evron, their discursive frameworks and, consequently, their critique of zionism were very different.

The critics discussed in this and the previous chapter brought to the surface problems and contradictions within zionist discourse. However, the hegemonic zionist discourse succeeded in effectively marginalizing them and neutralizing the effects of their critiques. In contrast, the postzionists whom I examine in the following chapters have succeeded in establishing space within Israeli culture from which to make their ideas heard. Although the postzionist critics comprise a small, elite group within Israeli society, they have succeeded in gaining a wider hearing both in the academy and in the popular press for many criticisms that the Israeli hegemonic culture had previously succeeded in silencing.

CHAPTER 4

POSTZIONISM:
THE ACADEMIC DEBATES

As we saw in the previous chapter, throughout the relatively brief existence of the state of Israel, critics have continually raised problems concerning the nature of Israeli collective identity, the relationship of Israeli culture to the larger Jewish world, the relationship of Israel to the Palestinian Arabs, and the ongoing viability of zionism in a post-state era. Yet until the late 1970s when the hegemony of labor zionism came to an end and Menachem Begin was elected prime minister, the issues raised by these critics remained marginal in Israeli culture.[1] However, groups like Mazpen and the Canaanites, notwithstanding their marginal position, succeeded in keeping alive the discussion of issues such as Israel's relation to the Palestinians and the relation of Israeli identity and culture to Judaism and the worldwide Jewish community. In the final analysis, however, neither Mazpen nor the Canaanites seriously threatened the domination of zionist discourse.[2]

However, beginning in the mid-1980s, a new form of critique emerged, one that continues to gain currency in Israeli culture. This critique, known as postzionism, has not been framed, as had earlier ones, purely in ideological terms. Instead, it has been framed in the discourse of the academy. Its beginnings may be traced to a group of scholarly writings that, beginning in the late 1970s, challenged the prevailing scholarly representations of Israeli history and society.[3] In the context of the debates precipitated by these studies, the issue of postzionism emerged. Postzionism is the most recent and, to date, most effective effort within Israel to problematize zionist discourse and the historical narratives it has produced.

Postzionism, like zionism, is in constant motion. The boundaries of postzionist discourse, like those of zionism, are in a constant state of flux. Comprised of nomadic concepts that assume different meanings in different contexts, postzionism lacks a distinct structure or organization, and its boundaries are often blurred.[4]

In the words of one observer cited earlier, the debate over postzionism reflects

> an identity crisis of a society that stands on the threshold of a period of peace, in which the national consensus, previously built upon threats to survival and security problems, clears a space for a debate across the society and its culture. (Pappe 1995b, 45)

Whether or not it is useful to speak of the identity crisis of an entire society, there is no doubt that Israel, since the 1960s, has been shaken by a series of events that have generated a widespread sense of disillusionment, instability, and uncertainty, particularly among intellectuals and academicians. Evidence of this is found in the writings of a younger group of scholars, most of whom were born around or immediately following the establishment of the state and who grew to maturity during a time in which Israel ruled over a resisting population of more than one million Palestinian Arabs.

As described by one scholar, Gershon Shafir (1989), the author of one of the more important studies subsumed under the rubric "new historiography," his interpretation

> was engendered by the dislocating experience of growing into maturity as part of the Israeli generation of 1967. For me, the aftermath of the Six Day War revealed the gap between the evidence of Israeli society's gradual but definite transformation through its manifold relationships with the Palestinian Arabs who came under Israeli occupation, and the Palestinians' invisibility in historical and sociological accounts of the early formation of Israeli society. (p. xi)

For Shafir, as for many others of his generation, the Israeli–Palestinian conflict became the key to understanding the history of the state and the social forms that it assumed. At the time, Israel's overwhelming victory during the 1967 War had appeared to many to signal the beginning of a new era in the life of the young state. The dramatic sounding of the ram's horn at the Western Wall by the chief rabbi of the Israeli Defense Forces proclaimed to all Israelis that Jerusalem, a divided city since the establishment of the state, was reunited, never to be split again. An emotion-laden photograph of a young praying soldier, head resting on his arm against the wall, his Uzi submachine gun at his side, was distributed throughout the international community. And at many public Jewish gatherings throughout the world, the recently composed "Jerusalem of Gold" displaced the zionist anthem "*Hatikvah*" [the hope].

While some viewed the war in messianic terms, others framed it in secular zionism's discourse of normalization and the fulfillment of a mission.

Yet there were some dissenting voices. Amos Oz warned of the destructive effects on Israel were they to retain control of the captured West Bank and Gaza with its population of more than one million Palestinians.[5] Eloquently expressing the ambivalent feeling of many young Israeli soldiers, Yitzhak Rabin, the commanding general of the Israeli forces, spoke at the Hebrew University campus on Mount Scopus, recently freed from Jordanian control, of the uncomfortable feelings that they felt being part of a conquering army.[6]

For the most part, however, Israelis were euphoric, seeing only the benefits that their victory had brought: defeated Arab armies; wider, more secure borders; the recovery of areas lost to Arab Armies in the 1948 War, and the reunification of Jerusalem. What few anticipated, however, was the extent to which the victory and the ensuing occupation of captured territories would be transformed into the glaring fault lines, dividing the country as it had never been divided before, and ultimately resulting in the assassination in 1995 of Prime Minister Yitzhak Rabin by a religious extremist who believed that he was ridding Israel, and Jewish people throughout the world, of a traitor.

In terms of our discussion, what has been labeled postzionism would most likely never have emerged, certainly not in its current forms, were it not for the Israeli victory in 1967. The ensuing occupation and the demands that it placed on young Israelis serving in the military sent a series of shock waves throughout the nation. The result was a growing disillusionment among Israeli intellectuals with zionism. Ironically, the event that to many was the ultimate confirmation of the zionist dream turned out for many others to be the beginning of its demise.

Among the unanticipated outcomes of the 1967 War was the emergence of a strong form of Palestinian nationalism that eventually gained for the Palestinians the international recognition they had previously been denied. Resisting the Israeli occupation with its accompanying oppression and daily indignities, the Palestinians demanded and attained legitimacy for their nation, and for their claim to a national homeland. Ironically, the Israeli victory in 1967 eventually won for the Palestinians what they were not able to win for themselves, that is, recognition as a distinct national group with legitimate national claims.

Strongly affected by the strength of the emerging Palestinian nationalism, and experiencing the difficulties of ruling over a resisting population, Israeli intellectuals and academicians slowly came to the realization that the Israeli–Palestinian conflict stood at the center of Israeli history and the formation of Israeli society. As Shafir (1989) comments:

> Although throwing off mental habits is always a slow process, I came eventu-
> ally to the conclusion that, during most of its history, Israeli society is best

understood not through the existing, inward-looking interpretations but rather in terms of the broader context of Israeli–Palestinian relations. (p. xi)

The sense of disillusionment with the prevailing interpretations of Israeli history is also conveyed by one of the more prominent new historians, Benny Morris. Morris (1994b), in an article in the Israeli daily *Haaretz,* reported on the powerful effect that his study of recently declassified documents relating to the exodus of Palestinians in 1948 had on him:

> From the new documents of that period it became clear that much of what had been told to the people—to children at school and adults in newspapers—in the memoirs and historical writings—was in the best instances distortion and in many other instances simply the ignoring of facts and plain lies. (p. 40)[7]

Morris' sense of betrayal was shared by other Israeli scholars, such as Dani Rabinowitz, a young anthropologist at the Hebrew University. Like Morris and Shafir, Rabinowitz, whose work I discuss in chapter 6, was shaken by the realization that the representations of Israeli history and society transmitted to him by his teachers were extremely biased and flawed. In a 1994 public debate with one of Israel's leading social scientists, Rabinowitz, in the words of a colleague,

> attributed his own radicalization to the realization as an adult, that the educators and authority figures responsible for his socialization had distorted and lied about the essential features of Israeli society and history. (Shalev 1996, 187–88, n. 15)[8]

As significant as it was, the Israeli–Palestinian conflict was by no means the only factor contributing to the disillusionment of Israeli scholars whose academic careers began in the 1970s and 1980s. Recounting what he describes as "one of my formative experiences as a sociologist," Shafir (1996b) tells of attending a lecture by the Israel's leading sociologist, Shmuel Eisenstadt of the Hebrew University. Speaking on social differentiation within Israeli society, Eisenstadt, as one questioner reminded him, had made no mention of the recent demonstration of the "Black Panthers," described by Shafir as "a group of Mizrahi youth, mostly from broken homes in the Musrara quarter of Jerusalem, [who] launched highly visible protests to object to the 'social gap' between Mizrahim and Ashkenazim in Israel." It struck Shafir that there was no room for "'social gap' or the attendant social conflict" in the functionalist sociological discourse that then prevailed in Israel (p. 189). This led him to conclude:

> [A] counterview of Israeli society was required, one in which social conflict and the contenders themselves would be accepted as a legitimate part of social analysis. (p. 189)

Actually, a group of radical Israeli sociologists had already begun to produce a critique of the Eisenstadt-dominated sociology in the late 1970s and early 1980s. In a series of articles published in the Hebrew journal *Notebooks for Research and Critique* (1978, 1984), sociologists like Shlomo Swirski, Deborah Bernstein, and others, taking issue with the dominant sociological discourse of adaption and integration, analyzed what Shalev (1996) describes as

> not just cynical manipulation of the Mizrachim [*sic*] for political purposes...but deep conflicts of interest between *olim* [new immigrants] and *vatikim* [veteran citizens], the privileged power position of the latter in the working out of these conflicts, and the role of Oriental immigrants [i.e., of Middle Eastern origin] in the dirty work of constructing a modern economy in Israel for the benefit of its "state-made" capitalists and salariat. (p. 185, n. 11)

Belying Israel's promise to welcome and integrate all Jews into a new secure and productive life, a large portion of Israeli Jews, those of Middle Eastern origin now referred to as Mizrahim, were not being granted an equal opportunity to share in the benefits or the power. Yet with rare exceptions, established Israel social science either ignored or minimized the gaps separating the dominant group of Jews of European origins (Ashkenazim) from the Marginalized Mizrahi Jews at the lower end of the socioeconomic ladder.

Alongside the 1967 War, the ensuing occupation of the captured territories, and the growing realization of social gaps and conflicts within Israeli society, other factors contributed to the growth of a widespread sense of skepticism toward the dominant Israeli historical narratives and social representations. While some of these are unique to the Middle East, others resulted from processes that were occurring in many nations across the globe. Within Israel, a spreading militancy among Israeli religious and right-wing secular groups advocating expanded settlement of the occupied territories led to a rethinking of the relation of zionism to the exercise of power. The intensification of national identity among Palestinians both in the occupied territories and in Israel forced Israelis to rethink their relation to the Palestinians. With the eruption of Palestinian resistance at the end of 1987, this issue acquired an urgency not previously felt.

The nearly disastrous outcome of the 1973 War, and revelations of Israel's unpreparedness and the negligence of its leaders were among the factors that contributed to the end of labor zionism's hegemony. The Likud victory in the 1977 elections opened the way to the rising power of such previously excluded groups as Jews of Middle Eastern origin, their religious leaders, and *Haredim* [ultra-Orthodox Ashkenazi Jews].

Israel's invasion of Lebanon in 1982—and the ensuing sense of shock, disillusionment, and demoralization—led to the emergence of peace groups previously unknown in Israel. In the wake of the invasion, many Israelis came to feel a previously unknown skepticism concerning Israel's officially stated commitment to fighting only defensive wars and to pursuing peace on all fronts. The trauma of Lebanon became the equivalent of the trauma of Vietnam in the United States of the 1960s and 1970s.

In the meantime, the effects of the long years of occupying territories conquered in the 1967 War and controlling a hostile and restless population rendered problematic the dominant representations of zionism as a humane, progressive movement. For many Israeli youth serving in the occupied territories, zionist discourse appeared ill-suited to render meaningful their daily confrontation with angry, fearful, and hostile Palestinians. This feeling was greatly exacerbated by the Palestinian uprising that erupted in 1987. Confronted with angry, rebellious women and children, Israeli soldiers found themselves called upon to carry out acts of violence and repression that tested their moral limits. Service in the military, previously considered to be an obligation and a source of great pride, now appeared much more complicated to many young Israelis and their parents. In the wake of the Intifada, the encounter of young Israeli intellectuals and academicians with their Palestinian counterparts led them to question the stereotypical representations of Palestinians that pervaded Isaeli society and found their way into school curricula.

Other than the events and conditions that are specific to Israel and the Middle East, processes that were occurring globally also played a major role in subverting the truths generated by zionist discourse and opening space for the emerging postzionist discourse. Like so many other countries in Asia and Africa, Israel, in recent decades, has experienced far-reaching demographic, economic, and cultural changes, which have been analyzed by University of Chicago anthropologist Arjun Appardurai (1996). These include a large influx of new populations, the rapid expansion of the media and technology, rapid financial growth, and the infusion of new ideas.[9] Within a relatively short period, the socialist structure of labor zionism had been dismantled and was being rapidly replaced by a privatized, market-driven, consumer-oriented economy. This contributed significantly to undermining labor zionism's collectivist pioneering ethos.

Israeli society in the 1980s and 1990s was also the scene of a massive influx of new ethnic groups, particularly from the former Soviet Union, a process referred to by Appardurai as an *ethnoscape*. Relatively few of these new immigrants had been motivated to emigrate by zionism, nor was Israel necessarily the first choice for many of them. Their decision to emigrate was often not based on the desire to live in the Jewish homeland or to experience an intensive Jewish cultural environment. Rather, what drove most of the immigrants from the Soviet Union was their intense desire for freedom from the oppressive Soviet system and for greater social and economic opportunities. Among the immigrants from the former Soviet Union there were many non-Jews as well as Jews whose Jewish credentials were challenged by the rabbinic authorities. This period also saw the influx of Thai laborers who were being used to replace Palestinian workers. When these new groups are combined with the large number (20 percent) of Israelis who are Palestinians and the increasingly activist antizionist *haredi* [ultra-Orthodox] community, the challenge to zionism's hegemony in Israeli culture becomes evident.[10]

The Israeli cultural landscape has also felt the effects of a rapidly expanding mediascape (Appardurai 1996).[11] Until recently, televised media in Israel had been controlled solely by the state, with little or no choice available to the viewer. However, with the arrival of cable and satellite television in the 1990s, this situation was radically altered. As the amount of non-government-controlled media space expanded, Israelis who only a few years ago depended on the government for news of domestic and external events now had other options. One result was the growing availability of non-Israeli perspectives on daily events, both in Israel and abroad. Like so many others throughout the world, Israelis have been experiencing a time/space compression that gave them immediate access to other places and other cultures. This, in turn, produced the desire for expanded cultural options.

Finally, Israel, like many other societies, has been experiencing a rapid process of Americanization.[12] This is evident in the rapid growth of shopping malls and the increasing presence of such American franchises as McDonald's throughout the country. Caught up in the pursuit of the good life, a growing number of Israelis, particularly among the younger generation, increasingly find the collectivist values of labor zionism to be unrelated to the realities of their daily lives.

Not surprisingly, the rapidly changing cultural, economic, and social landscapes and political conditions have led a growing number of Israelis to regard zionism as irrelevant to the new Israel. This, in turn, has led zionist leaders and representatives to adopt a highly defensive posture. On every front, the Israel of which previous generations had dreamed and for which they had fought seemed to be crumbling before their very eyes.[13] The rapid spread of Gush Emunim's ethos of militant messianic expansionism, the growing power within the government of antizionist *haredim*, and the increasing power of Jews from Middle Eastern countries through such parties as Shas all contributed to the rapid dissipation of the labor zionist dream of a socialist society grounded in European culture and serving as a "light unto the nations."

On the cultural front, Ahad Haam's dream of a comprehensive, organic, humanistic Hebraic culture seemed more and more remote. Increasingly, Jews of Middle Eastern origin as well as cultural goods imported from the

United States were rapidly changing the face of Israeli culture. In literature, film, art, and politics, the ethos of labor zionism—which since the establishment of the state had, for the majority of Israelis, been identified as authentic zionism—was slowly but surely eroding.

Given this complex combination of events, it is not at all surprising that a growing number of Israelis came to increasingly view zionist discourse, a product of late nineteenth-century nationalism, as ineffective, irrelevant, or obsolete.[14] The earlier skepticism toward zionism conveyed by the concept of "zionism in quotation marks" [*zionut bamerkhaot*] grew more intense.[15] Consequently, proponents of zionism, particularly labor zionism, felt besieged on all sides.[16] From their position, the emerging postzionist discourse was perceived as yet another manifestation of the subversion of zionist culture.

One concern shared by virtually all postzionists is the conflict between the zionist foundations of the state and its professed commitment to democracy.[17] Repeatedly, postzionists raise the question of whether Israel is primarily a Jewish state in which non-Jews, particularly Palestinians, do not share equally in the power, or a state of all its citizens in which the goal is to distribute power equitably among all groups.

Another major concern shared by most postzionists is to provide a hearing for marginalized minority voices within Israeli culture, including Palestinian Arabs and Jews of Middle Eastern origins. Postzionists are particularly concerned with rethinking the relationship between the state of Israel and the Palestinian Arabs. Others find Israel's collectivist orientation to be problematic and are concerned with creating a society that respects difference and allows for the nurturing of individual creative energies.

THE SCHOLARLY DEBATES: QUESTIONING ZIONISM'S HISTORICAL NARRATIVES AND SOCIAL AND CULTURAL REPRESENTATIONS

In the 1970s and 1980s, many younger Israeli scholars, pursuing graduate studies abroad and applying different methodological approaches, formulated alternative perspectives on Israeli history and culture. Their writings brought to the surface and highlighted questions that had previously been neglected and gained a hearing for voices previously muted or excluded from the dominant Israeli discourse. As described by one of these younger scholars:

> In the 1970s, in the face of painful evidence of social inequality, political turmoil, and military and economic vulnerability several strands of intellectual insurgency arose to challenge accepted thinking. Much of this work produced revisionist histories which cast the labour movement elite in a quite unflatter-

ing light. Critical scholarship was also driven by the search for theoretical alternatives to a sociological orthodoxy which had plainly failed to reckon with the conflicts and inequalities accompanying nation- and state-building and capitalist economic development. Israel's invasion of Lebanon, its continuing occupation of the West Bank and Gaza, and the intense political polarization surrounding these issues lent a further impetus to the critical social science in the 1980s. (Shalev 1992, 14)[18]

The writings of these younger scholars, taken together with interviews that I conducted in Israel in the winter of 1995–1996, indicate that much of these scholars' academic work was motivated by the disillusionment precipitated by the failure of the prevailing Israeli scholarship to come to grips with the blatant paradoxes and contradictions in Israeli life. While the dominant studies of zionism and the state presented them as humane, progressive, and liberal, all around them they saw evidence to the contrary.

A good sense of the key issues in the academic debates can be gained from the work of Tom Segev, an independent historian and journalist who was one of the first writers to challenge the prevailing scholarly representations of Israeli history and society.[19] Although academically trained, Segev wrote his *1949: The First Israelis* (in Hebrew, 1984) primarily for the nonacademic reader. Nevertheless, Segev grounded his book in careful historical research. Making extensive use of newly declassified documents, Segev challenged the prevailing scholarly interpretations of Israeli history and society while offering a clear overview of the broader cultural and political issues at stake in the academic debates. In the process, he sought to demonstrate that the conflicts afflicting Israeli society and culture in the 1980s were not abnormal. Rather, these conflicts were endemic to the zionist state.

Typifying the new scholarship emerging in the 1980s and 1990s, Segev (1984) argued that his book "shattered a firmly established self-image and exposed as mere myths a large number of long excepted truisms" (p. viii). These "myths," grounded in zionist discourse and produced and disseminated by the state apparatus, provided Israelis with the basic materials out of which they constructed their self-understanding as a collective. Additionally, they provided the state with its basic legitimation. Constituting the "common sense" of Israeli culture, they shaped the ways in which most Israelis viewed social, cultural, and political reality.

The "myths" under question included the following: (1) while the Israelis did everything possible to bring about peace in 1948 (and after), the Arabs continually refused all initiatives; (2) the Palestinian Arab refugees had willingly left their homes, deceived by leaders who promised them that they would soon return along with the conquering Arab armies; (3) the primary purpose of the state of Israel was to provide for persecuted Jews of the world a safe and secure place to which the "exiles" could be gathered;

(4) in addition to providing them with a safe haven, Israel provided Jewish immigrants with the opportunity to live freely as Jews, unhampered either by political persecution or economic and social discrimination such as had characterized life in "exile"; and (5) only in Israel could Judaism flourish, functioning as a unifying force for world Jewry.

Segev related the dispossession of the Palestinian Arabs to the conditions in which the state of Israel was established, the attitude of the state's leaders to peace, and the internal Israeli discourse on what had become known as "the Arab refugee problem." The dominant scholarly writings on these topics favorably compared Israel, a state committed to peace, with the Arab nations who were intent on waging war against Israel. In these accounts, Israel was depicted as pursuing every opportunity to bring about peace with its Arab neighbors, while the Arabs sought to subvert all peace efforts.

In the prevailing Israeli scholarly accounts, the flight of one-half to three-quarters of a million Arabs from the state in 1948 was attributed to the constant urging of the leaders of the Arab states. In these accounts, the Arab leaders promised the Palestinian Arabs that if they fled now, they could return with the conquering Arab armies. According to Segev (1986), a careful examination of newly released state documents makes it clear that these Israeli justifications were simply not true. For example, notwithstanding the claims of the Israeli government, these documents called into question the representation of Israel as the zealous pursuer of peace. In addition, they belied the dominant Israeli narrative explaining the flight of the Palestinian Arabs:

> It became apparent that the Arabs had not always refused to discuss peace with Israel and that Israel had not done all it could possibly do to reach peace with its neighbors at all costs. A large number of Palestinian Arabs were expelled from their homes, not only during the war of 1948-1949 but afterwards as well. (p. vii)

Segev's research further convinced him that the evidence contradicted the dominant zionist legitimation of Israel as the refuge for the Jewish people. In zionist discourse, Israel's primary mission was the "ingathering of the exiles." According to Segev, however,

> It was not the "gathering of exiles" in accordance with the Zionist ideal that was the primary purpose for Israel to encourage Jewish immigration, but rather its own needs for manpower in agriculture, industry and the army. Jewish immigrants from Arab countries have been discriminated against, partly as a result of explicit decisions, and many of them were deliberately stripped of their cultural and religious identity. (p. vii)

Scholarly studies, school texts, and popular literature all represented Israel as a nation striving to achieve a cohesive, integrated society dedicated to eliminating social inequities. Consistent with the zionist conception of Israel as the unifying site for world Jewry, Israelis were represented as comprising a family. This family comprised Jews from different parts of the world who had at last returned to their homeland. Freed from the fragmenting, destructive effects of life in exile, Jews, according to the prevailing discourse, would achieve in Israel the long-sought unity. Safe from the corrosive influence of foreign values and ideas, Jews could at last fulfill Ahad Haam's vision of a vibrant, creative, homogeneous Jewish culture thriving in its natural habitat.

The Israel represented by Segev was very different. From its inception, Israeli society was ridden with political, religious, social, and cultural conflicts. These included the ongoing conflicts between Arabs and Jews, European Jews and Jews of Middle Eastern origin, and religious Jews and secular Jews.[20] Challenging the zionist myths of progress and consensus, Segev (1986) represented Israeli society in the 1980s as plagued by the same conflicts that were present at the outset:

> 38 years after the Declaration of Independence, Israel still faces the very same problems and conflicts that troubled the first Israelis. It is a country still searching for its principles and its identity. (p. viii)

Segev's book was widely reviewed in the Israeli press and attracted much attention.[21] However, it did not provoke the widespread soul-searching about Israeli identity that we find in the 1990s. Also, insofar as it was not published as an academic book, it did not provoke widespread debate in the academic community. Soon, however, a series of academic books, many of which elaborated on themes presented by Segev, precipitated debates both within the academy and without, that eventually turned into debates over the basic character of Israeli identity and culture. The issues raised by Segev became, within the next decade, a basic part of debates over what came to be known as postzionism.

One of the most controversial and widely discussed books to emerge in this period was the detailed and comprehensive study *The Birth of the Palestinian Refugee Problem: 1947–1949* (1987) by Israeli scholar Benny Morris (b. 1948), a Cambridge University–educated historian and, at the time, a writer for the *Jerusalem Post*.[22] Morris' scholarly analysis focused on four premises informing the prevailing Israeli historical narratives surrounding the 1948 War: (1) While the leaders of the Israeli state were open to the United Nations partition plan in 1947, it was rejected by the Arab states; (2) the 1948 War "was waged between a relatively defenseless and weak (Jewish) David and a relatively strong (Arab) Goliath" (p. 21); (3) the Arab refugee problem resulted primarily from the actions of the Palestinian Arabs who, encouraged by the promises of their leaders that they would return as victors, fled their homes and villages; and (4) "at the war's end, Israel was interested in making peace, but the recalcitrant Arabs displayed no such interest, opting for a perpetual—if sporadic—war to the finish" (p. 21). Although, at times, individual scholars challenged one or another of these premises, they were generally accepted as a part of the prevailing knowledge within Israeli culture and widely taught to Israeli school children.[23]

Morris' work was distinguished, among other things, by extensive research into the historical records relating to the flight of more than 600,000 Palestinian Arabs from over 350 towns and villages in 1947 and 1948. Carefully studying newly released records of cabinet sessions, other government documents, and private papers of Israeli leaders, Morris reached conclusions that differed decidedly from the prevailing scholarly consensus. First, despite making every effort to uncover evidence supporting the widely disseminated Israeli claim that the primary cause of the mass Arab flight was the encouragement of their leaders, Morris found no such evidence. Morris instead concluded, through a nuanced, multicausal explanation, that the policies and decisions of Israeli political and military leadership and the actions of the Israeli military forces had played a decisive role in precipitating the flight.

Morris saw his work as related to that of two other Israeli scholars, Avi Shlaim and Ilan Pappe. Shlaim, who wrote *Collusion Across the Jordan* (1988), and Pappe, the author of *The Making of the Arab–Israeli Conflict: 1947–1951* (1992), had, like Morris, done their graduate studies in England. Their studies, like Morris', challenged the prevailing Israeli interpretations of the events surrounding the 1948 War. In a 1988 article published in the American Jewish journal *Tikkun,* Morris described the writings of the group as constituting a "new historiography."[24] The emergence of the "new historiography," argued Morris, was a result of two basic factors. On the one hand, because of Israel's Archives Law, hundreds of thousands of previously closed state papers had become available to researchers in the early 1980s. Among these documents were correspondence, memoranda, minutes of official government meetings, and the private papers of Israeli leaders. To Morris and other scholars of his generation born around the time of or soon after the establishment of the state, these documents shed new light on the conditions in which the state came into being.

A second but no less important factor contributing to the emergence of a group of "new historians" was generational. Coming of age following the establishment of the state, the new generation of Israeli historians was not burdened by the political and cultural baggage of their elders.[25] The perspective of the older generation of Israeli historians had been shaped by labor zionist ideology and the trauma of the 1948 War. In contrast, the new generation of historians had experienced a very different set of realities. Israel's occupation of the West Bank and Gaza in 1967, the Yom Kippur War of 1973, the 1982 War in Lebanon, and the Palestinian Intifada that erupted in 1987 produced in the younger generation a skeptical attitude toward the truths produced and disseminated by official Israeli discourse. Increasingly, the younger generation found that zionist discourse, addressing a very different set of circumstances, could not provide persuasive explanations of the changing realities.

Morris' book provoked strong reactions within the academic community. One of the sharpest criticisms was made by Shabtai Teveth, an independent scholar and historian, in a scathing three-part critique of the book in the Israeli daily *Haaretz*. The debate spilled over to the United States when Morris published the aforementioned article on the new historiography in the American nonacademic journal *Tikkun*, which has a declared left-wing agenda. Teveth published his response to this article in *Commentary*, a conservative Jewish-sponsored monthly.[26]

In *Haaretz* and *Commentary*, Teveth denounced Morris and the others for allowing political concerns to contaminate their scholarship. Casting doubt on Morris' scholarly qualifications, Teveth (1989b) also accused those associated with the new historiography of being sympathetic to the Palestinians and of seeking "to delegitimize Zionism":

> In other words, it is the commitment to the "purposes of peace" that determines eligibility in this new historical club. And what are the "purposes of peace"? While Morris does not attempt to define them, it would appear that one of their essentials is sympathy somewhat inclined to the side of the Palestinians. Another, therefore [*sic*] is the desire to delegitimate Zionism. (p. 24)

These criticisms were to recur frequently in the course of the debates.

According to Teveth, the writing of history should be independent of political concerns. Teveth argued that it is both possible and essential for a scholar to separate his or her political interests from scholarly analysis, interpretation, and writing. The goal of historical scholarship, according to this view, is to get the story "right," that is, to provide an account that corresponds to the objective events.

Morris concurred with Teveth's apolitical conception of historical interpretation. Identifying himself as a "positivist" historian, Morris agreed that the basic concern of the historian is to uncover the facts, independent of personal political views. Refusing to accept at face value the prevailing Israeli explanations for the flight of the Palestinian Arabs in 1948, Morris argued that he had carefully examined the evidence relating to the factors precipitating the flight. Morris acknowledged that he asked questions the answers to which previous generations of historians had taken for granted. These questions, his skepticism toward the accepted explanations, and the alternative narrative that developed out of his archival research produced "truths" Morris regarded as objectively "truer" than the ones presented by previous scholars.

However, from Morris' claims and Teveth's response, it is clear that far more than scholarly methods and historical accuracy were at stake. Extending far beyond the walls of academe, the questions raised by the younger scholars had the effect of problematizing prevailing notions of Israeli collective identity as well as the trustworthiness of the authorities of the state.

IS ZIONISM A FORM OF COLONIALISM?
OLD CRITIQUES, NEW ARGUMENTS

While the writings of Segev, Morris, Pappe, and Shlaim focused on the period of the establishment of the state, others extended the critique back into earlier periods of zionist history. In so doing, they challenged widely accepted axioms concerning the character of zionism and, by extension, the state that it helped to produce. Central to two of these studies was the question of whether or not zionism was a form of colonialism.

In *Zionism & Territory: The Socio-Territorial Dimension of Zionist Politics,* Baruch Kimmerling (1983) was the first Israeli academic to employ a colonial model. A Hebrew University sociologist and a student of the recognized dean of Israeli sociologists Shmuel Eisenstadt and his leading disciples Moshe Lissak and Dan Horowitz, Kimmerling took issue with their interpretations. Departing from his mentors, he drew comparisons between "the colonizing process of the Jews in Palestine and colonial type immigration and settlement movements in the Americas, Africa, Australia, etc." (p. 8).

Kimmerling was fully aware that "the entire Arab and Muslim worlds and thereafter...the Communist bloc and the Third World" regarded zionism "as being part of the colonialist world, as the expansion of the white man into the 'non-white' parts of the world for the purposes of exploitation" (p. 28). However, Kimmerling avoided "the question of the right of Jewish settlers to settle in Palestine and to transform the territory into an exclusivist national territory." Drawing a sharp boundary between academic fields, he insisted that questions of right and wrong belong to "the realm of philosophy, international law, ideology, theology, or political science" (pp. 29–30). Instead, he focused on the processes of legitimation employed by zionists and their effects on the structure of Israeli society.

Notwithstanding his hopes of avoiding political issues, Kimmerling's work brought to the surface a key problematic of Israeli society. Although refraining from challenging the validity of Israeli legitimations, Kimmerling also refused to take them at face value. In adopting this stance, he departed from the prevailing Israeli scholarship, raising issues and problems that it preferred to disregard. While not, at this point, openly criticizing zionist practices, Kimmerling, by classifying zionist practices as colonialist, clearly opened the way to a powerful critique of zionist discourse.[27]

The use of a colonial model to interpret zionist settlement was subsequently expanded and sharpened by another Israeli scholar, Gershon Shafir, now a professor at the University of California at San Diego.[28] Kimmerling, basing his analysis on the concept of frontier, had explored the ways in which the boundaries of the Israeli collective were represented and legitimated in Israeli scholarship. Shafir, for his part, focused on economic conditions, economic interests, labor practices, and their effects. Acknowledging the impact of the 1967 War and its aftermath on his thinking, Shafir (1989) placed the Israeli–Palestinian conflict at the center of his work.

Rejecting the interpretations that explained Israeli society in terms of the values of zionism, Shafir argued that the most decisive factor was "the conflict between the Jewish immigrant settlers and the Palestinian inhabitants of the land." This conflict, according to Shafir, also played a key role in the formation of Israeli collective identity: "[It] was in the context of this national conflict that both the Jewish and Arab sides assumed their modern identities" (p. 5). In shifting the focus of his analysis from the reasons and motivations for zionist settlement practices to their effects on Palestinian Arabs, Shafir departed from the prevailing Israeli academic practices. Specifically, he directly challenged the functionalist and elitist interpretive models that dominated Israeli social scientific scholarship.[29]

Utilizing, like Kimmerling, a comparative model, Shafir (1989) argues that Israel is best understood when compared with other European overseas societies "that were also shaped in the process of settlement and conflict with already existing societies" (p. xi). Shafir acknowledges that, as other scholars have claimed, zionism may be understood as "a variety of Eastern European nationalism, that is, an ethnic movement in search of a state" (p. 8). Nevertheless, he found a colonial model to be more useful in explaining the settlement of the land. Drawing on theories of colonialism developed by historians D. K. Fieldhouse and George Fredrickson, Shafir argues that zionism is regarded "more fruitfully as a late instance of European overseas expansion" (p. 8). Moreover, zionist settlement is a form of "the pure settlement of European overseas expansion in a frontier region, based on relatively homogeneous or relatively homogeneous population and on separate markets" (p. 10).[30]

Tracing the development of settlement and labor market practices back to the late nineteenth and early twentieth centuries, Shafir (1989) argues that economic realities combined with zionist ideology and practices to produce a society in which the indigenous Arab population was excluded from the labor market:

> The critical stage in Israeli state building and nation formation took place with the inauguration of the *fifth stage* in 1905 when the productivization drive of the Eastern European Jewish Enlightenment [Haskalah] was transformed, in Palestine, into "conquest of labor"—an aspiration to monopolize at first all manual labor, subsequently at least skilled jobs, by Jewish workers. Already in the "conquest of labor" phase the boundaries of the Israeli nation were determined. Yemenite, as well as other Mizrahi Jews were incorporated into Israeli society but placed in an inferior position in the labor market and social structure, while Palestinian Arabs were definitely excluded even as a labor force. This strategy, though not effective before the first World War, and even later yielding only modest results, left the legacy of *Jewish exclusivism*. (p. 188)

Moreover, like Kimmerling, Shafir criticized Israeli scholarship for focusing on internal conditions and processes while, at the same time, ignoring the wider context. Like Kimmerling, Shafir (1989) insisted that "during most of its history, Israeli society is best understood not through the existing, inward-looking, interpretations but rather in terms of the broader context of Israeli–Palestinian relations"(p. xi).

Shafir also emphasized the gap separating practical needs related to everyday realities from the ideological legitimations attributed to the settlers:

> When second Aliya members and leaders had to make choices, adopt or reject models, and change strategies of action, they constructed these not so much from the grand cloth of general ideologies as from the simpler materials of concrete methods of settlement. (p. 3)

Israeli functionalist social scientists studying the history of the second *aliyah* [wave of immigration] (1904–1914) had focused on ideological factors, while others had focused on political elites. Both groups emphasized "the interests of leaders and the organizations" while minimizing the importance of the economic conditions and the interests of members:

> Both perspectives neglect the impact of economic interests and the structure of production as phenomena in their own right. They see the participants in the process of state and nation formations as possessing greater freedom in the pursuit of their intrinsic designs than the study of economic conditions under which they operated would lead us to believe. (Shafir 1989, 4)

Notwithstanding differences in chronological focus and emphasis, Shafir acknowledged the connections linking his analysis to the new historiography. However, unlike those scholars who focused on the myths of the zionist movement, Shafir emphasized the ways in which the ideology of labor zionism concealed "social contradictions behind a facade of harmonious social relations" (p. xi).

Responding to critics in the Preface to the second edition of his book, Shafir elaborated on his colonial mode and answered those who claimed that zionism brought many social and economic benefits to the Arab population:

> Modernization, undertaken by the Zionist movement...was embedded in a colonial relationship and the goals of Jewish colonization, "conquest of labor," and "conquest of land," and the colonizing institutions that supported them—the Histadrut and the Jewish National Fund, were exclusivistic. "Conquest of labor" aimed at the displacement of Arab workers by Jewish workers in all branches and skill levels. Arab land, once purchased by the JNF [Jewish National Fund], could not be resold to the Arabs, and JNF land was not available for employment of Arab workers. The kibbutzim, that customarily were built on JNF land and had only Jewish members, were the most exclusivistic of all the creations of the Second Aliya, and in that fashion, also thoroughly nationalist! In fact, the Labor Movement's institutions were the ones that were least able to benefit the Arabs of Palestine. (Shafir 1996a, 5)

Notwithstanding the continued emphasis by Israeli scholars on the positive, creative, and constructive character of zionism and the benefits produced by its institutions, Shafir persisted in his counternarrative. In the process, he reiterated an interpretation that reveals the underside of values, practices, and institutions that, to most Israelis, are taken as models of social pioneering.

Critics of Shafir have also argued in journal and newspaper articles that insofar as there existed a "dual society" and "dual economy," zionism had little or no impact on the Palestinian population. In response, Shafir (1996a) insisted that

> as long as Jewish society was bent on expansion it could never remain self-contained and directly interacted with its Palestinian counterpart through the purchase, and later conquest of part of its land and the uprooting of a share of its sparse population. (p. 6)

A third criticism of Shafir was that while zionist settlement was a form of colonization, it was "colonization without colonialism."[31] Shafir (1996a) readily admitted that zionism does not conform precisely to European colonial models. Factors such as the absence of a metropolis, the decidedly nationalist character of zionism, and the secondary role of capitalistic expansion in zionist settlement clearly have distinguished zionism from other colonial undertakings. Nevertheless, zionism remained a movement "aimed at the creation of a homogeneous settler-immigrant population" (p. 7). Moreover, as long as zionist discourse represented the land as "empty," it produced and reproduced a colonialist view of "the native population as being part and parcel of the environment that was to be subdued, tamed, and made hospitable for themselves" (p. 6).

The claim that zionism was a colonialist enterprise and Israel a colonial state was not new. As we saw in the previous chapter, such claims had been previously made within Israel by radical leftist groups such as Mazpen, which had openly declared itself to be antizionist. In addition, hostile nations, including Arab, Soviet, and so-called "Third World" states, had repeatedly voiced this accusation in an effort to delegitimate the Israeli state.

What distinguished the new Israeli scholarly writings linking zionism and colonialism was that the scholars who produced them did not consider themselves to be hostile to the state. Notwithstanding the fact that their writings sharply contested the dominant Israeli representations of zionism as a humane, progressive enterprise, scholars like Baruch Kimmerling and Gershon Shafir considered themselves to be loyal Israelis for whom the legitimacy of the state was not in question. Nor did they identify with or support groups hostile to Israel.

Kimmerling and Shafir reflect a growing awareness among Israeli scholars that historical studies of zionism and the state of Israel must incorporate and treat seriously the previously excluded voices of the Palestinian other. Focusing on the position of marginalized or excluded groups, their studies significantly broadened the boundaries within which Israeli cultural identity is discussed. They thus departed from the dominant historical and sociological representations. Utilizing a comparative approach, both scholars produced works that strongly support the claim that the zionist settlement of Israel comprised a particular form of colonial settlement. Needless to say, this elicited sharp criticisms from other Israeli scholars, particularly those who identified with labor zionism.

In contrast to the scholarly interpretations that regarded Israel as a unique case demanding unique methodological approaches, Kimmerling and Shafir both argue that the analysis of zionist settlement practices requires a comparative model. Shifting attention away from the intentions and values of zionist leaders and settlers, they emphasize the destructive effects of zionist settlement patterns and practices on the native Palestinian population. In different ways and to differing degrees, both Kimmerling and Shafir challenge the dominant zionist view that represents the settlement of Palestine as a benign, progressive process that brought the benefits of modernity to Jews and Palestinian Arabs alike.

Another approach associated with postzionism is that of Ilan Pappe. Pappe is one of the few of these scholars to openly proclaim the relative, perspectival character of historical discourse. Pappe thus diverges from the positivistic position advocated by Morris, who had criticized Israeli historians for getting the story wrong.[32]

Pappe (1993d) agreed that the writings of historians such as Morris are more comprehensive than previous studies. This was, in part, a result of the fact that Morris asked questions that his predecessors had neglected. These included such questions as: (1) To what extent was the Yishuv in danger of destruction? (2) What was the level of preparation of Arab armies and the relative strength of the two sides? (3) What was the influence of the *Shoah* on diplomatic negotiations? (4) What caused the exodus of Palestinians from Israeli-held territory? (5) Who was responsible for the failure of the peace negotiations after the war?

However, Pappe departed from Morris and most of his colleagues by advocating a multiperspectival approach to history. One of the only postzionist scholars to draw upon recent critiques of objectivity, Pappe rejects the view that objectivity is a matter of the correspondence of interpretation to facts or events.[33] Given that events and facts are seen differently by different groups, the historian must incorporate multiple perspectives and alternative interpretations into his or her interpretation. In particular, historians of one group or nation must include in their narratives the narrative of the Other.[34] To demonstrate the cogency of this approach, Pappe edited several collections of scholarly articles of diverse, often conflicting viewpoints on such topics as the Intifada, Jews in the Ottoman Empire, and Islam and peace. Advocating a multiperspectival "Rashamon" type view of the Arab–Israeli conflict, Pappe (1993d) argues in favor of a "scholarly/research pluralism" (p. 110).[35]

The call for a multiperspectival approach to Israeli history was supported by Kimmerling, who with an American scholar, Joel Migdal, wrote a pioneering scholarly study of the Palestinians. Their book, *Palestinians: The Making of a People* (1993), represented the first effort by an Israeli scholar to produce a balanced, comprehensive account of the social and political development of the Palestinian nation. Depicting the prevailing Israeli scholarship as myopic, the authors criticized interpretations of Israeli history for excluding the Palestinian narrative. Adopting a position rare among both Israeli and non-Israeli Jewish scholars, Kimmerling and Migdal insisted that the narratives of Jews and Palestinians are intertwined:

> Zionists have been absorbed in a nationalist project rendering the Palestinians almost incidental. In the process, they have failed to grasp the extent to which

their own society has been shaped by its ongoing encounter with the Palestinians. (p. xviii)

Consequently, the history of one people cannot be understood without attending to the narrative of the other.

Challenging the zionist interpretation of history, Kimmerling and Migdal thus seek to provide space within Israeli scholarly discourse for the narrative of the previously silenced Palestinian. Whereas the dominant Israeli scholarship framed the history of zionism, the settlement of the land, and the creation of the state from a singularly Jewish perspective, Kimmerling and Migdal (1993) undertake to represent the Palestinian perspective:[36]

> As our own account may have suggested, it is impossible to tell the story of Zionism or Palestinism without understanding the impact they had on one another. For the Palestinians, the story centers on Al-Nakba, a catastrophe that produced ironically, a strong collective consciousness transcending all the fractures. (p. 279)

Kimmerling and Pappe further criticized the discourse of Israeli historians for its political bias. These scholars, using such value-laden terms as *aliyah* [immigration], *haluziut* [pioneering], *geulah* [redemption], *tekumah* [rebirth], and War of Liberation/Independence, neither critically analyzed these terms nor placed them in their ideological context. In using such terms, Israeli scholars actually reproduce zionist discourse and narratives (Pappe 1993d).[37] In place of this terminology, Kimmerling and Pappe advocate the use of more neutral terms, including immigration in place of ascent, purchase of lands in place of redemption of land, the attempt to actualize utopia in place of pioneering, the 1948 War in place of the War of Liberation, and fighting units or paramilitary groups in place of rioters or conspirators.[38]

Kimmerling presented a comprehensive summary of the new critical scholarship in a special (1995) edition of the journal *History & Memory.* Notwithstanding his refusal to accept the label postzionist, Kimmerling nonetheless provided a lucid and concise statement of the characteristics of postzionist scholarship.[39] Emphasizing the political effects of scholarly historical and sociological representations, Kimmerling critically assessed the basic principles that inform the dominant Israeli historiography and sociology and suggests alternatives.

According to Kimmerling, the dominant Israeli scholarly discourse is characterized by six practices: (1) periodizing Israeli history/prehistory according to the waves of Jewish settlement, wars, and the distinction between pre-state and post-state; (2) explaining the establishment of the state teleologically; (3) assuming the uniqueness of Jewish history, including the history of zionism and Israel; (4) using exclusionary, Judeocentric/ethnocentric categories to define the boundaries of the Israeli collective; (5) legitimating zionist territorial claims on the basis of the presumed antiquity of Jewish settlement in the land; and (6) analyzing and emphasizing the inner intentions of zionist and Israeli leaders, while ignoring the external effects of policies and actions on the Palestinians.

Kimmerling (1995a) asserted that ignoring the significant discontinuities among different waves of Jewish immigration and constructing "a 'reality' common to all the immigrants" significantly limited "the scope and questions of historical research." Moreover, the effects of zionist scholarship are by no means limited to the confines of the academy. Thus, by dividing Israeli history between pre-state and post-state periods, zionist scholarship clearly implies that "the process of state and society building had been concluded" by the end of the first five waves of immigration. Subsequent changes were thus regarded as "extensions or improvements (or even a worsening) of basic sociopolitical patterns established between 1882 and 1948" (p. 51). According to Kimmerling, this has the effect of minimizing the contribution of later, post-statehood immigrants, most of whom were from Middle Eastern countries.

Kimmerling (1995a) further argued that treating Israeli history as unique leads scholars to neglect patterns and characteristics that zionist immigration and settlement practices share with other immigrant-settler societies. Were scholars to utilize a comparative approach and refer to settlement processes in North and South America, Australia, New Zealand, Algeria, and South Africa, they would, argued Kimmerling, be forced "to deal with Israel's colonial legacy, the very allusion to which is taboo, in both Israeli society and Israeli historiography" (p. 53).

Kimmerling reiterated the argument that by focusing on intentions of the zionist settlers rather than on the effects of their practices, Israeli scholars have reinforced the zionist view that Jewish settlement was "a benevolent enterprise that would bring progress and prosperity to all the inhabitants of the land" (p. 56). This approach, which excludes the Palestinian perspective, ignores the disempowering, oppressive effects of this settlement on the indigenous Palestinian Arab population.

Another effect of the dominant scholarly discourse criticized by Kimmerling is its exclusionary effects. Treating Israel as if it were an exclusively Jewish society, Israeli sociologists and historians create "an almost 'exclusive' Jewish bubble which excludes the Arab population and the British state from serious consideration" (p. 53). This, in turn, legitimates the marginalizing or exclusion of non-Jews, particularly Palestinian Arabs. In this way, Israeli scholarship tends to confirm "the political and legal perception of Israel as the state of the Jewish people residing both within and outside its boundaries, rather than as the state of its citizens (which would also include Arabs)" (p. 54).

In Kimmerling's view, Israeli historians and sociologists are "caught in a cross-fire between their professional commitments on the one hand, and their commitment to the Israeli collective on the other." As a result, their academic discourse is "embedded in an active form of knowledge that shapes collective identity by bridging between different pasts (recovered, imagined, invented, and intentionally constructed) and creating meanings and boundaries for the collectivity." Consequently, historians and sociologists serve as "an ultimate 'supreme court' which deciphers from all the accumulated 'pieces of the past' the 'true' collective memories which are appropriate for inclusion in the canonical national historical narrative" (p. 57). Kimmerling called upon his fellow scholars to recognize that they are "part of a sociopolitical hegemony" and that the knowledge that they produce plays a key role in shaping that hegemony: "Only an awareness of those limitations can enable the historian to partially overcome their effect" (p. 57).

Kimmerling claimed that even the discourse used by scholars when referring to the land is politically laden. Israeli scholars repeatedly use the term "land of Israel" rather than Palestine even when discussing historical periods in which no Jews lived there or in which the land was ruled by other nations. In Kimmerling's view, this has the effect of granting "the Jews an eternal title over the territory, regardless of who populated or governed it, even in a situation when the 'legitimate ownership' was under dispute" (Kimmerling 1995a, 48). Similarly, the use of such ideological concepts as "ingathering of the exiles" has the effect of concealing the effects of settlement activities on the Palestinian "Others" who were already living in the land. This discourse also serves to close off discussion of these effects.[40]

In addition to emphasizing the power effects of scholarly discourse, the new historians and critical sociologists have also exhibited a concern for marginalized, excluded, or subjugated Others. Whereas zionist scholarship took for granted the legitimacy of the Jewish claim to the land, postzionist scholars juxtaposed these claims against those of the Palestinians living on the land. Rather than follow the conventional scholarly practice of privileging zionist claims, postzionist scholars seek to formulate a more neutral discourse so as to include the previously silenced voices of the Palestinian "Other."

Pappe is representative of the postzionist scholars who, like their critics, readily acknowledged that the issues at stake in the scholarly debates reverberate far beyond the boundaries of the academic community. Like Ram, he saw a clear connection between these debates and the crisis of Israeli collective identity. Torn between democracy and nationalism, which includes religious identity, secular Israelis are experiencing a crisis of identity (Pappe 1995c, 447). Although Israel has clearly achieved a type of democracy, insofar as it privileges nationalism over democracy, it diverges from the dominant Western liberal models. Moreover, by imposing Jewish nationalism on a non-Jewish minority, Israel puts limits on democracy. In the final analysis, concluded Pappe, while maintaining many democratic styles, Israel "is not democratic" (when compared with Western democracies).

Like others identified as postzionists, Pappe (1995c) favors a democratic state in which Israeli citizenship rather than religion or ethnic nationality is the primary identifying factor. In his view, even secular Israelis have accepted a religious, that is, Jewish, identity that, based upon the identity of the mother, is biologically grounded (p. 447). Such an identity, which is genetically determined, runs counter to an alternative, liberal-democratic-secular identity. Instead, Pappe advocates a pluralistic, heterogeneous Israel, whether it be a heterogeneity of east/west, of tradition/modernity, or of Jews/Palestinians. Consequently, he favors rescinding the Law of Return as a necessary step away from the position that identifies Israel with zionism and loyalty to Israel with loyalty to zionism. However, like Kimmerling, he eschewed the postzionist label. Pappe (1995c) preferred instead the label azionist or nonzionist.[41] In this, he differs from Kimmerling, who eschews all labels. However, notwithstanding their differing positions with regard to the use of the term postzionist, Morris, Pappe, and Kimmerling have each posed serious challenges to zionist discourse and have problematized the scholarship that they identify with it.

TOWARD A POSTZIONIST SOCIOLOGY

A highly significant moment in the formation of postzionist discourse was the publication of a selection of writings by critical social scientists edited by Uri Ram (Ram 1993). Ram was one of the first scholars to openly embrace the postzionist label. In this volume, he gathered together and put before the public a collection of sociological essays that had previously been published in academic journals. Interestingly, a number of the articles in Ram's book had originally appeared as early as the 1970s. These included essays by Haifa University sociologists Sammy Smooha, Shlomo Swirski, and Deborah Bernstein, each of whom focused on groups considered to be marginal by the dominant scholarship.[42]

Ram argued that the social scientists included in this volume laid the foundations for a new, postzionist sociology. Whereas the dominant Israeli social science identified with the discourse of labor zionism, postzionist scholars, producing alternative representations of Israeli society and culture, sought to break free from the effects of zionist discourse. Thus, these social scientific studies paralleled the new historiography in significant ways.

Rejecting the organic, integrationist model of society, Swirski, Bernstein, and Smooha highlighted the conflicts in Israeli society, along with exclusionary practices and ongoing power struggles. In place of assimilation and integration, they emphasized marginalization and exclusion. Consequently, their representation of Israel society differed significantly from that of the dominant scholarship. While their writings were frequently rejected or ignored by the dominant social science, the publication of Ram's anthology brought them into prominence and positioned them as a new critical school of Israeli sociology.

In his 1995 English study *The Changing Agenda of Israeli Sociology: Theory, Ideology, and Identity* (1995a), published in the United States, Ram elaborated on the background and context of the new postzionist social science:[43]

> While the agenda of Zionist sociology has been congruous with the founding of the Israeli nation-state, the time is now ripe for the formulation of a post-Zionist sociological agenda that would be congruous with the consolidation of a democratic Israeli civil society; a society of free and equal civilians and of diverse identities. Rather than national integration, the focus of such an agenda should be the issue of citizenship in a modern democratic society. (p. 206)

This integration of scholarly practice with the values of pluralistic democracy and the strengthening of Israeli civil society is a recurring theme among postzionist scholars.

Ram, in the tradition of Alvin Gouldner's critical sociology, sought to produce "a historically informed critique of [Israeli] sociology as a theory and as a social institution" (Gouldner, cited in Ram 1995a, vii). Ram made it clear from the outset that his study is politically engaged and shaped by his "personal, social and political involvement" and participation in "the Israeli left and the peace movement." Contrasting his approach with the prevailing objectivistic Israeli scholarship, Ram (1995a) described critical sociology as a platform upon which "a new Israeli identity struggles for emergence" (p. 206).

Ram linked conventional Israeli sociology to zionist ideology on the one hand and to particular moments in the political, social, and cultural life of Israel on the other. To Ram, the academic sociology that first emerged at the Hebrew University with the establishment of the state was a conscripted sociology that both legitimated and reinforced the dominant zionist ideology. In contrast, the writings of the critical sociologists represent a "wider political and cultural process of diversification and pluralization" as well as the "democratization of the public sphere" (Ram 1995a, 206). Critical of the positivist tradition that informs conventional Israeli social science, Ram considers "scientific practices to be embedded within cultural traditions and social contexts, and guided by social and cognitive interests"(p. 3).[44]

Accordingly, the efforts of objectivist scholars to separate academic discourse from the broader social and cultural discourse are futile. Declaring his intention to intervene in Israeli cultural debates, Ram considers postzionist sociology to be consistent with the kind of society he wants to see emerge in Israel.[45]

Ram's announcement of a postzionist agenda for Israeli sociology appears to be the first instance in which an Israeli scholar openly identified with postzionism. As the scholarly debates over new historiography and critical Israeli social science clearly revealed, the contested issues penetrate to the deepest levels of Israeli culture and society. Understandably, the critique of the dominant Israeli scholarship by Ram and others precipitated a major debate among Israeli historians and social scientists. In both scope and intensity, these debates differed significantly from previous debates over zionism.

THE PUBLIC DEBATES OVER POSTZIONISM: DEFINING THE BOUNDARIES OF ISRAELI NATIONAL DISCOURSE

In 1995, within a matter of months, the controversies over the new scholarship spread throughout the academy. This is evident in the several academic symposia devoted to the new scholarship and to postzionism held at each of the major Israeli universities and in published collections.[46] In addition, the debate was carried forward in such respectable academic journals as *History & Memory* and *Israel Studies*. The previous year, however, the academic debates had already flowed out of the restricted spaces of the academy and into the public sphere in such newspapers as *Haaretz, Yediot Aharonot,* and *Davar.* What first appeared to be academic debates among scholars were quickly transformed into debates about the character of Israeli society, its past, and its future. In the early stages of these public debates, we encounter the increasing use of the term postzionism as the key concept around which the conflict was framed.

The early attacks in the press give a sense of the urgency with which the academic debates over postzionism were received by a larger readership. In one of the first public attacks, published in the Israeli daily *Davar,* Yisrael Landers (1994) drew the lines of battle. In an article provocatively titled "The Sins that We Committed in Establishing the State," he wrote:

> What has previously been known in limited academic circles should now be revealed to the community at large: There has arisen a scholarly school among Israeli social scientists that challenges the zionist worldview, the zionist settlement of the land of Israel, and the right of the state of Israel to exist. (p. 8)[47]

According to Landers, a new wave of Israeli scholars, believing that "the state of Israel was born in sin," have depicted zionism as "a violent and oppressive movement." To Landers, these scholars, having allowed their ideology to intrude on their academic research, cannot be considered zionists. Instead, Landers designated them postzionists. Clarifying his use of the term, Landers (1994) applied it to those who believe that "Israel should be a normal democratic society without a specifically Jewish mission" (p. 8).[48]

Bypassing the scholarly issues, Landers emphasized the dangers that he considered the new historians and critical sociologists to pose to zionism and to the state of Israel:

> These critical scholars are presently only a minority among their colleagues in the various social sciences. But owing to their abilities as scholars and debaters, their views are receiving a wider hearing. They are directing generations of students in research, and their subversion of the zionist narrative will contribute, intentionally or unintentionally, to a delegitimation of the Jewish state at home and abroad. (p. 8)

Landers further accused the postzionist scholars of constructing a counternarrative that located the origins of the state in a series of sinful acts. In representing zionist practices as violent and oppressive, they were, he argued, calling into question the legitimacy of the state.

Landers also accused the new historians and critical sociologists of rejecting the zionist conception of the mission of the state. Denying that Israel had a specific Jewish mission, these scholars were guilty of trying to transform the state into a "normal democratic society."

Shortly after Landers' article appeared, the well-known novelist Aaron Megged carried forward the assault on postzionism. In an article in the daily *Haaretz* entitled "The Israeli Propensity for Self-Destruction," Megged attacked the postzionist scholars for their suicidal drive:

> Is zionism approaching the stage of its "Spenglerian" decline? As she stands on the threshold of this stage, is she driven by some blind biological force to self-destruction? (p. 27)

Purportedly aiming his criticisms at the 1993 Oslo Accords and the ensuing peace process, Megged (1994a) focused his attack on scholars such as Morris, Kimmerling, and Pappe. According to Megged, these scholars view zionism as "a kind of evil, colonialistic conspiracy to exploit the people [*am*] living in Palestine, to subjugate them, to dispossess them." Furthermore, they regard basic zionist values such as "redemption of the land," "conquest through labor," "ingathering of the exiles," and "defense," to be no more than hypocrisy and "euphemisms" for a depraved, base plot (p. 27). In Megged's view, these "postzionist" scholars attack the very zionist values that provide the state of Israel with its foundations.

Taking up a theme that was to recur in other attacks on postzionism, Megged (1994a) accused the postzionist scholars of abetting Israel's anti-Semitic enemies who seek the destruction of the state. In his view, the interpretations promulgated by the postzionist scholars are not really new, but a replay of earlier attacks on zionism and the state that had emanated from the Soviet Union and from other Marxist-Leninist circles:

> What is then the message of the new historians...whose words many truth-seeking and righteous Israelis are ingesting with masochistic thirst and pleasure? The message is that most of the certainties that are fixed in our consciousness and our experience are lies. (p. 27)

To Megged, the new historians were guilty of casting aspersions on all Israelis, present and past, who, motivated only by the highest moral ideals, had devoted themselves to reclaiming the land and defending the nation. Referring to the moral values, ideals, and motives of the settlers, Megged ignored the effects of their actions on the minority Palestinian population. Instead, he reiterated an argument disseminated by labor zionist discourse. The early zionist settlers, he insisted, never intended "to exploit the cheap labor of the natives, to steal their lands by force, to subjugate them through denying them rights, individually or collectively. Just the opposite: [Their goal was] to create an independent economic and cultural system alongside the Arab system, independent and nonexploitative." Far from seeking to harm the Arab economic system, the labor zionist movement only sought "to develop and advance it" (p. 28).

Insofar as they ignored the consciousness and experiences of the zionist settlers, postzionists were guilty of slandering all of those pioneers who fought malaria to clear swamps, established collective settlements, and risked their lives to defend the state. Following Landers, Megged accused Kimmerling and Migdal in their book *Palestinians* (1993) of reiterating antizionist attacks that had their roots in Soviet propaganda. In that propaganda, as in the writings of the postzionist scholars, the kibbutz had been represented "not as the realization of an elevated social dream, but rather [as] an economic tool for carrying out numerous oppressive acts against the Arab population" (p. 92).

Identifying Kimmerling and Migdal's position with that of enemies of the state, Megged (1994a) sought to discredit the work of the postzionist scholars:

> What motivates these Israeli scholars to distort and make ugly the face of the Jewish national liberation movement, whose only desire was to realize "the

hope of two millennia" to return to Zion, where the individual Jew as well as the Jewish People "will return to rebirth"…a movement which, even if it committed many errors on the way and caused many wrongs/injustices, never was there a national liberation movement in human history that tried like it did to actualize its goals nonviolently and to guide itself by moral principles. What drove them to portray it before the world as a movement grounded in conspiracies of subjugation and oppression? (p. 29)

Although acknowledging that there is no purely objective history and that historians can tell the story in a variety of ways, Megged nonetheless denounced those Israeli scholars who,

with great pleasure, demonstrate that our defensive wars were actually wars whose purpose was to destroy the other and attribute to the Israeli soldier, whom we know very well as our flesh and blood, the countenance of the Kluges SS. (p. 28)

Megged also accused postzionists of denying the historical bond linking the Jewish people to their ancestral homeland. In so doing, he insisted, they deny the very connection that had made possible the establishment of the Jewish state, the revival of Hebrew language and culture, and the ingathering of millions of Jews from all parts of the diaspora.

The articles by Landers and Megged unearthed a stream of impassioned responses by both defenders and critics of postzionism. Defenders of the academic "postzionists" accused Megged of failing to address the scholarly arguments of those whom he attacked. They further accused him of espousing a form of romantic nationalism in which the nation, driven by a biological force, was considered to be mystically tied to the land. They claimed that for Megged and critics like him, the only true Israeli intellectual is one who supports the zionist political establishment.

Kimmerling, who had been singled out for criticism by both Landers and Megged, denied that he was a postzionist. At the same time, he vehemently defended the position of "postzionist scholars." In his view, the debates over the new historiography and critical sociology are, among other things, a struggle for power. The attacks by Landers and Megged, he argued, reflect the position of senior scholars who, sensing that the ground beneath them is shaking, fear that "their views cannot withstand the changes that are occurring in the social sciences and in historiography" (Kimmerling 1994a, 52). Unable to win their point in the academic forum, these scholars now seek to win over the general public by manipulating public fear.

According to Kimmerling, Israeli scholars have traditionally been caught in a bind, torn between their commitment to scholarly objectivity on the one hand and their need to legitimate the state on the other. To support his claim, Kimmerling (1994a) pointed to the prevailing scholarly interpretations of the 1948 War. While historians and Middle Eastern specialists were well aware of the circumstances surrounding the expulsion of the Arabs in 1948, there was, he insisted, a taboo against discussing it. Thus, while claiming to establish an objective scholarship free of ideological bias, scholars committed to zionism produced a "zionist science" that legitimated the zionist enterprise (p. 50).

Kimmerling thus criticized the prevailing Israeli social science for being a "conscripted science" [*mada meguyas*] that served the interests of labor zionism. Not only did this social science exclude the voices of the Palestinians, it also allowed no space for the voices of Jewish women or Jews of Middle Eastern origin. In Kimmerling's view, critics like Megged, desiring to perpetuate this conscripted scholarship, yearn for the renewal of "a 'zionist science,' that is, an ideological science which is actually no science" (p. 51).

Kimmerling also criticized Megged for fomenting a general "fear of peace" that, like McCarthyism in the United States, encouraged a search for traitors. Thus, Megged, a nonacademician, served as

a mouthpiece for a highly respected group of senior academicians and part of a growing effort to delegitimate the works of younger scholars who, usually not yet having earned a permanent position in the academic establishment, are vulnerable to being hurt. (p. 54)

Pappe, denying that he in any way questioned the legitimacy of the state, accused journalists like Megged and Landers of engaging in ideological rather than scholarly criticism. From the perspective of these critics, the only crime committed by postzionist scholars is their refusal to accept "zionist truth." Taking a more extreme position than Kimmerling, Pappe (1994b) argued that the zionists had intentionally uprooted the Palestinian population and retroactively legitimated this action by their appeal to the "uniqueness of Jewish history that derives from the Shoah" (p. 54). Pursuing this line of legitimation, zionist historiography, according to Pappe, "used the unique historical event, the Shoah, as a means of exempting itself from any kind of academic or moral criticism" (p. 54).

Landers' critique of the postzionist scholars found a strong supporter in the highly respected Hebrew University sociologist, Moshe Lissak. Lissak, coauthor of two highly regarded studies of Israeli social and political life, had received the coveted Israel Prize for his contributions to Israeli scholarship. While acknowledging the validity of some of the claims of the postzionist scholars, Lissak nonetheless accused them of being driven by political ideology and allowing the Israeli–Palestinian conflict to dominate their scholarly analysis.[49] Lissak also accused them of having allowed their postzionist dream of a secular, democratic, Israeli society to intrude on their scholarship. Such ideological concerns, insisted Lissak, have no place in the scholarly enterprise.[50]

THE SHOAH AND ZIONIST DISCOURSE

Megged's position was vehemently supported by Shlomo Aronson, a professor of political science at the Hebrew University. Shifting the focus of the debate, Aronson raised the issue of the *Shoah,* the Nazi destruction of European Jewry. The *Shoah,* argued Aronson, is particularly troublesome to scholars like Ilan Pappe,[51] who accuse the zionists of using it as a political weapon to legitimate unjust acts against the Palestinians. Reiterating the accusations leveled by Landers and Megged, Aronson accused the postzionists of denying Israel's right to speak in the name of the dead victims. Consequently, he argued, they are guilty of resurrecting the accusation regularly leveled at Israel by her enemies, namely, that Israel was born in sin. To Aronson (1994)

> the Shoah destroys this claim, insofar as it establishes who were the real victims, how far the tragedy extended, who were the secondary victims, and to what extent they were sealed off from the suffering of others and their right to a piece of land to which their culture was linked for two thousand years. (p. 53)

In Aronson's comments we find an excellent example of the use of the *Shoah* in zionist discourse. Privileging the suffering of European Jews over the suffering of Palestinian Arabs in 1948, Aaronson sought to silence critical debate. Aronson (1994) further criticized Pappe for using ideas imported from England, France, and the United States, an accusation that was repeated by others, including Lissak (p. 52). According to Aronson, Pappe's antipositivist, narrative approach to history leads him "to view history with Arab, Soviet and Western eyes" (p. 53).

As Aronson's comment makes clear, the debates over the new scholarship and postzionism revolve around issues of territory and space. The denunciation of those using foreign or imported ideas implies that there are clearly defined cultural boundaries within which the production of meaning may be legitimately carried out. Those, like the postzionists, who draw upon concepts and categories developed outside of Israel are guilty of importing alien ideas and introducing them into Israeli culture. Assuming the unique character of Israeli society, culture, and history, Aronson accepts only particularly "local" conceptual frameworks as appropriate and legitimate. Those like Pappe and the other academicians associated with the new scholarship, who apply perspectives "brought in from" such places as Europe and the United States, are smuggling alien products into Israeli cultural discourse. Given the fact that all Israeli scholarship draws upon scholarship emanating from American and European universities, this accusation appears very strange indeed.

To critics like Landers, Megged, Aronson, and Lissak, the scholars whom they labeled as postzionists had transgressed the legitimate limits of zionist discourse. By calling into question the prevailing representations of Israeli history and society, new historians and their sociologist counterparts questioned the basic premises of zionist claims concerning the legitimacy of the state.[52] In the view of the critics, new historians and critical sociologists, positioning themselves outside the boundaries of legitimate zionist discourse, had provided support to those who sought to destroy the state of Israel.

It seems clear, therefore, that one of the central issues in the debates over postzionism is that of cultural borders. Aronson appears to be linking ideas and intellectual orientations with specific geographical areas. According to this view, which is subsequently reiterated by Lissak, one can evaluate ideas and scholarly methods according to the places in which they are produced. Conversely, it implies that Israeli history is best interpreted by ideas and methods unique to Israel, a highly problematic claim that significantly parochializes Israeli scholarship.

In raising the question of the Shoah, Aronson called attention to yet another issue that plays a prominent role in the debates over postzionism. The use of the Shoah to legitimate Israel's existence is clearly reflected in Israel's Declaration of Independence:

> The Nazi Holocaust, which engulfed millions of Jews in Europe, proved anew the urgency of the reestablishment of the Jewish State, which would solve the problem of Jewish homelessness by opening the gates to all Jews and lifting the Jewish people to equality in the family of nations. (Mendes-Flohr and Reinharz 1995, 629)

The *Shoah* occupies a distinct and powerful role in Israeli culture, particularly in relation to the construction of Israel national identity.[53] Zionists in Israel have regularly emphasized the contrast between new Hebrews and Israelis on the one hand and what they regarded as the unproductive, subservient, weak, parasitic diaspora Jew on the other. Not surprisingly, one question that troubled first-generation Israelis was the passive behavior of those diaspora Jews who had gone to their deaths "as sheep to the slaughter."[54] At the same time, many zionists viewed the destruction of European Jewry as confirmation of the zionist axiom that there was no hope for Jewish life in exile.

As we saw in chapter 1, zionism represented itself as a movement committed to providing a homeland that could serve as a refuge to persecuted Jews. For the Herzlian strain, zionism's primary objective was to transform the homeless nation from a defenseless and persecuted group vulnerable to the whims of exile into a nation secure in its own land. Thus, at the heart of the zionist enterprise was the well-being of world Jewry.

To the zionist founders of the state, the destruction of Europe's Jews under the Nazis was the ultimate proof of the truth of zionism's critique of exile. The fact that European Jews, many of whom thought that they were well-integrated into the nations in which they lived, could suffer the fate that they did was sufficient confirmation of the inherently unstable, insecure, and life-threatening character of life in exile.

In recent years, however, a number of scholarly studies have raised questions concerning the attitude and the actions of zionist and early state leaders toward the victims and survivors of the *Shoah*. One of the first to raise this question was Shabtai Beit Zvi, an independent scholar who authored a controversial but pioneering study published in 1973. Exploring the attitudes and behavior of zionist leaders to the survivors and victims, Beit Zvi concluded that in rejecting the option of Uganda as an alternative to a Jewish homeland in Palestine, the zionist movement had privileged the building of a homeland in Palestine over and above the goal of providing a refuge for persecuted Jews.[55] This claim, and the subsequent scholarship that provided support for it, was considered by opponents to be part and parcel of postzionist discourse.

THE DEBATES CONTINUE

Throughout 1994 and 1995, the debates over the new scholarship and postzionism escalated rapidly throughout Israel. It was clear that the issues raised by the scholars labeled as postzionists struck a responsive chord among many Israelis. In newspapers, scholarly journals, public forums, and academic symposia, the issue of postzionism was repeatedly echoed. In addition to Lissak and Aronson, attacks on postzionist scholars were leveled by Anita Shapira, a historian, and Eliezer Schweid, a professor of Jewish philosophy.

In these criticisms by academicians there are a number of recurring arguments. In response to the accusation that conventional Israeli scholarship was infused with political interests, the defenders of zionism argue that, in fact, it is the postzionists who are guilty of politicizing scholarship. Zionist scholars claimed that the new historians and critical sociologists had made the mistake of allowing their ideological interests to guide their academic research and determine their conclusions. Another recurring criticism made by Israeli academicians hostile to postzionism is that the new historians were guilty of blurring the lines separating past from present. Viewing past events through the prism of the present, they decontextualized the behavior of zionist leaders and their followers, thereby ignoring those very factors that are central to any historical interpretation.

These criticisms by Lissak, Shapira, and other academicians evoked strong responses from two critical social scientists, Michael Shalev of the Hebrew University and Gershon Shafir. Their articles, taken together with those of Kimmerling, Pappe, and Ram discussed earlier, help to further clarify the gulf separating the younger generation of postzionist social scientists from their zionist elders.[56] Citing Ram, Shalev and Shafir take issue with those who would separate a researcher's interpretation from his or her social and biographical context. To Shalev (1996), Lissak's attempt to "pose a rigid distinction between defenders of science, like himself, and those who would prostitute it to their political agenda" is "so absurd that it cannot be taken seriously" (p. 171). The very efforts of senior scholars to delegitimate the position of the postzionist scholars is a clear example of the politicized character of conservative and radical scholarship alike (p. 187, n. 30). At the same time, scholars would not consider ideological arguments sufficient. Thus, Shalev asserts, it is "the responsibility of scholars to justify and debate competing perspectives on theoretical and empirical grounds" (p. 183).

However, Shalev refuses to frame the divisions separating the scholars in terms of loyalty to zionism:

> The common denominator of the members of the critical community is not rejection of Zionist premises (some do, others do not). Instead, it can best be described as what I referred to in my own case as the "disappointment" that ensued when myths are shattered. (pp. 173–74)

While not denying that the issues of zionism and antizionism have an appropriate place in the discussion, Shalev refuses to make it the central point. As he sees it, those like Lissak and Landers who make the charge of antizionism are using witch-hunting tactics like those used by McCarthy in the United States in the 1950s:

> I have no intention of playing this game by McCarthyist rules. However, if the political agenda of critical scholars is to be clarified, then the issue of anti-Zionism must be addressed, but in general and not personal terms. (p. 185, n. 13)

Defenders of the critical social science also contest the adequacy of the previous generation's functionalist approach.[57] Privileging order, consensus, and integration, such an approach is inadequate to those "dealing with a context shot through with inequality and conflict" (p. 171). Moreover, those advocating a functionalist approach are themselves clearly influenced by the political context.

The younger scholars also distinguish between those who engage in a critique of a discourse such as zionism and those who, positioned in the discourse, criticize specific points. Thus, whereas Lissak and others of the previous generation of social scientists might very well have criticized specific government actions or policies, they nevertheless accepted as given the premises of zionist discourse. Thus, the older generation of scholars failed to grasp "the difference between criticism and critique; between an argument over means, conducted within the discourse of the powerful and privileged, and the untried alternative of disputing their very definition of the problem" (Shalev 1996, 172).

Both Shalev and Shafir also criticize those historians who emphasize intentionality and ideology and neglect concrete effects and material factors.[58] Reiterating in *Israel Studies* arguments they had each made in earlier works, Shafir (1996b) and Shalev (1996) argue that this approach ignores the central role of economic needs and interests and the desire of the labor movement to "advance its organizational and political interests."

Like Kimmerling, both men also criticize the establishment scholars for treating the "Yishuv largely as a self-contained unit." Instead, each argues the need for a comparative approach to the interpretation of zionist settlement practices and economic policies. Of particular concern to them is "the contingent role of the Jewish settlers' economic and political conflicts with the indigenous Arab population in shaping Zionist strategy and Yishuv society" (Shalev 1996, 171).

The younger scholars also criticize the zionist scholars' narrow concept of colonialism. They thus reject the arguments of those like Lissak and Shapira who insist on the "purity of zionist intentions." Instead, they insist that zionist settlement practices, although distinguished by the specificity of circumstances, clearly conform to models of colonialism utilized by contemporary scholars. Scholars like Lissak, however, are "simply unable to conceive of colonialization as a theoretical concept and an empirical variable" (Shalev 1996, 175).

As mentioned previously, one of the differences between the prior generation of scholars and the younger group associated with postzionism relates to the historical conditions in which they grew to maturity. In contrast to their elders, the perspective of the younger scholars was strongly affected by post-1967 realities. Many of the scholars who identified with labor zionism viewed the post-1967 realities, particularly the expansion of Israeli settlements in the captured territories, as a deviation from labor zionist intentions and practices. The younger scholars' examination of those policies and practices led them to the opposite conclusion. In their view, the post-1967 policies and practices are not a deviation from, but are consistent with the labor zionist practices that predate the establishment of the state.[59]

THE POST IN POSTZIONISM:
THE PROBLEM OF TERMINOLOGY

As previously indicated, the recurring use of the concept of postzionism throughout these debates is by no means consistent.[60] While some represent postzionism as an approach to scholarly inquiry, others represent it as a political position. Still others tend to integrate the two, denying that one can separate political interests from academic inquiry. The matter is further complicated by the reluctance of some who have been identified with the postzionist camp, such as Morris, Pappe, and Kimmerling, to accept the label.

Earlier, postzionism had been used to refer to the fact that the era of zionist hegemony in Israeli society had ended and a new, postzionist era had begun.[61] To those who hold this position, postzionism may be seen as a stage in the process of normalization that formed part of zionist discourse. Consequently, those who adopt such a view do not consider it necessary to resist or engage in a critique of zionist discourse.[62] Other intellectuals sympathetic to basic postzionist themes fault this form of postzionism for being too conservative. According to these critics, this type of noncritical postzionism ignores the fact that zionist discourse continues to shape the basic mechanisms and structures of Israeli society, politics, and culture. Consequently, it contributes, intentionally or not, to the reproduction of conditions that are oppressive to Palestinian Arabs and other minority groups.[63]

While not organized into a distinct political group, most of those who position themselves within postzionist discourse or are sympathetic to it share a common vision of Israel as a pluralistic democratic state of all of its citizens. Accordingly, they reject the axiom embedded in zionist discourse and materialized in the Declaration of Independence that Israel is the state of the Jewish people. Yet there is no consensus among postzionists as to how to realize such a goal. While some, like Pappe and Ram, advocate a repeal of the Law of Return, others, while advocating full and equal rights for the Palestinian minority, continue to support the law.

At the same time, notwithstanding the claims of zionist critics, all of the scholars who identify with postzionism or who have been so labeled by critics vehemently reject the attempt to equate postzionism with antizionism. While critical of many aspects of Israeli military policy and actions, postzionists consider themselves to be loyal citizens of the state who are prepared to risk their life to defend the country.[64] At the same time, they reject the claim that loyalty to Israel presupposes loyalty to zionism. The object of their critique, therefore, is not the state of Israel, but the zionist discourse that shapes its policies and positions. Rejecting the continued identification of Israel as a zionist state, they seek to generate an alternative basis for Israeli collective identity.

POSTZIONISM AND POSTMODERNISM:
A CASE OF OVERSIMPLIFICATION

A recurring strategy used by critics seeking to discredit postzionism is to identify it with postmodernism. Unfortunately, these critics offer only a schematic, highly reductionistic caricature of postmodernism. Without providing any support from postmodernist writings, they dismiss it as anarchistic, relativistic, and nihilistic. Insofar as they view postzionists as guilty by association, they, too, are vulnerable to the criticism of anarchism, relativism, and nihilism. In the forefront of those who identify postzionism with postmodernism are Hebrew University professors Elie Schweid, Yosef Dan, and Lissak.[65] Schweid, a professor of Jewish philosophy, and Dan, a professor of Jewish mysticism and thought, are both highly regarded in their respective fields.

Lissak argued that the positions of the critical sociologists and their historian counterparts are informed by "post-modernist moods." Without providing any substantiation for his claim, Lissak (1996) insists that writings of this kind regard all narratives as equally valid:[66]

> The idea of the absolute equality of narratives is predominant. No one narrative is preferable to another. Each one can choose from among the "supermarket" of narratives that which most appeals to him. (p. 254)[67]

Rather than treat historical narratives as "the focus of research," postzionist scholars, argues Lissak, regard them as "normative-ideological sources which support the researcher in a non-critical way" (pp. 254–55).

Refusing to separate their academic research from their political orientations, critical social scientists, according to Lissak, position theories in the context of "a power field of cultural stances" (p. 254). At the heart of the methodological controversy is the question of "whether or not an objective sociological and historical truth exists, and whether or not it is obtainable" (p. 253). At best, the critical sociologists are skeptical that such truth is possible; "at worst, they completely negate it" (p. 253). Insofar as they reject functionalist and positivist approaches, the postzionist social scientists transgress what Lissak regards as the boundaries of scientific scholarship. In his view, it all comes down to "the struggle between positivism and anti-positivism" (p. 254).

Lissak further criticizes the postmodernist postzionist scholars for having roamed far afield into "such areas as social psychology, the collective memory, symbolic anthropology and the like." While acknowledging that these are "weighty areas of study," Lissak faults interdisciplinary studies for their tendency to separate "research and teaching from central questions of Israeli society and politics"(p. 288).

Responding to the criticism that establishment sociologists were captive to the "zionist dream," Lissak argues that postzionist scholars, too, are captive to a dream. In their case, they "are captive to the dreams of those who are alien to Israeli society" (p. 289). Although he does not clarify who those aliens are, it seems clear that by using this term, Lissak, like other critics of postzionism, seeks to establish protective borders around Israeli academic discourse.[68]

As we saw earlier, some postzionists have argued that the discourse of zionist scholars is itself ideologically laden. Accordingly, they wish not only to revise historical narratives and social scientific representations but also to transform the discourse used to construct them. Seeking to reveal the power effects produced by the dominant Israeli scholarship, they raise the issue of the relationship of power and knowledge that is central to postmodern theory.

Nevertheless, the effort of critics like Lissak, Schweid, and Dan to identify postzionism with postmodernism is highly problematic. First, nowhere in their writings do they make a serious attempt to analyze the premises on which postmodernism is said to rest. Moreover, at no point do they cite writings by theorists of postmodernism. Instead, simplistically identifying postmodernism with anarchy, nihilism, and relativism, they attribute to postmodernists, and by association to postzionists, the position that any historical narrative is as good as any other.[69] As we shall see in chapter 6, they not only distort postmodern critiques of historical discourse, but they also exaggerate the perspectivalist positions advocated by Pappe, Kimmerling, and Migdal. Thus, not only do the critics refrain from engaging postmodernism seriously, but they also proceed to attack postzionist scholars for positions that they do not hold.[70]

Another problem with the efforts of critics to identify postzionism with postmodernism derives from the fact that virtually all of the scholars discussed thus far ground their interpretations in modern rather than postmodern discourse.[71] With rare exceptions, they understand themselves to be engaged in an effort to produce truer historical and sociological representations that correspond more fully to the "facts."[72]

Only rarely do those identified as postzionists display any firsthand knowledge of postmodern theory. Although critical of established Israeli scholarship, scholars such as Ram, Kimmerling, and Shafir do not problematize the modernist notion that scholars have the ability to render an objective and accurate representation of history and society. Grounded in modern, rather than postmodern, theory, the postzionist scholars discussed here do not indicate any in-depth knowledge of postmodern theory. In this sense, therefore, there is little to connect the new historiography and critical sociology with postmodernism.[73]

Although the identification of postzionism with postmodernism is problematic, the attempt to link the two reflects a deep concern among veteran Israeli scholars over recent changes within Israeli culture. As a result of far-reaching demographic, economic, media, and cultural changes discussed at the beginning of this chapter, Israel has been subject to a rapidly spreading individualism, consumerism, and careerism. Increasingly, young Israelis value the well-being of the individual over the collective well-being of the state. To committed zionists, this represents an incursion into Israeli cultural space of alien elements that are eroding the zionist foundations on which the state had rested. Defenders of zionism, like Schweid and Lissak, connect these unwanted changes to the critical discourse of the postzionists. Unfortunately, they have yet to produce a rigorous, persuasive theoretical analysis to support this linking.

Nevertheless, the introduction of the issue of alien methodologies and interpretations by zionist defenders makes it clear that the debates surrounding postzionism constitute a struggle over cultural space. Lissak and his colleagues, designating these methods and positions as imported or alien, seek to establish and protect what they regard as the legitimate borders of Israeli academic and public discourse determined by zionism. Scholars like Kimmerling, Shafir, Pappe, and Ram, utilizing comparative modes of interpretation developed in the United States and Europe, are struggling to open the spaces of Israeli culture to new methodologies and intellectual positions.

CHAPTER 5

PALESTINIAN CRITICS AND POSTZIONIST DISCOURSE: ANTON SHAMMAS AND EMILE HABIBY

I am located in the margin. I make a definite distinction between the marginality which is imposed by oppressive structures and that marginality one chooses as a site of resistance—as location of radical openness and possibility. This site of resistance is continually formed in that segregated culture of opposition that is our critical response to domination. (hooks 1990, 153)

I believe it needs to be made clear about cultural discourse and exchange within a culture that what is commonly circulated by it is not "truth" but representations. It hardly needs to be demonstrated again that language itself is a highly organized and encoded system, which employs many devices to express, indicate, exchange messages and information, represent, and so forth. In any instance of at least written language, there is no such thing as a delivered presence, but a "re-presence," or a representation. (Said 1989, 21–22)

Nations are contested systems of cultural representation that limit and legitimate people's access to the resources of the nation-state. (McClintock 1996, 260)

As we saw in the previous chapter, Israeli scholars, particularly those labeled as postzionists, have increasingly argued that the formation of Israeli culture and national identity cannot be understood without acknowledging the contribution of Palestinian Arabs. As Kimmerling and Migdal (1993) argue:

Zionists have been absorbed in a nationalist project rendering the Palestinians almost incidental. In the process, they have failed to grasp the extent to which their own society has been shaped by its ongoing encounter with the Palestinians. (p. xviii)[1]

Taking issue with conventional Israeli historiography, postzionist scholars have incorporated into their narratives the previously silenced voices of the Palestinian "Other." In their view, Jewish and Palestinian Arab narratives are intertwined. Moving beyond the limits of zionist discourse, these postzionist scholars help reveal its problems and inadequacies. In the process, they render problematic the zionist identification of Israeli culture with Jewish culture.

As critics like Homi Bhabha (1994) have argued, the presence of a subordinate, colonialized group has the effect of revealing national space as "a contentious performative space of the perplexity of the living in the midst of the pedagogical representations of the fullness of life." Minority writers thus problematize such notions as "the monumentality of historical memory, the sociological totality of society, or the homogeneity of cultural experience." Writing from the margins, such writers reveal "the insurmountable ambivalence that structures the 'equivocal' movement of historical time" (157).[2]

In Israel, those in the best position to reveal what Bhabha (1994), a University of Chicago postcolonial theorist of Indian origin, would call the contradictory and ambivalent space of Israeli culture are the Palestinian Arabs. Their writings have the effect of revealing the extent to which "hierarchical claims to the inherent originality or 'purity' of cultures are untenable" (37). The exclusion of Palestinian voices from Israeli cultural space, therefore, occludes the complex, often contradictory character of Israeli culture and identity formation.[3]

In two widely circulated books, *The Yellow Wind* (1989) and *Sleeping on a Wire* (1993), writer and novelist David Grossman has made an important effort to describe for his fellow Israelis the oppressive effects of zionist discourse and practices on Palestinians living in the conquered territories as well as those holding Israeli citizenship. Seeking to convey, through extensive quotes from Palestinians, what it feels like to be a Palestinian inside and outside of Israel, Grossman also succeeds in revealing the effects of practices that Jewish Israelis have come to accept as necessary and legitimate. To my knowledge, Grossman, a nonacademician, has never declared himself to be a postzionist and his name is never mentioned in the postzionism debates.

While a number of postzionist scholars make the concerns of the Palestinians central to Israeli discourse, rarely are Palestinians invited to represent their own positions in public discussions of postzionism. Instead, the representation of the attitudes and feelings of the Palestinians is left to scholars and writers of the hegemonic Jewish group. Yet, as Kimmerling and Migdal (1993), among others, have argued,

> It is impossible to tell the story of Zionism or Palestinism without understanding the impact they had on one another. For the Palestinians, the story centers on Al-Nakba, a catastrophe that produced ironically, a strong collective consciousness transcending all the fractures. (p. 279)

Consequently, no critique of zionism would be adequate, according to Kimmerling and Migdal, without allowing Palestinians to tell their own story and present their own criticisms.

Of the many Palestinian critics of zionism and Israel, few have contributed more to the problematizing of hegemonic zionist representations of Israeli culture and society than Anton Shammas and Emile Habiby. As Israeli citizens, both Shammas and Habiby participated actively is shaping Israeli public discourse. Shammas, besides working in Israeli television, regularly contributed articles of social and cultural criticism to the Hebrew press. As one of the first Palestinians to write and publish a Hebrew novel, Shammas, as Hannan Hever has argued, poses a unique challenge to the zionist representation of Hebrew as the Jewish national language.[4]

Habiby, an active participant in Israeli political life, served for many years as a representative of the Israeli Communist Party in the Knesset. In addition, Habiby edited an Arabic newspaper. Habiby's most significant contribution to Israeli cultural discourse has been his two novels, one novella, and a collection of short stories. Although originally written in Arabic, they have been made available to the Jewish Israeli reader through translations by none other than Anton Shammas.[5] Recognizing Habiby's distinctive contribution to Israeli culture, the government bestowed upon him in 1992 the prestigious Israel Prize for Literature.

Notwithstanding their significant impact on Israeli cultural space, both Shammas and Habiby write from the margins. However, they both succeeded in transforming the margin from a position of weakness and silence to one of resistance and power.[6] Thus, both writers effectively made the spaces of the margin into sites for the production of powerful critiques of the Israeli state and its dominant Jewish culture.

Neither Habiby nor Shammas question the legitimacy of the state. Unlike many other Palestinian writers, neither call for its dismantling. Instead, positioning themselves as loyal and responsible citizens of the state, they struggled to subvert and transform the dominant cultural and political framework. In the process, they produced some of the most trenchant criticisms of hegemonic Israeli/zionist discourse and practices.

While neither writer explicitly uses colonialism as a central critical category, both are extremely effective in revealing the colonialist effects of zionist practices and discourse on the Palestinian community. In this respect, they render a major contribution to the formation of postzionist discourse.

ANTON SHAMMAS: THE FAULT LINES
OF ISRAELI CULTURAL IDENTITY

In his pioneering work of Hebrew fiction *Arabesques* (1986a; in English, 1988a) and in numerous writings on social and cultural criticism, Shammas has significantly problematized the dominant Jewish Israeli representations of history, nationhood, and culture. In the process, he has represented the destructive effects of hegemonic Israeli social and cultural practices on the Palestinian Arabs. In fiction and nonfiction, Shammas repeatedly reveals the complexities and contradictions of Israeli society and culture as seen by the internal Palestinian Other.

At the same time, Shammas persuasively represents the oppressive, silencing, marginalizing, exclusionary effects of zionist discourse and practice as they are inscribed in the apparatus of the state. In so doing, he has effectively represented to a Hebrew readership the cultural violence that zionism has perpetrated on the Palestinian Other. He has also effectively demonstrated the various ways in which the process of shaping a distinctly "Israeli" culture and cultural identity, like the process of shaping any national culture, is embedded in power relations and infused with power-laden discourse and practices.

In Israeli liberal discourse, one finds many critiques of the effects of Jewish Israeli political hegemony on the political and civil rights of the Palestinians. Shammas, however, has been particularly forceful in raising cultural and identity problems. By showing the destructive effects of Israeli cultural hegemony on the practices through which Palestinians represent and make sense of the reality around them, Shammas reveals to his readers, Israeli and non-Israeli alike, the consequences of cultural discourse and practices taken by the Jewish majority to be natural and positive. At the same time, Shammas' powerful voice contributes to the construction of a Palestinian counternarrative.

Regarding Cultural Hegemony

Focusing his narrative on the everyday life of Palestinian villagers, Shammas, in *Arabesques,* engages in what literary scholars Gary Morson and Carol Emerson (1990), in their study of the Russian literary theorist Mikhael Bakhtin, refer to as "prosaics," "a form of thinking that presumes the importance of the everyday, the ordinary" (p. 15). Shammas' fiction represents an alternative reality to the everyday reality of the Israeli Jew.

According to the Israeli literary scholar Hannan Hever, the publication of Shammas' Hebrew novel *Arabesques* (1986a) had the effect of subverting the dominant notion of a Jewish-Hebrew literary canon and significantly problematizing the zionist view of Hebrew as the Jewish national language. Demonstrating a mastery of a rich and complex Hebrew style, Shammas, as interpreted by Hever (1990), transforms the language of the majority into a weapon of the colonialized minority in its struggle against hegemonic culture. By problematizing the classical zionist view of Hebrew literature as Jewish national literature, *Arabesques,* in Hever's words, "forces a fundamental revision in some of the political assumptions underlying Israeli public discourse" (p. 290).

Building on Hever's suggestive interpretation, I would like to expand the discussion to include what I see as Shammas' problematizing of Israeli culture and the prevailing conception of Israeli identity. I read Shammas against the background of recent writings in the field of cultural studies, which treat culture as a power-ridden, conflicted site of signifying practices that produce and disseminate meaning.[7] Shammas repeatedly draws our attention to the power and the paradoxes inherent in the processes whereby meaning is constructed and disseminated in Israeli society.

Through numerous examples, Shammas educates his readers to the fact that "culture," far from being a benign, humanizing realm, is a power-ridden process in which one continually struggles for hegemony. Positioning his readers to read Israeli culture from the perspective of the excluded "Other," he makes it difficult for his Jewish Israeli readers to ignore the power effects and the violence that Israeli culture entails for the Palestinian minority.

In particular, Shammas' writings provide powerful examples that supports French philosopher Jacques Derrida's (1984) claim that violence is inherent in the processes of collective identity formation:

> The rapport of self-identity is itself always a rapport of violence with the other; so that the notions of property, appropriation and self-presence, so central to logocentric metaphysics, are essentially dependent on an oppositional relation with otherness. In this sense, identity presupposes alterity. (p. 117)

Shammas makes us aware that alongside the physical destruction of Arab villages and the confiscation of land, another form of violence has been unleashed at the Palestinians, the violence engendered by zionist/Jewish cultural practices. Describing the cultural struggle between Israeli Jews and Palestinians as a "cruel bullfight between two cultures," Shammas (1983a) sees the Palestinians cast into the role of the "ill-fated bull" (p. 35), but in this bullfight,

> no one knows which role he is supposed to play. The roles change, and the rules of the game are lost. This war between the two cultures, the Jewish and the Arabic, is becoming increasingly like a "corrida" [bullfight], and many voices, on either side, are hoarse from yelling "Ole! Ole!" (pp. 35–36)

One site of this struggle is the Israeli educational system, which seeks to impose on the minority the perspective of the majority:

> The policy of Mapai [Israeli Labor Party] and later the Alignment [a left of center coalition that included Mapai] was devised, at least in the field of education, to attenuate the Arab personality, and then to demand that it [the attenuated Arab personality] integrate into the system of the state. The integration is carried out in the well-established tradition of Arab taste. (p. 36)

Shammas (1988b) provides us with numerous descriptions of the destructive effects of statehood on the indigenous Arab population:

> Since 1948, they [Palestinian Arabs living within Israel's borders] had been exposed to the state, which had defined itself, from the very beginning, as a Jewish state. This sudden exposure after 1948 knocked the ground—in the literal sense of the word—from under their cultural confidence. Those were the days of the military administration and land appropriations. (p. 48)

Whereas, to Jews, the establishment of the state was the culmination of their dream of national liberation, to Palestinian Arabs, Shammas reminds us, it was a disaster that deprived them of their independence and freedom of movement. Similarly, the Israeli Declaration of Independence, the official document proclaiming the new state, like Independence Day, the day established to commemorate the establishment of the state, and the flag, which is the material representation of the state, have entirely different, negative meanings for the Palestinian Arab citizens of Israel. Recounting a ceremony celebrating Independence Day in his school, Shammas (1991) writes:

> Little did we know that the state whose flags these were was not ours. Come to think of it, nobody knew, not even the young teacher who had taught us the Arabic translation of the Israeli Declaration of Independence from a brand new Reader, which also had a relatively detailed biography of Herzl. We were told, through some outlandish reasoning, to learn those texts by heart, and to this day some sentences of the Declaration will occasionally pop up out of the blue inside my head. (p. 220)

On another occasion he observes (1983a), in passing: "It was on May 2, 1979, Independence Day—not an occasion of celebration for me, I regret to say—I was on my way to Tel Aviv" (p. 34).

As Shammas (1991) repeatedly demonstrates, the documents and artifacts, the discourse and practices that, to Israeli Jews, represent liberation and freedom are, for the Arab citizens, constant reminders of their subordinate, disenfranchised condition:

> Even according to the Arabic translation of the Declaration, the state was defined as a Jewish state, but nobody seemed to pay any attention to that fact.

You see, we had the flags in our hands, so declarations did not matter, nor did the fact which we discovered later—that there was an utter rift between the signified and the signifier; those flags did not signify a single thing. (p. 220)

Shammas (1987b) represents the Palestinians as aliens living in exile in their own homeland. In a passage that rings familiar to students of European Jewish history, he writes:

Transit permits were necessary for Arabs of the 50's if they wished to travel from place to place in their homeland which had now become "the homeland of the Jewish people." Transit permits were not given to Arabs (in Israel) to move around in the cultural spaces in which he had grown up. His separation from the existence from which he had been cut off, which had found its way to the refugee camps, was complete. This was also the case in regard to his separation from his spatial cultural surroundings. Until finally, he finds himself in an ongoing cultural quarantine. (p. 24)

Insofar as it defined itself as the state of the Jewish people, the

state of Israel...did not even define itself by territory or space, but rather by time...the last link of sorts in the Jewish chain of time, the chain [that] will lead, as the Zionist movement believed, to a secular Geulah, salvation on earth. (Shammas 1988b, 9)

To further represent the disempowering effects of Israeli cultural hegemony, Shammas (1987b) uses the metaphor of playing the piano, which he compares with the arabesques of the Alhambra. In both instances, secondary designs emerge from the primary one, in variations on a theme, and in the end, they all come together in one arabesque:

"How" he asks, "can the Arabs learn to play the piano with the right hand, while the left hand of the Jewish majority provides the dominant chords from which the transitions emerge and to which they return, whether or not they want to." (p. 26)

Referring to the Hebrew writer A. B. Yehoshua, Shammas (1987b) adds, "What he [Yehoshua] does not know is that his left hand is already a part of my Israeli experience, just as at least one finger on his right hand is one of my own fingers" (p. 26).

Linguistic Hegemony

Shammas, like many thinkers in this generation, sees the sphere of language as a site of ongoing cultural struggle. In the Ahad Haamian form of zionist discourse, the establishment of a Jewish state is depicted as the culmination of a quest for a natural habitat, a natural space in which Jewish national culture could grow and flourish. Similarly, the establishment of Hebrew as the national language of Israel represents the renewal of the Jewish national spirit and the normalization of Jewish national cultural life.

To Israel's Palestinian Arabs, however, Hebrew symbolizes the cultural hegemony imposed by a conquering majority on the conquered minority: Portraying his father's first encounter with Hebrew as the official language of the new state, Shammas (1991) describes its marginalizing and exclusionary effects:

> My father, those days, was continuously and pensively struggling with the new [Hebrew] language that had invaded his small world and ours, imposing upon him confusion and a new type of illiteracy. He needed a special permit, like all the fathers of his generation, to move around in the scenes of his homeland which had turned overnight into "the homeland of the Jewish people"; but no such permits were available for moving around in the cultural scenes. (p. 217)

Lacking the linguistic means by which to navigate their way through the new Israeli culture, Palestinians like his father, whose families had dwelled in the land for generations, were suddenly transformed into outsiders, strangers, the Other.

However, it was not only people like his father who found themselves in an alien linguistic setting. Palestinian writers also experienced a sense of internal exile:

> Nowadays, to write in Arabic in Israel is a very lonely undertaking and a courageous one. It is lonely because the infrastructure is missing. The outline plan is blurred and the writers cannot come home again. The traditional house has given way to the modern villa, wherein everything is counterfeit. The walls are no longer built of stone—they are, at best, surfaced with it. The village society which remained in the country after the establishment of the State has not yet lost the sense of isolation. (Shammas 1991, 43)

Shammas (1989a) describes the success of zionism in establishing Hebrew as the Israeli national language as "the only triumph of Zionism":

> It is the only homeland that Zionism could ever offer to the Jewish people.... Hebrew is the only Israeli thing that Zionism managed to accomplish. The rest, albeit spectacular at times, is a moot, sometimes a very lethal one, grounded on plastic and kitsch. (p. 10)

Shammas, however, challenges the notion that Hebrew, the national language of Israel, is the exclusive possession of the Jewish people. Thus, in a dialogue between Israeli and American writers in Los Angeles in November 1988, Shammas (1989a) made the following highly provocative statement:

What I'm trying to do—mulishly, it seems—is to un-Jew the Hebrew language (to use a Philip Roth verb), to make it more Israeli and less Jewish, thus bringing it back to its Semitic origins, to its Place. This is a parallel to what I think the state should be. As English is the language of those who speak it, so is Hebrew; and so the state should be the state of those who live in it, not of those who play with its destiny with a remote control in hand. (p. 10)[8]

While the 1967 War presented Palestinians in Israel with unforeseen opportunities for renewed contact with the wider Arab world, the resulting contact only served to intensify their experience of cultural emptiness:

For twenty years the Arabs of Israel breathed with one lung, and the sudden exposure to contemporary Arab culture, which took place following the 1967 War, only intensified the feeling of suffocation. Under the circumstances, Arabic literature in Israel appears miraculous, impossible. The system of Arab education in Israel, at least in my time, produced tongueless people, more at home with 7th century Arab poetry than with that of the 20th century. These are people without a cultural past and without a future. There is only a makeshift present and an attenuated personality. The tongue has been cut out, like that of the old Arab in A. B. Yehoshua's "Facing the Forests." (Shammas 1983a, 43)

Kitsch

Shammas utilizes the concept of kitsch, which he borrows from the contemporary writer Milan Kundera, to represent the destructive effects of Israeli culture on the Palestinians. Kitsch, according to Shammas (1987b), "transforms the stupidity of accepted opinions to the language of beauty and feeling" (p. 24). In his eyes, "the hegemonic Israeli politics towards the Arabs, in all of its institutionalized forms, is based first and foremost on kitsch." According to Shammas (1983a) kitsch has "spread into the local councils of the Arab villages, and even sits in the Knesset" (p. 36).

The contemporary Arab house in Israel is "one of the many monuments [*Andratah*] that perpetuates the cultural oppression [*remisah*] of the third world by European kitsch" (Shammas 1987b, 24). This is reflected in the changing character of the walls of the Arab home. The classical (prezionist) Arab house was, to Shammas, an outstanding example of integration of function/aesthetic form. However, over three generations, under the impact of Western/zionist culture, the house became a monument to kitsch.

In "Kitsch 22," Shammas (1987b) describes the way in which the state imposed a new, alien culture on the Palestinian generation of 1948:

One can say by way of metaphor, that the Jewish-zionist reality, encasing things in a wrapping of government [*shilton*], not only wrested the walls of the stone from his [the Arabs] possession, with the help of his neighbors, but also forced him to hang on the walls items that he never would have hung there on his own (a poster of Ben Gurion hung in my father's shoe repair shop) just as it forced him to carry a transit permit from place to place. (p. 24)

Similarly, "in the reality of cultural and political threat, in the atmosphere of military government," with the ground pulled out from under him, the son lost the sense of cultural security that his father had and was made to "stand naked and barren before all new challenges" (Shammas 1987b, 24). Thus, couples were led to decorate the walls of their house with all of the gifts they received for wedding presents, whether they liked them or not. This changed the character of the wall/house to one of kitsch:

> The grandchild, the third generation Palestinian, the child of the '67 war, is forbidden to build a "house in Israel." His only recourse is to take his grandfather's house and renovate it. The kitsch that this produces is a consequence of the fact that the "Arab is asked to come to terms with the new complex reality of the Jewish state, with the complex reality of living bi-lingually." (Shammas 1987b, 26)

The Critique of Israeli Political-Legal Discourse

To Shammas, the paradox of Israeli cultural discourse is imbricated in political and legal discourse. This paradox is manifest in two basic documents of Israeli political life, the Declaration of Independence and the Law of Return. On the one hand, the Declaration proclaims Israel to be "the Jewish state in Palestine." At the same time, the Declaration pledges that the state will

> promote the development of the country for the benefit of all its inhabitants [and] will uphold the full social and political equality of all its citizens without distinction of race, creed or sex; will guarantee full freedom of conscience, worship, education and culture. (Mendes-Flohr and Reinharz 1995, 630)

To the Palestinian population, Shammas (1985b) insists, the Declaration, with its inherent paradox, is analogous to AIDS:

> The Declaration of Independence, which still has a good name as a liberal document (in the absence of a constitution), is, in my eyes, the AIDS of "a Jewish state in the land of Israel, the State of Israel." (p. 17)

Just as AIDS breaks down the immune system, so "the mononational state of Israel conceals, in its very definition, the seeds of catastrophe: the breakdown of the immunizing system of every state, that is, every democratic state" (Shammas 1985b, 17).

According to Shammas, the exclusionary discourse of the Declaration is further disseminated and institutionalized in the 1950 Israeli Law of Return, which legislates that

> any Jew who comes to Israel and after his arrival expresses his desire to settle there, is entitled to obtain an immigrant certificate. (Mendes-Flohr and Reinharz 1995, 633)

Commenting on this law in a debate in the Knesset on July 3, 1950, then–prime minister David Ben Gurion stated:

> The State of Israel is not a Jewish state merely because the majority of its inhabitants are Jews. It is a state for all the Jews wherever they may be and for every Jew who so desires. (Mendes-Flohr and Reinharz 1995, 631)

In Shammas' (1988c) view, the Law of Return is nothing short of racist:

> If we exclude its application to those Jews in the diaspora who are still persecuted because of who they are—an application that should not be excluded—the Israeli Law of Return is, in effect, a racist law. (p. 48)

The Law of Return entitles the American Jew to automatically claim citizenship, even though this Jew lacks the bond to the land that the Palestinian Arab living in Israel has. Accordingly, Shammas (1989a) characterizes the Law of Return as

> the Israeli-made pacemaker, installed in the chests of perfectly healthy Diaspora Jews. Just in case, the state of Israel being the ever hovering battery over an uncharted territory, undefined land. (p. 10)

Meanwhile, Palestinian Arabs who had lived in Israel prior to the establishment of the state but had fled or been driven off in the 1948 War were and are denied the right to return.[9]

To Shammas, an amendment to section 7A of Israel's Basic Laws passed by the Knesset in 1985 that disqualified parties espousing racism from participating in Israeli elections reproduced the racist discourse of the Law of Return by continuing to define Israel as "the State of the Jewish people." Thus, the inherent paradox of the Declaration continues to be disseminated throughout Israeli legal discourse.

As long as Israel remains a Jewish state and a state without a constitution, the situation of the Palestinian citizens is an impossible one. Lacking the protection of a constitution, they live at the mercy of the majority and are subject to the changing favors, whims, and moods of the majority: "The only protection that I can receive is the protection of a constitution, law, and justice" (Shammas 1983b, 34).

According to Shammas (1988b), Palestinians living in Israel are caught in a catch-22:

> The state of Israel demands that its Arab citizens take their citizenship serious-
> ly; but when they try to do so it promptly informs them that their participation
> in the state is merely social, and that for the political fulfillment of their iden-
> tity, they must look somewhere else (i.e., to the Palestinian nation). When they
> do look elsewhere for their national identity, the state at once charges them
> with subversion; and needless to say—as subversives they cannot be accepted
> as Israelis. Back to square one. (p. 9)

Rather than advocate the immediate repeal of the law, Shammas has suggested that in 1998, on Israel's fiftieth birthday, a ten-year moratorium be instituted whereby "all Jews can immigrate to Israel under its protec-tion." This would allow any Jew who is the victim of persecution because of that Jewishness to apply for refuge. In 2008, the law would be repealed and Israel will finally become a democratic state of all of its citizens.

One hears echoes of Shammas' critique in a recent lecture delivered by the Israeli Jewish political scientist Yaron Ezrahi (1993):

> The very insistence on the notion that Israel is a "Jewish state" despite its inher-
> ent ambiguities, rationalizes the role of the state as the promoter of a national
> Jewish culture. This role is clearly incompatible with notions of the relative
> neutrality of the state and the basic norms of democratic civil culture and their
> expressions in the educational system. In such a context, cultural forms not
> sanctioned within the established Jewish religious-national traditions in Israel
> are bound to appear "foreign" and to be at least partly rejected as inimical both
> to the values promoted by the Israeli educational system and to the policies of
> state sponsored cultural institutions. (p. 262)

Reconfiguring Israeli Identity

Shammas also targets the legal apparatus, the practices by means of which the dominant conception of Israeli identity is reproduced and disseminated. It is ironic, he argues, that on identity cards that are carried by all citizens there is no place that defines one's nationality as Israeli. Instead, the term Israeli comes under the category "citizenship," while under "nationality" is listed one's ethnic or religious community. The fact that there is no place for the category of Israeli national identity is yet another indication of the para-dox that lies at the heart of the official definition of the state:

> My nationality according to the Israeli Ministry of the Interior is "Arab"; and
> my Israeli passport doesn't specify my nationality at all. Instead, it states on the
> front page that I'm an Israeli citizen. (Shammas 1995a, 25)

Accordingly, when filling out a disembarkation card prior to landing in France, Shammas (1995a), like all Palestinian Arabs with Israeli citizenship, is confronted with the problem of having to write "Arab" under "Nationality":

> If I wrote Arab under Nationalité, in the French form, I would be telling the truth according to the state that had issued my identity card and my passport, but then it may complicate things with the French authorities. On the other hand, writing "Israeli" under Nationalité is worse still, because in that case I would be telling a lie; my passport doesn't say that at all, and neither does my I.D. (p. 25)

To Shammas (1995b), the confusion in Israeli official discourse between nationality and citizenship is at the root of what is referred to in that discourse as "the Arab problem." This confusion is indicative of the ongoing problematic of a group identity that is based upon unclear distinctions between citizenship, nationality, and people:

> I do not know many people in the Middle East who can differentiate between "citizenship," "nation" [*leom*], "nationalism" [*leumiut*], "nationalism" [*leumanut*], "people" [*Am*], and "nation" [*umah*]. In Arabic, as in Hebrew, there is no equivalent for the English word nationality. (p. 30)

According to Shammas, the solution is to establish an "Israeli" identity that is determined by citizenship in the state rather than a historical link to a particular ethnic, religious, or national group.

SHAMMAS AND HIS JEWISH CRITICS:
A. B. YEHOSHUA AND SAMI MIKHAEL

Not surprisingly, Shammas' arguments have elicited strong responses from Israeli critics. Among the most articulate and forceful of these critics is author and social critic A. B. Yehoshua, a leading voice of the Israeli left. In a widely cited statement in the left wing journal *Politika*, Yehoshua (1985) leveled the following challenge to Shammas:

> If you want your full identity, if you want to live in a state with a Palestinian character [*Ishiut*], an original Palestinian culture, arise, take your belongings [*metaltelekhah*], and move one hundred meters east, to the independent Palestinian state that will exist alongside Israel. (p. 11)

Acknowledging that he and Shammas are in conflict over the nature of Israeli identity, Yehoshua argues that Israel is a Jewish state in the same way that Spain is a Spanish state. Seen in this light, Israeliness is not only citizenship but an essence that can be quantified or measured. What Yehoshua has said to Shammas, he would also say to Jewish settlers living in territories that have been or will be returned to Palestinian authority:

> Anton Shammas wants to place upon me his dual identity [Palestinian and Israeli] (which for him is a source of richness). And I refuse. There are enough Jews in the world with dual identity, and I do not want to be of dual identity [Jewish and Israeli] here. (Yehoshua 1986, 23)

Yehoshua criticizes Shammas for not speaking out against Arab/Palestinian acts of terror. For the Israeli left not to lose its moral force in its debate with the right, it must continuously demand of the Arabs, particularly the Palestinians, "Where are your Arie Eliav's? Your Shalom Akshav (Peace Now)?" (Yehoshua 1986, 22).

In response, Shammas argued that just as he rejects the notion of a Jewish state, he likewise rejects the notion of a Palestinian state. What he advocates is a state called Palestine, whose citizens will be Palestinians, alongside a state called Israel, whose citizens are Israelis. Taking issue with Yehoshua's argument that just as Spain is a Spanish state, Israel is a Jewish state, Shammas (1986b) argues, "Israel is an Israeli state in the same way that Spain is a Spanish state" (p. 44):

> In spite of everything I have said, if time passes and Yehoshua still insists that it is better that I seek my full identity elsewhere, I shall leave my land and my birthplace. For if Yehoshua prefers to establish a state together with his brethren from the Jewish terrorist organization, may he and they be healthy. (p. 45)

The debate between Yehoshua and Shammas over the limits of Israeli identity was resumed six years later in 1992, when Shammas, who had since moved to the United States, returned to Israel for a visit, and he and liberal Israeli writer David Grossman met with Yehoshua at the latter's home on Mt. Carmel. The confrontation, described at length in Grossman's book *Sleeping on a Wire* (1993), brings to the surface in a particularly lucid way the ongoing points of difference that separate Yehoshua and Shammas:

> "My problem and debate with Anton are not about equality, but about identity. Because as a national minority in an Israeli state..."

> "What's an Israeli state?" Shammas interrupted him. "There's no such thing!"

> "What do you mean there's no such thing?... For me, 'Israeli' is the authentic, complete, and consummate word for the concept 'Jewish.' Israeliness is the total, perfect, and original Judaism, one that should provide answers in all areas of life." (pp. 253–254)

To which Shammas responded: "How can you want to make me a partner in an Israeli identity, if Israel is the totality of Judaism?" (p. 272).

Yehoshua compared Shammas to a Pakistani who comes to England with a British passport and insists on being a partner in the creation of the British nationality, seeking to introduce Pakistani, Muslim symbols and languages. In response, Shammas argued:

> "Buli, the minute a man like you does not understand the basic difference between the Pakistani who comes to England and the Galilean who has been in Fasuta for untold generations, then what do you want us to talk about?"(p. 254)

When Yeshoshua argues that to separate Israeli and Jewish is like trying to separate France from Frenchness, Shammas replies:

> "France and Frenchness come from the same root, but Judaism and Israeliness is a different matter. That's why I advocate the de-Judaization and de-Zionization of Israel...I'm asking you for a new definition of the word 'Israeli,' so that it will include me as well, a definition in territorial terms that you distort, because you're looking at it from the Jewish point of view." (p. 255)

Shammas accepts the notion that as a state in which the majority is Jewish, Israel has the right to impose an educational system that reflects the composition of the population:

> "These are legitimate political power struggles as part of the game of democracy. But the minute you tell me that not only is the country's ambience Jewish, but also its very character as a national state; the minute the law faculty at Tel Aviv university drafts a constitution for Israel that opens with the sentence 'Israel is the eternal state of the Jewish people'; the minute the Knesset inserts a racist definition into its amendment of the Knesset basic law, as it did in 1985, then I've got a problem with you, because you exclude me from that definition." (p. 261)

One can read the debate between Shammas and Yehoshua as one of conflicting interpretations of culture and cultural identity.[10] On the one hand, in contrast to Yehoshua's apparently essentialistic definition of Israeli identity, Shammas' antiessentialistic position resembles the recent nonessentialistic, strongly contested conceptions of identity that have been espoused by writers such as postcolonial critics Edward Said and Homi Bhabha, cultural critic Stuart Hall, and feminist critic Judith Butler. In their writings, and in the writings of others in the field of cultural studies, cultural identity is viewed as a dynamic process that can best be understood in relation to the cultural Others over and against which a group defines itself.[11] As articulated by Jacques Derrida (1984):

> No culture is closed in on itself, especially in our own times when the impact of European civilization is so all-pervasive. Similarly, what we call the deconstruction of our own Western culture is aided and abetted by the fact that Europe has always registered the impact of heterogeneous, non-European influences. Because it has always been thus exposed to, and shadowed by, its other, it has been compelled to question itself. Every culture is haunted by its other. (p. 116)[12]

This position blurs the sharp boundaries between insiders and outsiders, natives and foreigners, we and they. Instead, emphasizing the mutual impact of colonizing and colonized, dominant and subordinate, hegemonic and minority cultures on one another, they have urged us to be simultaneously attuned both to voices "within" and voices "without."

At the same time, Shammas (1995a) reads identity in terms of power: "Ultimately we are dealing with the question of identity; the identity which is given to us by those who have the power to do so" (p. 24). Shammas thus represents Israeli culture and identity as a contested, power-ridden set of discourses and practices through which meaning is produced, disseminated, and legitimated.

Shammas effectively depicts the cultural violence with which the dominant Israeli culture treats Palestinians who are Israeli citizens. He thus poses a unique challenge to those on the Jewish Israeli left like Yehoshua, who frame the problems of Palestinians in Israel solely in the discourse of legal rights and political equality. While the problems of political and economic inequality are complex and challenging, to the liberal Israeli they can be largely resolved through legal and political reforms. However, if, as Shammas argues, the basic conflicts are embedded in the dominant Israeli discourse and practices, then political and social reforms are not adequate. To achieve the desired goal as understood by Shammas, it would be necessary to change the "character" of the society by revising the prevailing cultural discourse and the practices related to it. As Shammas repeatedly argues, this entails a far-reaching revision of the dominant notion of Israel as a Jewish state and Israeli culture as basically Jewish culture, a revision that, like Yehoshua, most Jewish Israelis would oppose.

Sami Mikhael, an Israeli Jew originally from Iraq, has taken up Shammas' challenge. Mikhael, a novelist, has been a leading critic of Israel's marginalization or exclusion of Jews of Middle Eastern origin, the so-called Mizrahi Jews. However, pointing to the case of Lebanon as an example of a failed attempt at democracy in the Middle East, Mikhael (1986) states his opposition to making Israel a democratic, as opposed to a Jewish, state:

I am willing to fight shoulder to shoulder with him [Shammas] against every injustice against the Arab minority. But, no more than that. I am willing to gamble my personal fate, but not my national fate. (p. 17)

While empathizing with Shammas' suffering, Mikhael (1986), like Yehoshua, refuses to contemplate a situation that would result in Israeli Jews becoming a minority:

Many Jews from every camp understand his pain and identify with his suffering as a member of a minority. Many are ready to pay a price in order to make it easer for him but not to the point where they make themselves into a minority. (p. 17)

In a bristling reply to Mikhael, Shammas (1986d) again summarizes his position: (1) After the establishment of the state of Palestine, Israel, the state of the Jewish people, should be declared the state of Israel, "medinat Yisrael." (2) In the box reserved for "nationality" [*leom*] on both Shammas' and Mikhael's Israeli identity card, the word "Israeli" should be written:

What, essentially, is Israeli identity? In my view, Israeli identity is the identity of a citizen of Israel who asks of the Ministry of the Interior that the word "Israeli" be written in the box marked "nationality" on his identification certificate. (Shammas 1987c, 27)

Shammas (1987c) then states the following additional propositions:

1) Zionism, as a national movement, ended its function with the establishment of the state; 2) Everyone living within the green line who is a citizen of the state of Israel should be defined as an "Israeli." 3) The Law of Return...is the strictest kind of racist law [*lemehadrin*]. One generation is sufficient time for a mature man to decide if he will immigrate to Israel or not. And a situation in which an individual, always a Jew, decides whether or not to adopt the state as his home is absurd. The time has come to transform the law of return into a regular immigration law, as in the Western states (secular and democratic!). The state will have the authority to decide who may be called Israeli, but Israeliness should no longer be automatic or self-understood [*muvan meelov*]; 4) All Israelis should be equal with regard to rights and responsibilities; 5) Currently, the state of Israel is not democratic, even for Jews (as it was prior to 1967); occupation and democracy can only exist in tandem in a fountain by Agam; 6) All of the above can come about only when the state of Israel returns to its legitimate boundaries. Terribly simple! (p. 27)

He then concludes,

If we have fumbled the chance for "we, the members of the Israeli nation," should we then wait, with Levantine patience, for the first Jew to proclaim at the head of the camp, in hope that the entire camp will follow after him: "Zionism is dead, long live the Israeli nation."(p. 27)

With the establishment of a Palestinian state, the Palestinian citizens of Israel who choose to remain in Israel will be confronted with the following dilemma:

If this is the national homeland of the Jewish people, what are you—Palestinian Arabs whom we forgot to drive out in 1948—doing here? Are you *benei bayit*? Renters on a monthly basis? Protected renters [*dayarim muganim*]? Renters with key money? Do you have a document of ownership? [*yesh lakhem tabu*]? Allah knows! (Shammas 1989b, 25)

Shammas has thus problematized the prevailing zionist conception of Israel as a Jewish state, a state belonging to the Jewish people worldwide. Calling into question the hegemonic notions of Israeli identity and culture, he has effectively revealed the contradiction between the claim of the state to be democratic and the claim of the state to be Jewish, a motif that, as mentioned earlier, recurs in the ongoing debate over postzionism and in the writings of particular groups of Israeli social scientists. Shammas' name rarely if ever is introduced into the debates over postzionism. Nonetheless, as I have argued, his writings problematize zionist discourse in general and the zionist definition of the state of Israel far more effectively that those of Jewish critics.

As Homi Bhabha reminds us, there is an inherent tension between the official representations of the nation and the everyday life of the people. Distinguishing between official, pedagogical discourse and practices and the ways in which national life is enacted in daily practice, Bhabha helps us understand the ways in which the presence of Palestinian Arabs, like other minority populations, subverts efforts to represent the state and its culture as homogeneous. Differentiating between "the people" as represented in official nationalist or state discourse and "the people" as enacted in the course of everyday practice, Bhabha problematizes the concept of "the people," conventionally taken to be the foundation, core, or essence of the nation.

Far from being a natural entity, a people is the product of complex cultural and social processes. In Bhabha's (1994) terms, the people, like the nation, must be written:

The scraps, patches, and rags of daily life must be repeatedly turned into the signs of a national culture, while the very act of the narrative performance interpellates a growing circle of national subjects. In the production of the nation as narration there is a split between the continuist, accumulative temporality of the pedagogical, and the repetitious, recursive strategy of the performative. It is through this process of splitting that the conceptual ambivalence of modern society becomes the site of writing the nation. (pp. 145–46)

Bhabha (1994) also stresses the liminality of the nation. On the one hand, a nation is the object/subject of a national narrative grounded in historical past. At the same time, it is the product of the everyday performance by those belonging to the nation that constantly rubs against the grain of that narrative. Thus, in all nations, the people are the site of ongoing conflict:

> The people are neither the beginning nor the end of national narrative; they represent the cutting edge between the totalizing powers of the "social" as homogeneous, consensual community, and the forces that signify the more specific address to contentious, unequal interests and identities within the population. (p. 146)

As Shammas has shown us, the existence of a large population of Palestinians renders problematic the zionist premise that Israeli identity, Israeli culture, and the Israeli people are exclusively Jewish.

EMILE HABIBY: UNMASKING THE ZIONIST APPARATUS

In contrast to Shammas, Emile Habiby (1922–1996) was actively engaged in Israeli political life for most of his career. A major figure in the Israeli Communist Party since the early 1940s, he served as its representative in the Knesset for nineteen years (1953–1972). Hoping to improve conditions of Palestinians in Israel through political means, he subordinated his artistic career to his political activities. In the end, however, Habiby acknowledged that his political activities failed to yield the sought-after results. Realizing the futility of trying to juggle a political career and writing, he abandoned politics.

In his last novel, *Sarayah* (1993), Habiby describes his inner conflict:

> The true identity of Sarayah was not revealed to me until the final pages. I was amazed [*nidhamti*], as was a poet friend who read the manuscript, by the truth that was revealed to me. But I have not allowed myself to hide it, although it contradicts the path I have chosen [based on] my faith that it is both possible and beneficial "to carry two watermelons with one hand, actively engaging in politics and in literature." (p. 9)[13]

Toward the end of his life, Habiby recognized the futility of his dreams of working simultaneously in literature and politics. Describing the protagonist/narrator in *Sarayah* as representing his lost youth, full of hope, Habiby (1992) observed:

> Sarayah is the noble dreams of justice, equality and freedom. She is the essence of the early period of my youth, when I believed that the communist ship would fulfill my hopes. However, the ship did not bring us to a safe shore, exploding before arriving there. (p. 15)

Unlike Shammas, Habiby wrote his fiction and most of his political commentary in Arabic. Owing to the editorial efforts of Anton Shammas, he became known to the Hebrew reading public. Through Shammas' translations, the Jewish reading public was exposed to Habiby's powerful satirical style. Using satire and irony, Habiby's writings problematize an apparatus that most Israeli Jews take for granted.[14]

Habiby is widely recognized as one of the most talented writers in the Arabic language, and his works have been widely disseminated throughout the Middle East. Arabs, particularly Palestinians, claim Habiby as one of theirs. Thus, the announcement in 1992 that Habiby was awarded the prestigious Israel Prize for Literature, the first Arab writer ever to be so recognized, precipitated an uproar in both Jewish and Arab circles.[15]

To many Palestinians, like the poet Muhmad Darwish, to accept the award from the Israeli conquerors would be an act of betrayal and a confirmation of Israel's legitimacy. Jewish critics, particularly from the right wing, considered it inappropriate to award the Israel Prize to one who wrote in Arabic.

According to zionism, Israel is a Jewish state, and Israeli culture is Jewish culture. When Israeli Jews speak about Israeli literature, they almost always mean literature written by Jews in Hebrew. And when they speak about Israeli culture, they almost always mean Israeli Jewish culture, the culture of the majority. Thus, the awarding of the Israel Prize was a powerful statement on the parameters of Israeli culture. By acknowledging the significance of Habiby's contribution to Israeli literature and culture, the committee was, intentionally or not, expanding the boundaries of that culture far beyond the limits of the dominant zionist view.

As a public figure active in Israeli politics, Habiby represented the views of Palestinian Arab citizens of Israel in numerous articles in journals and newspapers in both Arabic and Hebrew. In these articles, as in his fiction, Habiby revealed the perspective of a minority that, since 1948, has found itself subordinated to the Jewish majority and to the apparatuses of a state grounded in the discourse of zionism. Many of his articles depict the insecurities and fears of the Palestinians living in Israel.

Habiby's writings present a Palestinian counternarrative to the dominant zionist historical narrative. His writings thus contribute to what Homi Bhabha (1994) describes as

> the emergence of a hybrid national narrative that turns the nostalgic past into the disruptive "anterior" and displaces the historical present—opens it up to other histories and incommensurable narrative subjects. (p. 167)

Habiby organizes his narrative, like the Jewish historical one, around major wars and acts of violence. However, unlike the dominant Israeli narrative, Habiby's is written from the perspective of those Palestinians who remained in the state. For Palestinians as for Israelis, the defining moment in the history of the state was the 1948 War. However, whereas Jews represent that war as the War of Liberation/Independence, Palestinians represent it as "the Catastrophe," the equivalent of the Hebrew term *Shoah,* which for Jews represents the destruction of European Jewry.

According to Habiby (1988c):

> The tragedy of the Palestinian Arabs is a total tragedy, encompassing those who fled and became refugees, and those who, becoming refugees, remained in their homeland. The poet Tufik Zayid, who was also the mayor of Nazareth, was right when he said to one of his brethren, a refugee (who had fled), "The tragedy that I live is part of your tragedy." It became clear to me that the tragedy of the Palestinian urbanites was even more tragic—those who fled and those who remained, "alone like a sword" in the hands of the lone master, surrounded by people who do not know him. Not only do they not know that he is an knight, but do not recognize that he, like them, is a human being. (p. 8)[16]

Habiby is considered to be one of the most compelling narrators of the destructive effects of the 1948 War on the Palestinian nation.[17] Describing the Palestinians' expulsion from their homes, he (1993) depicts the tragic splitting of villages and families and the redrawing of boundaries (pp. 103, 107).[18]

One of the most powerful effects of Habiby's writings is the continuous subversion and problematizing of the "collective remembering/forgetting" inscribed in the hegemonic Israeli narrative. As postcolonial theorists remind us, every national memory entails a national forgetting. Behind the events that are narrated in a nation's myth of beginnings are events that are eclipsed and "forgotten." In the wake of the 1948 War, this collective remembering/forgetting was aided by physically erasing the sites of Arab villages, building new Jewish settlements over them, and giving them new Hebrew names. In larger urban areas such as Haifa, streets previously known by Arabic names were assigned new Hebrew names and new street signs were erected to replace the old ones. With the passing of time, as the old names were forgotten, it came to be assumed that the space had always been "Jewish" space.

As our previous discussion of Benvenisti in chapter 2 showed, this process of erasure and collective forgetting was embedded in the discourse and practices of labor zionism. Moreover, as discussed in chapter 4, it was disseminated throughout Israeli culture by means of academic writings and school texts. In scholarly historical studies, popular books, and school texts, the official version placed responsibility for the displacement and flight of the Arab populations solely on the Palestinians themselves.

As Habiby began in 1970 to publish his short stories and novels, the narratives dominating Israeli culture with very few exceptions, were silent about the Palestinian version of events. As we saw in chapter 4, not until the late 1980s did Jewish scholars begin to produce alternative narratives that challenged the official Israeli versions of the 1948 War and its consequences.

Within Israeli society, there were few Jewish Israelis who were aware of or considered credible the Palestinian counternarrative presented by Habiby. This situation had changed little when the first English translation of his novel *Saeed* appeared in 1985. Even at that time, most Jewish Israeli readers dismissed Habiby's alternative narrative as Palestinian propaganda. However, with the subsequent appearance of numerous studies by Jewish Israeli scholars, an emerging Jewish counternarrative about the events of 1948 has provided a more supportive context for Habiby's counternarrative, thus rendering it more credible to Jewish Israeli readers.

Habiby's confrontation with death during the 1948 War was a precipitating factor in his writing. Returning home to Haifa during the war, he encountered death face-to-face in the form of Israeli soldiers. In Haifa, he found his family and his neighbors scattered in all directions. Habiby (1991a) swore to himself:

> [I]f I survive, I will not forgive those who led my people and my family into desolation [*asher holikhu et ami umishpahti sholel*]. I will do all that is in my power to ensure that my people not forget that bitter experience. (p. 5)

Most of Habiby's fiction, particularly his novels, is devoted to fulfilling that vow of not allowing his people to forget. Habiby accomplishes this through a number of strategies. One strategy is the recurring recital of the "forgotten" Arabic names of those "forgotten" villages conquered by the Israelis in 1948. While some, left unoccupied following the war, were nonetheless assigned new Hebrew names, others were destroyed by the Israelis, who built on the sites new Jewish settlements bearing Hebrew names. In *The Secret Life of Saeed: The Pessoptimist* (1985), the protagonist, shortly after crossing (infiltrating) into Israel from Lebanon, is besieged by a group of Palestinian refugees who have been assembled by the Israeli authorities in a school courtyard. Relating their conversation, Habiby succinctly recounts the fate of hundreds of Palestinian villages destroyed by the Israelis in the 1948 War, thereby providing an alternative to the dominant Israeli narrative:

> Cooled down at last, they began to accept me and bombarded me with questions about their relatives who had taken refuge in Lebanon.
> "We're from Kwaykaat. They demolished it and evicted everyone. Did you meet anyone from Kwaykaat?... I am from al-Manshiyya. There's not a stone left standing there except the tombs. Did you meet anyone from al-Manshiyya?"
>
> "No."
>
> "We are from Amqa. They plowed all its houses under and spilled its oil onto the ground. Did you meet anyone from Amqa?"
>
> "No."
>
> "We over here are from Berwah. They forced us out and obliterated it. Did you meet anyone from Berwah?"...
>
> "We are from Ruwais." "We are from al-Hadatha." "We are from el-Damun."
>
> "We are from Mazraa." "We are from Shaab." "We are from Miy'ar."
>
> "We are from Waarat el-Sarris." "We are from Al-Zeeb."
>
> "We are from el-Bassa."
>
> "We are from el-Kabri." "We are from Iqrit." "We are from Kufr Bir'im."
>
> "We are from Dair el-Quasi." "We are from Saasaa." "We are from el-Ghabisiy."
>
> "We are from Suhmata." "We are from al-Safsaf." "We are from Kufr "Inan."
> (pp. 21–22)[19]

Following this litany of destroyed villages, Habiby (1985) sardonically adds: "Please do not expect me, dear sir, after all this time, to remember the names of all the villages laid waste to which these figures made claim that evening in the courtyard of the Jazzazr mosque." And, as if to further accentuate the effects of collective forgetting, he adds:

We of Haifa used to know more about the villages of Scotland than we did about those of Galilee. Most of those villages I have never heard mentioned except for that one evening. (p. 22)

This then has the effect of subverting the efforts of the hegemonic power to erase or cover over that conflicted, violent past, thereby enforcing a forgetting that is so often inscribed into the establishment of a nation-state. By reciting Arabic place names, Habiby represents for his readers the conflict and violence that marked these spaces and that the Hebrew narrative with its Hebrew site-names sought to conceal. Far from being "empty," as implied in the zionist narrative, the land was the site of villages and towns in which Palestinians carried on their daily lives, raised their children, and dreamed their dreams.

Another strategy used by Habiby is to ridicule the effects of the Israeli practice of changing Arabic street names into Hebrew names. In the process, Habiby (1988a) does not allow his readers to forget that many places now known by their Hebrew names were formerly known by their Arab names:

I traveled by way of the street of heroes [*derekh hagibburim*], the heroes who expelled the inhabitants of Wadi Rushmiya from their homes, and reached the street of the pioneers, the street had been paved by the first Jewish pioneers in Haifa. (pp. 36–37)

After commenting on how, during the British Mandate, the street had been filled with Arab shops and houses, Habiby continues:

They called the street "pioneer," which in Arabic means Talii. But we, for historical reasons, are not permitted to translate it into Arabic, unlike our Jewish brothers, who translated or changed the names of many old Arab streets in the city. (p. 38)

The Israeli practice of transliterating Hebrew names into Arabic letters often produced humorous results:

They changed the name of Feisal square at the entrance to the Hijazit railroad station to the Street of the Golani Brigade [Hativat Golani]. In Arabic, this means "Golani's betrothed/fiancee." Before I had acquired the necessary military vocabulary, I thought that Golani was a Don Juan who had many lovers, but out of courtesy referred to them as betrotheds/fiances. (pp. 38–39)

Citing a humorous incident in which a university student in Milan, in asking a question, used a literal Arabic translation for the name of the city Tel Aviv, Habiby (1988a) observed:

From the perspective of the received/inherited wisdom there is no difference between that student...and our brothers the Jewish historians of Haifa, except that he translates with words only, while they translate with both words and deeds. (p. 39)

The continued mention of Arabic place and street names serves to counteract for the reader the effects of the official Israeli practice. As one Jewish Israeli commentator observes:

The political statement aimed at the Zionist presence in the Arab world is transmitted with a light, sharp irony, as wells as with true humor. The main hinge is the emphasis on the changing of place names mentioned in the book. The names are almost always mentioned by their Arabic name by which the places were known prior to the 1948 War ("the war which liberated the land of its inhabitants" in the language of the book), along with the indication of the new Hebrew name of the place, as a sign of the new times that came upon the land. (Yizhaki 1993, 13)

Another strategy employed by Habiby to subvert, undercut, and destabilize the dominant Israeli representation of the 1948 War is the use of alternative/competing/counter nomenclature. As we saw in chapter 4, Israeli scholars like Kimmerling and Pappe speak of the need for a neutral historical discourse; Habiby, in contrast, wishes to represent the silenced voices of the displaced Palestinian. Thus, whereas the 1948 War is referred to in Israeli public discourse as the War of Liberation or the War for Independence, Habiby (1993) ironically refers to it as "the day on which the land was liberated of its dwellers" (p. 96). Speaking of his father's death, he refers to 1948 as "the year that the earth split open and the state came into being" (literally, "into the light of day") (p. 103).

Habiby reveals another dimension of the erasure of memories in a passage about his elderly mother. Bereft of hope, she speaks of her prior friendship with Jewish neighbors, first in their village of Shefaram and later in Haifa, in the years before the establishment of the state. Commenting on his mother's remembering, Habiby (1988c) suggests that the eclipsing of memories contributes to the conflict and hostility between Jews and Palestinian Arabs:

Do the Jews who lived in Shefaram in those days tell others about their memories of visits in the house of "the teacher Shukri" in Haifa? I think not. Were they to do so, Kahanism would never have occurred. (p. 9)

Whereas Jewish Istraelis take it for granted that the 1948 War was "The War of Liberation," Palestinians take it for granted that it was but another extreme instance in a series of disasters. In *Life of Saeed,* Habiby's protagonist recounts the ongoing series of invasions and conquests by foreign powers. In this counternarrative, the Israelis are represented as but the most recent invaders. Habiby's stories thus have the effect of interrupting the dominant Jewish Israeli narrative, counterposing to it an alternative narrative that never ceases to place it under question and threaten its hegemony.

Habiby also seeks to counteract the official state erasure of the memory of the Palestinian presence by references to the length of the Arab presence in the land and to the ancient roots of Arabic culture. In *Sarayah*, his last novel (1993), he traces the history of some villages back to the era of the Crusades and to the pre-Islamic era. In this history, his recounting of the string of invasions dating back to the medieval period has the effect of diminishing the uniqueness of the Israeli conquest. At the same time, the reader is told that just as in the case with past conquerors, this conqueror, too, will also pass from the scene.[20]

Reinforcing the antiquity of Arabic culture through frequent references to medieval Arabic philosophers and writers, Habiby highlights the idea of an indigenous Arab culture. At the same time, he juxtaposes an alternative Arabic claim to the Jewish claim of an ancient and continuing presence in the land. It is as if he is saying, "We, too, have a culture with roots in the distant past. We too have an intellectual tradition filled with philosophers, scholars, etc. Our history and our culture are much older than that of the zionists, who are newcomers on the scene."

Habiby (1985) represents the process of historical forgetting/remembering and erasure/fabrication in an encounter between Saeed and his former teacher. The teacher, representing the history of the land as a series of brutal massacres, informs him that the land is made holy by the spilling of human blood, and that "After every massacre there was no one left to tell the new generation about their origins":

"But why didn't you teach us about all this holiness, sir?"

"Well, the British do have the right to boast about their own history, you know, especially about that great king of theirs, Richard the Lionhearted. But even without our teaching you all this, they were participating in the process of rendering our country holy by spilling our blood. Conquerors, my son, consider as true history only what they have themselves fabricated."

"Will we be permitted to study this history after the conquerors have left and the country obtains its independence?"

"You'll have to wait and see." (pp. 24–25)

Habiby represents the sense of humiliation and powerlessness that the war inflicted on the Palestinians in a scene describing his encounter with an

Israeli soldier in his family home in Haifa in 1948. The scene represents the good and bad in Israelis. In 1948, when Israeli troops invaded Arab homes in Haifa, a Jewish friend from HaShomer HaZair drove Habiby from Nazareth to Haifa. Arriving home, Habiby found an Israeli soldier sitting in his house with his elderly mother, his wife, and young daughter. After a long night sitting opposite one another and staring one another down, a night in which Habiby felt embarrassed by his helplessness, the soldier, himself, became embarrassed and left (Habiby 1988c, 9).[21]

Habiby brings to the surface the violence caused by Jewish settlement practices undertaken in the name of zionism. What the dominant Jewish narratives represent as marks of progress or redemption are, in Habiby's Palestinian counternarrative, depicted as acts of violence. Thus, whereas zionist discourse speaks in terms of the "ingathering of the exiles," Habiby (1993) speaks of "the great scattering of the Palestinians" (p. 107). Similarly, over and against the Jewish practice of recounting the story of their exodus and liberation on the festival of Passover, Habiby (1988a) depicts Palestinians performing the reenactment of their more recent "exodus" from Palestine (pp. 147 ff.). In addition, alongside the zionist discourse of exile and return, Habiby presents a Palestinian discourse of exile and the yearning to return.

Habiby's history, like many Jewish Israeli accounts, builds the narrative around wars. For Israeli Jews, the narrative would include the war with Egypt in 1956 in which Israel, with the help of England and France, captured the Sinai; the 1967 War, in which Israel captured the West Bank and Gaza; the Yom Kippur War of 1973, which caught Israel by surprise and revealed its military vulnerability; the Invasion of Lebanon in 1982, which helped to undermine the prevailing notion of Israel using its military power for peace and defense; and the Palestinian uprising, the Intifada, beginning at the end of 1987. While using many of the same dates, Habiby transformed them to conform to the Palestinian memory. For Habiby and his fellow Palestinians, 1956 marked the year in which forty-nine unarmed Palestinian villagers, returning from working in the fields at the village of Kfar Kassem unaware that a curfew had been imposed, were shot and killed by a contingent of Israeli soldiers. According to Habiby, that date serves to remind the Palestinian minority of their insecure position, their continuing vulnerability to violence, and their fear of renewed expulsions.

For Habiby and his fellow Palestinians, 1967 represents the year in which they were reunited with their Palestinian brothers and sisters who had fled Palestine in 1948. Habiby recounts how, following Israel's victory, he renewed his acquaintance with childhood friends in the West Bank and Gaza. Habiby frequently refers in his stories to the ambivalent feelings, including a sense of guilt, of those Palestinians who had remained in Israel. Now, from those who did flee, he learns that the Palestinians who remained were a source of inspiration to the Palestinians in the territories who, amidst continuing dangers, remained in their new homes in the West Bank, thus constituting a constant reminder of the catastrophic effects of the war.

To Jewish Israelis, the Gulf War of 1991 was a reminder of their vulnerability and the complexity of their military situation. Compelled by the United States to refrain from engaging in military action against Iraq, Israelis were forced to sit by passively, dependent upon the military might of the United States, while Iraqi missiles rained on their land. To Habiby, the fear experienced by the Jewish Israelis sitting in rooms sealed against the dangers of biochemical weapons mirrored the fear and sense of impotence that are daily felt by Palestinians. During the days of the Gulf War, Palestinians also lived in fear. In their case, according to Habiby, what they feared were pogroms and expulsions initiated by the Israeli right. Nevertheless, unlike 1948 when many Palestinians packed their belongings and fled, in 1991, reflecting their confidence that they had a rightful place in the land, they held fast and refused to leave.

Reports of Palestinians standing on rooftops and cheering when they sighted Iraqi missiles angered many Israelis. While these reports reinforced the prior hostile feelings of those on the right, they also shook the confidence of those on the left who had been engaged in the pursuit of avenues of reconciliation and peace. To Habiby (1991a), however, the reaction of those Palestinians should not have surprised Jewish Israelis. Habiby, who personally opposed the behavior of the young Palestinians, denied that it was representative of the Palestinians as a community. At the same time, responding to liberal Israelis who were shaken up and angered by the murderous looks from Palestinians during the Gulf War, Habiby connects those looks to the blindness of the Israeli politicians who failed to grasp the pain of the same Palestinians. Denying that such looks represent "an abyss of hatred that will be difficult to bridge," he accused Israelis of exaggerating their significance and, at the same time, of having only a superficial understanding of the Palestinian position.

Habiby insisted that he, like all Palestinians, encounters "murderous looks" from Jews every time that he speaks Arabic in a restaurant or in the street. However, notwithstanding the chants of "death to the Arabs" that were frequently heard during the year preceding the Gulf War, Habiby (1991b) is prepared to ignore these things and focus, instead, on the hopeful signs:

> I do not build my future in this state, my homeland, my only homeland, on the murderous looks, but on the wise and human looks of my writer friends and my fisherman friends. (p. 7)

Contrasting the position of the dominant Jewish Israeli community with that of the subordinate, vulnerable Palestinians, Habiby speaks of the loneliness of Palestinians who looked at those (Israelis) around him "with hopeful eyes." The decisive question—"Is there anyone with whom to talk?"—is always the question of the Abir/Knight who remains alone like the sword (Habiby 1988c). Insisting that as the dominant group, the Israelis have a greater responsibility, Habiby challenges Jewish Israelis to recognize the humanity of the Palestinians in their midst:

> The first obligation of people of conscience, especially in an oppressive, conquering people, is to do all that they can, every hour of every day, to excise from the hearts of the oppressed, their natural suspicion, which is self-understood, of the will to peace and coexistence among a people whose government oppresses, conquers, and tries daily to totally destroy the "other people." (p. 9)

During the Intifada, Habiby spoke out in support of the uprising. Insisting on the right of Palestinian citizens of Israel to support their fellow Palestinians living under an oppressive Israeli occupation, he proclaimed (1991a):

> I support the Intifada because and to the extent that it is not a war, but a nonviolent communal struggle for peace. I am opposed to the war that the Israeli occupying forces are waging against the Intafada. (p. 5)

In a similar fashion, Habiby upholds the rights of Palestinian citizens to publicly demonstrate in support of the struggle of the Palestinians in the territories. Thus, when Motta Gur, a former chief of staff of the Israel Defense Forces and a member of the Knesset, publicly questioned the loyalty of the Palestinian citizens of Israel who participated in a strike against the Israeli occupation of the territories captured in the 1967 War, Habiby (1988b) responded sharply. Writing in the Israeli Hebrew daily *Davar,* he denied that the demonstrations on what the Palestinians called "Peace Day" were directed against the Israeli sovereignty over its Palestinian citizens. Habiby insisted instead that the demonstrations were "a protest against the cruelty against their brothers and sisters in the occupied territories" and that "they were only expressing their opposition to the continuation of Israeli 'sovereignty' in those territories." These demonstrations, argued Habiby, were a prideful demonstration by Palestinian citizens who were seeking to make the state and its parties understand that there is a second community in Israel and that the time has come when their voice must be heeded:

> The minimal right of Arab citizens in Israel, like all other citizens in the state, is to try to influence the state and its direction. This right is denied them. It is not the Arabs who strike a blow against the "state's right of national existence and our physical right to exist as human beings, as Jews, and as the masters of the state and its defenders" as Gur claims, but the opposite. The question is, how long can the captains of the state ignore the existence of its Arab citizens? (p. 5)

Only if they were accepted as legitimate members of society would Palestinians finally lose the sense of tragedy, fear, and frustration that permeates their community.

A recurring theme in Habiby's writings is the rift that the 1948 War created within the Palestinian people. At the war's end, while some Palestinians were allowed to remain within the borders of Israel and become citizens of the state, others were forced to remain outside. Many of those on the outside viewed their brothers and sisters who remained in the new state as guilty of complicity with the oppressive, deterritorializing zionist apparatus. Palestinians who remained in Israel felt compelled to justify themselves to their brothers and sisters in exile.

In a particularly poignant passage about his mother, Habiby (1988c) represents the trauma experienced by Palestinian families split apart in 1948.[22] Attending a meeting of Jewish and Palestinian women, his mother hears a Jewish speaker refer to a struggle for the return of the Palestinian refugees:

> Crying out: "Will my sons return?" she heard the amazed speaker respond: "They will return when there is peace." "Liar" Ema Varda cried out. "My son Emile does not lie to me. He told me that many years will pass before they return, if they return. I'll no longer be alive then." (p. 9)

Following this encounter, he writes, his mother was never the same:

> Since then, my mother would go off by herself and sit on a lone rock in the Bahai Gardens near our home, and cry out alone over the loss of her sons, and particularly her younger son Naim. "Yo Naim, what happened to you after me?" (p. 9)[23]

Determined to seek out her children who cannot return, his mother decides to leave her children in Israel in search of her children who cannot return. In a poignant passage, Habiby describes how he accompanied his mother to the Mandelbaum Gate and watched her cross the border, never to return. The sense of abandonment and loss that recurs in numerous passages in his writings is graphically depicted:

> Ema left us that same year, by way of Mandelbaum Gate, to her children who had found refuge in Damascus. There in Damascus Al Shaam, she died, not in Shefaram. "You can remain, your life is before you" she said to me when we separated on the Israeli side of the Mandelbaum Gate.
>
> It seems to me that Ema Varda still remains. Don't the mothers remain? (p. 9)

In a particularly powerful scene that in a staged performance of *Saeed* brought a mostly Jewish audience to its feet cheering, Habiby depicts the conflicts among the generations. Whereas Saeed, a member of the "48 generation," continually attempts to accommodate and appease the Israeli authorities, his son, whom he encounters after a long separation, chooses armed resistance. The Israeli authorities, hoping to dissuade the young man and defuse the situation, bring Saeed and his wife, Baqiyya, to a beach where the boy has been trapped:

> "Lay down your arms, Walaa, my son, and come on out," implores the mother.[24]

> "You, woman who came with them, you tell me where I should come."

> "Out in the open air, my son. That cellar is too small, too shut in. You'll suffocate down there."

> "Suffocate? It was to breathe free that I came to this cellar, to breathe in freedom just once. In my cradle you stifled my crying. As I grew and tried to learn how to talk from what you said, I heard only whispers."

> "As I went to school you warned me, 'Careful what you say.' When I told you my teacher was my friend you whispered, 'He may be spying on you.' When I heard what had happened to Tanturah and cursed them, you murmured, 'Careful what you say.' When he cursed me, you repeated, 'Careful what you say.' When I met with my schoolmates to announce a strike, they told me, 'Careful what you say.'"

> "One morning you told me, mother, 'You talk in your sleep; careful what you say in your sleep!' I used to sing in the bath, but Father would shout at me, 'Change that tune! The walls have ears. Careful what you say!' 'Careful what you say!' 'Careful what you say!' Always, 'Careful what you say!' Just for once, just once, I want to be careless about what I say. I was suffocating! This may be a poky little cellar, Mother, but there's more room here than you have ever had! Shut in it may be, but it's a way out." (Habiby 1985, 109–110)

When the mother cries out: "But we aren't your enemies," the son, reflecting the destructive effects of Israeli domination on the Palestinian family, cries out: "But you are not on my side, either."

Skeptical of the efficacy of armed resistance, the mother challenges the son's claim that he is free: "If only we were free, my son, we wouldn't quarrel. You'd not bear arms and we would not ask you to be 'careful.' We act this way because we do seek freedom" (p. 110).

This scene is one of several in his fiction in which Habiby reveals the catch-22 situation of Palestinians in Israel, a situation taken by some theorists to be a sign of an oppressed minority.[25] If they wish to preserve their limited freedom and their limited rights as citizens, Palestinians must remain silent. By so doing, however, they acquiesce to their oppressed and repressed condition. When the mother argues that the Palestinians are not prepared to follow the path of armed rebellion, the son moans:

"Mother, mother, how long must we wait for the lilies to bud?"

"Don't think of it as waiting, son. We must simply plow and plant and bear our burden until it is harvest time."

"When will the harvest be ready?"

"Just stick it out."

"All my life I've 'stuck it out.'"

"Stick it out some more." (p. 111)

And the young man, in a comment that puts into question his father's entire life, responds: "I'm sick of your submissiveness" (p. 111). In the end, the mother, joining the son in the cellar, picks up a machine gun.

Saeed, meanwhile, remains passive. His Israeli "benefactors" warn him that he must "keep secret all that happened." In return, the Israelis will "pardon" him for the actions of his wife and son and permit him to return to work (p. 113).

Habiby repeatedly seeks to defamiliarize everyday occurrences, thereby revealing the absurdity of circumstances that Jewish Israelis have come to regard as normal or natural. In the process, he presents his Jewish Israeli readers with a reality that is totally alien. He thus effectively problematizes the unstated premises on which Jewish Israelis construct their collective identity.[26]

Irony is a major technique employed by Habiby to achieve these effects. In his first novel, *The Secret Life of Saeed: The Pessoptimist* (1985), Habiby represents the ways in which Palestinians in the new state lived immediately following statehood. While ostensibly appearing to be humorous, Habiby uses events in Saeed's life to reveal the cruelty of the system that victimizes him, rendering him an outsider in his own homeland. Notwithstanding Saeed's repeated efforts to serve his new masters, he can never escape the veil of suspicion. Habiby thus brings to the surface the twisting paths followed by Palestinians as they seek to make sense of their position in the newly formed "Jewish state."[27]

Like many other Palestinians in Israel, Saeed seeks to survive by playing according to the rules of those in power. Returning to Israel from Lebanon, he seeks to ingratiate himself with the Israeli power apparatus, represented by the ever-present but never-seen Mr. Safsarshek. Despite Saeed's repeated efforts, the Israeli continues to doubt his loyalty. Thus,

Habiby seems to be telling us, no matter how obsequious the Palestinian makes himself or herself, no matter how much a Palestinian complies with or assists the Israeli authorities, he or she will always be treated with suspicion and his or her loyalty will always be questioned.

Habiby's narrative often has the effect of rendering Kafkaesque the condition of the Palestinians in Israel. In *Saeed* (1985), he talks of the system of punishments used by the state authorities against Palestinians suspected of acts against the state. This system, which the Israeli administrator insists is fair and just, includes nighttime searches of homes, destroying suspects' homes, and imprisonment, as well as forced exile:

> "I have merely noticed according to your account of prison rules of etiquette and behavior that your prisons treat inmates with great humanitarianism and compassion—just as you treat us on the outside. And we behave the same, too. But how do you punish Arabs who are criminals, sir?"

> "This bothers us considerably. That's why our minister general has said that our occupation has been the most compassionate known on earth ever since Paradise was liberated from its occupation by Adam and Eve."

> "Take for example our policy of punishing people with exile. This we award them without their going to jail. If they once entered jail, they would become as firmly established there as the British occupation once was."

> "Yes, God bless you sir!"

> "And we demolish their homes when they're outside, but when they're inside prison we let them occupy themselves building."

> "That's really great! God bless you. But what do they build?"

> "New prisons and new cells in old jails; and they plant shade trees around them too."

> "God bless you again! But why do you demolish their homes outside the prison?"

> "To demolish the rats that build their nests in them. This way we save them from the plague."

> "God bless and save you!" (pp. 124–25)

In his second novel, *Ehtayeh* [Pity] (1988a), Habiby offers a vivid representation of the surrealistic plight of the Palestinians. Set in the city of Haifa, a city with a dense Palestinian population until 1948, the narrative centers around a traffic jam. The narrator, who after many years abroad has returned to Haifa in search of Ehtayeh, his lost love, finds himself trapped in the massive traffic tie-up.[28]

Habiby's use of the traffic jam represents what Palestinians take to be the distorting effects of an exaggerated Israeli preoccupation with security and terrorism. The traffic jam begins when a driver's attention is diverted by an attractive blonde woman in the next car. Unable to account for the cause of the traffic problem, the Israeli police, encouraged by the testimony of anxious eye witnesses and encouraged by newspaper accounts, take the event to be a terrorist attack. The hapless narrator, an attorney, becomes a victim. Accused of being a terrorist, he is detained and interrogated by the police. While the accusation strikes the reader as absurd, it represents a situation that, according to Habiby (1988a), sooner or later confronts all Palestinians: "Every Palestinian wonders at some point if he is not perhaps a terrorist [*mehabel*]" (p. 65). Habiby thus conveys the sense of futility felt by Palestinian Arabs struggling to escape the apparatus erected by the Israelis. No matter how much they endeavor to become integrated into the state, life remains one big cordon (Habiby 1985, 141–43).

Habiby also seeks to reveal the absurdity of the Israeli practice of representing Palestinians seeking to return to their homes as "infiltrators." Yuad, the object of Saeed's love, has traveled from Nazareth to Haifa to inform her sister that their father had been arrested. Having traveled without permission, she was labeled an infiltrator by the Israelis who seize her and forcibly remove her from her sister's house. To a soldier's cry: "She's an infiltrator," Yuad responds: "This is my country, this is my house, and this is my husband" (Habiby 1985, 62).

Satirizing the Israeli government's practice of labeling all who travel without permits as infiltrators, Habiby writes: "They had taken her with other 'infiltrators' to Haifa; people from Nazareth, Jaffa, Maalul, Shafa Amir, Iblin, and Tamrah. Many an Arab worker who had slipped into the city to feed his family had also been seized" (p. 63).[29]

Habiby effectively represents to his readers the everyday humiliations to which Palestinians were subjected. In *Saeed,* he satirizes the strip searches undergone by "Arab prisoners of either sex, on land, on sea, and in the air, in the airport at Lydda, at the port of Haifa, and over the 'open bridges.'" Referring to the description of strip searches in Voltaire's *Candide,* Habiby comments, "That's why our 'Turks of either sex,' when they decide to travel, take such pains to clean out their pockets, suitcases, and clothes, inside and out. And our 'Turkish' ladies are careful to wear the very finest nylon underwear, to inspire awe and envy in the policewomen who search them and so ensure they behave themselves" (p. 74).

In *Sarayah* (1993), Habiby describes in detail how his ninety-year-old aunt was subjected to the indignity of two strip searches because, he wryly comments, "they suspected that perhaps I had hidden in the folds of her blouse...a molotov cocktail or a package bomb which Auntie Nezihah would throw from over Idlewild (later Kennedy) Airport in New York, when the plane began its descent and American Jews applauded the captain on his successful landing." Referring to his previous reference to strip searches in *Saeed,* he injects a more serious tone:

> There (in *Pessoptimist*) I described faithfully what was done and continues to be done at Ben Gurion Airport beneath the clothes of departing Arab passengers. I thought that by mentioning it there, I had forever avenged them, an eternal vengeance [*ledorei dorot*] for what happened to Aunt Nezihah. Because this personal revenge did not achieve its purpose, and why should it have, I have here prepared a more comprehensive revenge. (p. 110)

Habiby offers graphic descriptions of other degradations to which Palestinians were subjected, particularly during the period of the military government imposed on them from 1948 to 1966. These include confiscation of land (see Habiby 1985, 90, 96, 126), house searches, and the cordoning off of villages.

As discussed in chapter 4, the *Shoah,* the destruction of European Jewry under the Nazi machine, is a central component in Israeli discourse.[30] Writing in 1971, Amos Elon observed:

> The trauma of the holocaust leaves an indelible mark on the national psychology, the tenor and content of public life, the conduct of foreign affairs, on politics, education, literature, and the arts. (pp. 198–99)

It is not surprising, therefore, that the Holocaust has been a recurring theme in all discussions concerning the treatment of Israel's Palestinian citizens. When objections are made to the practices described earlier, the *Shoah* is frequently invoked as a legitimation. It is to be expected, therefore, that Habiby, in his efforts to challenge the dominant Israeli discourse, would address this topic.

One argument used by Israeli liberals, among others, is that the displacement and deterritorialization inflicted on the Palestinians was the tragic result of circumstances in which the Jews had no choice. Large numbers of Jews, brutalized and rendered homeless by the Nazis, were in dire need of a safe and secure homeland. For Jews, the *Shoah* was a clear indication that only in their own homeland could Jews ever be safe.

When asked by the editors of a left-wing Israeli journal, "How do Arabs view the *Shoah?*" Habiby acknowledged the terrible fate of the Jews under the Nazis. However, he rejected the idea that the *Shoah* somehow legitimates the terrible fate inflicted on the Palestinians. To Arabs, the *Shoah* was the outcome of the Nazi war against humanity. Without minimizing the suffering of the Jews, Arabs nonetheless view it in terms of the surge of widespread international sympathy for the plight of the Jews.

Consequently, they relate it to the conditions that made it possible for zionists to persuade millions of Jews and non-Jews of the righteousness of its cause:

> Certainly there is no comparison between the suffering of European Jews and that of the Palestinian people. But the latter still suffer, and the survival of the Palestinian people in their homeland is endangered. (Habiby 1986, 27)

For the Palestinians, argues Habiby, the *Shoah* represents the original sin. As a result of it, the zionists were able to persuade millions of Jews of the righteousness of their cause. However, according to Habiby (1986), the *Shoah* has distorted the moral sensitivity of the Jews:

> I cannot imagine that the brothers and sisters of Heine, Rambam, Berthold Brecht, Stefan Zweig, Albert Einstein, and the Arab-Jewish poet Ben Haalmovet Alsaval [Shlomo ben Ovadiah] would permit a Jewish government to expel another Semitic people from its homeland were it not for the *Shoah*! (p. 27)

Although written in Arabic, Habiby's novels have become, through the Hebrew translations of Shammas, a part of Israeli culture. At the same time, they effectively problematize dominant notions of Israeli literature:

> It appears that the historians of Hebrew literature don't know what to make of and what place to assign to them [writings in Hebrew by Palestinians, and writings in Arabic, translated into Hebrew, by Israeli Palestinian citizens], if any. Nevertheless, it appears that literature written in Israel by Arab writers splits [*mavkiah leatzmah*] the path of canonical Hebrew literature, especially through the merit of these two important creators, Emile Habiby and Anton Shammas. It seems to me that there is no way to ignore it and its outstanding Israeli character, notwithstanding the many problems, which also we cannot ignore, bound up in its presence in Israeli literature. (Yizhaki 1993, 12)

Hever (1993) sees Habiby, as he does Shammas, as a minority writer who effectively subverts both the dominant Israeli political discourse and the dominant Israeli equation of Israeli culture with Jewish culture and Israeli literature with Jewish literature. Whereas Shammas uses the language of the majority, Hebrew, to subvert the discourse of the majority, Habiby's use of the language of the minority, Arabic, problematizes the dominant notion of Israeli culture as a Hebrew culture:

> Habiby writes texts that have a dual political status. On the one hand, through their universal vision, they are able to gain acceptance into the canon of the majority culture. On the other hand, they subvert the majority culture by assigning to the Palestinian voice an independent particular place that is not easily integrated into the universal model. (p. 113)[31]

Habiby, like Shammas, effectively problematizes the dominant zionist conception of Israeli culture as a Jewish culture, as well as the literary and cultural canon that is derived from it.

Notwithstanding his apparent acceptance into Israeli culture, Habiby's legitimacy, argues Hever (1993), is borderline:

> In the final analysis, Habiby stands on the border of legitimacy. While the sharp political dimension of his creativity undergoes processes of adaption and uprooting [by the majority culture], the principal way in which he joins with the cultural majority's hegemony is through subverting it. (p. 114)

Through his pioneering analyses of Shammas and Habiby, Hever has effectively revealed their significance for the postzionist debates. By representing the literary canon as a site of power relations in a way that distinguishes him from most of his colleagues, Hever (1989) as I shall discuss further in the next chapter, has shed light on an important but often neglected aspect of the debates:[32]

> Previously a body of writing that accepted its marginal status in order to preserve its uniqueness, Arabic literature in Israel now poses an increasingly strong challenge to the canon of the majority.... As the minority literature becomes increasingly cognizant of its potential, it may find its place much closer to the core of the canon. In so doing it will also gradually leave behind its marginal role as the literature of the ethnic minority and will be incorporated—so we may hope—as a legitmate and potent partner in Israeli literature. (p. 33)

CHAPTER 6

POSTZIONISM, POSTMODERNISM, AND POSTCOLONIAL THEORY: A RADICAL POSTZIONIST CRITIQUE

If we continue to speak the same language to each other, we will reproduce the same story. Begin the same stories all over again. Don't you feel it? Listen: men and women around us all sound the same. Same arguments, same quarrels, same scenes. Same attractions and separations. Same difficulties, the impossibility of reaching each other. Same...same...always the same.... This currency of alternatives and oppositions, choices and negotiations, has no value for us. (Irigary 1988, 205)

The essential political problem for the intellectual [is] that of ascertaining the possibility of constituting a new politics of truth. The problem is not changing people's consciousnesses—or what's in their heads—but the political, economic, institutional regime of the production of truth. (Foucault 1984a, 74)

INTRODUCTION

As we have seen, Shammas and Habiby effectively represent the powerful impact of zionist discourse and practices on the everyday life of Palestinian Arabs, particularly those living in Israel. As depicted by Shammas and Habiby, zionism has helped create conditions that have rendered the Palestinians a colonized people, culturally as well as physically. Positioned at the margins of Israeli society and speaking in the voices of the minority, Shammas and Habiby have revealed the exclusionary effects of zionist discourse that represents Israel as a Jewish state or a state of the Jewish people. Uncovering the fault lines of Israeli democracy, they show the inherent contradiction between the official claim that Israel is "an independent Jewish state in Palestine" and the promise that the state will "promote the development of the country for the benefit of all of its inhabitants" and "uphold the full social and political equality of all its citizens, without distinction of race, creed or sex; will guarantee full freedom of conscience, worship, education and culture."[1]

Shammas and Habiby also subvert the process of "forgetting" that informs the historical narratives of nation-states.[2] They convincingly depict the violence, physical as well as cultural, inscribed in the beginnings of the state and the technologies of power that continue to operate in Israeli society. Whether or not one chooses to call it colonialism, their graphic depictions of the multiple and diverse ways in which power is imbricated in the prevailing Israeli political, social, and cultural discourse reveal the limitations of conventional academic discourse in uncovering the power relations that permeate all social and cultural formations.

As discussed in chapter 4, Israeli scholars like Kimmerling and Shafir designate zionist settlement practices as colonialist. Comparing these practices to those of other colonialist nations, they significantly problematize conventional Israeli academic discourse and the historical narratives that it produced.[3] Most Israeli historians and social scientists, resisting their interpretations, have tended to ignore or minimize the power relations brought about and legitimated by zionism. Instead, they get caught up in such formalistic issues as whether or not zionism actually fits the colonialism category.[4] Emphasizing the uniqueness of zionism as a nationalist movement driven by humane concerns, most Israeli scholars continue to argue that colonialist motives were lacking among zionist leaders. Thus, the debates surrounding the work of Kimmerling and Shafir tend to assume the form of: "Was zionism 'really' a colonialist enterprise?" When we read the writings of Shammas and Habiby, however, these debates appear quite superficial.

The reluctance in Israel to seriously confront the power effects of zionist discourse is not unique to the academy. Throughout Israel, in the academic community, in the government, in school curricula, and in the popular media, the powerful exclusionary effects of essentialistic zionist discourse continue to be felt. Notwithstanding the new historians and critical sociologists, serious efforts to represent the complex power relations within Israeli society continue to be the exception throughout Israeli culture. As Dominguez (1989) has argued, for a nation to acknowledge such relations is to "acknowledge...having more power than we may wish to have or be comfortable having" (p. 191).

Nonetheless, a small group of Israeli intellectuals and academicians, whose writings form the subject matter of this chapter, argue that the refusal to acknowledge the centrality of power relations occludes the actual conditions of Israeli life, particularly as they relate to Palestinian Arabs both inside and outside of Israel. Deeply affected by the Israeli–Palestinian conflict and by what they see as Israel's oppressive and exclusionary practices, they find unacceptable the taken-for-granted discursive framework within which Israeli public debates are carried out. This has led them to take postzionist discourse in a new direction.

Thus, even as the debates over the new historiography and critical sociology were heating up, another group of critics, a distinct minority, was already formulating an alternative form of postzionist critique. To distinguish this newer, theoretically reflective form of postzionist critique from that which I discussed in chapter 4, I shall, notwithstanding the problems of such a designation, refer to it as postmodern postzionism.[5] As I shall soon make clear, my usage of the concept "postmodern" differs decidedly from the loose and superficial usage by critics of postzionism discussed in chapter 4.

Combining theoretical reflection and research with social and cultural critique, these writers draw extensively on cultural studies, postcolonial studies, feminist criticism, and other theories commonly subsumed under the term postmodernism. Influenced by Foucault, Derrida, Deleuze, Guattari, Bourdieu, White, Bhabha, and French feminist theorist and psychotherapist Kristeva, they consider problematic many of the premises that the new historians and critical sociologists take for granted. Rather than engage in questions of historical and social scientific methodology, they focus on the discursive and representational practices through which scholars produce their representations and interpretations.[6]

However, the primary concerns driving these critics are by no means theoretical. For them, theory is significant only insofar as it can affect social and cultural realities. Their turn to theory, for the most part, is a function of their commitment to changing the power relations in Israeli life, particularly, but by no means limited to, those involving Palestinians. The major site for the production of their postmodern critique of zionism is the journal *Theory and Criticism* [*Teoria Uvikoret*].[7]

The events leading up to the establishing of this journal help clarify the factors contributing to the formation of this distinctive form of postzionist critique.[8] In October 1987, Adi Ophir of Tel Aviv University and Hanan Hever, then teaching at the Hebrew University, formed a protest group called 21st Year (*Shanah esrim veehad*—a reference to the twenty-one years of Israeli occupation of the West Bank and Gaza).[9] Dissatisfied with the form and pace of protest by the existing peace movements in which they were active participants, the group sought, in the words of one of its founders, "a framework for active involvement and ongoing practical activity" in ways not currently available within the existing peace movements.[10] Its charter states:

> The presence of the occupation [in Israeli life] is total. Our struggle against the
> occupation must therefore also be total. We shall resolutely refuse to collabo-
> rate with the system of occupation in all of its manifestations. Refusal is the
> only morally and politically sound form of participation in Israeli society dur-
> ing the occupation. Refusal is...a source of hope for our moral integrity as
> Israelis. (in Bar On 1996a, 196)

In June 1988, Ophir went to prison for his refusal to perform reserve
duty in the occupied territories. In his statement to Yitzhak Rabin, then
minister of defense, Ophir explained why, after twenty years of regular and
reserve duty, he felt "compelled to disobey an order." Referring to the
Intifada as "a fight for freedom, whose only aim is release from Israeli
rule," he spoke of the grave injustices and human rights violations perpetrated by Israel against the Palestinians: "Under the present circumstances,"
he wrote, "you are not calling on me to defend Israel's security, but to participate in the enslavement of another people." Objecting to what he saw as
the erosion of Israeli democracy, Ophir argued that "the continued occupation is far more threatening to Israeli democracy than my own refusal to
serve, or the past or future refusal of my friends."[11]

In early 1989, Ophir, Hever, and a number of fellow members of 21st
Year went to the Palestinian town of Qualqilya to protest the demolition of
the house of a family whose son was a suspected terrorist. Unbeknownst to
the group, the Israeli army had closed off the area that morning. Refusing
the army's order to leave the area, twenty-seven of the protesters who
entered the town were arrested and imprisoned for seven days.[12] This experience, together with the differing positions within the group, led them to
reflect on the long-term implications of ongoing political protest for their
future professional and personal lives and their responsibilities as intellectuals.[13]

Several members concluded that they would be most effective by formulating and disseminating a critical discourse that could reveal the unjust
manifestations of power in Israeli society and culture.[14] One of their basic
concerns was the role that the intellectual could and should play in Israeli
culture. An unpublished document written by Hever and Ophir (n.d.) indicates their basic concerns at that time:

> The current political and moral situation in Israel has sharpened the question
> of the role of the intellectual and the academician in Israeli culture. Many of us
> participate in different forms of political action and activities in opposition to
> the occupation. But there is no [adequate] intellectual response to the challenge
> presented to us by the current historical situation. (p. 1)

Ophir and Hever argued that the need to respond immediately to the
demands of the political struggle had taken its toll on their intellectual prac-

tice and had "deepened the gap between that political practice and the theory that feeds it." In the academy, their efforts to integrate critical-political reflection with their academic work were met by "indifference, expressions of contempt, or explicit opposition." In their view, their inability to distance themselves in order to engage in theoretical, critical reflection is tantamount to "participating in the culture of occupation and the apparatuses that legitimate and reproduce it." What was needed, they argued, was a context that would enable them to combine the study of culture and its critique. Such a critique had to be, insofar as possible, free of excessive limits imposed by disciplinary boundaries.

Clearly reflecting the impact of Foucault, Ophir and Hever spoke of the need for linking theoretical debates to the study of local realities, the historicization of the sociocultural field, the genealogical reconstruction of key cultural and political concepts, and the identification of the culture's fault lines:

> Historicization is necessary in order to make possible the critical understanding of the competing theories of the Israeli culture. We are basically speaking of the foundational categories and the key concepts of Israeli discourse (zionist, pioneering, nation, state, religion) and the accepted descriptions of the recognized lines of division (Jew/Gentile; secular/religious; Eastern/Western; National/leftist; and so on.) We wish to try to understand the focal points of conflict in terms that are free of the imprint of the reigning ideologies. (p. 2)

Toward this end, Ophir and Hever suggested the formation of an interdisciplinary group devoted to the study and critique of culture that, meeting regularly, would focus on specific questions and agreed-upon texts. The vision underlying this group was that of "a kind of radical academy, that would develop and examine its analytic tools through critical reflection on the society in which it lives."

The group met for more than a year during which time many members clarified their theoretical positions and honed their critical skills. One highly significant result was a decision to publish a journal. In 1991 *Theory and Criticism* began publication. Published by the Van Leer Institute in Jerusalem and edited since its inception by Ophir, *Theory and Criticism* quickly emerged as the primary site of a distinctive, theoretically informed critique of zionist discourse and Israeli culture.

THEORY AND CRITICISM: THE SEARCH FOR AN ALTERNATIVE ISRAELI CRITICAL DISCOURSE

Before examining specific articles published in the journal over the past eight years, it will be helpful to briefly describe some of the characteristic themes and theoretical approaches that distinguish it from other journals in Israel.[15] Like the proposal formulated by Ophir and Hever, the journal clearly shows the impact of Foucault, whose writings are frequently cited by many contributors. One of *Theory and Criticism*'s distinguishing characteristics is the emphasis on power as the fundamental organizing force in social and cultural life. Many writers analyze discursive and material practices in Israel—the rules, regulations, social arrangements, institutions, and cultural forms—that produce and disseminate power.[16]

Expanding on themes only touched upon by the postzionist critics discussed in chapter 4, many articles emphasize the ways in which knowledge, particularly the knowledge produced by academic discourse, is implicated in power relations. Of particular concern are the practices through which this knowledge functions to marginalize and exclude such "Others" as Palestinians, women, and Jews of Middle Eastern origin. This concern is one that the journal clearly shares with postmodern theory:[17]

> We can, rather brutally, characterize postmodern thought (the phrase is useful rather than happy) as that thought which refuses to turn the Other into the Same. Thus it provides a theoretical space for what postmodernity denies: otherness. Postmodern thought also recognizes, however, that the Other can never speak for itself as the Other. (During 1993, 449)

A second distinguishing characteristic of the postmodern and postcolonial critique produced in *Theory and Criticism* is the shift in focus from historical and social scientific methodology to discursive and representational practices. This is reflected in the writings of historians Gabi Piterberg and Amnon Raz-Krakotzkin, anthropologists Dani Rabinowitz and Gil Eyal, cultural critics such as Ariella Azoulay and Sara Chinski, and literary scholar Hannan Hever. Each analyzes practices by which Israeli scholars have constructed specifically zionist interpretations of history, culture, and space and their exclusionary effects. Informing their critique is Foucault's (1984c) insight that discourse is not only "that which expresses struggles or systems of domination, but that for which and by which, one struggles; it is power which one is struggling to seize" (p. 110).

In contrast to the postzionist scholars discussed in chapter 4, many of the contributors to *Theory and Criticism* deprivilege academic discourse. They thus regard academic discourses such as history and social science as no more than, but no less than, alternative ways of organizing, conceptualizing, analyzing, producing, and disseminating knowledge. While several new historians and critical sociologists called attention to the power effects of historical discourse, they continued to assign it a privileged position. In contrast, writers in *Theory and Criticism* subject historical and social scientific discourse to an extensive critique. A basic concern of this critique is the role of power in the construction of representations of the past and the ways in which these representations empower or disempower specific groups.

A third recurring theme in the journal is the problematization of modernistic discourses that privilege time over space and history over geography.[18] Historians and social scientists, focusing on the temporal rather than the spatial, tend to treat space as fixed, passive, and given. Dissenting from this position, writers like Azoulay, Chinski, and Eyal criticize the spatializing practices that impose specific meanings on particular territories such as the land of Israel. In the process, they make clear the power effects of those practices.

A fourth distinctive theme in the journal is the critique of essentialistic notions of identity and the ways in which they are imbricated in power relations. A number of authors analyze the discursive processes through which identities, individual as well as collective, are produced in Israeli culture. Providing space for the voices of women, the journal analyzes the ways in which gender differences are constructed and inscribed in Israeli society. It also analyzes the discursive practices with which Palestinian Arabs are positioned in Israeli society. Through contributions from the philospher Azmi Bishara, now a member of Knesset, and Ahmad Saidi, a social scientist, the journal also provides space for Palestinian voices.

These articles form part of the critique of what the editor referred to as the "complex social and cultural mechanisms through which identity is constructed or negated." Emphasizing the contingency of these mechanisms, the journal calls attention to the power relations that make it possible for them "to represent the combination of events that gave rise to them as natural law, as essence or mission" (Volume 5, p. 3). Analyzing the common cultural practice of essentializing or naturalizing identities, the journal provides numerous examples of how Israeli culture is, to paraphrase Derrida, haunted by its Others.[19]

Finally, many of the writers, eschewing essentialistic conceptions of nation, society, culture, and history, highlight their contingency.[20] Rather than trace the historical origin and development of supposedly preexisting entities such as the Israeli nation, society, or culture, they analyze the discursive processes by means of which these "entities" are constructed. In the process, they problematize concepts that most Israelis take for granted. This, again, connects them to a basic component of postmodern criticism:

> A postmodern conception deviates from a modern one in understanding the categories by which social life is organized as historically emergent rather than naturally given, as multivalent rather than unified in meaning, and as the frequent result and possible present instrument in struggles of power. (Nicholson and Seidman 1995, 26)

Theory and Criticism effectively incorporates postcolonial, poststructural, and feminist theory into Israeli critical discourse.[21] One strategy for doing this is to publish translated excerpts from the writings of Foucault, Bhabha, feminist postcolonial critic Gayatri Chakravorty Spivak, social theorist Slavoj Žižek, and French postmodern philosopher Jean François Lyotard. However, beyond simply publishing these excerpts, the editor seeks to position them so as to frame political and cultural debates in Israel.

A clear example of this practice is the following editorial comment on a translated excerpt from Homi Bhabha:

> The system of knowledge/power involved in the establishment of identity and the establishing of the other always includes the multiple meanings and values of the different subject positions spread over the field of power relations between the hegemonic "I" (which could be, for example, western, male, Christian, Jewish) and the dominated "other" (mizrahi, female, Jew, Goy, respectively). Thus, we need complex strategies of cultural or political activity, because every resistance—including artistic and theoretical—contains a grain of cooperation, and vice versa. Bhabha's discussion focuses on the relations of rule and the systems of knowledge/power in the colonial or post-colonial culture, and is also relevant [literally, its writing is good], I propose, for our culture. (Volume 5, pp. 3–4)

Extending the postzionist critique far beyond the point to which it had been taken by critical social scientists and "new historians," the postmodern postzionists writing in *Theory and Criticism* have uncovered power relations inscribed in such areas of Israeli culture as art, ethnography, museums, education, literature, law, and the academy.[22]

For complex reasons that fall outside the purview of this study, Israeli intellectuals and the Israeli academic community have been slow to make use of postmodern and postcolonial theory, cultural studies, and feminist theory.[23] As a result, theoretical problems heatedly debated by scholars in Europe, North America, and Australia have produced few echoes in Israel. Rarely in Israeli does one encounter academic journals or conferences that highlight the names of Derrida, Foucault, feminist theorists Judith Butler and Joan Wallach Scott, cultural critics Stuart Hall and Paul Gilroy, or postcolonial critics Edward Said, Homi Bhabha, and Gayatri Chakravorty Spivak. For a growing number of Western academicians and intellectuals these names are household words and their writings have had a profound impact on the ways in which scholars outside Israel talk about politics, culture, and society. In Israel, this is not the case.

Outside Israel, a select group of scholars have grounded critiques of zionism and Israeli culture in postmodern, postcolonial, and cultural theory. These include cultural critics Ella Shohat and Ammiel Alcalay, the anthropologist Virginia Dominguez, who is strongly influenced by poststructuralist theory, and the cultural critic and scholar of Talmudic culture Daniel

Boyarin. The fact that these writings, mostly products of what zionists call exile, have been essentially excluded from the postzionism debates in Israel is an important commentary on the intellectual boundaries that circumscribe Israeli cultural discourse and the continuing effects of the zionist spatial binary of homeland and exile.[24]

Although a critique of zionist discourse and practice is a recurring theme in *Theory and Criticism,* neither the journal nor all of its contributors openly identify as postzionist or postmodern. Moreover, contributors do not share a common perspective on zionism or postzionism. Nonetheless, numerous articles critically explore the various ways in which zionist discourse continues to produce, perpetuate, and legitimate distinct forms of power relations. Problematizing and deconstructing such foundational zionist concepts as nation, history, identity, subject, culture, homeland, and exile, the journal provides a forum for a new, reflective, theoretically informed postzionist critique.

Although many articles use modernist discourse, the effects of postmodern theory is evident throughout.[25] Arguing in *Theory and Criticism* that "the representation of reality is the political question with a capital P" (Volume 2, p. 3), the editors repeatedly call attention to the production of meaning in Israeli culture and the resulting power effects. Repeatedly, one encounters the recurring usage of such concepts as discourse, power, representation, positioning, and the "Other," which are common to postmodern and postcolonial discourse. In contrast to the modernist view of culture as inherently benign and humanizing, *Theory and Criticism* represents it as a site of conflict. This is consistent with the postmodern conception

> [that] deviates from a modern one in understanding the categories by which social life is organized as historically emergent rather than naturally given, as multivalent rather than unified in meaning, and as the frequent result and possible present instrument in struggles of power. (Nicholson and Seidman 1995, 26)[26]

POSTCOLONIAL THEORY AND THE CRITIQUE OF COLONIALISM

Not satisfied with the ways in which conventional historical and social science discourse frames the discussion of colonialism, theorists like Edward Said (a Palestinian-born professor of literature and theory at Columbia University), Homi Bhabha (an Indian-born scholar who teaches at the University of Chicago), and Gayatri Spivak (an Indian-born feminist and postcolonial theorist) have contributed to the production of an alternative critical postcolonial discourse.[27] Drawing on writers such as Foucault and Derrida, they have played a decisive role in moving the discussion of colonialism beyond the limitations imposed by conventional academic discourse.[28] Critically exploring the discourse and practices of Western scholars and writers and the knowledge that these produce, they have shown how they function to establish and preserve colonialist structures and relations. What literary scholars read as benign, humanizing expressions of truth and beauty is, to these critics, part of an oppressive apparatus. They have, therefore, opened new avenues for the critique of colonialism and other oppressive practices.[29]

One of the few Israeli scholars to apply postcolonial theory to the analysis of Israeli culture is Hannan Hever, a founder of *Theory and Criticism* and a regular contributor. In an article entitled "Hebrew through the Pen of An Arab: Six Chapters on Anton Shammas's *Arabesques*," Hever, a professor of Hebrew literature at Tel Aviv University, analyzed the political effects of Shammas' writings and their significance for a critique of Israeli culture. In this and subsequent articles on Shammas, Hever provides an important link between Israeli critical discourse and the writings of Shammas discussed in the previous chapter.[30]

Hever's article first appeared in a special edition of the English-language American journal *Cultural Critique* devoted to the problem of minority discourse. As formulated by the editors of the book that resulted, minority discourse is best understood as "a theoretical articulation of the political and cultural structures that connect different minority cultures in their subjugation and opposition to majority culture" (JanMohamed and Lloyd 1990, ix). In this article and others, Hever reads Shammas' Hebrew novel *Arabesques* as a powerful exemplar of what French philosophers Deleuze and Guattari call a minority literature.[31] While written in the language of the majority, minority literature problematizes the premises on which the majority literature rests.[32] As an Arab writing in Hebrew, Hever argues, Shammas problematizes the dominant zionist conception of Hebrew literature as Jewish literature and the dominant conception of Israel/Hebrew culture.

According to Hever (1990), "Shammas's decision to write in the Other's language provides a glimmer of hope, a possible way out of the political and cultural dead end in which Israeli society now finds itself" (p. 267). In fact, asserts Hever, "Shammas may well have written the most truly Hebrew novel yet written" (p. 267). In Hever's reading, Shammas' novel, written from the perspective of the oppressed minority, has the effect of revealing several paradoxes in Israeli culture. While Israel claims to be a democracy, it disenfranchises its non-Jewish minority, proclaiming itself a state of the Jewish people. At the same time, although an occupying majority, Israelis adopt "the linguistic and behavioral style of the minority" (p. 272). In addition, although 20 percent of the citizens of the state are Palestinian Arabs, the dominant Israeli discourse, excluding the Palestinian population, represents the cultural identity of the state as Jewish. Finally, by framing his narrative in terms of the experiences of Palestinian minority,

Shammas subverts the notion of time that pervades the dominant Jewish discourse.

Shammas, according to Hever (1990), demands of Israeli Jews "that they change the rules of the game—that, as Jews, they reexamine the function that keeping old scores and accounts has in confusing the issues of their political and moral situation today" (p. 274). Shammas also brings the dominant Israeli linear historical discourse into confrontation with a cyclical discourse that finds its paradigm in the arabesque, with its interweaving lines.

Of particular concern to Hever is Shammas' challenge to Israeli liberal discourse, which desires "to change the surface formulation of the stereotype [of the Arab] without addressing the presuppositions of their own discourse" (p. 283). Hever thus reiterates *Theory and Criticism*'s basic premise that to effectively change Israeli cultural and political realities, one must first unmask and then change the rules and practices of zionist discourse itself. As read by Hever, Shammas' novel is, as I indicated in chapter 5, a powerful form of postzionist critique.

THE CRITIQUE OF HISTORICAL DISCOURSE

Central to the postmodernist critique of zionism is the emphasis on history as a discursive practice. The critique of historical discourse in the pages of *Theory and Criticism* provides a clear example of the differences separating a postmodern form of postzionism from the postzionism of the new historians and critical sociologists. Scholars like Kimmerling, Pappe, and Ram, although pushing up against the limits of historical and social scientific discourse, nonetheless continue to operate according to the disciplinary practices that determine the boundaries of these fields. Notwithstanding significant differences among the practices of historians and social scientists, they both operate on a playing field with particular rules. While it is still somewhat of an overgeneralization, for our purposes, let us say that these scholars operate according to particular evidentiary standards, rules of documentation, and forms of argumentation.

Moreover, while scholars like Kimmerling, Pappe, and Ram called attention to the exclusionary effects of scholarly discourse, they nonetheless continue to adhere to a representational view of language. Distinguishing between events, reality, and the language used to talk about them, they treat language as a means of mirroring or reflecting them. In their view, a major task of scholars still appears to be developing interpretations that more accurately represent events, past and present.[33]

Postmodern critics of historical and social scientific discourse refuse to accept the rules established by these disciplines as universally binding. Following Foucault (1984c, 118–20), they regard the setting and policing of disciplinary boundaries to be part of scholars' efforts to retain control over the production and distribution of knowledge.

Other postmodern critics, like cultural critic Hayden White and literary critic Elizabeth Ermarth, focus on the linguistic and literary practices used by scholars to produce their interpretations.[34] Rejecting the representational concept of language that informs these academic disciplines, they argue that our only access to reality is through the discourse that we employ, and it is this discourse, rather than the inaccessible "reality" it is supposed to mirror, that should be the object of our analysis and critique. Postmodern critics thus avoid arguments over methodology and evidence, analyzing instead the discursive practices through which representations of the past and present are constructed. Accordingly, it is on discourse, rather than scholarly methodology, evidence, and accuracy, that they focus their critique.[35] Underlying their critique is an approach to language that focuses on effects and functions rather than meaning.[36]

According to postmodernist critics like philosopher Hans Kellner (1989):

> rather than merely providing a record of facts about the past, historical discourse and the scholars that produce it are engaged in creating meanings from the scattered, and profoundly meaningless debris we find around us. (p. 10)

According to Kellner, rather than discovering or uncovering the truth of past events, historians "create events from a seamless flow and invent meanings that produce patterns within that flow" (p. 24).[37]

Either unaware of or concealing their discursive strategies, historians present their work as descriptions of reality. While postmodern critics do not necessarily deny the existence of a "reality" independent of discourse, they insist that our only access to that reality is through discourse.[38]

> Facts themselves are invariably constituted by communities through defining, naming parts, sorting these designated objects, devising conceptions of the relations between them, distinguishing opportunities and contraries, selecting beginnings and endings, eliding gaps, evaluating relative importance among objects or categories, creating hierarchies, finding or creating new objects that will differ from existing objects in detail while resembling them in kind (as evidence), and so forth. (Kellner 1989, 326)

Thus, instead of presenting accurate representations of reality, historians produce what French cultural critic Roland Barthes has referred to as "reality effects."[39]

These distinctions are very important to the postzionism debates. Critics of postzionists take it for granted that they and their opponents are both playing by the same disciplinary rules of the academy. Insofar as new historians and critical social scientists accept those rules, then they and their critics do seem to share a common set of rules and criteria of evaluation.

On the other hand, the postmodern critics discussed in this chapter are critical of modernist academic discourse. Accordingly, to criticize them for not adhering to the rules and practices of that discourse is to mistakenly assume that they share the same interpretive premises as their zionist critics. However, the postmodern postzionists operate with a different set of assumptions than their academic critics. Consequently, as we shall shortly see, the critique leveled against them by these critics is based on what philosophers have called a category error, that is, they have placed the practices of those whom they are criticizing in the wrong category or discursive framework.

We can gain a clearer idea of these differences by turning to two contributors to *Theory and Criticism,* Ben Gurion University scholars Amnon Raz-Krakotzkin and Gabi Piterberg. Influenced by Said and Hayden White, among others, they aim their critique at Israeli historical discourse and the Orientalist, colonialist premises that inform it. Far from accepting the premises of that historical discourse, they deconstruct the binary foundations that ground zionist interpretations of history. In so doing, they introduce into Israeli cultural discourse a way of talking about the past that differs significantly from that of conventional historians.

Raz-Krakotzkin (1993), combining ideas drawn from the writings of Foucault, Said, and Walter Benjamin, advocates a historical approach in which the past is explored not to uncover what happened, but rather as the basis for changing the consciousness of the present. His goal, therefore, is to see if the critical study of the past "is able to suggest possibilities for the present" (p. 49). The question that concerns him is not "what actually happened," but how the images of the past influence the present reality in which we read that past (p. 49). For Raz-Krakotzkin, this critical approach to the study of the past serves as the basis of a critique of zionist discourse.

In a two-part article entitled "Exile in the Midst of Sovereignty," Raz-Krakotzkin (1993 and 1994) focuses his critique of zionist discourse on the fundamental concept of "negation of the diaspora." In his view, those postzionists who, characterizing the present as "postzionist," see no need to engage in a critique of zionist discourse, are only reinforcing zionism:

> The conclusion that there is no need to analyze the foundations of zionist ideology actually strengthens its foundational assumptions, making it possible to ignore the central function played by "negation of the diaspora" in forming Israeli political and cultural discourse. (1993, 26)[40]

Raz-Krakotzkin, acknowledging his indebtedness to Said and other postcolonial theorists, is particularly concerned with the effects of zionist discourse in Israeli historical writing. In these particular essays, Raz-Krakotzkin builds his critique of Israeli historical discourse around the writings of the German cultural critic Walter Benjamin.[41]

Like Foucault and Said, Raz-Krakotzkin approaches history as discourse.[42] Of particular concern to Raz-Krakotzkin are the discursive processes in Israeli historical discourse, which have resulted in the silencing of the voices of the other. As Benjamin sought to combat fascism by criticizing its conception of history, Raz-Krakotzkin (1993) uses his critique of zionist historiography as the grounds for a critique of exclusionary, oppressive Israeli practices (p. 37). Like Benjamin, his interpretation of history is particularly concerned with "the ways in which the events of the past are grasped from the perspective of the oppressed" (p. 38). Seeking to provide a hearing for the silenced voices of the victims of zionist discourse and practice, Raz-Krakotzkin, in this essay, emphasizes the need to recover and restore the voices of the oppressed Palestinian minority.

Eschewing the view of history as a detached and objective enterprise, Raz-Krakotzkin regards it as praxis, a politically engaged act. Critical of the positivistic scholarly approach of "new historians" such as Benny Morris, Raz-Krakotzkin describes the study of the past as "a practice that exists in the present in order to form 'a history of the present' in the full sense of the term." Raz-Krakotzkin thus rejects the positivistic premise that the past is fixed and closed and, therefore, susceptible to objective representation. Instead, the past is an active process carried on in the present. Consequently, the goal of historical practice is neither to uncover the events of the past nor to engage in self-flagellation by uncovering the "sins" of the past. The historian, critically appropriating the past, can actually help change it:

> Such a critical engagement with the past reveals the limits of the consciousness that was inherited through the authoritative representation of the past and opens possibilities of a new consciousness. The purpose is not to return to the past in any way...but to return to the present that same past whose denial is a part of the present. (p. 49)

Proclaiming his desire to restore to Israeli cultural discourse the foundations of which it has been systematically dispossessed, Raz-Krakotzkin asks: "How do the images of the past influence the reality within which we read that past?" (p. 49).

Central to Raz-Krakotzkin's critique is the historical fate of the Palestinian Arabs, their expulsion in 1949, and the implication of zionist discourse and practice in creating the conditions for that fate. What is needed, he argues, is a critique of that discourse and of the current forms of Israeli political culture that enable Israelis to systematically deny and forget the events of the past. Specifically, Raz-Krakotzkin singles out the concepts of *shelilat hagalut* [negation of the diaspora] and the "new Hebrew."

In an analysis that problematically emphasizes ideas with little attention to practice, Raz-Krakotzkin attributes to the notion of *shelilat hagalut* a central role in the subordination and marginalization of Jews of Middle Eastern origin.[43] The zionist image of the "new Hebrew," constructed by Ashkenazi zionist leaders, privileged European Jews while disempowering non-European Jews. Raz-Krakotzkin sees a parallel between the early zionists' critique of the European Jewish culture as a culture of exile and the later denigration of the "exilic" culture of Mizrahi Jews following the establishment of the state.[44] Mizrahi Jews did not view the move to Israel as a means of abandoning the distinctive patterns of life they had developed in their lands of origin, but rather as a means of preserving and fulfilling them. However, entering a culture that was shaped and controlled by Ashkenazi Jews, the Mizrahi Jews soon learned the price for becoming Israeli. To become integrated into Israeli society, it was necessary to divest themselves of exactly what they treasured, the specific cultural practices that they had brought with them and through which they constructed their identity. In addition to being victims of this process of cultural domination, Mizrahi Jews were positioned at the bottom of the socioeconomic ladder.

However, for all of the oppressive effects of zionist discourse on the Mizrahi Jews, they, according to Raz-Krakotzkin, were not the primary victims of its exclusionary effects. The primary victims, he argues, were the Palestinian Arabs. In zionist discourse, as discussed in chapter 1, the oppressive conditions of exile can only be ended through the return of the Jews to their homeland. Consequently, the conflict between the indigenous Palestinian population and the Jews was situated within the context of zionism's teleological reading of history. By contextualizing the Jewish return to the land and the conflict that it precipitated with the Palestinians in terms of European Jewish history, zionist discourse, and the historiography that it produced, decontextualized the Israeli–Palestinian conflict from its Middle Eastern setting. It thereby neutralized the role of zionist settlement practices as a precipitating factor in the conflict. At the same time, in framing the Jewish settlement of the land within the discourse of exile and return, zionism has the effect of excluding Palestinians from Israeli public discourse:

> The definition of zionist settlement as an expression of "shelilat hagalut" [negation of diaspora] and "shivat haam" [the return of the nation] to its homeland prevented relating to the collective yearnings of the local Arab population and its perspective. It [also] undoubtedly made it impossible to turn the fact of this collective's existence into an essential foundation for establishing a new Jewish identity. The historical conception of shelilat hagalut, the emptiness of Jewish time that separates the loss of sovereignty over the land and its renewed settle-

ment is completed in a direct way through the image of the land—the place for the realization and resolution of history—as an "empty land." (Raz-Krakotzkin 1993, 44)

The discourse of *shelilat hagalut,* argues Raz-Krakotzkin, has the further effect of excluding Palestinian perspectives from Israeli interpretations of history. This is evident in Israeli historiography's refusal to seriously engage in such central issues as the dispossession of the Arabs from their lands, the relation of the Palestinians to the British mandate, the reasons for their opposition to the Balfour Declaration, and the factors leading to the creation of the Palestinian refugee problem.

According to Raz-Krakotzkin (1993), the discourse of the "negation of the diaspora" continues to define the self-consciousness of Israeli Jews, shaping their conception of history, their collective memory, and the collective identity that is grounded in them (p. 23). It thus has "far-reaching consequences for determining the cultural and political boundaries within which the political consensus is defined." Linked to such ideas as "right to the land" and "ownership of the land," the discourse of negation of the diaspora legitimates the zionist/Israeli practice of denying the "existence" of the Palestinian Other.

Representing the land as the Jewish homeland and the culture produced there as Jewish culture has the effect of concealing the role of the Palestinians in the formation of Israeli and, consequently, Jewish cultural identity. Moreover, it renders Palestinian claims to the land irrelevant to the formation of Israeli identity and collective consciousness. This exclusion is reinforced by a sophisticated cultural apparatus that prevents a discussion of these and other historical topics, resulting in

> a kind of active cultural practice that defines the boundaries of the consensus and prevents any discussion of the fate of the refugees—whether out of an inability to deal with the guilt feelings, or because of the tendency to preserve the myth.[45]

Raz-Krakotzkin includes left-wing parties in his critique. Although advocating peace and reconciliation with the Palestinians, such groups refuse to grant a hearing to the historical memories/perspectives of the Palestinians. Refusing to honestly confront the yearnings and memories of the Palestinian Other, the Israeli left, argues Raz-Krakotzkin, wishes only to get rid of the territories.[46]

Alongside his deconstructive analysis of "negation of the diaspora," Raz-Krakotzkin (1994) makes a constructive move in which he tries to recover the concept of exile and transform it into a positive, albeit dezionized category. He finds the sources for such a dezionized concept in traditional Jewish sources:

The Jewish language makes it possible to criticize these distinctions, pouring a concrete cultural content into the abstract political demand for pluralism, without slipping into a dangerous particularism. Here the significance of the concept "galut" as historical consciousness becomes clear. Such a concept makes it possible to preserve the relative autonomy of different histories without ignoring the connection, that the present creates, without ignoring the power of definitions of the present. (p. 130)

Turning again to Benjamin, Raz-Krakotzkin (1993) attempts to integrate political and theological discourse, a move that separates him from other postmodernist postzionists and from postmodern discourse in general. Just as Benjamin regarded redemption as a recurring possibility, the concept of *galut* incorporates the yearning for redemption. Thus, the concept of *galut* represents an "absence, the consciousness of being in an incomplete present, the consciousness of a blemished world." To yearn for redemption means to engage in political activity "that values the perspective of the oppressed, the only perspective from which a moral stance can develop" (p. 39).[47]

Raz-Krakotzkin also makes the somewhat surprising claim that the concept of *galut* he advocates is in fact compatible with central zionist concerns. In no way, he argues, does the zionist concept of Israel as a refuge or the fundamental connection of the Jewish people to the land depend upon negating the diaspora. On the contrary, the concept of *galut* enables "a Jewish identity based on the recognition of the potential embodied in the bi-nationality of the land" (p. 49). This, in turn, sets the conditions for a political discourse whose starting point is "the recognition of the Palestinian collective as a group with a historical consciousness." This entails remembering both "the denied Jewish past and the denied Palestinian past." By identifying with and assuming responsibility for, attending to, and responding to "the consciousness of the conquered Palestinian," the Jew recovers the "principles embodied in the theological concept of galut" (p. 49).

However, Raz-Krakotzkin stops short of advocating a binational state. His goal is less to prescribe political solutions than to enable a change in consciousness. His call for "a decolonization of the Jewish-Israeli entity" entails not only ending the occupation but also changing the basic colonialist consciousness embodied in the concept of *shelilat hagalut*. Colonialism, in this sense, refers to the memory work that directs the forgetting. Decolonialization, in this sense, is a kind of deterritorialization that doesn't mean leaving the land. It does, however, require creating a space for the memories of the vanquished.

Raz-Krakotzkin also criticizes the ways in which the *Shoah* has been appropriated as a major vehicle for legitimating zionism, another effect of shelilat hagalut. The influence of these concepts on Israeli education and culture had the effect of isolating the discussion of the *Shoah* from the historical issues and events leading up to it. In addition, the negative attitude toward exile and privileging the building of the state helped produce a representation of the victims/survivors as passive sheep, who were contrasted with those heroes who built the new country.[48]

Raz-Krakotzkin criticizes Israeli historical scholarship for neglecting the history of the land while focusing on its significance for Jewish time. A true history of the land would discuss all of the people who dwelled in it, not just Jews. In Habiby's notion of *galut betokh hamakom,* he detects a call for recognizing the "freedom of longing for the land within the land" (Habiby 1988a, 9). He considers this to be "a new starting point of all who dwell in the land, a basis for their partnership, a basis for their separate consciousness" (Raz-Krakotzkin 1993, 52).

Another writer who engages in a postcolonial critique of zionist discourse, particularly historical discourse, is Gabi Piterberg. Of particular concern to Piterberg are the ways in which the Orientalist mentality analyzed by Said is implicated in zionist discourse. A particular object of his criticism is the Orientalist perspective that informs the dominant Israeli social scientific discourse formulated by Hebrew University sociologist S. N. Eisenstadt and his disciples (Piterberg 1995a, 98). According to Piterberg, this discourse, infused with Orientalist assumptions, has an exclusionary effect in relation to Mizrahi Jews. There is, he argues, a clear connection between the marginalized position of Mizrahi Jews and the ways in which they are represented in Israeli social scientific discourse.

Citing a study of Israeli school curricula published by the Hebrew University scholar Ruth Firer (1985), Piterberg argues that the recurring application to Mizrahi Jews of the Orientalist discourse of petrification, impotence, primitivism, decadence, backwardness, superstition, poverty, squalor, lack of culture, defective education, inferiority, and baseness clearly privileges Jews of European origin. This rhetoric, which is also characteristic of Israeli academic discourse, shapes Israeli collective memory and popular cultural discourse.

Piterberg (1995a) also finds clear evidence of an Orientalist, antidiaspora discourse in zionist historiography. Zionist historians, accepting zionism's premise that the return to the land of Israel is the ultimate goal of Jewish history, "related to Jews not as they were, but as they were supposed to be according to that same historiography."[49] Piterberg acknowledges that some zionist historians were critical of the zionist historiography's Palestine-centered approach to Jewish history. However, he argues, most of them embraced this approach together with the essentialistic notion of nation that it entailed (p. 96).[50]

According to Piterberg (1995a) "the writing and teaching of history [is]...part of the process in which modern Middle Eastern communities imagine themselves as territorial nations" (p. 81, n. 1). However, the perpetuation of the zionist-territorialist perspective in Israeli historical discourse precludes the emergence of a genuine pluralism. Acknowledging recent efforts of scholars such as Hebrew University historian Shmuel Ettinger to produce a history of Jews of the Middle East, by representing Jews as a "continuous, unified, territorial nation," such studies actually perpetuate an orientalist discourse.

In his analysis of Israeli academic discourse, Piterberg also draws upon Hayden White's critique of historical discourse and Benedict Anderson's critique of essentialistic discourses of nationalism. Piterberg rejects the essentialistic concept nation that grounds zionist discourse. Insisting that nations are culturally constructed and historically contingent, Piterberg proceeds to deconstruct such binaries as form/content, historical/imaginative (or literary) narrative, and representation/reality, which are foundational to the dominant Israeli historical discourse.

Piterberg and Raz-Krakotzkin are among a very small number of Israeli scholars who are indebted to the theoretical perspectives of Said, Young, Anderson, and White. Drawing on their works, the writers in *Theory and Criticism* open new avenues of inquiry previously neglected in Israeli scholarship. Given that these theorists have had a far-reaching impact on American and European scholars for decades, the recentness of this development in Israel is indicative of the great suspicion of current critical theory among Israeli academics. While Said's Palestinian origins and his active involvement in the Palestinian cause undoubtedly arouse suspicion among Israeli scholars, their reluctance to take his theoretical writings and those of Young, Anderson, and White seriously significantly limits their ability to critically analyze the colonialist effects of zionist discourse and Israeli practices.[51]

ISRAELI IDENTITY, ZIONIST DISCOURSE, AND THE PALESTINIAN OTHER

In *Theory and Criticism*, we encounter a heightened awareness of the relation of collective identity construction and the practices by means of which groups such as women, Jewish ethnic minorities, and Palestinians are disempowered, marginalized, or excluded. The role of the "Other" in the formation of hegemonic conceptions of Israeli collective identity is, therefore, a recurring theme.

These critics, in keeping with contemporary cultural theory, reject essentialistic notions of identity. Although postzionists have repeatedly called for Israel to become a state of all of its citizens, new historians and critical sociologists paid little attention to the cultural practices through which identity is constructed. Rejecting the underlying zionist representation of Israeli cultural identity as fixed and continuous, postmodern critics of zionism have highlighted its hybrid, heterogeneous, and fluid character.[52] Criticizing the identification of Israeli with Jewish and Jewish with Eastern European, they emphasize the diverse, often conflicted character of Israeli culture and identity.

Dani Rabinowitz, an anthropologist at the Hebrew University, analyzes the discourse used to identify and categorize the Palestinian citizens of Israel as a group, listing six basic terms used to label them: (1) The Arabs of Israel/*Arviei Yisrael,* (2) Israeli Arabs/*Aravim Yisraelim,* (3) Arabs/*Aravim,* (4) Palestinians/*Palestinim,* (5) Palestinians in Israel/*Palestinim baYisrael,* (6) Palestinians who are citizens of Israel/*Palestinim ezrahei Yisrael.*

Israelis, argues Rabinowitz (1993), find it problematic to relate to the Arab citizens of the state as "Palestinians":

> This concept alludes to one who experiences the state as an slender institutional veil that masks the true identity of the place. Terms that include the concept "Palestine" hint at the fact that the place has a primordial identity that competes with the identity assigned to it by Zionism, an identity that many Israelis see as exclusive. The changing image of the place forms a crouching shadow—an elusive essence that waits for the right moment to come out of hiding, to break the conspiracy of silence, and to impose a new old order on the place which had ignored it. (p. 145)

Yet when speaking of Arabs outside of Israel, Israelis have no difficulty referring to their national identity (Jordanians, Egyptians, etc.) rather than their (Arabic) cultural identity.[53] By using the generic concept "Arabs" to refer to the Palestinians, Israeli Jews

> divert attention from the painful topic of a place that is mired in controversy [and shift it] to the less threatening topic of cultural difference—[which] in the liberal Israeli discourse of cultural pluralism, is much more legitimate. (Rabinowitz 1993, 145)

According to Rabinowitz, "*Arviei Yisrael*" [Israeli Arabs] is actually a more politically laden term than Palestinian citizens of Israel. Although commonly used, the term is no more natural, neutral, or precise than other terms:

> Especially its having become, in the course of time, a part of the canon of describing reality makes it very difficult to remove the political baggage hidden in it. The concept "Israeli Arabs" is one of the political-historical foundations of the historical political doxa of zionist Israel, to use a term from Bourdieu. (p. 149)

Emphasizing the role of discourse in shaping identity and the political character of the struggle over discourse, Rabinowitz advocates the creation of new deliberative space with new parameters and fresh patterns of thought. In time, the Palestinians could enter such a space and struggle much more effectively for what is theirs. (p. 150)

Grounding his critique of Israeli social scientific discourse in the writings of Edward Said, and the poststructuralist anthropological theorists James Clifford and Virginia Dominguez, Rabinowitz describes his article as an exercise in "poetics of representation which is tied to the politics of representation" (p. 143). Like Clifford, he considers poetics, which simultaneously results from and reproduces power relations, as political.

SPACE AND POWER IN ISRAELI DISCOURSE

As we saw in chapter 1, territory and space comprise basic components of zionist discourse. It is not surprising, therefore, that those engaged in a critique of zionist discourse will turn to the spatializing practices whereby space is imbued with particular meanings and its boundaries are defined. Accordingly, several writers in *Theory and Criticism* focus on the power effects of spatializing practices, a recurring theme in postmodern theory. In the process, they significantly expand the scope of the postcolonial postzionist critique to areas such as art, museums, and the discourse used to represent Palestinian space.

Applying concepts drawn from Said and Bhabha to Israeli culture, Gil Eyal, then a graduate student at Tel Aviv University, examined the ways in which the dominant Israeli cultural discourse marginalizes or excludes Palestinians and Jews of Middle Eastern origin. In an article in *Theory and Criticism,* "Between East and West: The Discourse on the 'Arab Village' in Israel," Eyal (1993) analyzed the ways in which Israeli representations of space contribute to marginalizing or excluding Palestinians. Whereas zionism, like other nationalist discourses, treats space as fixed, passive and given, postmodern critics emphasize dynamic, contingent processes of spatialization. It is through these processes that particular spaces, such as the land of Israel, are imbued with meaning.[54] Highlighting the power effects of those processes, writers like Eyal significantly problematize the essentialistic discourse of space that grounds zionist practice.[55]

Analyzing research conducted both prior to 1948 and in the 1960s, Eyal argues that the concept of the "Arab village," a concept widely circulated within Israeli culture, objectified and categorized Arab space. Informing this discourse are such binaries as modern/traditional and Jew/Arab. Drawing on Said, Eyal (1993) criticizes the Orientalist, Eurocentric perspective imbedded in the dominant Israeli discourse on Arab space:

> The discourse on the history of the Arab village illustrates the manner in which Orientalism has contributed to the construction of a separate/distinctive Israeli identity [i.e., separate from the Arabs]. (p. 41)

According to Eyal, a key component of the discourse of identity is the concept of the "Arab village." In the pre-state era, there were some who stressed the Jewish connection to the East. However, after 1948, this virtually disappeared and the concept of the Arab village as an object of study and control was linked to the security needs of the state. In the discourse and practices that made possible the notion of the "village" as a distinct unit, differences between villages as well as the fact that some of the villages were actually cities were overlooked.

Eyal's analysis helps to further clarify the differences between the new historians and critical sociologists and the postmodernist critics of zionism. To Eyal, the discussion of the Arab village is (a marginal) comment on the sources/nature of "Israeli separatism." Most Israeli academicians treat the separation between Jew and Arab as given, natural, and necessary. A second, more radical group, including Gershon Shafir, have recognized that this separation was produced by an institutionalized system grounded in political, military, and economic interests on the one hand and the subordination of the Arabs on the other. However, argues Eyal, these more radical scholars fail to recognize the culturally constructed character of this separatist notion of identity, the product of particular interests and power relations. Moreover, they, like their more conservative counterparts in the academy, blind themselves to the role of the academy in producing and disseminating this notion of identity.

Drawing on Said, Eyal (1993) also analyzes the cultural processes whereby Arabs have been excluded from the boundaries of Israeli collective identity as Orientalist:

> It is important to emphasize that as a practice of establishing Israeli identity, Orientalism is a discursive practice through which the Jews supervise/watch over themselves. For when the Jew speaks the orientalist discourse, he is separated [separates him/herself] from the "oriental" and the "mesorati" that is within him, and distances himself from them. By force of this, he establishes himself as the subject of a certain manner of rule. (p. 41)

Nor is the Palestinian Arab the only victim of the dominant, Eurocentric Israeli cultural discourse. Like Piterberg and Raz-Krakotzkin, Eyal sees a clear link between Israeli Orientalist discourse and the processes that marginalize and exclude Israeli Jews of Middle Eastern origin (Mizrahim). Eyal also connects the Orientalist discourse on the Arab village, the dichotomy of Jew/Arab, and the program of development towns.

In the case of the latter, Mizrahi Jews are placed at outlying sites, which distances them from the dominant Ashkenazi population.

Eyal emphasizes the hybridity of Israeli identity, a concept that is basic to the writings of Homi Bhabha, arguing that the Arab and Middle Eastern elements in Israeli identity construction are commonly concealed or ignored. The dominant Israeli view, which rejects the Arab ("*Araviut*") dimension of Jewish culture, positions Arabs and Arab culture as "Other,"[56] as is clearly evident "in the cultural realm where representations of the collective are formulated" (p. 40). As a result of the neglect of the Arab dimension of Israeli culture, Israelis have produced only "a partially consistent identity" (p. 40).

Applying a postmodernist critique of essentialistic conceptions of space,[57] Ariella Azoulay, a social critic and art critic, and Sara Chinski problematize the zionist representation of the land of Israel as Jewish national space, the natural homeland of the Jewish people. Calling attention to the aesthetic processes and spatial practices that shape a society's collective memory, they introduce the theories of Foucault, French cultural critics Roland Barthes and Pierre Bourdieu, and French postmodern philosopher Jean-François Lyotard into Israeli discourse on space.

Azoulay (1992), highlighting such issues as borders, limits, boundaries, rules of classification and gradation, and canonization, criticizes the dominant Israeli discourse on space (p. 89).[58] Rejecting formalistic notions of representation, Azoulay advocates a critical, political approach to art that

> reveals the seams in the representational acts...the perspective/position of the representational act...and the order of power that makes possible the existence of one viewpoint while eliminating others. (p. 105)[59]

In what she deems the contemporary, postmodern situation, each individual has his/her own rhythm of time, own pace, own space. Azoulay objects to efforts to quantify, grasp, or commodify time as well as space. Like space, time has lost its organizing structure.

Azoulay (1993) also applies her critique to the cultural practices that shape historical memory. In treating spatial divisions as natural and given, nationalist movements like zionism legitimate particular hierarchies of power.[60] This is evident in zionism's representation of the land as the "homeland."[61] The zionist practice of controlling the ways in which the homeland is represented is part of an effort to "to make it possible for them to gradually control that space until they achieved control over all or part of it" (p. 89).

Among the practices that Azoulay singles out as establishing and legitimating zionist control of the land are creating archaeological sites, establishing settlements, setting up road signs, constructing public structures and monuments, carving out urban/rural spaces, and establishing museums. She is particularly concerned with the ways in which public sites and museums are used to legitimate the zionist dream of a Jewish homeland. To Azoulay (1993) these places actually function as sites for a struggle for power,

> one of the primary sites of struggle in which the certificate of ownership of the land of Israel is written and represented. This has been a continuous practice since the beginnings of the Zionist movement, through remembering/forgetting, settlement activities, maps, archaeological excavations, planning, and carving out new landscapes [*nofim*]. In Israeli society, the establishment and control of historical sites [*atarim*] through the representations created in them and disseminated through them was and remains a "hot" [*boeret*] political issue. (p. 80)

Zionists, as Habiby has so effectively shown, have sought to simultaneously remember and forget the past by erasing all traces of Arab villages and establishing in their place "authentic" Jewish historical places. In zionist discourse and in Israeli culture, sites have been represented as passive places that lie around covered by dust. When the dust is removed, "authentic" documents/objects are revealed. Zionism, regarding such sites as evidence of Jewish continuity in the land, has removed all traces of the power struggles and conflicts that had transformed them into zones of memory. It has represented cultural objects, which are the products of willful and intentional power practices, as "natural."

According to Azoulay (1993), historical museums are a microcosm of zionist practices that represent the past. As she reads them, historical museums have the effect of standardizing and controlling the (representations of the) "past," the identity of individuals and groups, and the ways in which they affiliate with the national collective. In displaying or representing the (culture of the) past, historical museums actually participate in managing the present. Museums thus play a major role in establishing a particular type of relationship between individual and collective, between citizen and nation. They thus function as "silent monuments of a time that has passed, a time in which there was a public space for memory" (p. 80).

Azoulay specifically mentions two museums, the Bezalel Institute in Jerusalem, established in 1906 as the first Jewish school of art and museum in Palestine, and the Museum of the Diaspora in Tel Aviv [*Beit HaTefuzot*].[62] The past, in Bezalel's representation, appears as simply given, with no indication of conflict. Such a representation was made possible, according to Azoulay (1993), because "the Jews who immigrated to Israel were the only ones who invested time and resources in the conquest and signification of the public space and in controlling the representations scattered in it" (p. 90). In the Museum of the Diaspora, Beit HaTefuzot, the narrative represents all Jewish communities as comprising a unity, which fosters the idea that the nation's dream of return has been realized (p. 91).

Azoulay sees the Likud victory in 1977 as a turning point in the internal Israeli struggle for control over the representation of the past. Prior to that time, a secular, Jewish, and male-dominated labor zionist hegemony controlled Israeli culture. Ignoring all competing representations of the past, including those produced by Jewish religious groups and the minority revisionist party, labor zionists marginalized such Israeli groups as Jews of Middle Eastern origin, women, revisionists, and Palestinians. In the wake of the Likud victory, new public spaces were created that subverted the previously dominant labor zionist narrative. In the decade following Likud's ascendancy in 1977, eighty new museums, 60 percent of all of the current museums in Israel, were built. Also, in the 1970s, while the ability of Palestinians to display and represent their past continued to be severely restricted, some Jewish minorities did succeed in producing their own narratives. However, these were absorbed by the dominant labor zionist narrative (Azoulay 1993, 80–90).[63]

In the 1970s, a new stage in the politicization of artistic discourse was initiated. At that time, cracks began to appear in the dominant narrative of the past leading to a struggle for control of representations and the mechanisms for their distribution. This challenge to zionism's control over processes and forms of representation became part of a larger struggle over control of land and the state. Although the 1982 war in Lebanon and the Intifada opened cracks in the dominant representations that subsequently grew larger, historical museums have not kept pace.[64] Moreover, warns Azoulay, the emergence of voice/representation of marginalized/minor groups in public space is not a sufficient indication that their uniqueness and the significance of their narratives have been recognized.[65]

Another important critique of zionist spatializing discourse and practice has been formulated by Sarah Chinski (1993, 1994). Concerned, like Azoulay, with the power effects of Israeli art, Chinski focuses on the ideological, colonialist assumptions that ground zionist and Israeli discourse. Zionism "grasps artistic endeavor as participation in the zionist project with unquestioning faith and certainty" (1993, 110).[66] According to Chinski, much Israeli art is rooted in a colonial territorialization of the artistic text. Such an approach legitimates the authenticity of a work of art in terms of cognitive geography and inscribes symbolic maps that reflect the power relations of the field. Although the constructed character of these premises are, she argues, evident for all to see, zionist discourse presents them as "natural."

To deconstruct the dominant interpretive discourse of art, Chinski advocates two moves. First, the critic must dismantle the narrative proclaimed by the discourse. At the same time, he/she must unravel the processes by means of which the interpretive discourse is produced and disseminated. Drawing upon Foucault, Chinski argues that power is a necessary part of artistic creation. A genealogical critique of zionist art reveals struggle, conquest, oppression, and the violent conquest of space (1993, 121).[67]

According to Chinski (1993, 111 ff.), devotion to progress is one of the ideological pillars of Israeli society. It follows, therefore, that a critique of that society entails a critique of modernization, a point also made by Piterberg, Rabinowitz, and Eyal. Chinski finds the tools for subverting the modernist premises that underlie Israeli culture and society in postmodernism. Calling into question the basic social and cultural premises that ground zionist discourse, postmodernism problematizes zionism.

The canonical Israeli discourse on art is, according to Chinski, premised on modernist notions of art for art's sake, the autonomy of art, and art as the basis for a critical perspective on society. However, at the same time, the prevailing Israeli notion of critical art is based on conformity to the society's values, preservation of the existing order, and enhancement of that order's embodiment of the image of authority (1993, 109).

Drawing on Benjamin, Chinski identifies the artist as a social subject who is formed by social forces, not an ingenious individual who takes a stand in relation to social forces and even seeks [*mityamer*] to influence them:

> Therefore, I will represent the artistic creation as a social practice born out of a specific system of knowledge and participating in its creation, rather than a idiosyncratic sign floating above the social forces. (1993, 113)

To support her argument, Chinski analyzes Avital Geva's "Greenhouse" project (in which the artist constructed a greenhouse for study and research) exhibited at the 1993 Venice Biennial. Criticizing the socially "engaged art" that Geva took over from Yizhak Danziger, Chinski connects it to the dominant Israeli/zionist discourse on nature and land. Seen in this way, Danziger's "engaged art," negating individualism, privileged, like zionism, the collective. In this sense, argues Chinski, engaged art simply meant art that functioned to strengthen the state and further its hegemonic goals (1993, 108–09).[68]

According to Chinksi, Geva's "Greenhouse" project also reflects the zionist commitment to doing/praxis. A consummate pragmatist, Geva pays little attention to the sociopolitical context in which he works. Chinski, through a genealogical analysis, seeks to reveal the relationship between Geva's discourse on art and such zionist values as "land" as exchange value, suppression of the other, art as a "contribution" to the zionist enterprise, the principle of *bitzua* [execution/performance] as a ritual, technology as a qualitative moral value, all of them comprising different aspects of the modernization perspective (1993, 111).

Chinski ascribes to Geva a "fetishism" of doing/making: "like a magic ritual of the collective, doing as religion, the religion of labor" (1993, 110).

This she takes to be consistent with zionism's fetishization of the Marxist notion of productive labor, "a vulgarization and a reduction" (p. 110). The zionist notion of activity/labor served as a slogan in the battle against (1) inactivity, and (2) passivity/intellectuality of *galut*.

Chinski reads the greenhouse as a metaphor for both the progressive as well as the oppressive dimensions of modernistic Israeli society. She thus describes the greenhouse as a site of total viewing [panopticon] and total policing/managing (1993, 111). In addition, the greenhouse serves as a part of an educational system that carries out the ideological work of creating docile subjects needed by a rationalist, useful, technical society (1993, 112).

Within the greenhouse itself, the technology of power operates on nature: "The nature within the greenhouse represents the positioning of the other. It is a nature lacking presence, which is inscribed, supervised, administered and exploited" (1993, 112). And in the case of one fruit: "The watermelon is objectified, subjected to cold, distant, invasive, obsessive, scientific, gaze."

Chinski, like Azoulay, also criticizes zionist practices of representing space. The dominant Israeli notion of space/homeland, the one that is taught to all elementary school children (1993, 115–116), by equating Israeli art with Jewish art, eliminates the Palestinian other. Drawing on Deleuze and Guattari, Chinski speaks of the territorialization of the (artistic/interpretive) text (1993, 115).

In the 1986 exhibit "Dalut Hahomer" [the poverty of the material], Chinski sees a reflection of the zionist discourse on territory, homeland, and homeborn (1993, 118). Placing the "dispossessed Sabra" [*zabar menushal*], the narcissistic Tel Avivian, at the center, it totally ignored the "dispossession" and marginalization of the Other effected by the palmah and the youth movements (1993, 118). By disregarding the marginalized others of the Israeli population, the exhibit participated in the marginalization of non-Ashkenazic and non-Jewish citizens.

Drawing on Said, Chinski finds a parallel between the Eurocentric, Orientalist zionist conception of Israeli art and the ideas of Palestine as a territory devoid of existing culture and a land devoid of dwellers. She considers both to be central to zionist discourse. Whereas in Orientalist discourse the Middle East is represented as the silent or subjugated "Other," in zionist discourse it is the Palestinian Arab (1993, 120).

ZIONISM'S POSITIONING OF WOMEN: TOWARD A FEMINIST CRITIQUE OF ZIONIST DISCOURSE

Showing the influence of recent feminist theory, a number of writers in *Theory and Criticism* call attention to the ways in which women have been positioned by Israeli cultural discourse. In so doing, they have helped to shape a theoretically informed feminist critique that is rare in Israeli society and culture. While feminists have been active on the public scene in Israel since the 1960s, most of the discussion reflects the liberal concerns of that form of American feminism that focused primarily on the struggle for equal rights. Israeli feminist scholars like Deborah Bernstein, whose writings form a part of the critical sociology group, sought to recover the voices of women in Israeli history and reveal their distinctive role in the formation of the nation. While providing a counternarrative to the hegemonic male narrative, this critique, consistent with modernist social scientific critiques, stopped short of exploring the discursive processes by means of which women were marginalized or excluded.

The critique of discursive and representational practices that inscribe gender differences, a commonplace among Western feminists, has only recently emerged in Israel. Focusing on the ways in which women have been positioned by the dominant Israeli cultural discourse, *Theory and Criticism* has provided one of the few cultural sites in Israel for a theoretically informed feminist critique.[69] Several writers employ feminist theory to challenge prevailing zionist cultural narratives and problematize the assumptions on which zionist discourse is grounded. In the process, they reveal the contingency of dominant zionist narratives and the conception of history that they support, and suggest the possibility of alternative narratives. Comprising distinctive voices within Israeli feminist criticism, these writers render problematic many of the cultural assumptions of zionism and Israeli nationalism.[70]

One of the effects of a feminist critique of zionism and Israeli culture has been to problematize the dominant notions of Israeli identity. Delilah Amir, in a study of practices relating to abortion and educating new immigrant women on sexual practices and birth control, calls into question such taken-for-granted terms as "Israeli," "Israelis," "Jew," and "Sabra." According to Amir (1995), these terms have the effect of concealing the ethnic, gender, religious, age, and class differences within Israeli society. Utilizing the concept of gender as a critical category, Amir focuses on the different processes by means of which female and male identities are constructed in Israeli society. This entails a critique of the dominant Israeli discourse of national identity (p. 7).

Other articles employ recent feminist theory to highlight the oppressive effects of the positioning of women in zionist and Israeli cultural discourse. Drawing on Julia Kristeva's critique of identity and language, Rivkah Feldhay of Tel Aviv University's Cohn Institute of the History of Science and Ideas analyzes the psychological dimensions of zionist discourse. Criticizing dominant zionist views of individual and national identity, Feldhay (1992) argues that nationalist discourses like zionism are grounded either in a conventional, symbolic interpretation of identity or a psychotic, fantastic notion.

Feldhay (1992) explores three options that can assist feminists in their struggle (p. 82). The first option is political activism in the form of fighting for equal rights for women. A second alternative is to engage in a critique of patriarchal hegemonic discourse in an effort to uncover the underlying power relations. This is cathartic but dangerous insofar as it is likely to reproduce the patriarchal discourse (p. 89). The third alternative, which she attributes to the writer Amalia Kahana-Carmon, is to work within the existing patriarchal discourse to subvert it.

Feldhay urges Israeli Jewish women to recognize the link between their position as Others and that of Palestinian Arabs. Although somewhat cryptic, her analysis presents Israeli women with new possibilities. Rejecting total identification with or total rejection of the dominant discourse, she advocates that women consider themselves as "Others" who, while positioned within the dominant discourse, simultaneously assume a critical, subversive stance toward it.

Feldhay finds that novelist Amalia Kahana-Carmon's notion of subjectivity as created through the act of relating to the Other, which is based upon Kristeva, applies to national identity as well. National identity is nonessentialistic and does not preexist performative acts. Instead, one creates oneself as a national subject through national practices and acts of national identification.

Other contributors to *Theory and Criticism*, applying feminist theory, produce fresh readings of the writings of several women authors. Orly Lubin, a cultural critic teaching at Tel Aviv University, and Hamutal Zamir challenge the prevalent Israeli critical practice of incorporating women authors within the Hebrew national canon. In the process, they seek to demonstrate the subversive effects of their writings on zionist discourse. They thus seek to reveal an alternative to the hegemonic zionist narrative.

Drawing on Benedict Anderson, Frederic Jameson, and feminist critic Monique Wittig, Lubin (1995) argues that, in general, nationalist discourse has allowed little space for women. Although the nation is represented as female, the story of the nation is, as Anderson has shown, "the story of male bonding" [*ahvah*]."Imagining the nation as woman-mother in the establishing of the imagined nation conceals and covers up the fact that we are talking about arrangements [*sedarim*] between men—a totally male history" (p. 164).

To the extent that the national subject, in national imagining, is represented as male, the female, too, is subsumed under 'male,' the universal category. At the same time, as Wittig (1983) has argued, gender is viewed as a category applicable only to women: "Here are not two genders, only one, the female, for 'male' is not a gender. Male is not a gender, but rather the general [the universal]" (p. 64).

Analyzing the writings of Devora Baron, an author who lived in prestate Palestine, Lubin challenges the dominant critical practice of historical realism that emphasizes the theme of national continuity. To Lubin, reading Baron through a gender-sensitive lens produces an alternative interpretation. Notwithstanding the efforts of many critics, Lubin finds it difficult to read Baron's work as reinforcing zionist discourse, the reading that justifies including her in the Hebrew literary canon. Focusing on the details of everyday life, Baron pays little if any attention to the nation and its history. Nationalist critics, desiring to bridge the breach between the individual and the national, impute to Baron's writings a coherence that, in Lubin's view, does not exist. To Lubin, Baron's narrative, with its focus on the everyday, the individual, and the private, has a fragmenting effect that is incompatible with a zionist reading.

Critics, desiring to erase the centrality of gender in Baron's writings, have subsumed it under such universal concepts as the general voice of the oppressed. According to Lubin, this move simply cannot work. Women are central to such works as Baron's novel *haGolim,* with men appearing only by virtue of their relation to women. It is women, however, rather than men, who are active.

Lubin also finds in Baron's writings an alternative organization of time, one that runs counter to the nationalist organization of time. In her work, time is based on everyday events rather than being eternalized in dates. This alternative time contrasts with the unified, serial, continuous, logical time that underlies nationalist narratives (Lubin 1995, 167).

Similarly, Baron emphasizes emotion over logical action. In addition, in her work, the causal force of the historical-national is displaced by the causal force of the body and its material needs, such as food: "All of these prevent the possibility of organizing an orderly, consistent national narrative." Although the national narrative is not totally eliminated, it is subordinated to the other narrative.

Lubin thus finds in Baron's novel two alternative narratives. On the one hand, there is the hegemonic, national narrative, and on the other, a counternarrative that subverts it, or at least challenges its hegemonic position:

> A broken narrative and an alternative meaning, another national narrative in which the woman is able to establish herself as a national zionist female subject. (Lubin 1995, 168)

Rather than eliminate or struggle with national hegemony, Baron's subversive narrative exists alongside it, but independently. In that sense, the novel, thematically and rhetorically, may be considered subversive rather than revolutionary.

According to Lubin (1995), when viewed from a feminist perspective,

> there is little room for woman to position herself as an autonomous national subject in the hegemonic channel of the [universalistic, territorial nationalist

zionist] discourse, in the ideational channel of the universal, male (which eras-
es its gender and sex), spiritual, territorial discourse—therefore she can only
position herself in the margins, in the discourse that has been pushed to the outside: the bodily, sexual discourse, and not as an image of spirit and territory, as
women are made to function in the hegemonic discourse, but as an authority
unto itself. (p. 172)

Like Lubin, Hamutal Zamir (1995) emphasizes the masculine character of modern nationalism, which requires of women that they subordinate
their female identity to the basically masculine universalism of the national
collective:

> Any sexuality that is not bound up with fertility and birth (including homo-
> sexuality, both among men and women) is excluded [*mutzet*] from the nation-
> al discourse. In every instance, therefore, the national discourse denies women
> the possibility of subjectivity, sexuality, and her own voice. (133–34)

According to Zamir, a careful reading of the writings of Esther Raab
reveals her efforts to resist this situation and position herself as a woman.
Although adopting the conventional national discourse that treats the land
as female, Raab, as a woman, subverts the normal nationalistic hierarchical
relation to the land in order to establish a unique dialogue with it.

Hannan Hever (1995), whose writings on Anton Shammas I discussed
earlier, finds the women poets of the 1948 War to be excellent examples of
the silencing or exclusionary effects of the canonization of Hebrew literature. The metaphorical structure of the womens' poetry differs from that
found in the poetry produced by men:

> The representation of war in women's poetry of the War of Independence is
> based, therefore, on a dual process: the first and obvious step is the represen-
> tation of the living dead on the level of national metaphor, that is, as part of the
> hegemonic discourse and the representation of the fighting living dead.... But at
> the same time, on the other hand, the speaker [in Esther Raab's poems]
> responds to her other position as one who has been pushed outside of the
> canonic center. Her conflicted positioning as a woman—who writes in the lan-
> guage of the canonic center but is distanced from it; who testifies to the event
> of war but is prevented from being a legitimate witness to them—this position-
> ing brings her to choose a poetic perspective that is unique, one which suggests
> an alternative representation of the metaphor of the living dead. (p. 110)

In the nationalist, zionist narrative, the death of the individual is subsumed within the collective experience of the nation. In this way, Hever
(1995) argues, it is assigned a mythic meaning that occludes the corporeal:

> The image of the individual death is transformed in the mythic life of the col-
> lective life which elevates death in battle to the plane of transcendent national

experience. According to the cultural logic, one may say that to the extent that the individual identity is blurred, the power of the collective national identity increases. (p. 104)

Women poets, too, appropriate the metaphor of the living dead. However, in women's poetry, the language of the body functions as an alternative to the male myth of the living dead. It thus focuses on the individual physical body rather than subsume it within the national collective. Whereas, according to Hever (1995), the hegemonic myth, framed in a masculine, militaristic discourse, marginalized women, the emphasis on the body helped to subvert that hegemony:

> The national hegemony of the metaphor of the living dead is essentially a male hegemony. Therefore, the choice by women of the metaphor of the living dead did not eliminate, in general, the double state of their literary positioning: it made it possible for them to enter the heart of the canonical literary representation of the period, but together with this, it did not have the power to remove/rescue them from their representation as the holders of a marginal position at the rear, far from the fire line. (p. 104)

Hever acknowledges that in the final analysis, the women poets of the 1948 War remain within the boundaries of nationalist discourse. While the shift in emphasis to the body allows us to hear their voices, it leaves in place ethnic identity. In the end,

> they lead to the "nationalization" of the feminine and teach the woman to come to terms with the sacrifice. Thus they fulfill the function in the economy of the national emergency, the masculine arsenal, of the representation of war. (p. 122)

A significant contribution to gender criticism of zionist discourse appears in the Winter, 1997 issue of *Theory and Criticism* (volume 11). In a special section devoted to the one hundredth anniversary of the first Zionist Congress, Daniel Boyarin, Michael Gluzman, and Sarah Chinski analyze the ways in which binaries, hierarchies, and relations of power built around gender differences are embedded in zionist discourse. Applying theories of gender construction and gender difference to the writings of two of the early shapers of zionist discourse, Theodor Herzl and Max Nordau, Boyarin and Gluzman open areas of inquiry into a basic dimension of zionist discourse neglected by most other scholars. In bringing before the Israeli reader the writings of Boyarin, an American scholar who has pioneered in applying gender criticism and cultural studies to the field of Jewish studies, *Theory and Criticism* again introduces into the postzionist discussion new avenues of inquiry rarely found in the writings of Israeli scholars. Thus, the journal once again significantly expands the scope of the postzionist critique, linking it to critical currents familiar to intellectuals in many other parts of the world.

Boyarin explores the central role that the quest for the renewal of manliness played in zionist discourse. Teasing out the gender discourse in both Freud's and Herzl's discussion of zionism, Boyarin sees the quest to recover a lost manliness as a key to understanding Herzl's vision as well as that of Max Nordau. Thus, for example, dueling, an important theme in Herzl's play, *The New Ghetto*, is a means for Jewish men to recover their lost sense of honor.

> Herzlian Zionism, I suggest, is dueling carried on by other means, yet another desperate attempt to win Jewish honor and cultural disappearance as a deformed alterity by 'doing our Christian duty.'(1997b, 295)

Building upon earlier work by Sander Gilman, George Mosse and Michael Berkowitz, and integrating insights drawn from gender theory and postcolonial theory, Boyarin's analysis reveals how a particular vision of masculinity, one borrowed from the dominant European culture, is inscribed in early zionist discourse.

Herzl, in analyzing the Jewish condition, internalized the dominant European view of the Jew as weak and effeminate. While recognizing the obvious differences, Boyarin nevertheless sees clear parallels between the Europeans' relation to Jews, and the relation of colonizer to colonized. Represented by the dominant society as strangers and aliens, Jews, in exchange for being granted Emancipation, had to remake themselves in keeping with the dominant European male image. For Herzl, "that which distinguishes Jews from gentiles is a deformation" (1997b, 280). The goal of Herzl's zionism, argues Boyarin, was to correct this deformity by creating conditions in which Jews could "remain loyal to some memory of Jewish identity, as long as it did not distinguish them in any ways from gentiles" (280). This entailed finding a way for Jews to assimilate the dominant European male characteristics without losing their honor. According to Boyarin, the zionist goal that Jews become "like all of the nations" [kekhol hagoyim] really meant becoming manly. To do this, concluded Herzl, the Jews would have to go elsewhere.

Boyarin, adding a new twist to the discussion of zionism's relation to colonialism, identifies Herzl as

> an almost perfect example of that condition of the colonial subject so brilliantly anatomized in Frantz Fanon's *Black Skins, White Masks;* a book about Herzl and his compatriots could be called Black Pates, Blonde Wigs. (302)

Just as colonized peoples yearn to transform themselves in the image of the colonizers, Herzl wanted to transform the Jews into European "white men." One way in which that could be done was for Jews to themselves become colonizers:

> Herzlian zionism imagined itself as colonialism because such a representation was pivotal to the entire project of becoming 'white men.' What greater Christian duty could there be in the late nineteenth century than carrying on the civilizing mission, exporting manliness to the Eastern Jews and to darkest Palestine.... Herzlian zionism is thus itself the civilizing mission, first and foremost directed by Jews at other Jews and then at whatever native happen to be there, if indeed, these natives were noticed at all. (303)

An important component of pre-emancipation Jewry's identity was its abjection of the gentile (goy) as "a creature stereotyped as violent, aggressive, coarse, drunk, and given to such nonsense as dueling, seeking honor in war, and falling in romantic 'love'" (304). In contrast, the post-emancipation, postcolonialist Jews, as envisioned by Herzl, would, through zionism, recover their lost manliness by appropriating the dominant European values and transforming them into a key Jewish virtue through the colonization of a new territory.

The colonialist image is further buttressed by Herzl's inattention to any indigenous population that might be living in the projected Jewish colony.

> If in other national movement's, 'manliness' is made to serve nationalism, for Herzl nationalism was an instrument in the search for manliness. (302)

Boyarin's project of critiquing zionist discourse through the framework of gender studies is taken up by Michael Gluzman of the program in Hebrew literature at Ben Gurion University. Like Boyarin, Gluzman is interested in the key role played by the concept of manliness in zionist discourse. According to Gluzman (1997), at the turn of the century, the image of the Jew was that of a homosexual, with both Jews and homosexuals depicted as threatening "the natural gender order" (147). In the writings of Max Nordau, one of the major zionist theorists, the goal of creating a new strong, muscular Jewish man "is an outstanding example of the moment in which the male body is turned into a symbol of the new society and a means for the establishment of the nation" (148). According to Gluzman, "the [zionist] striving for the physical renewal of the Jewish body is anchored in the national that is formulated through the concepts of normal masculinity" (148).

Gluzman, who is critical of Israeli scholarship's neglect of the gender issues in zionism, is one of the few Israeli scholars to read zionism through the lens of gender criticism. Following Boyarin, Gluzman speaks of Herzl's zionist discourse as being "to a large extent, a discourse of masculinity or, more precisely, of the yearning for masculinity" (149). Whereas Boyarin focused on *The New Ghetto,* Gluzman turns his attention to Herzl's utopian novel, *Altneuland,* which "treats the 'code of masculinity,' a code that is simultaneously ethical and bodily" (149). To Gluzman, Herzl's novel is "a document that deals in an exciting and revealing way with zionism as a gender and sexual question" (149). A key theme in the novel is "the effort to 'cure' the emotional illness of the melancholy and effeminate Jewish male." Gluzman finds repeated evidence of the homoerotic character of the relationship between the Jewish protagonist Dr. Friedrich Loewenberg and the aristocrat Kingscourt.

Like Nordau, Herzl wanted

> to refute the anti-Semitic caricature of the Jew as effeminate, a stereotype that both men had internalized. Interpreting the Jews' effeminate character as the outcome of the conditions of life in exile, Herzlian zionism assumed that "the transition to Palestine would bring about, almost instantly, a transformation in the body and the character of the Jew. (154)

According to Gluzman, Herzl yearned, first and foremost, for a "normal" masculinity. His concept of "normalcy" was based on "the denial of the feminine" as explained by another Viennese Jew, Sigmund Freud. Herzl, as encoded in *Altneuland* through the heterosexualization of the Jewish male, "promotes an ideology of gender polarization that motivates the male to deepen as far as possible the differences between him and the woman" (156). Herzl's yearning for a normal masculinity, a "non-Jewish" masculinity (represented in the novel by Kingsport), leads him to present zionism as a process of gender redemption, whose culminating point is marriage.

Following the American scholar David Biale, Gluzman describes the zionist project as seeking a renewal of Jewish masculinity through the creation of the new, masculine Hebrew. At the same time, Herzlian zionism aims to eliminate the inequities suffered by women. This double vision, however, is grounded in the hierarchical polarization of the sexes (156). This striving of gender polarization has the effect of marginalizing women. In *Altneuland,* "zionism is represented as a male idea, while the woman is the one who assists the male in realizing his dreams" (158). Arabs in the novel are, like women, represented as a marginal minority. In both instances, the "acquisition of full equal rights would endanger the marginal group's position in relation to the Jewish male hegemony" (158). Herzl, as encoded in *Altneuland* as through the heterosexualization of the Jewish male, promotes an ideology of gender polarization, an ideology that motivates the male to deepen as far as possible the differences between him and the woman (156). Whereas Jewish women would have freedom of movement and subjectivity in the new society, equality of the Arab would be based on his readiness to cooperate with the hegemonic Jewish powers.

Although Boyarin's and Gluzman's ideas are extremely suggestive and helpful when read in tandem with the many critical writings by Israeli feminists on the positioning of women in Israeli culture, neither of them undertake to analyze the connection between zionism's quest for manliness and the apparatuses through which zionist discourse was produced and disseminated. This task, however, is partly taken up by Sarah Chinski, whose critique of Israeli art we discussed earlier in this chapter. Chinski analyzes the role of Jewish art in constructing the boundaries of the new Hebrew identity being shaped under zionism in the early part of the century. Chinski argues that the Bezalel Academy of Art in Jerusalem, under the direction of Boris Schatz, played a key role in the production and dissemination of a new artistic enterprise in Jerusalem that was woven into the zionist narrative in two ways. First, it contributed to the formation of a new mapping "of the metaphorical geography of the zionist movement"—geography that confirmed "zion" as legitimate while defining the "golah" (diaspora) as substandard. Similarly, the art produced in Israel was considered to be authentic, while the art produced in the diaspora was not. In addition, just as in zionist discourse, only in the land of Israel could the Jewish worker find fulfillment, there, alone, could the soul of the Jewish artist find fulfillment. Thus, the discourse of Hebrew art converged with the zionist discourse in which life in the land of Israel was viewed as basic to the realization (hagshamah) of authentic Jewish national life.

Bezalel also played a key role in "organizing a cosmology of objects that would be defined and distinguished as Hebrew" (199). The different departments in the school were identified with different manifestations of Hebraism—botanical, zoological, archaeological, anthropological, and daily life. Establishing the identity of Jewish art, the product produced by Bezalel was rendered "a political subject worthy of political discussion"(178).

Specific objects produced at Bezalel, such as carpets, mezuzot affixed to the doorposts of Jewish homes, and lamps served as vehicles for disseminating the new Hebrew culture that was set up in opposition to the Jewish culture produced in the lands of exile. To Schatz, the Hebrew room, containing a variety of objects viewed as creations of the new Hebrew spirit, instilled in those who dwelled in the home a strong identification with the past and present as conceived within zionist discourse. The Hebrew artifacts were seen by him as having the power to shape the structure of feelings of those who connected to them. Thus, according to Chinski, artistic objects were not only expressions of identity, but also functioned to construct that identity by positioning those who viewed and used them.

Under the regime of Bezalel, Hebrew art contributed to the expansion of zionism's political project into everyday life. In Foucault's terms, Hebrew popular art constituted an apparatus encompassing "institutions, discursive fields, objects, administrative practices and geographic spaces" (178). In the

Hebrew room, Jews, according to Schatz, "learn to take pride in our past and be prepared to make sacrifices for our spiritual burdens and their future" (quoted in Chinski 1997, 203). Thus, Bezalel became a major "political-cultural agent of the zionist movement" (178), acquiring, in the process, a mythic status in the writings of historians of Israeli art. Insofar as the zionist enterprise was political and national as well as cultural, the inscribing of Hebrew culture in domestic space thus transformed that space into "a center for the shaping of a political agenda, one that was engraved on the body" (203).

Chinski is particularly concerned with the ways in which women are positioned in the dominant Israeli discourse relating to the arts. Analyzing manifests describing the organization and structure of Bezalel, the writings of Schatz, and historical studies of Israeli art, Chinski teases out the ways in which that discourse marginalized and excluded women. Of particular concern to Chinski are the practices through which women were relegated to certain areas of "popular culture," while the field of high culture was reserved for male artists. Thus, crafts such as lace making and weaving, considered from an artistic perspective to be less significant, were reserved for women. Insofar as the crafts with which women artisans were identified were connected to the home rather than the pubic realm, women were excluded from the public realm and constructed as an internal "Other." Taking as a given the binary that privileged high culture over low or popular culture, Israeli art, as developed and shaped at Bezalel, constructed the identity of the Hebrew woman around her absence (from the realm of high culture), and her silence.

The fact that women constituted the majority of the artists and artisans working at Bezalel at the beginning of the century is effectively concealed in the available documents and historical accounts in which women artists are represented primarily by their absence. Whereas works of high art are identified as the product of specific creators, works of popular art are viewed as a product of the people. Thus, whereas male artists were identified by their professions, women artists were relegated to anonymity. While the former were identified by name as the creators of specific works of art, women were identified as members of families, as somebody's mother, sister, or wife.

INTERROGATING THE LITERARY CANON

Hever's analysis of the women poets forms part of a larger project in which he critically analyzes the construction of the Hebrew national canon. Again drawing on insights produced by postcolonial theory, Hever analyzes the impact of Hebrew literature in constructing Israeli national identity and a unified national culture.

Whereas the prevailing forms of Israeli literary criticism focus on history, structure, and meaning, Hever emphasizes the power effects of Hebrew literature and the power mechanisms and practices that shape the Hebrew literary canon. Grounded in poststructuralist and postcolonial criticism, Hever seeks to formulate and put into practice an alternative approach to interpreting the Hebrew literary canon. Emphasizing the ways in which the narratives produced by Hebrew writers have produced and disseminated the dominant representations of Israeli national identity and collective culture, he challenges the modernist, nationalistic premises that ground most Hebrew literary analysis. Focusing on the ways in which this literature constructs the national subject, Hever also seeks to show how narratives produced by Hebrew writers participate in producing the dominant Israeli representations of national identity and collective memory.

As his critics have noted, Hever frames Hebrew literature, in part, through the struggle over power. Rather than concentrate primarily on what the texts say, their plot structure, or their characters, he focuses our attention on what the text does, its effects, particularly its cultural and social power effects. Drawing from Deleuze and Guattari, he represents the construction of the Israeli literary canon as an ongoing struggle between various forms of minor literature and the dominant, hegemonic, major literature.

Hever (1994) represents the formation of the Hebrew literary canon in terms of a continuing struggle between the hegemonic group's efforts to construct and disseminate a national identity and culture grounded in zionist discourse and the ongoing efforts of "minority" writers to construct an alternative notion:

> The activity of literary canonization was an integral part of the effort to establish an ideological consensus of modern nationalism in Hebrew literature. (p. 59)

The historiography of Hebrew literature played a fundamental role in the canonization process in which "a consistent line which presented throughout the years a more or less fixed image of a normative national subject" (pp. 59–60) was maintained. The basic tendency of this historiographical tradition "was to remove from its lists anyone who sought to subvert the dominant version of the zionist canon" (p. 60). To support his political reading of the history of Hebrew literature and highlight its imbrication in the zionist power apparatus, Hever focuses on key moments in that history. Beginning with debates among early framers of zionist discourse such as Ahad Haam, Yosef Haim Brenner, and Mikhah Yosef Berdiczewski, he focuses on writings that he sees as subverting the conventional theorization of Hebrew literary development. Thus, alongside his study of little-known Galician Hebrew writers from the early part of the century such as Yitzhak Fernhoff and Reuven Fahan, he analyzes the writings of the Palestinian author Anton Shammas and women poets of the 1948 War.

Hever believes that an alternative approach to Hebrew literature, based in part on the writings of Walter Benjamin and Benedict Anderson, was made possible by the conditions of Hebrew culture in the 1980s and 1990s. A key moment, according to Hever (1994), was "the flowering in the 1980s of a Palestinian literature transformed, through translations and through the originals, into an outstanding component in the Hebrew canon" (p. 76). As a result, in place of a canon of Hebrew literature, identified as Jewish, there emerged a canon of Israeli literature:

> But now, in contrast to the point at which modern Hebrew literature arose, the Palestinian, the non-Jews, are the minority, while the Jews now occupy the position of the majority. (p. 76)

Shammas' novel, written in Hebrew, revealed the contingency and the precariousness of the bond, which zionist discourse treats as natural and necessary, between Hebrew literature and Jewish literature.

The current subversion of the "necessity" of the literary structure of the Hebrew literary subject makes possible a consideration of alternative Hebrew literary subjects that had been previously marginalized or silenced. Thus, it is now possible to distinguish between national literature written in a national language and an ethnic literature written in that language. The present conditions thus make it possible to question

> the current historical perspective which represents the national literary subject as a natural structure, seemingly independent of and non-contingent on historical circumstances, thus opening possibilities for analyzing the apparatuses of representation and the political strategies that shape and form it. (Hever 1994, 60)

To Hever (1994), the debate over literature is by no means limited to aesthetic practices of representation. At the heart of the debate is the struggle over the authoritative representation of the Jewish national subject. The voices of the individual Hebrew writers have not been seen simply as their own, but have also been seen as representative voices, "universal" voices that speak not simply for themselves, but as voices of the entire nation (p. 62). Through their writings, the image of the national subject, the normative national subject, has been formed.

Drawing from Deleuze and Guattari, Hever depicts the dominant or major literature, here represented by territorialized zionist writers, as providing a legitimation for the dominant culture. In the process, this major literature obscures political, racial, and class divisions behind a universalistic concept of the nation. In contrast, the minor literature, employing the same language as the major, endeavors to actualize the aesthetic values of the major. At the same time, the minor literature struggles against the dominant, "normative" literature along with its representation of the national subject.

Taking issue with the dominant historiographical trends that read the history of Hebrew literature in the context of national renewal, Hever advocates a genealogical approach that can bring to light the conditions of struggle out of which the modern Hebrew canon emerged. Attending to texts that have been marginalized or excluded from the canon, Hever seeks to widen the circles of possibilities that existed in the past and to present the outcomes/remnants of that past not as natural and authoritative, but as a product of historical processes that entailed choices and decisions. Demonstrating that the apparatuses that brought about the elimination of texts from the canon are bound up with the cultural and material contexts in which they were formed serves to uncover the interests and power relations in which these practices are grounded.

Hever (1994) treats practices of reappraising marginalized writers and literary works as both cultural/aesthetic and political. Besides producing a renewed appraisal of forgotten or marginalized writers and literary works, this practice can also produce "a renewed integration of marginal texts into the dynamic of modern Hebrew literature as establishing a new national identity" (p. 60). Thus, debates over Hebrew literature are also debates among competing views of the Jewish/Hebrew national subject.

While acknowledging that these debates are framed by the protagonists themselves as disputes over aesthetic practices, Hever (1994) insists that they can also be read "as disputes over the representation of power relations in the field of culture and as political conflicts" (p. 67; cf. p. 70). Accordingly,

> If we reflect on it [Hebrew literature] not as natural and self-explanatory, but rather as an institutionalized, historical description of images of reality, then we are able to break it down to its component parts and investigate the power apparatuses that it serves. (p. 67)

To support his reading, Hever turns to debates from the early years of zionism. To Hever, these debates over Hebrew literature were not simply debates over aesthetic practices. One of the major functions of Hebrew literature was to form/represent the national subject by providing a "normative" representation of the national collective. Analyzing debates between Brenner and Berdiczewski on the one hand and between Yitzhak Fernhoff and Reuven Fahan on the other, Hever focuses on their conflicting attitudes toward the *galut*.[71] Brenner, rejecting the possibility of a creative Jewish diaspora culture, sought to marginalize and exclude from the Hebrew canon Galician writers whose writings promote the creative potential of diaspora Jewish life. Placing the literary debate in the context of political debates within the Austro-Hungarian empire, and within the zionist movement over autonomous national minorities, Hever shows Fernhoff and Fahan as representing a view that believes in the possibility of national autonomy apart from one's homeland, in the midst of another dominant national culture.

According to Hever (1994), "behind the aesthetic discourse that shaped the canon, there were hidden political conflicts as well as representations of power relations in the field of culture" (p. 67). Similar conflicts are evident in the debates discussed in chapter 1 between Brenner and Berdiczewski on the one hand and Ahad Haam on the other. Hever reads these debates as debates over the representation of the national subject (p. 68). Ahad Haam offered a positivistic, collectivistic, organic vision of Jewish society and culture. In contrast, Berdiczewski's representation was a highly individualistic, antipositivistic, conflicted one:

> Berdiczewski's position repeatedly challenged the collective identity of the national subject. In place of collective authority, the national subject, for Berdiczewski, subordinates the collective to the individual, thereby awarding universal authority and power to a particularistic, nationalistic position. (p. 69)

Hever (1994) thus analyzes the discursive processes by means of which Brenner and Berdiczewski, in their efforts to establish a canon of Hebrew national literature, construct their critique of the Galician writers (pp. 72–73).

CONCLUSION

Applying postmodern, postcolonial, and feminist theory to the critique of Israeli society and culture, postzionist writers in *Theory and Criticism* have taken the critique of zionism, and of Israeli culture and identity, to a new place. In the process, they have shifted the grounds of the debates over postzionism in Israeli culture. Despite this, for the most part, the debate continues to be carried out according to the very premises and practices that the postmodern postzionists have criticized.

Undoubtedly, the new historians and critical sociologists have raised issues and precipitated debates of great significance in Israeli culture. Insofar as their writings opened to public debate issues and problems that had been, for the most part, suppressed, they rendered a major contribution to Israeli public discourse. Yet the ways in which they framed their critique imposed distinct limits on the debates. Within the academic community, these debates have revolved around such issues as: Did they get the story right? Are their interpretations of the past and present accurate? Do they use the right methods? Have they considered all of the available evidence? Are they objective, or do they allow their political concerns to inform their scholarship?

However, these kinds of questions presuppose assumptions that postmodern theory has rendered highly problematic. This is not to say that critics like Kimmerling, Pappe, Ram, or Shafir are oblivious to issues raised by these theories. However, only the postzionist critics discussed in this chapter have made discourse, and the relation of power and knowledge, central to their critique of zionism and Israeli culture. This is not to imply that their positions are impervious to criticism. Many cogent critiques of postmodern theory have been formulated by philosophers and social critics.[72]

Unfortunately, those who undertake to criticize the postmodern postzionists proceed as if the premises of zionist discourse have not been significantly problematized by postmodern, postcolonial, poststructuralist, and feminist theory. Israeli critics of postmodernism, like Eliezer Schweid, Yosef Dan, and Moshe Lissak, have refused to relate to the critique of postmodern postzionists with the seriousness that it warrants. Instead, they have set up and subsequently demolished straw persons. In so doing, they have done a disservice to cultural debates in Israel.

Problematizing objectivistic academic discourse and essentialistic notions of nation, identity, and space, postmodern postzionists have attempted to shift the ground of critical debate in Israel. Whether or not one is persuaded by their arguments, those who participate in Israeli cultural discourse do a disservice to that discourse by disregarding the epistemological issues that they raise. Only if those participating in the cultural debates in Israel seriously engage the arguments of these postzionist critics can the debates over postzionism and the future of Israeli collective identity move forward.

CONCLUDING REFLECTIONS

On September 11, 1993, the headlines in the English language Israeli daily *The Jerusalem Post* read: "Taboos Shattered in Peace Process." Only a short time before, Israelis had become aware that since May 1993, Israel and the Palestinian Liberation Organization (PLO) had been conducting secret negotiations in Oslo, Norway. Uri Savir, a seasoned Israeli diplomat, and Abu Ala (Ahmed Querei), a high official in the PLO, had led the two teams of negotiators whose efforts resulted in a Declaration of Principles. The signing of this document on September 13 at the White House brought about a cessation in the armed hostilities between Israel and the Palestinian people that had been going on since the state came into being in 1948. In the words of Yitzhak Rabin at the White House ceremony, a new era was dawning on the Middle East.

As Savir (1998) reports, the momentous event was made possible by the willingness of the two sides to draw "a new road map" (p. 15). In other words, serious peace negotiations between Israel and the Palestinians required a new mapping of the Middle East. According to Savir, central to this new mapping was separating the events of the past from the realities of the present and the hopes and promises of the future. To move forward, both sides agreed, references to the past had to be suspended.

According to Savir (1998), in an early meeting he and Abu Ala spoke warningly of the need to change the pernicious categories that they had inherited. They both agreed that if their efforts were to prove successful, it would be necessary to change the prevailing discourse in the Middle East:

> "You know," I warned Abu Ala, "as far as most Israelis are concerned, you're just a gang of terrorists."

> "And as far as most Palestinians are concerned, you are a nation of cruel oppressors, robbing us of our lands." (p. 21)

Although I seriously doubt that either of these men had ever read Foucault, they instinctively sensed what Foucault had argued throughout his career: For a significant social and cultural transformation to occur, a change must first occur in the discourse through which events are framed and assigned meaning.

In this book, I have analyzed the conflicts in Israeli society surrounding the efforts of a small group of intellectuals and academicians to effect a change in the dominant discourse. This effort, which has been given the name "postzionism," is based on the assumption that democratic processes in Israel require a new mapping of the power relations within Israeli society. As these postzionists realize, a process of change that builds only from the top down will not succeed. The historians and sociologists who first began to challenge the dominant historical narratives were not acting in isolation. As I have argued, postzionism could only have emerged as the result of far-reaching changes at the grassroots level, for example, the generational shift in attitude brought on by the occupation. These changes, brought about by a series of powerful moments in the history of the state, opened the way to and provided the motivation for postzionism.

However, as the postzionists' analysis reveals, even if the currently stalled peace process is resumed and brought to a successful conclusion, the problems of Israeli society and culture will continue. As Foucault (1996) reminds us, power relations are a basic part of any society, and the conflicts over meaning will not disappear: "Power operates in all spheres of life.... We cannot escape." In this situation, the intellectual's role is to "struggle against the forms of power that transforms him/her/us into its object and instrument in the sphere of 'knowledge,' 'truth,' 'consciousness,' and 'discourse'"(p. 75).

The dissonance in Israeli culture of which postzionists speak is shared by many Israelis. As intellectuals, the postzionists seek to formulate a theoretical framework through which to position this dissonance. While the theoretical writings of those postzionists I have labeled as postmodern often appear to the uninitiated to be abstract and remote from the realities of daily life, they would reject this reading. As Foucault (1996) has argued, "[T]heory does not express, translate, or serve to apply practice; it is practice...local and regional, not totalizing" (p. 75). Thus, to theorize is to engage in a struggle against certain forms of power. In Foucault's words, it is:

> a struggle aimed at revealing and undermining power where it is most visible and invidious. It is not to "awaken consciousness" that we struggle...but to sap power, to take power; it is an activity conducted alongside those who struggle for power, and not their illumination from a safe distance. (pp. 75–76)

As Israeli intellectuals, postzionists have accepted the responsibility of speaking out against what they consider to be unjust power relations in their society. In so doing, they have undertaken:

> to speak on this subject, to force the institutionalized networks of information to listen, to produce names, to point the finger of accusations, to find targets.... [This is] the first step in the reversal of power and the initiation of new struggles against existing forms of power. (Foucault 1996, 79)

However, those whom I have called postmodern postzionists are not so naive as to believe that academic or pedagogic practice is sufficient to bring about the end of these unjust power relations. What they may hope, however, is that their struggle against them might help to create conditions in which

> all those on whom power is exercised to their detriment, all who find it intolerable, can begin the struggle on their own terrain and on the basis of their proper activity (or passivity). In engaging in a struggle that concerns their own interests, whose objectives they clearly understand and whose methods only they can determine, they enter into a revolutionary process. (Foucault 1996, 81)

As understood by postzionists, a prerequisite to changing existing power relations in Israel is revealing the ways in which the dominant zionist discourse has produced and sustained forms of exclusion and domination. Working within the constraints that have prevailed thus far in Israeli culture, postzionists have invested their energies in the deconstructive task. In the context of the oppressive effects, both inside and outside of Israel, produced by Israel's continuing occupation of the West Bank and Gaza and its control of more than one million resistant Palestinians, postzionists have operated, for the most part, on the margins of Israeli public and academic discourse. However, if my analysis is correct, this is slowly changing.

If the peace process is allowed to move forward, this change will occur more rapidly. Should this happen, it will then be possible for postzionists and other Israeli intellectuals to turn their attention to formulating and putting into practice a vision of democracy appropriate to Israeli society. While the details of this vision must be left to Israelis to formulate, it should, at the very least, entail maximizing the opportunities for equitable and just relations in a democratic context that values difference and diversity.

Introduction

1. www.nytimes.com, April 10, 1998.
2. Ibid.
3. www.haaretzco.il/eng, December 25, 1997.
4. Ibid.
5. www.nytimes.com, April 10, 1998.
6. I use the concept of culture as it is currently employed in cultural studies to refer not to a "set of things or objects," but rather to "a contested process whereby meanings are produced and distributed." Hall and others, such as Foucault, see power relations as intricately connected to this process. In recent writings, Hall has used Foucault's concept of discourse and has emphasized the effects or function of cultural processes more so than the question of meaning. See Hall (1997) and Jordon and Weedon (1995). See also other references cited in chapter 5, note 7, and chapter 6, note 26.
7. Insofar as Israel is considered by zionists to be the legitimate form of contemporary Jewish life, to accuse postzionism of being hostile to zionism is to equate it to anti-Israel and, therefore, anti-Semitic, propaganda. This is clear in the position of Aaron Megged, Shlomo Aronson, Yisrael Landers, and other critics of postzionism, whom I discuss in chapter 4.
8. For a useful distinction between the terms antizionist and nonzionist, see Aronoff (1989). Aronoff defines as antizionist "those groups that reject all aspects of the Zionist civil religion and deny even de-facto recognition of the right of Israel to exist as an independent state. They do not participate in the electoral parliamentary process, and individuals belonging to these groups (or categories) do not serve in the army. We define as non-Zionist those groups that reject Zionist civil religion (or at least its most central values), but give de-facto recognition to the existence of the state of Israel and pragmatically cooperate with its institutions, including competing in elections. Some individuals belonging to these groups serve in the army but, when they do, are likely to engage in dissident activity" (p. 130). For a response to the antizionism charge, see Ram (1994b).
9. Their position is complicated by the fact, mentioned by Aronoff (note 8), that some who identify themselves as antizionist also served in the military. See the interview with Eli Amigov, a member of the radical antizionist group Mazpen, in *Haaretz*, February 20, 1987, 22. Amigov states clearly that he is antizionist. However, asked about his military service he replies: "Serving in the military by itself poses no problem for me. You do not remove yourself from your people.

Even though I do not love this state, I pay taxes. The Army is a kind of tax. Even in the military, our task is to influence people, to serve as a polar opposite to the dominant apparatus." Mazpen is discussed further in chapter 3.

10. See for example, the discussions of Benvenisti in chapter 2. Ruth Firer (1985, 1989) has analyzed school curricula in Israel and the pre-state Yishuv (community). Kimmerling (1995a) discusses the role of the university in disseminating zionist discourse. See also Myers (1995) and Ram (1995c). For an analysis of the production and distribution of collective memories and myths, see Zerubavel (1995) and Ben-Yehuda (1995). Valuable discussions of the nationalist functions of archaeology in Israel are in Silberman (1993) and the chapters by Elon, Silberman, and Shavit in Silberman and Small (1997).

11. According to Dominguez (1989, 70–191), our reluctance to acknowledge the power effects of identity construction on others leads us to regard it as a benign process. For a group to recognize that the construction of its identity entails the power to constitute "Others" is "to acknowledge having more power than they may wish to have or be comfortable having" (p. 191). Consequently, most zionist discussions of Israeli identity avoid the issue of power. For an overview of the ways in which sociologists who challenge the dominant trends in Israeli sociology have addressed the issue of marginalized or excluded others, see Ram (1995a, 97–117). Ram is one of the leading representatives of postzionism in Israel. Among the most powerful voices of the Palestinian "Other" in Israeli society are Anton Shammas and Emile Habiby (see chapter 5).

12. The following paragraphs are based on Silberstein (1997).

13. From "Proclamation of the State of Israel," in Mendes-Flohr and Reinharz (1995, 629). Dominguez (1989) provides one of the few efforts to formulate an alternative, nonessentialist approach to the problem of Jewish group identity. Rather than take concepts such as people and peoplehood as natural givens, Dominguez problematizes them: "What is peoplehood? In what ways is it a representation, an objectification? How is it shaped, molded, altered, and perpetuated? And how can it help us learn about the very processes of objectification in which we all participate?" (p. 19). Dominguez's assumption is that "collective identities are conceptual representations masquerading as objects (positivities in Foucault's sense) and that they are in perpetual need of nurturing." I discuss Dominguez in relation to postzionism in Silberstein (1995, 189). Recent works that treat nationhood and peoplehood as socially constructed and culturally imagined include Anderson (1991), Hobsbawm (1990), and Smith (1986, 1991). For postcolonialist perspectives on nationalism, see Chatterjee (1993) and Bhabha (1990). See also the important collection of articles in Eley and Suny (1996b), which connects recent developments in cultural studies, feminist studies, and other fields with the analysis of nations and nationalism.

14. See chapters 4–6.

15. "Basically in any society, there are manifold relations of power which permeate, characterize and constitute the social body, and these relations of power cannot themselves be established, consolidated nor implemented without the production, accumulation, circulation and functioning of a discourse [e.g., the

discourse of law, the various "social sciences" and the race relations industry].
We are subjected to the production of truth through power and we cannot
exercise power except through the production of truth" (Foucault 1980, 93).

16. Recent Israeli scholarship, which is discussed in chapter 4, offers many examples of the changing position of Israeli scholars on this issue. Yonathan Shapiro
(1985) was one of the first Israeli sociologists to emphasize the role of power,
which he defined in a more conventional way, in Israeli political life. Ram
(1995a) discusses Shapiro (see his chap. 5).

17. See, for example, Shapira (1992) and Gorny (1987). An alternative perpective
that emphasizes the power effects of zionism is Shafir (1989). While Morris
(1988) clearly shows the power effects of zionism on the Palestinians, he does
not discuss their connection to zionist discourse.

18. See, for example, the collection of articles in Avni and Shimoni (1990). The
title of the book, *Zionism and Its Jewish Opponents,* positions zionism in the
center and takes it for granted that those who criticize it are "its opponents."
It thus structures the discussion from a zionist perspective.

19. The confusion over the meaning of the term is clearly reflected in a symposium
published in the Israeli daily *Haaretz* in 1995 (Margalit 1995). For a brief but
useful overview of the various dimensions of postzionism in Israeli society and
culture, see Sheleg (1995).

20. Writings by Israeli scholars advocating the strengthening of democratic
processes in Israel who do not openly identify with postzionism are found in
Diamond and Sprinzack (1993), and Ezrahi (1997). While Ezrahi's position
borders on that of the postzionists, he shies away from the term, preferring to
speak of a post-epic Israel (pp. 282–283). One may also point to a number of
younger Israeli political leaders, such as Yossi Beilin, Uri Savir, and Ron
Pundak, all of whom speak in a discourse that appears to be postzionist. Each
of them played a significant role in the negotiations between Israel and the
Palestinians that formulated the Declaration of Principles signed by Yitzhak
Rabin and Yasir Arafat at the White House in September 1993.

21. A series of articles on postzionism appeared in *Haaretz,* beginning with an article by Urit Shohat, "Who Is a Postzionist?" (September 1, 1995). Responses by
Amnon Rubinstein, Zeev Sternhell, Shlomo Avineri, and Baruch Kimmerling
appeared in *Haaretz* on September 12, 15, 22, and 29. The debate led to a
symposium published in *Haaretz* (Margalit 1995) that reflects the ongoing
confusion over the meaning of the term. Symposium participants included
Amnon Rubinstein, Yosef Gorni, Avi Gissar, and Yoav Gelber, all of whom are
critical of postzionism, and Benny Morris, Tom Segev, and Ilan Pappe, who are
sympathetic to it. For earlier usages of the term see chapter 4, note 4.

22. See, for example, Cohen, (1983, chap. 8), Woocher (1986, chaps. 3–5), and
Fein (1988, chaps. 5 and 6).

23. At the time of the signing of the Declaration of Principles in Washington, many
American Jewish newspapers and journals carried discussions about the implications of peace in the Middle East for American Jewish identity.

24. For recent discussions of the problems of Israeli democracy see Dowty (1998)
Diamond and Sprinzack (1993), and Rouhanna (1997).

25. See Lovejoy (1965, chap. 1) and Veyne (1997). I develop this theme in chapter 1 as well as in other places throughout this book.

26. Thus, for example, zionism translates the cosmic mapping of traditional religious Judaism into a material, that is, a symbolic, imaginary, and representational mapping. For a discussion of mapping, see Deleuze and Guattari (1989). See also Harvey (1996, pp. 111–112, 282–285), and Kaufman and Heller (1998, Introduction, and 145–162). On the role of mapping in the zionist enterprise see Benvenisti (1986, pp. 191–267), and Benvenisti (1997).

27. In addition to the writers whom I discuss in this book, there are clear manifestations of postzionism in other areas of Israeli culture which fall beyond the purview of the current work. Thus, in the field of literature one can point to two novelists, Orly Castel-Bloom and Ronit Matalon. I am grateful to Stacy Beckwith for helping me to clarify the place of postzionist motifs in the work of Matalon and to Deborah Starr for doing the same with the works of Castel-Bloom. Two recent exhibitions of Israeli art, "Desert Cliches" and "To The East: Orientalism in the Arts in Israel," also show clear postzionist motifs. See the references cited below, chapter 6, nn. 51 and 58. I thank Tami Katz-Freiman and Ariella Azoulay for their inisghts into this phenomenon in Israeli art.

Chapter 1

1. Foucault (1997a), explaining his genealogical approach, wrote: "[A]s opposed to a genesis oriented towards the unity of some principal cause burdened with multiple descendants, what is proposed instead is a genealogy, that is, something that attempts to restore the conditions for the appearance of a singularity born out of multiple determining elements of which it is not the product, but rather the effect" (p. 57). In another essay in which he attributed this approach to Nietzsche, he wrote that searching for descent rather than origin, the genealogical approach "disturbs what was previously considered immobile; it fragments what was thought unified; it shows the heterogeneity of what was imagined consistent with itself" (p. 82).

2. Of course, no one seeking to represent a subject like zionism can avoid talking or writing from a particular position. Consequently, like those scholars who are positioned in a zionist space, I, too, am already positioned by particular discourse(s). In addition to the writings of Foucault, Deleuze, and Guattari, the discourses from which I draw to construct my representations of zionism derive mainly from cultural studies, postfoundational philosophy, feminist theory, and postcolonial theory. The representation that results from the application of these discourses differs significantly from those that one finds in conventional studies. For a discussion of the significance of these theories for the interpretation of zionism, see chapter 6.

3. As formulated by Foucault (1980), apparatus refers to "[a] thoroughly heterogeneous ensemble consisting of discourses, institutions, architectural forms, regulatory decisions, laws, administrative measures, scientific statements, philosophical, moral and philanthropic propositions—in short, the said as

much as the unsaid" (p. 194). Foucault goes on to explain: "The apparatus is thus always inscribed in a play of power, but it is also always linked to certain coordinates of knowledge which issue from it, but, to an equal degree, condition it. This is what the apparatus consists in: strategies of relations of forces supporting and supported by types of knowledge" (p. 196).

4. Studies which depict the multiple competing movements among Eastern European Jewry in the late nineteenth and early twentieth centuries are Frankel (1981) and more recently Peled (1997a and b). As I shall discuss later, there were many conflicts among zionists. At the same time, it is possible to isolate certain truths or shared knowledge to which all zionists are expected to assent. To the extent that zionism became hegemonic, these truths and the knowledge surrounding them came to be taken as common sense, as givens.

5. For a classic critique of the concepts ending in "ism" and "ity" see Lovejoy (1965, 5–7). A more recent critique, drawing on Foucault, is Veyne (1997, 172).

6. As stated in the Introduction, following Foucault, I do not consider the ubiquity of power relations within society to be a cause for despair. Far from being rendered immobile and helpless by such revelations, we are, instead, confronted with a different kind of political task, that is, to bring to the surface the relationship between and functioning of discourse, knowledge, power, and social relations.

7. As we see in the following chapters, zionism's effectiveness in doing this has been increasingly subverted in recent decades. This has produced a crisis of collective identity and meaning that is revealed in the debates surrounding postzionism.

8. See Bove (1990) and sources cited above in Introduction, n. 26.

9. The fact that these terms no longer carry the same connotations to most Israelis is a sign of the weakening hold of zionist discourse. I discuss the factors surrounding the decline in the force of zionist discourse in chapter 4.

10. "Far from being differentiated by their objects, discursive formations produce the object about which they speak. Madness [author note: read Zionism] was not...an object or limit experience outside of discourse which each age had attempted to capture in its own terms.... [Zionism is] constituted by all that was said in all the statements that named it, divided it up, described it, explained it, traced its developments, indicated its various correlations, judged it, and possibly gave it speech by articulating, in its name, discourses that were taken to be its own" (Foucault 1972, 32).

11. For the attitudes of zionists toward the indigenous Arab population, see Gorny (1987), Shapira (1992), and Almog (1983). For a leftwing perspective, see Cohen (1970).

12. See the discussions in Swirski (1989), Dominguez (1989, chaps. 4 and 5), Segev (1986, chap. 6), Dowty (1998), Shohat (1988, 1989), Alcalay (1993, 1996), and Smooha (1993a, 1993b).

13. Among recent efforts, see Avineri (1981) and Shimoni (1995). Similarly, Vital entitles the first volume of his multivolume study, *The Origins of Zionism*. I am not claiming that these authors ignore the differences among differing conceptions of zionism. What I am saying is that they still believe that it is possi-

ble to speak of zionist ideology or zionism, implying that notwithstanding the differences among different zionist parties, there remains a unity that transcends all differences. An exception to this is Mitchell Cohen (1992), who suggests in the preface to the revised edition that it is more appropriate to speak of zionisms in the plural.

14. As we see later, writers like Ahad Haam, a seminal figure in shaping zionist discourse, framed a new way of talking about Judaism, Jewish identity, and Jewish history. In Ahad Haam's case, the binary structure underlying his representation of the Jewish condition is evident in the titles of many of his essays. See, for example, the titles of articles in Ahad Haam (1947, 73–92). An awareness of these binaries and their status as "givens" is essential to an understanding of zionist discourse.

15. As I discuss in chapter 6, the dominant discourse in Israel spoke of the Arab population not as Palestinians, but as Israeli Arabs or Arabs of Israel. There was no room in this discourse for the term "Palestinians." Thus, Golda Meir's famous 1969 statement: "There was no such thing as Palestinians. When was there an independent Palestinian people with a Palestinian state?... It was not as though there was a Palestinian people and we came and threw them out and took their country from them. They did not exist" (in Kimmerling & Migdal 1993, xvi). To my knowledge, Yitzhak Rabin, in his White House speech in 1993, was the first Israeli leader to break with previous patterns and speak of a Palestinian people. This is not to say that there were not many zionists who were aware of and sensitive to the national aspirations of the Arabs in Palestine. Such an awareness and concern are clearly evident in the positions of groups such as Brith Shalom and Ihud, movements such as HaShomer Hazair, and political parties such as Mapam (see references in note 11).

16. The same applies to the culture produced by these subjects.

17. Salo Baron, Simon Dubnow, and other historians have argued that the zionist narrative is far too simplistic and ignores the fact that many Jews willingly left to establish communities in the "diaspora" (Babylonia, the Roman Empire) and that the majority of these were not "driven" from the land by Romans. For a critique of the zionist representation of the diaspora, see Evron (1995).

18. The narratives produced by secular zionist discourse often obscure the fact that zionism appropriated many religious concepts and symbols. See Canaani (1976), Luz (1988), and Evron (1995), as well as the discussion on Evron in chapter 2 and on the postzionist critique in chapter 6. Religious zionists, on the other hand, argued that the role of religion was central to authentic zionism and sought to integrate religious and nationalist discourse.

19. See, for example, Dinur (1969). On Dinur and zionist historiography in general, see Myers (1995). For a more critical perspective, see Raz-Krakotzkin (1996) and Ram (1995c).

20. For an overview of modern Jewish views on the concept of exile, see Eisen (1986) and Levine (1983).

21. To map the controversy among Ahad Haam and his interlocutors is to map the diverse meanings attributed to the basic concepts of zionist discourse. This, in turn, affords an excellent opportunity to see how these concepts, articulating with diverse conceptual/political/cultural frameworks, acquired different, often conflicting, meanings. Such a mapping clearly demonstrates the futility of zion-

ist efforts to impose essentialistic meaning on the basic terms of its discourse. Other examples of these conflicting representations and efforts to demarcate specific boundaries abound. These include conflicts between religious and secular zionists; Marxist, socialist, and liberal zionists; labor zionists and revisionists; zionists and Canaanites; secular humanists and Gush Emunim; and secular territorial expansionists and members of the Israeli left who advocate exchanging territory for peace.

22. Foucault (1984a, 101–120). "What Is an Author."

23. See Anderson (1991).

24. Foucault's analysis of the concept of problematization is useful for grasping the dynamic involved in framing the Jewish problem. According to Foucault (1996), it "doesn't mean the representation of a pre-existent object, nor the creation through discourse of an object that doesn't exist. It is the set of discursive or nondiscursive practices that makes something enter into the play of the true or false, and constitutes it as an object of thought" (pp. 456–57).

25. Ahad Haam recognized that there were ongoing processes of adaption throughout Jewish history (see Ahad Haam 1947, 86–89).

26. One term widely used to describe these processes is modernity. For a recent discussion of the effects of modernity on group identity, see Hall et al. (1996).

27. This in no way implies that Jewish communities in different parts of the world were not confronted by actual physical, social, political, and cultural dangers or problems. However, these were represented in diverse ways in keeping with the diverse discourses within which they were represented. Thus, to take one example, what zionists represented as problems of assimilation among European Jews were alternatively represented by nonzionists as problems of integration. Similarly, whereas zionists attributed the problems confronted by diaspora Jews to an essential anti-Semitism that was inherent in European culture, political liberals and socialists defined the problems in terms of specific sociopolitical conditions.

28. See Ahad Haam (1947, 399–404); translated in Hertzberg (1970, 270–77).

29. For Dubnow's theory of diaspora nationalism, see Dubnow (1961).

30. This description of the effects of zionism on Jewish identity applies primarily to Ashkenazic Jews of European origin. The impact of zionism on the Jews from Middle Eastern countries is a complex phenomenon that is only recently being told. See Alcalay (1993) and Shohat (1988), both of whom emphasize the marginalization/otherization of Sephardic Jews and their culture under the Ashkenazic hegemony first in the pre-state *yishuv* and subsequently in the state. See also references listed in note 12.

31. In various places, Ahad Haam (1970a) acknowledges his indebtedness to nineteenth-century social theory, including the writings of Fustel de Coulanges, E. B. Tylor, Gabriel Tarde, and Herbert Spencer (see pp. 69, 82, 107, 163, and 237).

32. Although Berkowitz focuses on the spread of zionist culture among Jews in Central and Western Europe, his description could also apply, with modifications, to Jewish communities in Russia and Poland. Berkowitz's pioneering study, one of the few efforts to analyze the ways in which zionist culture was produced and disseminated among European Jews, significantly broadens the framework through which the spread of zionism had previously been dis-

cussed. Although citing Foucault and Said, Berkowitz operates with a more benign view of culture, shying away from analyzing the power–knowledge connection and its specific effects.

33. Like so much of his discourse of Jewish nationalism, Ahad Haam's representation of intellectual freedom was derived not from traditional Jewish discourse, but from the Western European Enlightenment.

34. In addition to conflicting with the representations of the Jewish problem and its solution as set forth by Herzl and by Western liberal Jews, Ahad Haam's discourse also conflicted with those of nonzionists such as historian Simon Dubnow (see Dubnow 1961). Dubnow agreed with Ahad Haam's representation of Jews as a nation, but drew different implications from it. For example, Dubnow believed that a vibrant national life was possible for Jews in the lands of the diaspora. Depicting Jews in previous generations as having succeeded in building a vibrant social and cultural life in different societies and among different nations, Dubnow embraced the discourse of minority rights and national autonomy.

35. See Ahad Haam (1947, 271, 286, 288).

36. For other instances of Ahad Haam's efforts to define the limits of Jewish culture, see Ahad Haam (1947, 133–34; also "The Transvaluation of Values" and "Judaism and the Gospels" in 1962).

37. Berdiczewski's discourse, like that of all zionists, was masculine and androcentric.

38. Here, again, the differences between Berdiczewski's basic point of view and that of Nietzsche are readily apparent (Brinker 1988, 248, n. 13).

39. On the debates between Ahad Haam, Berdiczewski and Brenner, see Brinker (1990a, b).

40. See on this controversy Guvrin (1985). Cf. Haam's letter to Barukh Ledizinsky, a member of the board of *HaShiloah*, dated December 14, 1910, in Guvrin (1985, 32); see also Ahad Haam (1946, 289–90). See also responses by Berdiczewski (Guvrin 1985, 194–95) and Brenner (Guvrin 1985, 195–97).

41. Ahad Haam (1947) argued that the Hebrew Bible embodies the spirit of the Jewish people from an earlier period. It doesn't matter why biblical books were incorporated into the canon. Once they were, he insisted, they became "an essential part of our national identity/ego/self, which cannot be imagined without it." Comparing those who reject exclusive power of Tanakh to those "who reject their mother because they found another more beautiful," he accused them of suffering "absolute atrophy of national feeling" (p. 408).

42. Guvrin (1985) frames the debate as one over freedom of expression; Brinker (1988), in his recent study of Brenner, frames the debate in terms of their relation to Judaism/Jewish tradition.

Chapter 2

1. On Brith Shalom, see Yehoshua and Kedar (1978, 97–114).

2. For a discussion of Buber's spiritual interpretation of zionism see Silberstein (1989, chap. 8), on which this section is based.

3. For a thorough statement of Buber's views on the Jewish claim to the land see Buber (1983, 81–91); see also Buber's letter to Gandhi (111–26).

4. These comments are from Buber's response to Gandhi's sharp rebuke of the Jewish claims in Palestine (see note 3).

5. See Buber (1983, 239–44, 295–303) for examples of his encounters with Israeli leaders.

6. Buber's statement aroused the anger of one of his own disciples who felt that Buber had gone too far. See Buber (1983, 228–35), and Buber's reply (pp. 236–39).

7. According to Mendes-Flohr (Buber 1983) Buber also alluded to covert actions by the Israeli military to encourage the flight of the Arabs. On this issue, see Segev (1986, chaps. 1–3) and Morris (1988, 1991).

8. Buber (1983, 239–44, 294–97). See also Keren (1983, 63–99) and Simon (1965).

9. Buber spoke out in the wake of Israeli attacks on the Jordanian village of Kibya in 1953 and the village of K'far Kassem in 1956; see Friedman (1983, Vol. 3, 337–38 and the sources he cites on 455–57).

10. Bar On served for twenty years as an officer in the Israeli military and was, for a time, the chief education officer. An active member of Peace Now, Bar On has been a leading proponent of peaceful coexistence with the Palestinians. See Bar On (1996a, xvii–xviii).

11. This is a common motif with many Israeli liberals, who distinguish between the authentic or essential character of the state and those aberrations or distortions that are responsible for the problems. Others, however, like Tom Segev, argue that the contradictions and conflicts within Israeli culture and society were inherent from the outset. For a critique of the liberal zionist position such as that espoused by Bar On, see Peled and Levi (1993).

12. Bar On (1983), using a rationalistic notion of ideology, makes a somewhat strange distinction between zionism as a phenomenon, that is, a historical movement, and zionist consciousness, which he relates to "a particular set of ideas" (p. 2). This differs significantly from Foucault's conception of discourse, which links together language, thought, practice, and apparatuses. For more recent uses of the concept of ideology and a discussion of the relationship of Foucault's concept of discourse to the concept of ideology, see Barrett (1991); for a discussion of ideology by a leading cultural studies theorist, see Hall (1985, 1988). In recent years, Hall, speaking decreasingly of ideology, has adopted Foucault's concept of discourse; see Hall (1997).

13. While sympathetic to some of their concerns, Bar On (1996b) is basically critical of the postzionist scholars discussed in chapter 4. See also chapter 4, note 25.

14. Amos Oz (1984, 163–65, 170–72) suggests parallels between the practices of early Jewish nationalism and Palestinian nationalism.

15. For a critique of the ideology of the "tragic metaphor" from the radical antizionist left (Mazpen) see VanTeefelen (1981).

16. Elon here represents the official zionist rationale for the practice. For an alternative interpretation of *avodah ivrit,* see Shafir (1989, 1996b).

17. Elon was one of the first to use the term postzionist, albeit in a very different way than it is used in the current debates. Speaking of the younger, postzionist generation, he used it to refer to those Israelis who had been born after the state had come into existence (1971, 158). In his recent work (1997), he refers

to the current use of the term: "The recent talk of 'Post-Zionism' has nothing to do with the current 'postmodern' discourse. It reflects a conviction that the Zionist revolution has achieved its aim, as well as a growing desire to move away from 'official Jewish ideology,' especially since a fifth of its citizens are Arab. It reflects a desire to move ahead to a more Western, more pluralistic, less 'ideological' form of patriotism and of citizenship" (p. 11). For a more thorough and nuanced discussion of the concept see below chapters 4 and 6.

18. While Oz, in his fiction, poses countermodels and images to those of the dominant zionist ideology of the 1940s and 1950s, this chapter focuses on his non-fiction. For a discussion of the challenge to hegemonic notions expressed in Oz's fiction, see Shaked (1991, esp. 129–39).

19. Lubin (1990) argues that Oz's narrative enables him to avoid telling the reader exactly where he, Oz, stands on political issues. Lubin is speaking as a member of the Israeli left who would like specifics. However, Oz's general political stance does come through to the reader, especially when the work is read in the context of his other writings of social and political criticism.

20. Recent neo- or post-Marxist theorists such as Althusser, Williams, and Hall assign a far greater significance to the realm of culture than was traditionally assigned in Marxist thought. In these writings, culture is regarded as an independent social force rather than simply a reflection of material processes. See Williams (1977), Hall (1985), and Barrett (1991).

21. For academic discussions of labor zionism see Shapira (1992, chaps. 1–3), Shimoni (1995, chap. 5), and Gorny (1987, 207–33).

22. A recent postzionist exploration of the discourse and practices of labor zionism relating to the land is Gurevitch and Aran (in Hebrew, 1991; in English, 1994). They discuss such concepts as *yediat haaretz, kibbush haaretz,* and *ahavat haaretz,* as well as the institutions and practices by means of which such ideas are materialized and actualized.

23. For an insightful discussion of the ways in which nations construct history so as to silence the voices of subordinate or conquered groups, see Trouillot (1995).

24. Emile Habiby, the late Israeli Palestinian writer whom I discuss in chapter 5, has graphically depicted the effects of silencing on the Palestinian population of Israel in his fiction.

25. Benvenisti refers to Said's *Orientalism* (1989) as describing the same phenomenon.

26. On the problem of representation and the real in mapping the spaces of a colonized land, see Mitchell (1988). Benvenisti (1997) elaborates and expands his analysis of mapping. In this article he focuses on the Israeli practice of replacing Arabic names of sites with Hebrew names, many of them derived from the Bible.

27. As I argue in chapter 6, this is true of many liberal zionists who work with similar models. The shortcomings of the modernist structural model of colonialism has been subjected to extensive critique by those whom I designate as postmodern postzionists.

28. See Benvenisti (1986, 161 ff.) for further discussion. In a subsequent work (1992), Benvenisti, after showing clear points of convergence between Israel's occupation of the territories and colonialism, again rejects the colonial model in favor of the intercommunal conflict model. There he argues that since no clear-cut borders separate Israel from the Palestinians, it is difficult to speak of colonialism.

Chapter 3

1. For a powerful statement of the extreme Canaanite position on the negation of the diaspora, see the short story by Hazaz (1975).

2. Scholars disagree as to the precise relationship of Canaanism to zionism. To some critics, Canaanism, a counterdiscourse to zionism, reflected the ethos of native-born Israelis in the 1940s and 1950s (Kurzweil 1971). In the eyes of one scholar, Canaanism is best understood as "a secular anti-Zionist heresy" (Shavit 1987, 5). According to this view, Canaanism represents a "new myth" within Israeli society which, since the end of the 1940s, "has been hovering over the Zeitgeist, or climate of ideas, of Israeli political culture" (Shavit 1987, 2). To yet other interpreters (e.g., Diamond 1986), Canaanist discourse can best be seen as a dialectical outgrowth of inherent contradictions in zionist ideology. Seen in this way, Canaanism is a prototypical postzionist discourse that sought to move beyond the limits of zionist discourse in an effort to transcend these contradictions.

3. The enormous outpouring of support, material and moral alike, from diaspora Jews during the 1967 War, led to a greater sense of connection on the part of Israelis.

4. See Kurzweil (1971) and Diamond (1986, chap. 6).

5. Evron was highly disturbed by the fact that many of the Canaanite leaders had identified with the colonialist goals of Gush Emunim, a movement informed by a highly particularistic ethnocentrism mixed with Jewish religious ideology.

6. See Friedman (1995) and Dowty (1998, chap. 8).

7. Regarding the Uganda controversy, see Vital (1988, chaps. 9 and 10).

8. This is evident from the wording of Israel's Declaration of Independence. See chapter 4, pp. 119–20.

9. Published independently, Beit Zvi's study was, until the late 1980s, either ignored or outright rejected by the academic establishment. On the controversy surrounding Beit Zvi, see Grodzinski (1994 b,c,d).

10. For Evron's critique and the response by Yehuda Bauer, a leading Holocaust scholar, see Evron (1980; reprinted in Michman 1997, 565–76).

11. Evron does not deny that there is a growing emphasis on ethnic distinctiveness. Nevertheless, he argues, separatist nationalism, which created the conditions for the anti-Semitism of the nineteenth and early twentieth centuries, while in no way disappearing, is clearly losing its effectiveness as a major political force. At the same time, even in the former Soviet Union, Jews feel less and less motivation to emigrate and, when they do, their first choice is frequently not Israel. Evron criticizes the efforts of Israeli leaders to bring pressure on European governments and the United States to discourage or prevent Jews from settling there in large numbers so that they will turn to Israel. For recent studies that provide support to Evron's overall transnational perspective, see Appardurai (1996) and Grewal and Kaplan (1994).

12. Evron also speaks of the unequal distribution of power between Ashkenazi Jews of European origin and Mizrahi Jews of Middle-Eastern origin as further evidence of the inherent contradictions of zionism.

13. On the structure of Israel's civic society, see Dowty (1998, chap. 4). Regarding the unique problem of the Palestinian Arab citizens, see Dowty (1998, chap. 9) and the fine study by Rouhanna (1997, chap. 2).

14. Several years prior to the current widespread use of the term postzionist in Israeli cultural debates, Diamond (1990) applied the term to Evron. In his foreword to Evron (1995), Diamond describes Evron as "post-Zionist and post-'Canaanite.'"

15. This statement is quoted from the document "The Palestine Problem and the Israeli-Arab Dispute," issued by Mazpen, May 18, 1967. It was first read at a public gathering of Israeli and Palestinian students in Paris and was Mazpen's first public statement on the Middle East situation.

16. For disagreement within Mazpen on the two-state solution, see Orr (1994, chap. 12).

17. See Machover and Offenberg (1978).

18. On Beit Zvi, see note 9.

19. See Hecht and Yuval-Davis (1978) and Erlich (1980).

Chapter 4

1. On the decline of labor zionism's hegemony see Dowty (1998, chap. 6).

2. According to Kimmerling (1992), "There has been a growing tendency to treat their [groups such as Mazpen's] criticism selectively and seriously. This recognition is limited, however, and is usually not expressed by direct reference to their writings" (p. 456). For an account of the ways in which academicians sought to neutralize the arguments of radical critics, see Shalev (1996, 187, n. 30).

3. See Shalev (1992, 18, n. 23) and Ram (1993, 1995a).

4. The term postzionism was not unknown in Israeli culture prior to the 1990s. However, it was usually used by those questioning the necessity of maintaining a zionist apparatus in a post-state era. Thus, critics such as Menahem Brinker (1986) and Amos Elon (1971) used the term to indicate not the failure of zionism, but rather its success. Having achieved its goal of a Jewish state, they suggested, perhaps zionism could now quietly pass from the scene and allow the state to carry on the fulfillment of its vision. Mordecai Bar On (1996b, n. 42) reports that Brinker, in the face of the large immigration from the former Soviet Union and Ethiopia, recanted and acknowledged the need of the continuation of zionism. In contrast to Elon and Brinker, Uri Avneri (1968) used the term as a way of talking about the inadequate ways in which zionism addressed the problems of the Middle East. However, Avneri, while engaging in an ongoing critique of zionism, continued to operate within its spaces, serving for a time in the Knesset. For a recent use of the term in a similar way see Erik Cohen (1995).

5. Oz (1979, 69–108; 1995, 79–101).

6. For Rabin's speech see Laqueur and Rubin (1984, 230–32); for the responses of groups of soldiers from kibbutzim, see Shapira (1970).

7. The shock and disappointment experienced by many in the current generation upon learning that they had been lied to is a common theme among younger, critical scholars. See autobiographical recollections by Shafir and Shalev (1992 preface, 1996, n. 14). See also Ben-Yehuda (1995, 3–7). For an expression of disillusionment of a different kind over the changes in Israeli life by a member of the 1984 generation, see Horowitz (1993).

8. This sense of shock over learning the "truth" about Israeli history, particularly the 1948 War, was a recurring theme in interviews that I conducted in Israel in December 1995 and January 1996.

9. I am grateful to Miriam Peskowitz for calling Appardurai's valuable work to my attention.

10. The discourse of labor zionism has also been both challenged and co-opted by the militant, expansionist movement known as Gush Emunim. Rejecting the Western humanist discourse of secular zionists, Gush Emunim seeks to put in its place a religious, messianic, expansionist discourse that often evokes feelings of identification among otherwise secular Israelis. See Lustick (1988) and Sprinzak (1991) (cf. Oz 1984, 103–53).

11. See Weimann (1995, 1996).

12. On Americanization, see Mehlman's lively journalistic account (1992, chap. 13) and Eric Zakim (1998).

13. See Benvenisti (1986) and Oz (1984, 193–217). On the far-reaching shifts in Israeli society and culture see Schmemann (1998).

14. Zerubavel (1995) speaks of the rapid decline of the power of the basic myths that had shaped the collective memory of the Yishuv and the state in its early years, as does Ben-Yehuda (1995). An early and important work that significantly contributed to the debunking process is by Harkabi (1983).

15. See Bar On (1994, 266, n. 3), Dowty (1998, 108), and Gonen (1975, 118–19).

16. See Hillel Halkin (1998) and Shapira (1995, 15–16).

17. See comments of Yoav Gelbar and Amnon Rubenstein in the symposium in Haaretz (Margalit 1995).

18. Shalev succinctly summarizes the critique leveled by critical sociologists at Haifa University (1996, 185, n. 11). See also Ram (1995a, chaps. 6–8).

19. The Hebrew edition, which appeared in 1984, was followed in 1986 by an English translation.

20. These conflicts continue to plague Israeli society. See Yehoshua (1995). Yehoshua outlines the conflicts confronting Israeli society in a post-Oslo era. The rifts that will continue to divide Israeli society after peace is achieved include those between religion-secular, Ashkenazim-Mizrahim, and Israelis-diaspora Jewry. Yehoshua, an ardent although often critical defender of zionist ideology, anticipates the ultimate resolution of these conflicts in the context of the zionist state. Oz (1984), discussed in chapter 2, has described these rifts in a different way. For other perspectives on the issues dividing Israeli society, see Ezrahi (1997), Sprinzak (1991), and Lustick (1988). Horowitz (1993) focuses on generational issues, Ezrahi on the conflict between the dominant collectivist ethos and that of liberal Western individualism, and Sprinzak and Lustick on right-wing settler and militant religious and nonreligious groups, particularly Gush Emunim.

21. Reviews appeared in all of the Israeli daily newspapers and in local city newspapers and weeklies. The book elicited many letters to the editor.

22. Morris eventually received an academic position at Ben Gurion University of the Negev, which is home to many of those scholars considered to be postzionists.

23. Among those who challenged the conventional wisdom were Cohen (1970), Buber (see chapter 2), and the members of Mazpen (see chapter 3).

24. In keeping with the terminology regularly used by both sides in the debates, I shall use the terms new historians and critical sociologists to refer to those historians and sociologists who, because they challenged the prevailing interpretations of Israeli history and society, have been accused by their critics as being postzionists.

25. An interesting study of the stages in the revision of Israeli history is in Bar On (1990). Bar On elaborates on the forms of such revisions, the different functions they are meant to fulfill, and the variety of factors motivating such historiography. Bar On has recently extended this interpretation. See also Bar On (1996c).

26. See Teveth (1989 a-d). Morris responded to Teveth's criticisms in "The Eel and History: A Reply to Shabtai Teveth" (1990). For a convenient summary of Morris' basic historical claims see Silberstein (1991, 42–56). For Morris' more recent reflections on the debates see Morris (1994a).

27. For Kimmerling's later critique of zionist scholarship see below, pages 107–110.

28. Shafir, born and educated in Israel, now lives and teaches in the United States and publishes in English. However, his work has made a strong impact on the debates over postzionism and his name is increasingly included on lists of "postzionist" scholars.

29. For a broader discussion of the dominant schools of Israeli social science, see Ram (1995a).

30. In the new Preface written for the second edition of his book (1996a), Shafir situates his work in the context of the new historiography.

31. See Tsahor (in Hebrew, 1994).

32. Pappe's multiple perspective approach to history is often labeled postmodern by his critics. For the postmodern interpretation of historical discourse, see chapter 6.

33. For examples of recent critiques of historians' claims to objectivity, see works cited in chapter 6, notes 34 and 35.

34. Pappe published an early extensive critique of Israeli historiography in *Theory and Criticism*, the most important site of a theoretically grounded postzionist discourse. I discuss this journal extensively in chapter 6.

35. See Pappe (1995a) and Pappe and Swirski (1992).

36. As significant as Morris' work was for broadening and altering the dominant historical representations of the 1948 War, it does not incorporate Palestinian voices. Nor is he particularly concerned with the ways in which the narratives of the two peoples were intertwined.

37. Pappe, like Kimmerling, criticizes zionist historiography for treating zionist/Jewish/Israeli history as unique. This results in a neglect of comparative approaches and little or no concern with the broader, non-Jewish context. Criticizing highly regarded historians of zionism such as David Vital, Pappe (1993d) argues that their studies should compare the history of zionism with that of other nationalist movements and the history of Israel with that of other new nations. For a recent collection of essays emphasizing a comparative approach, see Barnett (1996).

38. Kimmerling (1995a) makes this argument.
39. As indicated earlier, both Kimmerling and Pappe resist the postzionist designation. See also Margalit (1995).
40. Kimmerling focuses on the ideologically embedded character of historiography more clearly and incisively than most other Israeli scholars. However, although acknowledging the importance of discourse and practices of periodization, he does not, as do postmodern critics, undertake to analyze the processes through which these become inscribed as a part of Israeli hegemonic culture. In contrast, as indicated earlier, a postmodernist critique would focus on the rhetorical processes by means of which the scholarly discourse is constructed and disseminated. In addition, postmodern critics like Derrida and Foucault would problematize and critically analyze notions such as structure, history, identity, subject, nation, society, continuity, history, agency, context, and representation. Kimmerling (1992) sharply criticized the effort by Gurevitch and Aran (1991 and 1994) to critically analyze the discourse of homeland. Aran and Gurevitch sought to demonstrate that rather than being "natural" categories, terms such as homeland and exile are culturally, that is, discursively, constructed and disseminated. Kimmerling objected to what he perceived as a tendency to "dematerialize" or render "imaginary" the material, physical effects of the Jewish notion of homeland and the practices based upon it on the Palestinians. For the application of postmodern theory to the critique of zionism see chapter 6.
41. Morris, while openly challenging the prevailing Israeli versions of the 1948 War and its aftermath, nevertheless continues to identify as a zionist.
42. In contrast to Haifa, one of the newer Israeli universities, the Hebrew University in Jerusalem, established in 1925, was considered to be the most prestigious. The dominant scholarship, shaped by Hebrew University professor Shmuel Eisenstadt and his disciples, was strongly influenced by structural functionalism. Privileging social integration and cohesion, the dominant school either ignored minority groups such as Jews of Middle Eastern origin, Palestinian Arabs living in Israel, and women, or relegated them to the margins. When they did discuss these groups, the emphasis was on the processes by which they were being integrated into mainstream Israeli society and culture, and the factors that impeded this integration. See Ram (1995a).
43. The following draws upon Silberstein (1996). See also Shalev (1996, 185, n. 11).
44. Ram (1995a) acknowledges his indebtedness to the philosopher of science Thomas Kuhn. His mapping of Israeli sociology is built around seven major theoretical orientations or, as he refers to them, "soft" paradigms. These include structural functionalism (Shmuel Eisenstadt and his disciples); revised functionalism (Moshe Shokeid, Dan Horowitz, and Moshe Lissak); Yonatan Shapiro's elitist orientation; the pluralistic model (Sammy Smooha); Marxist sociology (Shlomo Swirski, Deborah Bernstein, S. Carmi, and Henry Rosenfeld); feminism (Deborah Bernstein, Marilyn Safir, Barbara Swirski, Dafna Izraeli, and Yael Azmon); and colonization (Baruch Kimmerling and Gershon Shafir). In his anthology, Ram (1993) also included excerpts from the

writings of Ella Shochat, whose critique of Israeli culture is consistent with postcolonial theory; Michael Shalev; and the Palestinian philosopher Azmi Bishara.

45. The title of his 1995 Epilogue, "Towards a Post-Zionist Sociology," clearly states his objective, as does the Introduction to his Hebrew anthology (1993).

46. See Ginosar and Bareli (1996) and Weitz (1997). A comprehensive collection of materials appearing in the press and journals that conveys a good sense of the intensity and breadth of the debate over postzionism is Michman (1997).

47. Landers cites extensively the Hebrew University sociologist Moshe Lissak, a leading academic critic of postzionism. See below, pp. 119, 124–126.

48. Landers singled out Kimmerling and Migdal, whom he accused of subverting the zionist narrative and aiding the crystallization of "an opposing Palestinian narrative" (p. 8).

49. Lissak agreed that the first generation of Israeli sociologists did not pay sufficient attention to the ways in which the political establishment exploited the new immigrants for political purposes. Lissak also acknowledged that the image of the "melting pot" is flawed. He insisted, however, that the sociologists of the Jerusalem school had been the first to criticize that model. He further argued that the fact that the writings of the Jerusalem group actually helped to bring about changes in government policies and practices indicates that they were not pawns of the political establishment, as critics claimed.

50. While seeming to imply that the sense of "a Jewish mission" formed an appropriate component of Israeli scholarly research, Lissak claimed that advocating the secular democratic character did not. Kimmerling, whose views are discussed later, responded in 1994c.

51. A similar connection is made by Dan (1994).

52. In an expansion of his original *Tikkun* essay, Morris (1994a) reviews the scholarly controversy precipitated by his book and defends himself against the criticisms of such scholars as Asher Susser, Itamar Rabinovich, Michael Oren, and Immanuel Sivan.

53. On the role of the *Shoah* in Israeli culture and identity, see Segev (1993) and the interesting article by Diner (1995).

54. See the discussion of martyrdom and resistance in relation to the myth of Masada in Zerubavel (1995, chap. 5).

55. On Beit Zvi, see a series of articles in *Haaretz* by Grodzinski (1994a–d) and comments of critics. Diner (1995) describes Beit Zvi's work as an "early and amateurish, but nonetheless important study" (p. 168, n. 6).

56. While their criticisms were written in direct response to Lissak, they apply, for the most part, to Shapira as well.

57. Shalev (1996), like Morris and others, cites generational differences between "the generation that grew to maturity when the state was established, versus those like myself who have no personal memories of the heroic period, and for whom Israel has always been a regional power with far greater strength than the competing claimants to this land" (p. 174) as a major factor in the debates.

58. Shalev/Shafir cite the work of Yonatan Shapiro in the 1970s, which focused on the hegemonic labor party's political interests and quest for power. For a discussion of Shapiro's contribution, see Ram (1995a, chap. 5).

59. Shalev points out that the initial expansion of settlements occurred under a labor government. The subsequent expansion by the right-wing Likud government was simply a continuation of what labor had already initiated, a claim often made by Likud leaders. On postzionism as a critique of labor zionism see Shapira (1995, 15–17); see also Halkin (1998).

60. See Introduction, note 19.

61. See note 4.

62. A useful discussion of the problems connected to "post" terms is McClintock (1995, 9–17). Although her critique revolves around the term postcolonialism, it is relevant to the concept of postzionism as well. On this issue see also Shohat (1992) and the criticisms of Hall (1996b).

63. This is the position of Amnon Raz-Krakotzkin (interview, December 1995).

64. Shapira (1995) agrees that there are clear differences between "the old anti-Zionism of the Communist or Bundist variety or that of the New Left and 'Matzpen' of the 1970's" and the postzionists, of whom she says, "Its proponents do not question the existence of Israel, but their attitude toward it is, at best, indifferent and, in more extreme cases, a priori suspicious and critical" (p. 11). See Introduction, p. 3.

65. Shapira (1995) also makes this claim, speaking of its "deconstructionist trends" without attempting in any way to clarify how she uses this term.

66. To my knowledge, this position has never been argued by any postzionist scholar or, for that matter, any postmodernist. What they do argue, however, is that there are no absolute, foundational premises upon which the truth claims of a narrative can be based. Nor, they argue, can any metanarrative be considered as universally binding. On this point, see Berkhofer (1995b, chap. 1).

67. The only social scientists whom Lissak names are Shafir and Kimmerling. Ignoring their books and numerous articles, he chooses to dwell only on the selections included in Ram's anthology. Classifying Shafir's work as positivist and functionalist, an identification that Shafir vigorously denies, he attributes to him a voluntaristic, somewhat psychological explanatory framework that is nowhere to be found in Shafir. Similarly, in briefly summarizing Kimmerling's position, he makes no reference to such concepts as frontier or legitimation, both of which, as we have seen, are basic to Kimmerling's analysis.

68. In a fascinating comment on the relationship of politics and historical scholarship, Shapira (1995), a critic of the new historiography, recently explained the reluctance of historians to apply a colonial model to Israeli history by claiming that such a model fed into the hands of Israel's enemies: "Today, with the dissolution of the Soviet Union, which made colonialism the white bogey of the Third World, and with the liberation of that world from the patronage of the West [sic], there is room for dispassionate thought, free of ideologies, on the subject of colonialism." In a statement that is indicative of the impact of the postzionist perspective on the Israeli academic establishment, Shapira acknowledges that "defining a movement as settlement-colonialism may well help to clarify the relations between the settling nation and the native one." At the same time, continuing the binary discourse of outsiders/insiders, she argues: "To complete the picture, we need the perspective 'from within' as well" (p. 30).

69. For example, Lissak (1996) asserts, without citing any sources, that "'post-modernism' rebels against every metanarrative and every meta-theory and, in practice, encourages spiritual anarchism or nihilism, dissolving all of those rules and ethos which have been created within the frame of the social sciences over the past 100 to 150 years" (p. 253). In addition, claiming that the critical sociologists ignore conceptual-theoretical or metatheoretical issues, he accuses them, without specific references, of "focusing, instead, upon several psuedo-theoretical axioms such as 'relativism,' 'reflexivity,' 'post-modernism' [*sic*], or 'equality between the narratives'" (p. 250). I discuss the postmodern critique of zionism in chapter 6.

70. Schweid wrote an extensive article in which he purported to trace the history of postmodernism while never providing any support for his interpretation. As Shalev (1996) has pointed out, none of the social scientists included in Ram's anthology "has either expressly or by implication taken a post-modern position" but have, rather, based their work on "traditional scientific practices of analytical reasoning and empirical evidence" (p. 173). With the exception of Pappe, and this only to a limited degree, the same could be said of the so-called "new historians."

71. As I make clear in chapter 6, with the exception of Ilan Pappe, one finds few connections between the writings of the "new historians" and critical sociologists and postmodernism or postmodern theory. Only rarely do they display any firsthand knowledge of postmodern theory. Although questioning the established Israeli scholarship, scholars such as Ram, Kimmerling, and Shafir do not problematize the notion that scholars can achieve an objective and accurate representation of history and society, a distinctly modernist position. Overall, as Shalev argues (see note 70), the methodologies within which they work are grounded in modern, rather than postmodern, theory. Only Pappe, emphasizing a perspectival approach, rejects, in the spirit of Lyotard, the validity of any (meta)narrative. As I discuss in chapter 6, another group of postzionist critics are strongly influenced by postcolonial and postmodern theory.

72. As discussed earlier, Morris insisted that the new historians succeeded in producing a "truer" picture of past events than did their predecessors. In his usage, truer clearly means corresponding more faithfully to the events that occurred.

73. One possible exception is Pappe, who, rejecting all metanarratives, advocates a multiperspectival approach to history. Although there is no indication that Pappe's views are connected to postmodernist theorists, there are some indications that he is receptive to selected positions associated with postmodern theory. Scholars like Kimmerling, who have raised the issue of the political effects of academic discourse, touch on the issue of the relation of discourse, knowledge, and power that is a central concern of postmodern theory. However, Kimmerling would clearly reject the label postmodern. See chapter 6, note 33.

Chapter 5

1. Palestinians are by no means the exclusive bearers of Arab culture in Israel. As Alcalay (1993) has persuasively argued, the culture of Jews of Middle Eastern origins bears more affinites with Arabic culture than with European Jewish culture.

2. The transformation of a marginal position to a position of strength is asserted by writer bell hooks (1990): "I am located in the margin. I make a definite distinction between the marginality that is imposed by oppressive structures and that marginality one chooses as site of resistance—as location of radical openness and possibility" (p. 153). For other discussions see Soja (1996) and Bhabha, later in this chapter.

3. For an extensive discussion of the conditions of Palestinian citizens in Israel and the problems relating to their identity, see Rouhanna (1997) and Dowty (1998, chap. 9).

4. The first Palestinian to write a novel in Hebrew was Attalah Mansur. I am grateful to Hannan Hever for this reference.

5. The fact that Habiby's novels have been made available to the Hebrew reader through the translations of Anton Shammas is further indication of Shammas' contribution to Israeli cultural discourse.

6. On the idea of the margin as a site of empowerment, see bell hooks (1990, esp. chap. 15); see also Soja (1996, chap. 3) and Bhabha (1994, 36–39).

7. "Culture as a field of struggle: the notion drives important strains of thinking on the problem of social discourse. Such a characterization of the network within which our meanings are made meaningful has a strategic advantage: it draws attention to the intensity of social contradiction within the linguistic and symbolic realms. It conceives these as the loci within which, the mediums by which, such contradictions receive expression and determine representation. Much of the bearing of recent materialist criticism has been to show how deeply the struggle for control of meaning inscribes itself in the language of culture" (Terdiman 1985, 25). For an extensive analysis of cultural conflicts, see Jordon and Weedon (1995).

8. Cf. comment by Alcalay (1993, 286–87, n. 21). Interestingly, one of Shammas' critics, the Jewish writer Sami Mikhael, provides, albeit unintentionally, support for Shammas' position. In a revealing comment on the hybrid character of Palestinian Israeli identity, Mikhael (1986) describes a scene that he witnessed in Cairo. There, in a square, he found a group of Israeli Arab youths sitting and speaking Hebrew. To Mikhael, this scene reflects the identity problem of Arabs in Israel. Unlike Egyptian Arabs, their home is Israel. Unlike Israeli Jews, they are Arabs whose "homeland is fighting with my people" (p. 12).

9. See the discussions in Dowty (1998, 197–200), and Grossman (1993, chap. 5).

10. As Hannan Hever has reminded me, Yehoshua, in his novel *Mr. Mani,* has also set forth a dynamic conception of identity. However, Yehoshua maintaining a sharp distinction between the identity of Israeli Jews and that of Israeli Palestinians does not accept Shammas' complex, hybrid conception of Israeli identity. This seems to be a contradiction between two conceptions of identity employed by Yehoshua. I briefly discuss the concept of identity in *Mr. Mani* in Silberstein (1995), where I argue that reading Yehoshua, a professed zionist, against the grain reveals ideas that border on postzionism.

11. "Cultural poesis—and politics—is the constant reconstitution of selves and others through specific exclusions, conventions, and discursive practices" Clifford and Marcus (1986, 24).

12. For recent discussions of the concept of culture as viewed in cultural studies, see Grossberg et al. (1992), Turner (1990), and Dirks et al. One of the major

texts suggesting a postmodern approach to culture is Clifford and Marcus (1986).

13. Habiby (1993, 9) describes his writing process as one in which he allows his consciousness to roam without determining in advance where it would lead. At times, he acknowledges, the result borders on anarchy.

14. In his later years, while contributing to a number of Hebrew periodicals and newspapers, Habiby continued to write his fiction in Arabic.

15. For a background on the awarding of the prize, see Hever (1993).

16. Habiby (1988c) quotes from a poem about an Arab hero, "Omer ben Maadi Krav," whom he describes as a kind of Arab Robin Hood: "Those whom I loved have departed, and I remain alone like a sword" (p. 8). Habiby notes that he described these feelings in his novel *Ehtayeh* (1988a) which I discuss later in this chapter.

17. Cf. *Hamizrah Hahadashah (The New East): Journal on the Israeli Oriental Society.* Special Issue on "The Literature of the Arabs in Israel." vol. xxxv (1998, 46–114).

18. In *Saeed* (pp. 47–48), Habiby (1985) describes poignantly a Palestinian's visit to his former home, now occupied by Jews.

19. Writing of the coastal villages between Haifa and Tel Aviv that were destroyed by "the catastrophes of war and dispossession," he adds: "The list is long—al-Tirah, Ain Hawd, al-Mazar, Jaba, Ijzim, Sarafand, Kufr al-Burj, Qaisariyyah, Umm Khalid, Khirbat al-Zababidah, al-Haram, Jalil al-Shamaliyyah, and Jalil al-Qibliyyah."

20. Habiby (1992) discusses the symbolism of *Sarayah*.

21. Habiby (1988c) writes in the article: "This is the first time that I dare to recount my most personal childhood memories. Why do I do this for the first time in the Hebrew language?" (p. 6).

22. Habiby (1991c) said that the reason that he wrote often about women was that "I feel the evil that was done to the Arab woman. It disturbs me, it is part of my roots, and I want, not only in literature, to compensate her" (p. 24).

23. Habiby (1988c) says that he only learned about this when he heard his two daughters "playing Savta [grandma]" crying out "Yo Naim" (p. 9).

24. Here, as in many other places in his writings, Habiby makes a woman the active figure. See note 22.

25. Frye (1983, 2–10) speaks of the double-bind experienced by oppressed groups. For an insightful analysis of the five aspects contributing to oppression, see Young (1992). Like Foucault, Young makes it clear that oppression is effected through the everyday actions of well-meaning people: "The conscious actions of many individuals daily contribute to maintaining and reproducing oppression, but those people are usually simply doing their jobs or living their lives, not understanding themselves as agents of oppression" (p. 180).

26. At times, Habiby represents the Israelis as colonialists. Thus, he refers to the colonialist/Orientalist attitudes of Israeli soldiers in Ramalah in 1967. He also equates Israeli rule of the territories to the actions of the Americans in Vietnam and the French in Algeria (1988d, 38).

27. For the position and treatment of Palestinian Arabs in Israel in the first two decades of state, see Lustick (in Silberstein 1991); Pappe and Korn (in Troen

and Lucas (1995, 617–58, 659–82), Lustick (1980), Dowty (1998, chaps. 5 and 9), and Rouhanna (1997, 58–65).

28. In *Saeed* (pp. 141–42), Habiby (1985) had written of life for the Palestinians as being one big cordon.

29. On the Israeli practice of categorizing Palestinians seeking to return to their homes as "infiltrators," see Black and Morris (1991, 117–19). Black and Morris argue that most of those labeled "infiltrators" came for personal reasons, to visit family, or for material gain. However, "a small number of infiltrations were intended to kill Israelis, sabotage Israeli targets or gather intelligence" (p. 118).

30. See Dowty (1998, 87–88), Elon (1971, 189–221), and Segev (1993).

31. For more on Hever's analysis of the significance of writings of Palestinian citizens of Israel to the Israeli cultural and literary canon, see chapter 6. As Bhabha (1994) argues, "Minority discourse acknowledges the state of national culture—and the people—as a contentious performative space of the perplexity of the living in the midst of the pedagogical representations of the fullness of life" (p. 157).

32. For one criticism of Hever's emphasis on the relationship of politics to literature in Habiby's writings, see Har Even (1992, 26) and Hever's response (1992, 27).

Chapter 6

1. "Proclamation of the State of Israel," in Mendes-Flohr and Reinharz (1995, 629–30).

2. See Trouillot (1995).

3. The writings of Morris on the fate of the Palestinian Arabs during the 1948 War represented the deterritorializing effects of that War on the Palestinian population. However, Morris' narrative was centered on the practices of the Israelis. His research, analyzing the multiple and complex causes of the Palestinian flight, offered little insight into the social, cultural, economic, and psychological effects of that flight on the Palestinians, nor was it intended to.

4. Those who defend zionism from the "charge" of colonialism take it for granted that colonialism has its origins in and serves the interests of a metropolitan center. Insofar as zionism lacks these characteristics, it cannot be regarded as a colonialist enterprise. See chapter 4, pp. 102–107.

5. Mindful of the problems associated with the term postmodern, I nonetheless find it to be helpful in distinguishing between the kind of postzionist critique discussed in this chapter and the critique of zionism formulated by the historians and social scientists discussed in chapter 4. In referring to these postzionist critics as postmodern, I have in mind certain characteristics that they share with theory that is frequently characterized as postmodern. These characteristics have been usefully summarized by Nicholson and Seidman (1995) as follows: (1) viewing all historical metanarratives as contingent and historically positioned; (2) decentering essentialistic notions of identity and asserting that identities are always multiple, "always framed in discourses and practices in multiple, sometimes contradictory ways" (p. 28); (3) the interlocking relationship of knowledge and power and the view that "all categories of analysis—even

those used in the service of political opposition, are the effects of special relations of power"; (4) "rethinking the very categories through which the social whole is viewed and constituted" (p. 24); (5) viewing social and cultural phenomena as historically contingent and socially constructed and reconceptualizing gender and sexuality; (6) "understanding sexuality neither as nature nor discourse, but as a sphere of social practices that constitute social relations" (p. 33).

6. For a valuable discussion of postmodern theory's critique of historical discourse, see Berkhofer (1995b, chap. 1 and passim).

7. The moving force behind the journal is its editor, Adi Ophir, a philosopher at Tel Aviv University. The journal, sponsored by the Van Leer Foundation, emerged out of a series of conversations and seminars in the late 1980s.

8. Discussions at Van Leer during late 1988 and 1989 reveal a struggle to find an appropriate critical discourse with which to formulate a critique of Israeli social and cultural life. These concerns are summarized in unpublished documents in my possession including a document written by Ophir and Hannan Hever, a professor of Hebrew Literature at Tel Aviv University. I am grateful to Adi Ophir for providing me with copies of these documents.

9. Bar On (1996a, 196–97).

10. The words are those of Nurit Schleifman, a scholar of Russian history, and Rachel Freudental, a specialist in German Literature, from an interview conducted by Bar On, August 17, 1992. See Bar On (1996a, 196).

11. Adi Ophir, "Letter of Protest"; distributed by the American-Israel Civil Liberties Coalition (n.d.).

12. Bar On (1996a, 227) writes that the reason for the protest was violent acts by Israeli settlers. I have here followed Adi Ophir's recollection.

13. Interview with Ophir, June 16, 1996, Bethlehem, Pa.

14. Interview with Ophir, June 16, 1996. See also Bar On (1996a, 194–97).

15. Articles advocating a postmodernist critique of zionism and Israeli culture have also appeared in the journal *Alpayim*.

16. Foucault himself did not designate his work as postmodern and was skeptical about the usefulness of the concept. Nevertheless, most studies of postmodernism regard him as one of its leading theorists. Cf. Best and Kellner (1991) and Flynn (1994); see also Best (1994). On Foucault's contribution to the postmodern critique of historical discourse, see Berkhofer (1995b, chap. 8 and passim). Notwithstanding Foucault's own reluctance to accept the label, there is no doubt that his writings have had a formative effect on the discourse of postmodernism.

17. In a highly suggestive study of Foucault, Christopher Falson (1998) has persuasively argued that the ongoing interaction with others is a central motif in Foucault's writings:

> I want to argue that the ethic of openness to and respect for the other can be understood as underlying Foucault's very form of critical reflection, his critical interrogation of our contemporary forms of imprisonment. (62)

This concern for openness to, and respect for marginalized and excluded others within Israeli society, as well as Palestinian others without, is also basic to the thinking of those whom I label postmodern postzionists, most of whom are influenced by Foucault. As I argue in this chapter and in my Concluding Reflections, much of their critique of zionism and Israeli culture derives from a concern for the ways in which power relations engendered by zionist discourse impede this openness and respect in the diverse spheres of Israeli life. For a discussion of the significance of the Other for the construction of Jewish cultural identity, see Silberstein (1994). The chapters in Silberstein and Cohn (1994) provide useful examples of the various ways in which Jews in different periods have constructed their Others and, through them, their own identity.

18. The shift in focus from historical time to space is characteristic of many postmodern writings. See, for example, Harvey (1989), Soja (1996; Soja discusses Foucault's place in this discussion in chap. 5), Keith and Pile (1993), Massey (1994a), and Gregory (1994).

19. See Derrida (1984, 116).

20. For a discussion of these issues and problematics in postmodern social and cultural theory, see Nicholson and Seidman (1995).

21. Relating Bhabha's conceptions of "mimicry" and Otherness to the Israeli discourse on the Palestinian minority, the journal introduces the cultural dimension into the discussion of Israeli colonial practices. This is a dimension that was not discussed by Shafir and Kimmerling.

22. While I recognize that the term postmodern imposes a greater degree of coherence than actually exists among these theoretically oriented postzionists, I nonetheless find it to be useful. I am not claiming that all of those whom I designate as postmodernist postzionists would accept the label, nor do they all use the postmodern form of critique in the same ways.

23. In conversations with the author, Adi Ophir has indicated that it is difficult to find articles suitable for publication that are informed by a clearly articulated theoretical perspective.

24. Cf. Dominguez (1989), Shohat (1988, 1989), Alcalay (1993, 1996), and Boyarin (1997a). Alcalay, Shohat, and Boyarin show clear affinities to postcolonial theory and cultural studies. Dominguez's writings show the influence of poststructuralism and postmodern anthropological theory. On Boyarin's critique, see end of chapter 6. Although Shohat's writings have had an impact on Israeli film studies, they are rarely mentioned in the postzionism debates. I thank Hannan Hever and Orly Lubin for calling this to my attention. My decision not to discuss Alcalay, Dominguez, and Shohat should in no way be taken as a negative judgement on the significance of their work. Each of these writers makes a significant contribution to the theoretical critique of zionist discourse. However, having chosen to focus my study on Israeli cultural discourse, I have limited my discussion to writings that have come to be regarded in Israel as comprising a part of that discourse. A broader analysis of postzionist discourse both inside and outside of Israel should certainly include a discussion of their important work.

25. Modernist discourse in the journal includes Marxist theory and the critical theory associated with the Frankfurt School.

26. For recent discussions of the concept of culture as used in cultural studies, see Grossberg, Nelson, and Treischler (1992); Turner (1990); and Jordan and Weedon (1995). Jordan and Weedon discuss the relationship of cultural criticism and postmodernism in their Introduction. See also Grossberg (1997).

27. See Said (1989, 1993), Bhabha (1994), Spivak (1990).
28. For collections of writings on postcolonial theory, see Ashcroft, Griffiths, and Tiffin (1995); Williams and Chrisman (1994); and McClintock, Mufti and Shohat (1997). McClintock (1995) focuses on the role of gender in colonialist practices. Young (1990) focuses on the relationship of historical discourse and colonialism. See also Young (1995).
29. Young (1990, 1995) critically analyzes their contributions, as does Moore-Gilbert (1997).
30. See also Hever (1989).
31. Hever is one of the few Israeli scholars whose writings appear in Western journals on cultural and postcolonial criticism. The contribution of Deleuze and Guattari to the analysis of minority discourse is a theme that pervades the JanMohamed and Lloyd (1990) volume. Their significance for postcolonial studies has been highlighted by Young (1995, 166–74).
32. Previously published in English, Hever's essay on Shammas, a Hebrew version of which (1991) appears in *Theory & Criticism,* forms an important part of the postmodernist postzionist critique.
33. In a recent article, Kimmerling (1997) refers to a shared premise of Israeli historians: "If historians lack adequate tools, or if they do not have all of the required information and documentation, they can still be evaluated according to whether or not they have done everything possible to approach that singular truth" (p. 261). In a note, Kimmerling expresses his agreement: "A good theoretical framework, basically comparative, can do much to atone for the inaccessibility of [all] the facts and primary data. The force of this kind of theory will be determined by its ability to pass judgement after additional relevant materials have been uncovered" (p. 261, n. 8).
34. White (1987) and Ermarth (1992).
35. For a recently published collection of postmodern critiques of historical writing, see Jenkins (1997). See also Berkhofer (1995b) for one of the most extensive postmodern critiques of historical discourse. For other examples, see Kellner (1989) and Ankersmitt and Kellner (1995). From a literary perspective, see Hutcheon (1993). For a discussion of the crisis of objectivity in historical discourse, see Novick (1988).
36. For a suggestive discussion of the differences between representational and nonrepresentational views of language, see Thrift (1997). Thrift bases his conception of nonrepresentational thought on Foucault, Deleuze, and Guattari.
37. While, as discussed in chapter 4, critics had labeled some of the postzionist historians and sociologists as postmodernist, this is, as I argue there, an error. With rare exceptions, the historians and social scientists I discuss in chapter 4 clearly position themselves within modernist academic discourse. Moreover, there is little indication that they are familiar with the theoretical writings commonly subsumed under the postmodern category. While frequently raising issues that converge with some of those raised by postmodern theory, they frame these issues in a very different way. The most notable exception is Pappe, who argued for a multiperspective conception of history that incorporated multiple narratives. In the spirit of postmodern theorists like Lyotard, Pappe

rejects all metanarratives, preferring instead a multiperspectival approach to historical writing. Pappe has been criticized for this position by Raz-Krakotzkin (1997), whose views I discuss in this chapter. Notwithstanding his privileging of historians over the histories that they write, Pappe's discourse falls basically within the parameters of modernist discourse. Similarly, while Kimmerling and Pappe critically assess the power effects of academic discourse, their critiques are also framed within modernist discourse (see Kimmerling in Weitz 1997, 261, especially n. 8). Kimmerling has also criticized efforts by Gidon Aran and Zali Gurevitch to apply postmodern notions of space to Israel. See Gurevitch and Aran (1991, 1994) and Kimmerling (1992). Recently, Pappe and Uri Ram have incorporated current nonessentialistic theories of nationalism into their writings.

38. See, for example, Laclau and Mouffe (1990, 100–3). On the complexities involved in adjudicating disputes between narratives, see Lyotard (1988). Contrary to claims of critics of the new Israeli historiography (such as Anita Shapira), this approach does not demand that we treat all narratives of the past as equally true or valid. Instead, postmodern theory employs different criteria than the modernist criterion of "objectivity." For example, as feminist theorists such as Judith Butler (1990, 1993, 1995) have argued, our social or political perspectives may move us to privilege some narratives over others in anticipation of their social or political effects. What the postmodern critique of historical discourse does assume, however, is that all narratives, including those through which we position ourselves in establishing our identity, are socially constructed and historically contingent and entail specific power effects.

39. See Barthes (in Jenkins 1997, 129–33).

40. While Raz-Krakotzkin does not specifically identify those who advocate such a position, he is most likely referring to many or all of the postzionist critics discussed in chapter 4. However, as the discussion in chapter 4 shows, such a criticism is far too sweeping.

41. This raises serious questions, which cannot be taken up in this discussion, regarding the compatibility of Benjamin's approach, with its emphasis on human consciousness, with that of Foucault.

42. The influence of Said is clearly seen in Raz-Krakotzkin's doctoral dissertation (1996), in which he draws extensively on him. Without using the specific term colonialism, Raz-Krakotzkin (1993) nonetheless depicts Israeli sovereignty over the Palestinians as a colonialist situation. In the first part of the article, he does use the discourse of colonialism, speaking of zionism's/Israel's colonialist practices and the need for decolonialization (pp. 45, 51). Insofar as Benjamin is generally regarded as a modernist thinker, Raz-Krakotzkin's critique interweaves both modernist and postmodernist components.

43. There is much in Raz-Krakotzkin's representation of the power effects of zionist discourse that is highly problematic. For one thing, ignoring apparatuses through which the discourse is produced and disseminated, he relegates to ideas a causal force that has been seriously questioned by critics like Foucault, Deleuze, and Guattari. They concentrate simultaneously on practices and words, on what can be seen and what can be heard.

44. One could argue that this was far more an effect of the dominant Eurocentric or Orientalist discourse in Israeli culture. See the discussion on Piterberg later in this chapter.

45. See his note 57, in which Raz-Krakotzkin criticizes the limits of the liberal consciousness in Israel, referring to the furor caused by a poem by Mahmud Darwish.

46. Raz-Krakotzkin refers to the effects of zionist discourse in such left-wing Israeli groups as the Meretz party.

47. A distinctive feature of Raz-Krakotzkin's critique of zionism is his criticism of the masculinist character of zionist discourse. In the film *Against the Poison of Galut* by David ben Shitrit and Sinai ben David, Raz-Krakotzkin finds an alternative to the prevailing Israeli notion of "masculinity." Focusing on three Palestinian women who speak for themselves, the film shows masculinity as it relates to femininity. Referring to the critique in Feldhay's earlier essay (1992), which I discuss later, he draws a connection between this masculinist view and the unwillingness to relate to the Palestinian historical perspective.

48. Raz-Krakotzkin's references to the writings of Segev (note 11) and Evron (note 18) show the lines connecting his scholarship to that of critics of zionism discussed in chapters 3 and 4. Raz-Krakotzkin's call for a spiritualization of the concept of *galut* in the tradition of Jewish theology seems close to Gurevitch and Aran's position (1991 and 1994), although he criticizes them for dematerializing and depoliticizing the yearning for the land.

49. To support this claim, Piterberg cites the writings of Ben Zion Dinur, a professor of Jewish history at the Hebrew University and one of Israel's leading historians. See Dinur (1969), and his Introduction to the first volume of the historical journal *Zion*. For other critical perspectives on Dinur, see Ram (1995c) and Myers (1995). Meyers' important study analyzes the entire founding generation of Israeli historians.

50. Besides Dinur, Piterberg criticizes historians Yizhak Baer, Gershom Scholem, and Haim Hillel Ben Sasson for their Orientalist discourse.

51. Kimmerling, Pappe, and Ram have utilized Anderson in recent writings. The use of Said, however, remains rare. An example of Said's growing influence is the recent exhibit "To the East: Orientalism in the Arts in Israel" at the Israel Museum, Jerusalem. See in particular the catalogue articles by Graciella Trachtenberg (1998) and Yigal Zalmona (1998). A recent dissertation by Adriana Kemp (1997) is deeply indebted to discursive theorists of space such as Foucault, Soja, and David Harvey as well as to postcolonial theory. In a personal communication, Kemp indicated that her approach has been well received by anthropologists at the Hebrew University and by other scholars at Ben Gurion University. She sees this as a sign that the situation in Israel is slowly changing and becoming more receptive to the use of postcolonial and postmodern theory.

52. On the critique of essentialistic notions of identity see Hall (1990), and Alan Pred (1997), Grossberg (1997), and Butler (1990, 1993, 1995). For a preliminary discussion of the issue of identity in relation to postzionism, see Silberstein (1997).

53. Rabinowitz (1993), citing Ahmed Saidi, argues that the use by Israelis of the term "Arabs" to refer to Israeli Palestinians makes it easier to preach "transfer" to another Arab country (p. 146).

54. See the works cited in note 18.

55. While Kimmerling emphasized the processes whereby boundaries were constructed and legitimated, he did not analyze the discursive processes whereby the land was imbued with particular kinds of meaning; see Kemp (1997).

56. See Alcalay (1993).

57. On the postmodern shift in focus from time to space, see sources cited in note 18.

58. Azoulay describes three social and cultural conditions necessary for a critical art. First, conditions must allow for a struggle over reigning doxa, which she distinguishes from a pluralism based on "good taste." Second, critical art requires a fixed art market in which symbolic capital can be transformed into economic capital. Without this, there is little motivation to determine boundaries to preserve and transgress. Finally, there must be a tension between dealers and collectors. The presence of a strong critical art in Israel, which is clearly connected to the phenomenon of postzionism, is reflected in the "Desert Cliche" exhibit; see Katz-Freiman and Cappellazo (1996), in which clear connections between the art presented in the exhibit and the spreading postzionist discourse are established.

59. While she limits her focus to art, one can expand Azoulay's critique to apply to the general absence of cultural studies in Israel. Like Azoulay's critical approach to art, cultural studies seeks to uncover the relationship between cultural representation, the power relations that make them possible, and the power effects of cultural representation. Israeli culture and society, perhaps because of the obsession with security and survival, is not receptive to these forms of critical activity that subvert the very assumptions on which "official" or "canonical" artistic and cultural activities are based.

60. Cf. the discussions in this volume of Benvenisti (chapter 2) and Habiby (chapter 5), each of whom revealed the constructed character of national space and the practices through which the zionist representation of a Jewish "homeland" was produced and perpetuated.

61. Even before the zionists had actually gained possession of land, they represented it in narratives as belonging to them. See Evron (1995) and Berkowitz (1993, chaps. 5 and 6).

62. For the background and history of Bezalel, see Ofrat (1998, chap. 2).

63. Eventually, she argues (1993) the Palestinians were successful in establishing transitory modes for representing their space and their past through such practices as "land day" and the Intifada (p. 90).

64. What is most significant is that most of these were established by previously marginalized groups, including Jews from various Middle Eastern countries, members of the militant unofficial Ezel and Lehi groups, or particular units of the Israel Defense Forces. However, even prior to the Likud victory, alternative voices emerged and struggled for control of the means for representing the past and the present.

65. Azoulay points to a number of signs that are indicative of what she calls the maturation of Israeli society. It is now possible to: (1) denounce the manipulation of memory of the *Shoah*; (2) even suggest forgetting the *Shoah*; (3) denounce the torture of Palestinian prisoners; (4) publicize acts of the Security Services and the military in the territories; (5) talk of emigration in rational terms of individual gain rather than in moralistic, judgmental terms; (6) suggest repealing the Law of Return; and (7) oppose zionism and even talk openly about the end of zionism. While Azoulay takes these changes as indications of the maturing or "normalization" of Israeli society, they may also be seen as indications of a transition from a zionist to a postzionist culture. While not identifying herself as a postzionist, Azoulay's critique is both consistent with and serves to expand the parameters of the postzionist critique. Azoulay also edited a special edition of the Israeli art journal *Studio* (October 1992), which focused on the political use of space and spatializing practices in Israel.

66. Chinski specifically refers to Foucault, Benjamin, Deleuze and Guattari, Althusser, Harvey, and Said.

67. Chinski (1993) sees Israeli art as based on a functional perspective, with modernization being one of its concerns. Although in Israel, art is viewed as autonomous realm, independent of social practices, artistic creation is nonetheless analyzed in terms of its contribution to the society (p. 113).

68. For an alternative interpretation of Geva's project, see Ofrat (1998, 304–5). Ofrat emphasizes the political nature of Geva's art, at least prior to the "Greenhouse" project. He identifies Geva's work after 1972 as a part of the left-wing artists' war on art that came in to full bloom with the ascendancy of the Likud party in 1977. A comparison of Ofrat's discussion here and in vol. 3 of *Theory & Criticism* with Chinski's helps to clarify the differences between a modernist and postmodernist approach to (Israeli) art. Ofrat utilizes the modernist notion of the individual artist as creator, and emphasizes Geva's utopian educational goals. Chinski, criticizing the "romantic" conception of the artist as creator/hero, positions the artist within the discursive structure within which he/she works.

69. For other recent examples, see Shiran (1993). See also Sharoni (1995); and Emmett (1996). The absence in *Theory & Criticism* of specific attention to the plight of Mizrahi women has been called to my attention by Ella Shohat. I thank her for this observation.

70. In an oft-cited feminist critique of nationalist discourse, Anthias and Yuval-Davis (1994) describe the various "ways in which women have tended to participate in ethnic and national processes and in relation to state practices." The roles assigned to women include: (1) biological reproducers of members of ethnic collectivities; (2) reproducers of boundaries of ethnic/national groups; (3) participating centrally in ideological reproduction of collectivity and as transmitters of its culture; (4) signifiers of ethnic/national differences…in ideological discourses used in construction, reproduction, and transformation of ethnic/national categories; (5) participants in national, economic, political, and military struggles.

71. Hever frames the literary debates among these writers within the broader context of the debate over *gegenwartsarbeit*, that is, activities to develop and preserve Jewish culture in the diaspora.

72. For examples of serious critical engagements with the postmodern conceptions of history, see Appelby, Hunt, and Jacob (1994), and Jenkins (1997). Jenkins' anthology is the only one known to me that presents a good selection by both advocates and critics of the postmodern approach to history. I would argue that it behooves those Israeli scholars who are critical of the postmodern postzionist approach to history discussed in this chapter to familiarize themselves with these debates.

REFERENCES

Aaronson, Ran. 1993. "Baron Rothschild and the Initial Stage of Jewish Settlement in Palestine (1882–1890)." *Journal of Historical Geography* 19, 2.
———. 1996. "Settlement in Eretz Yisrael—Colonialist Enterprise?" "Critical Scholarship" and Historical Geography. *Israel Studies* 1, 2 (Fall): 214–29.
Ahad Haam. 1946. *Ahad Haam: Essays, Letters, Memoirs*. Translated and Edited by Leon Simon. Oxford: East and West Library.
———. 1947. Collected Writings (in Hebrew). Tel Aviv: Devir.
———. 1962. *Nationalism and the Jewish Ethic: Basic Writings of Ahad Haam*. Edited with an Introduction by Hans Kohn. New York: Schocken Books.
———. 1970a. *Ahad Haam Selected Essays*. Translated with an Introduction by Leon Simon. New York: Atheneum.
———. 1970b. "Negation of the Diaspora." Pp. 270–77 in *The Zionist Idea*, ed. Arthur Hertzberg. New York: Atheneum.
Alcalay, Amiel. 1993. *After Jews and Arabs: Remaking Levantine Culture*. Minneapolis: University of Minnesota Press.
———, ed. 1996. *Keys to the Garden*. San Francisco: City Lights Press.
Almog, Shmuel, ed. 1983. *Zionism and the Arabs: Essays*. Jerusalem: The Historical Society of Israel and the Zalman Shazar Center.
Amir, Delilah. 1995. "On the Committees to Prevent Pregnancy" (in Hebrew). *Theory and Criticism* (Winter): 247–54.
Anderson, Benedict. 1991. *Imagined Communities*. London: Verso.
Ankersmitt, Paul, and Hans Kellner, eds. 1995. *A New Philosophy of History*. Chicago: University of Chicago Press.
Anthias, Floya, and Nira Yuval-Davis. 1994. "Women and the Nation State," pp. 312–15 in *Nationalism*, ed. John Hutchinson and Anthony D. Smith. Oxford: Oxford University Press.
Appardurai, Arjun. 1996. *Modernity at Large: Cultural Dimensions of Globalization*. Minneapolis: University of Minnesota Press.
Appelby, Joyce, Lynn Hunt, and Margaret Jacob. 1994. *Telling the Truth about History*. New York: W. W. Norton.
Appiah, Kwame Anthony. 1992. *In My Father's House: Africa in the Philosophy of Culture*. New York: Oxford University Press.
Arian, Asher. 1998. *Israel: The Second Republic: Politics in Israel*. Chatham, N.J.: Chatham House Publishers.
Aronoff, Myron J. 1989. *Israeli Visions and Revisions*. New Brunswick, N.J.: Transaction Publishers.
Aronowitz, Stanley, and Henry Giroux. 1991. *Postmodern Education: Politics, Culture, and Social Criticsm*. Minneapolis: University of Minnesota Press.

Aronson, Shlomo. 1994. "The New Historians and the Challenge of the Shoah" (in Hebrew). *Musaf Haaretz* (24 June), 52–53.

———. 1996. "Postzionism & Peace" (in Hebrew). *Gesher* 42, 132: 104–7.

Ashcroft, B., A. Griffiths, and H. Tiffin, eds. 1995. *The Post Colonial Studies Reader.* New York: Routledge.

Avineri, Shlomo. 1981. *The Making of Modern Zionism: The Intellectual Origins of the Jewish State.* New York: Basic Books.

———. 1995. "Forward to the 18th Century" (in Hebrew). *Haaretz* (22 September), 6.

Avneri, Uri. 1968. *Israel without Zionists: A Plea for Peace in the Middle East.* New York: Macmillan.

Avni, Haim, and Gideon Shimoni, eds. 1990. *Zionism and Its Jewish Opponents* (in Hebrew). Jerusalem: Hassifriya Haziyonit.

Azoulay, Ariella. 1992. "On the Possiblity and Situation of Critical Art in Israel." *Theory and Criticism* 2 (Summer): 89–118.

———. 1993. "Open Doors: Museums of History in Israeli Public Space." *Theory and Criticism* 4 (Fall): 79–95.

Bakhtin, M. M. 1981. *The Dialogical Imagination: Four Essays by M. M. Bakhtin.* Edited by Michael Holquist, translated by M. Hol. Austin: University of Texas Press.

Bammer, Angelika, ed. 1994. *Displacements.* Indianapolis: Indiana University Press.

Barnett, Michael N., ed. 1996. *Israel in Comparative Perspective: Challenging the Conventional Wisdom.* Albany: State University of New York Press.

Bar On, Mordecai. 1983. "Post Revolutionary Zionism." *New Outlook* (October–December): 1–7.

———. 1990. "A Second Look at The Past—Revisions of Historiography of the 1948 Arab–Israeli War" (in Hebrew). *Contemporary Jewry: A Research Annual* 6: 89–115.

———. 1994. "Zionism into Its Second Century." Pp. 20–40 in *Whither Israel: The Domestic Challenges,* eds. Keith Kyle and Joel Peters. London: Tauris.

———. 1996a. *In Pursuit of Peace: A History of the Israeli Peace Movement.* Washington, D.C.: United States Institute of Peace Press.

———. 1996b. "Postzionism and Antizionism: Distinctions, Definitions, Clarification of Accomplishments, and Some Personal Evaluations" (in Hebrew). Pp. 475–508 in *Zionism: A Contemporary Debate,* eds. Pinhas Ginosar and Avi Bar Eli. Beer Sheva: Ben Gurion University Press.

———. 1996c. "History that Never Was" (in Hebrew). *Contemporary Jewry* 10.

Barrett, Michelle. 1991. *The Politics of Truth: From Marx to Foucault.* Stanford, Calif.: Stanford University Press.

Bauer, Yehuda. 1944. "It's Possible to Accuse, and It's Possible to Accuse and to Hate" (in Hebrew). *Haaretz* (23 June).

Bauman, Sygmunt. 1992. *Intimations of Postmodernity.* London: Routledge.

Beit Zvi, Shabtai B. 1977. *Post Ugandan Zionism in the Crisis of the Shoah* (in Hebrew). Tel Aviv: Bronfman.

Belsey, Catherine. 1980. *Critical Practice.* New York: Methuen.

———. 1993. "Towards Cultural History." Pp. 58–59 in *A Postmodern Reader,* ed. J. Natoli and L. Hutcheon. Albany: New York University Press.

Ben-Yehuda, Nachman. 1995. *The Masada Myth*. Madison: University of Wisconsin Press.

Ben Ezer, Ehud, ed. 1974. *Unease in Zion*. New York: Quadrangle Books.

———. 1986. *There Is No Peace in the Land* (in Hebrew). Tel Aviv: Am Oved.

Benko, Georges, and Ulf Strohmayer, eds. 1997. *Space and Social Theory: Interpreting Modernity and Postmodernity*. Oxford: Blackwell.

Benvenisti, Meron. 1986. *Conflicts & Contradictions*. New York: Villard Books.

———. 1992. *Fatal Embrace* (in Hebrew). Jerusalem: Maxwell-Macmillan-Keter Publishing Company.

———. 1995. *Intimate Enemies: Jews & Arabs in A Shared Land*. Berkeley: University of California Press.

———. 1997. "The Hebrew Map" (in Hebrew). *Theory and Criticism* (Winter): 7–29.

Berdiczewski, M. Y. 1960. *Writings of Micah Yosef Bin Gurion* (in Hebrew). Tel Aviv: Devir.

Berkhofer, Robert F. 1995a. "Viewpoints in Historical Practice." Pp. 174–91 in *A New Philosophy of History*, eds. F. Ankersmit and H. Kellner. Chicago: University of Chicago Press.

———. 1995b. *Beyond the Great Story: History as Text and Discourse*. Cambridge, Mass.: The Belknap Press of Harvard University Press.

Berkowitz, Michael. 1993. *Zionist Culture and West European Jewry before the First World War*. Cambridge: Cambridge University Press.

———. 1997. *Western Jewry and the Zionist Project: 1914–1933*. Cambridge: Cambridge University Press.

Best, Steven. 1994. "Foucault, Postmodernism and Social Theory." Pp. 25–52 in *Postmodernism & Social Theory*, eds. David Dickens and Andrea Fontana. New York: Guilford Press.

Best, Steven, and Douglas Kellner. 1991. *Postmodern Theory: Critical Interrogations*. New York: Guilford Press.

Bhabha, Homi K., ed. 1990. *Nation and Narration*. London: Routledge.

———. 1994. *The Location of Culture*. London: Routledge.

Black, Ian, and Benny Morris. 1991. *Israel's Secret Wars: A History of Israel's Intelligence Services*. New York: Grove Werdenfield.

Bober, Arie. 1972. *The Other Israel: The Radical Case Against Zionism*. New York: Doubleday Anchor.

Bove, Paul. 1990. "Discourse." Pp. 50–65 in *Critical Terms for Literary Study*, eds. Frank Lentricchia and Thomas McLaughlin. Chicago: University of Chicago Press.

Boyarin, Daniel. 1997a. *Unheroic Conduct: The Rise of Secularity and the Invention of the Jewish Man*. Berkeley and Los Angeles: University of California Press.

———. 1997b. "Colonial Drug: Zionism, Gender, and Mimicry" (in Hebrew). *Theory and Criticism* (Winter): 123–44.

Brenner, Yosef Haim. 1985. *Writings* (in Hebrew) (Volumes 3 and 4). Tel Aviv: Sifriat Poalim.

Brinker, Menahem. 1986. "Post-Zionism" (in Hebrew). *Siman Keriah* 19: 21–29.

———. 1988. "Brenner's Jewishness." Pp. 232–49 in *Studies in Contemporary Jewry IV. The Jews and the European Crisis, 1914–1921*, ed. Jonathan Frankel. Oxford: Oxford University Press.

————. 1990a. *Narrative Art and Social Thought in Brenner's World* [*Ad HaSimtah HaTeverianit*] (in Hebrew). Tel Aviv: Am Oved.

————. 1990b. "Ahad Haam, Berdichevski and Brenner: Three Secular Relationships to Obligatory Jewish Texts" (in Hebrew). *Kivvunim: A Journal of Zionism and Judaism* 2 (December): 7–24.

Buber, Martin. 1983. *A Land of Two Peoples*. Edited with commentary by Paul R. Mendes-Flohr. New York: Oxford University Press.

Butler, Judith. 1990. *Gender Trouble*. New York: Routledge.

————. 1993. *Bodies that Matter*. New York: Routledge.

————. 1995. "Contingent Foundations: Feminism and the Question of 'Postmodernism.'" Pp. 3–21 in *Feminist Contentions*, S. Ben Habib et al., eds. New York: Routledge.

Butler, Judith, and Joan Scott, eds. 1992. *Feminists Theorize the Political*. New York: Routledge.

Canaani, David. 1976. *The Relation of the Second (Labor) Aliyah to Religion and Tradition* (in Hebrew). Tel Aviv: Sifriat Poalim.

Castel-Bloom, Orly. 1990. *Where Am I* (in Hebrew). Tel Aviv: Zemora-Bitan.

————. 1992. *Dolly City*. Tel Aviv: Zemora-Bitan.

————. 1993. "The Lost Article" (in Hebrew). *Yediot Aharonot* (11 June): 29–30.

Chambers, Ian. 1994. *Migrancy, Culture, Identity*. New York: Routledge.

Chatterjee, Partha. 1993. *The Nation and Its Fragments: Colonial and Postcolonial Histories*. Princeton, N.J.: Princeton University Press.

Chinski, Sarah. 1993. "Silence of the Fishes: The Local and the Universal in the Israeli Discourse on Art" (in Hebrew). *Theory and Criticism* 4: (Fall): 105–22.

————. 1994. "Theoretical Clarifications" (in Hebrew). *Theory and Criticism* 5 (Fall): 187–190.

————. 1997. "The Lacemakers from Bezalel" (in Hebrew). *Theory and Criticism* 11: (Winter): 177–205.

Clifford, James, and George E. Marcus, eds. 1986. *Writing Culture: The Poetics and Politics of Ethnography*. Los Angeles: University of California Press.

Cohen, Aharon. 1970. *Israel and the Arab World*. New York: Funk and Wagnalls.

Cohen, Erik. 1995. "Israel as a Post-Zionist Society." Israel Affairs 1, 3 (Spring): 203–14.

Cohen, Mitchell. 1992. *Zion and State: Nation, Class and the Shaping of Modern Israel*. New York: Columbia University Press.

Cohen, Steven M. 1983. *American Modernity and Jewish Identity*. New York and London: Tavistock Publishers.

Culler, Jonathan. 1982. *On Deconstruction: Theory and Criticism after Structuralism*. Ithaca, N.Y.: Cornell University Press.

Dan, Yosef. 1994. "Postmodernism against the State of Israel" (in Hebrew). *Haaretz*, (24 June): 8b.

————. 1995. "On Postzionism, Oral Hebrew, and Futile Messianism" (in Hebrew). *Haaretz* (25 March), sec. V, 1.

Deleuze, Giles. 1988. *Foucault*. Translated by Sean Hand. Minneapolis: University of Minnesota Press.

————. 1993. *The Deleuze Reader*. Edited by Constantin Boundas. New York: Columbia University Press.

————. 1995. *Negotiations: 1972–1990*. Translated by Martin Joughin. New York: Columbia University Press.

Deleuze, Giles, and Felix Guattari. 1986. *Kafka: Toward A Minor Literature.* Translated by Dana Polan. Minneapolis: University of Minnesota Press.

———. 1989. *A Thousand Plateaus: Capitalism & Schizophrenia.* Translated and edited by Brian Massumi. Minneapolis: University of Minnesota Press.

Deleuze, Giles, and Claire Parnet. 1987. *Dialogues.* New York: Columbia University Press.

Derrida, Jacques. 1984. "Deconstruction and the Other." Pp. 105–26 in *Dialogues with Contemporary Continental Thinkers,* ed. Richard Kearney. Manchester: University of Manchester Press.

Diamond, James. 1986. *Homeland or Holy Land: The "Canaanite" Critique of Israel.* Indianapolis: Indiana University Press.

———. 1990. "We Are Not One: A Post-Zionist Perspective." *Tikkun* 5, 2 (March/April): 106–15.

Diamond, Larry, and Ehud Sprinzak, eds. 1993. *Israeli Democracy Under Stress. An Israel Democratic Institute Policy Study.* Boulder: Lynne Rienner Publishers.

Diner, Dan. 1995. "Cumulative Contingency: Historicizing Legitimacy in Israeli Discourse. *History and Memory* 7, 1 (Spring/Summer): 147–70.

Dinur, Benzion. 1969. *Israel and the Diaspora.* Philadelphia: Jewish Publication Society.

Dirks, Nicholas B., ed. 1992. *Colonialism and Culture.* Ann Arbor: University of Michigan Press.

Dirks, Nicholas B., Geoff Eley, and Sherry B. Ortner, eds. 1994. *Culture/Power/History: A Reader in Contemporary Social Theory.* Princeton, N.J.: Princeton University Press.

Dirlik, Arif. 1997. "The Postcolonial Aura: Third World Criticism in the Age of Global Capitalism." Pp. 501–28 in *Dangerous Liaisons: Gender, Nation, and Postcolonial Perspectives*, eds. Ann McClintock, Aamir Mufti, and Ella Shohat. Minneapolis: University of Minnesota Press.

Docherty, Thomas, ed. 1993. *Postmodernism: A Reader.* New York: Columbia University Press.

Doel, Marcus. 1995. "Bodies without Organs." Pp. 221–40 in *Mapping the Subject,* eds. Michael Keith and Steve Pile. New York: Routledge.

Dominguez, Virginia. 1989. *People as Subject, People as Object: Selfhood and Peoplehood in Contemporary Israel.* Madison: University of Wisconsin Press.

Dowty, Allan. 1998. *The Jewish State One Hundred Years Later.* Berkeley: University of California Press.

Dreyfus, Hubert, and Paul Rabinow. 1983. *Michel Foucault: Beyond Structuralism & Hermeneutics.* 2d ed. Chicago: University of Chicago Press.

Dubnow, Simon. 1961. *Nationalism and History: Essays on Old and New Judaism.* Edited and translated by Koppel S. Pinson. New York: Meridian Books: Philadelphia: Jewish Publication Society.

During, Simon. 1993. "Postmodernism or Post-colonialism Today." Pp. 448–62 in *Postmodernism: A Reader*, ed. Thomas Docherty. New York: Columbia University Press.

Ehrlich, Avishai. 1980. "Zionism, Demography, and Women's Work." *Khamsin* 7. 87–105.

Eisen, Arnold. 1986. *Galut: Modern Jewish Reflections on Homelessness and Homecoming.* Indianapolis: Indiana University Press.

Elam, Yigal. 1996. "A State of Its Citizens" (in Hebrew). *Gesher* 42 (132): 74–76.

Eley, Geoff, and Ronald Grigor Suny. 1996a. "Introduction: From the Moment of Social History to the Work of Cultural Representation." Pp. 3–37 in *Becoming National,* eds. G. Eley and R. Suny. New York: Oxford University Press.

———, eds. 1996b. *Becoming National.* New York: Oxford University Press.

Elon, Amos. 1971. *The Israelis: Founders and Sons.* New York: Holt, Rinehart & Winston.

———. 1997. *A Blood-Dimmed Tide: Dispatches from the Middle East.* New York: Columbia University Press.

Emmett, Ayala. 1996. *Our Sisters' Promised Land: Women, Politics, and Israeli–Palestinian Coexistence.* Ann Arbor: University of Michigan Press.

Erlich, Avishai. 1980. "Zionism, Demography, and Women's Work." *Khamsin* 7: 87–105.

Ermarth, Elizabeth Deeds. 1992. *Sequel to History: Postmodernism and the Crisis of Representational Time.* Princeton, N.J.: Princeton University Press.

Evron, Boaz. 1980. "The Shoah: Danger to the Nation." *Iton* 77, 21 (May–June): 12–15.

———. 1988. *A National Reckoning* [*HaHeshbon HaLeumi*] (in Hebrew). Tel Aviv: Devir.

———. 1995. *Jewish State or Israeli Nation.* Bloomington: Indiana University Press.

———. 1996. A Proper State. *Iton* 77 (May): 20–21.

Eyal, Gil. 1993. "Between East and West: The Discourse on the 'Arab Village' in Israel" (in Hebrew). *Theory and Criticism* 3 (Winter): 39–55.

Ezrahi, Yaron. 1993. "Democratic Politics and Culture in Modern Israel." In *Israeli Democracy Under Stress.* An Israel Democratic Institute *Policy Study,* ed. Larry Diamond and Ehud Sprinzak. Boulder, Colo.: Lynne Rienner Publishers.

———. 1997. *Rubber Bullets: Power & Conscience in Modern Israel.* New York: Farrar, Straus.

Falson, Christopher. 1998. *Foucault and Social Dialogue: Beyond Fragmentation.* New York: Routledge.

Fein, Leonard. 1988. *Where Are We? The Inner Life of America's Jews.* New York: Harper and Row.

Feldhay, Rivkah. 1992. "On Amalia Kahana-Carmon" (in Hebrew). *Theory and Criticism* 2 (Summer): 69–88.

Firer, Ruth. 1985. *Agents of Zionist Education* [*Sokhnim Shel HaHinukh HaZioni*] (in Hebrew). Tel Aviv: Sifriat HaPoalim/HaKibbutz HaMeuhad.

———. 1989. *Agents of the Holocaust* [Sokhnim shel HaLekah] (in Hebrew). Tel Aviv: HaKibbutz HaMeuhad.

Fisher, Shlomo. 1992. "Who Will Criticize the Critics? A Response" (in Hebrew). *Theory and Criticism* 2 (Summer): 147–54.

Flapan, Simcha. 1987. *The Birth of Israel: Myths & Realities.* New York: Pantheon.

Flynn, Thomas. 1994. "Foucault's Mapping of History." Pp. 28–46 in *The Cambridge Companion to Foucault,* ed. Gary Gutting. Cambridge: Cambridge University Press.

Foucault, Michel. 1972. *The Archaeology of Knowledge.* New York: Pantheon Books.

———. 1979. *Discipline & Punish: The Birth of the Prison.* Translated by Alan Sheridan. New York: Vintage/Random House.

―――. 1980. *Power/Knowledge: Selected Interviews & Other Writings, 1972–77*. Edited by Colin Gordon. New York: Pantheon Books.

―――. 1983. "The Subject and Power." Pp. 208–28, in *Michel Foucault: Beyond Structuralism & Hermeneutics*. 2d ed., eds. H. Dreyfus and P. Rabinow. Chicago: University of Chicago Press.

―――. 1984a. *The Foucault Reader*. Edited by Paul Rabinow. New York: Pantheon.

―――. 1984b. "Nietzsche, Genealogy, History." Pp. 76–100 in *The Foucault Reader*, ed. Paul Rabinow. Chicago: University of Chicago Press.

―――. 1984c. "The Order of Discourse." Pp. 108–38 in *Language and Politics*, ed. Michael J. Shapiro. New York: New York University Press. Originally published 1971.

―――. 1996. *Foucault Live. Collected Interviews, 1961–1984*. Edited by Sylvere Lotringer. New York: Semiotexte.

―――. 1997a. *The Politics of Truth*. New York: Semiotexte.

―――. 1997b. *Ethics, Subjectivity & Truth: The Essential Works of Michel Foucault*. Edited by Paul Rabinow. New York: The New Press.

Frankel, Jonathan. 1981. *Prophecy and Politics: Socialism, Nationalism, and the Russian Jews, 1862–1917*. Cambridge: Cambridge University Press.

Friedman, Maurice. 1983. *Martin Buber's Life and Work*, Vol. 3. New York: Dutton.

Friedman, Menahem. 1995. "The Structural Foundation for Religio-Political Accommodation in Israel: Fallacy and Reality." Pp. 51–82 in *Israel: The First Decade of Independency*, eds. I. S. Troen and N. Lucas. Albany, N.Y.: SUNY Press.

Frye, Marilyn. 1983. *The Politics of Reality*. Freedom, Calif.: The Crossing Press.

Gardiner, Michael. 1992. *The Dialogics of Critique: M. M. Bakhtin and the Theory of Ideology*. New York: Routledge.

Ginosar, Pinhas, and Avi Bar Bareli Eli, eds. 1996. *Zionism: A Contemporary Controversy* (in Hebrew). Beer Sheva: Ben Gurion University Press, The Ben Gurion Research Center.

Gluzman, Michael. 1997. "Longing for Heterosexuality: Zionism and Sexuality in Herzl's *Altneuland*" (in Hebrew). *Theory and Criticism* 11: (Winter, 1997): 145–62.

Gonen, Jay. 1975. *A Psychohistory of Zionism*. New York: Meridian.

Gorny, Yosef. 1987. *Zionism and the Arabs*: 1882-1948. Oxford: Clarendon Press.

Gossman, Lionel. 1990. *Between History & Literature*. Cambridge: Harvard University Press.

Gregory, Derek. 1994. *The Geographical Imagination*. Oxford: Blackwell.

Grewal, Inderpal, and Caren Kaplan, eds. 1994. *Scattered Hegemonies*. Minneapolis: University of Minnesota Press.

Groden, Michael, and Martin Kreiswirth, eds. 1994. *The Johns Hopkins Guide to Literary Theory and Criticism*. Baltimore: Johns Hopkins University Press.

Grodzinski, Yosef. 1994a. "The Shoah, The Yishuv, and Their Historians: The Case of Rav Weismandel from Bratslava as an Example" (in Hebrew). *Haaretz* (8 April).

―――. 1994b. "Refuted Claims, Erased Affairs" (in Hebrew). *Haaretz* (15 April).

―――. 1994c. "Historians or Propagandists?" (in Hebrew). *Haaretz* (27 May).

―――. 1994d. "To Struggle against the Zionization of the Shoah" (in Hebrew). *Haaretz* (15 July).

———. 1995. "There Is, Nonetheless, Something in That Story" (in Hebrew). *Haaretz* (5 March).

Grossberg, Lawrence. 1993. "Formations of Cultural Studies." Pp. 21–66 in *Relocating Cultural Studies*, eds. J. Shepherd and I. Taylor Blundell. New York: Routledge.

———. 1997. *Bringing It All Back Home: Essays on Cultural Studies*. Durham, N.C.: Duke University Press.

Grossberg, Lawrence, Cary Nelson, and Paula Treischler, eds. 1992. *Cultural Studies*. New York: Routledge.

Grossman, David. 1985. "The Meeting that Was and the Meeting that Wasn't" (in Hebrew). *Mooznayim*.

———. 1989. *The Yellow Wind*. Translated by Haim Watzman. New York: Delta.

———. 1993. *Sleeping on a Wire: Conversations with Palestinians in Israel*. New York: Farrar, Straus, Giroux.

Gurevitch, Zali, and Gidon Aran. 1991. "About the Place" (in Hebrew). *Alpaiim, A Multidisciplinary Publication for Contemporary Thought & Literature* 4: 9–44.

———. 1994. "The Land of Israel: Myth and Phenomenon." Pp. 195–200 in *Reshaping the Past: Jewish History and the Historians. Studies in Contemporary Jewry*, ed. Jonathan Frankel. Oxford: Oxford University Press.

Guvrin, Nurit. 1985. *The Brenner Affair: The Struggle over Freedom of Expression, 1911–1914* (in Hebrew). Jerusalem: Yad Yizhak Ben Zvi.

Guttman, Yisrael. 1994. "Was there Really a Dark Zionist Conspiracy?" (in Hebrew). *Haaretz* (22 July).

Habiby, Emile. 1985. *The Secret Life of Saeed: The Pessoptimist*. Translated by Salma Hkadra Jayyusi and Trevor LeGassick. London: Zed Books. Originally published in Arabic in 1974.

———. 1986. "Your Shoah, Our Tragedy!" (in Hebrew). *Politika 1986* 8 (June/July): 27.

———. 1988a. *Ehtayeh* (in Hebrew). Translated by Anton Shammas. Tel Aviv: Am Oved. Originally published in Arabic in 1985.

———. 1988b. "An Israeli Arab Replies to Motta Gur" (in Hebrew). *Devar* (10 January): 5.

———. 1988c. "Like a Wound" (in Hebrew). *Politika* 21: 6–9.

———. 1988d. Everything Passes, Habiby. (Interview with Yotam Levveni) (in Hebrew). 7 Days: weekly of Yediot Ahuronot (April): 37–39.

———. 1991a. "Jews and Arabs: We Have Encountered Death Enough" (in Hebrew). *Hadashot HaShavua* (18 January): 5.

———. 1991b. "The Days of the Witch with the Broom Are Over" [*Ovru Yemei HaMahashefah im Hametatei*]. *Davar* (3 March): 7–8.

———. 1991c. "Do You Call This Alienation?" (in Hebrew). *Iton 77*, 134 (March): 24–26.

———. 1992. "An Interview with the Writer Emile Habiby" (in Hebrew). *Mifgash* 20–22 (Spring/Fall): 5–17.

———. 1993. *Sarayah: Daughter of the Ghoul* (in Hebrew). Translated by Anton Shammas. Tel Aviv: HaSifriyah HaHadashah.

Halkin, Hillel. 1998. "Israel's Civil War within the Ranks of the Left." *Chronicle of Higher Education* (13 March): B7.

Hall, Stuart. 1985. "Signification, Representation, Ideology: Althusser and the Post Structuralist Debates." *Critical Studies in Mass Communication* (June): 91–114.

———. 1986. "Variants of Liberalism." Pp. 34–69 in *Politics & Ideology*, ed. by James Donald and Stuart Hall. Milton Keynes, England: Open University Press.

———. 1988. *The Hard Road to Renewal: Thatcherism and the Crisis of the Left.* London: Verso.

———. 1990. "Cultural Identity and Diaspora." Pp. 222–37 in *Identity, Community, Culture, Difference,* ed. Jonathan Rutheford. London: Lawrence & Wishart.

———, ed. 1996a. *Questions of Cultural Identity.* London: Sage.

———. 1996b. "When Was the 'post-colonial'? Thinking at the limit." Pp. 242–60 in *The Post-Colonial Question.* Eds. I. Chambers and L. Curti. New York: Routledge.

———. 1996c. *New Ethnicities in Stuart Hall: Critical Dialogues.* Edited by David Morley and Kuan-Hsing Chen. New York: Routledge.

———, ed. 1997. *Representation: Cultural Representations and Signifying Practices.* Thousand Oaks, Calif.: Sage Publications.

Hall, Stuart, et al. 1996. *Modernity: An Introduction to Modern Societies.* Oxford: Blackwell.

Har Even, Alouph, ed. 1983. *Every Sixth Israeli: The Relation between the Jewish Majority and the Arab Minority in Israel.* Jerusalem: Van Leer Jerusalem Foundation.

Har Even, Shulamit. 1992. "The Open City is Absurd" (in Hebrew). Yediot Aharonot, Hamusaf Leshabat (19 June): 26.

Harkabi, Yehoshafat. 1983. *The Bar Kokhba Syndrome.* Chappaqua, New York: Rossel Books.

Harvey, David. 1989. *The Postmodern Condition.* Oxford: Blackwell.

———. 1996. *Justice, Nature, and the Geography of Difference.* Oxford: Blackwell.

Hazaz, Haim. 1975. "The Sermon." Pp. 271–87 in *Modern Hebrew Literature*, ed. Robert Alter. New York: Behrman House.

Hecht, Dina, and Nira Yuval-Davis. 1978. "Ideology Without Revolution: Jewish Women in Israel." *Khamsin* 6: 97–117.

Hertzberg, Arthur, ed. 1970. *The Zionist Idea.* New York: Atheneum.

Hever, Hannan. 1989. "Israeli Literature's Achilles' Heel." *Tikkun* (Sept./Oct.): 30–33.

———. 1990. "Hebrew in an Israeli Arab Hand: Six Miniatures on Anton Shammas's *Arabesques.*" Pp. 264–293 in *The Nature and Context of Minority Discourse*, eds. Abdul R. JanMohamend and David Lloyd. New York: Oxford University Press.

———. 1991. "Hebrew in an Israeli Arab Hand" (in Hebrew). *Theory and Criticism* 1: 23–40.

———. 1992. "Optimist Is Not Just a Humanist" (in Hebrew). *Yediot Aharonot, Hallusaf Leshabot* (26 June): 27.

———. 1993. "The Refugee Women to the Refugees: Emile Habibi and the Canon of Hebrew Literature in Israel" (in Hebrew). *The New Middle East [HaMizrah HeHadash]* (special issue) 35: 102–14.

———. 1994. "The Struggle over the Canon in Hebrew Literature" (in Hebrew). *Theory and Criticism* 4 (Fall): 55–78.

———. 1995. "Women Poets of the War of Independence" (in Hebrew). *Theory and Criticism* 7 (Winter): 99–123.

Hever, Hannan, and Adi Ophir. n.d. "An Israeli Group for Culture Study and Critique: A draft on a Working Paper" (in Hebrew). VanLeer Institute, Jerusalem.

Hobsbawm, Eric. 1990. *Nations and Nationalism since 1780: Programme, Myth, Reality*. Cambridge: Cambridge University Press.

hooks, bell. 1990. *Yearning: Race, Gender, and Cultural Politics*. Boston: South End Press.

Horowitz, Dan. 1993. *The Heavens and The Earth: A Self Portrait of the 1948 Generation* (in Hebrew). Jerusalem: Keter.

Huggan, Graham. 1995. "Decolonializing the Map." Pp. 409–10 in *The Post-colonial Studies Reader*, edited by B. Ashcroft et al. New York: Routledge.

Hutcheon, Linda. 1988. *Poetics of Postmodernism: History, Theory, Fiction*. New York: Routledge.

———. 1989. *The Politics of Postmodernism*. New York: Routledge.

———. 1993. "Beginning to Theorize the Postmodern." Pp. 243–72 in *A Postmodern Reader*, ed. J. Natoli and L. Hutcheon. Albany: SUNY Press.

Irigary, Luce. 1988. *This Sex Which Is Not One*. Ithaca, N.Y.: Cornell University Press.

JanMohamed, Abdul R., and David Lloyd, eds. 1990. *The Nature and Context of Minority Discourse*. New York: Oxford University Press.

Jenkins, Keith, ed. 1997. *The Postzionism History Reader*. New York: Routledge.

Jordon, Glenn, and Chris Weedon. 1995. *Cultural Politics: Class, Gender, Race, and the Postmodern World*. Oxford: Blackwell.

Katz-Freiman, Tami, and Amy Cappellazo, eds. 1996. *Desert Cliche: Israel Now-Local Images*. Miami: Israeli Forum of Art Museums and the Bass Museum of Art.

Kaufman, Eleanor, and Kevin Jon Heller, eds. 1998. *Deleuze and Guattari: New Mappings in Politics, Philosophy, and Culture*. Minneapolis: Universiity of Minnesota Press.

Keith, Michael, and Steve Pile, eds. 1993. *Place and The Politics of Identity*. New York: Routledge.

Kellner, Hans. 1989. *Language and Historical Representation: Getting the Story Crooked*. Madison: University of Wisconsin Press.

Kemp, Adriana. 1997. *Talking Boundaries: The Making of Political Territory in Israel, 1949–1957* (in Hebrew). Unpublished doctoral dissertation, Tel Aviv University.

Keren, Michael. 1983. *Ben Gurion and the Intellectuals: Power, Knowledge and Charisma*. DeKalb: Northern Illinois University Press.

Khalidi, Rashid. 1995. "Contrasting Narratives of Palestinian Identity." In *The Geography of Identity,"* ed. Patricia Yeager. Ann Arbor: University of Michigan Press.

Kimmerling, Baruch. 1983. *Zionism & Territory: The Socio-Territorial Dimension of Zionist Politics.* Berkeley: University of California Press.

———. 1992. "On the Knowledge of the Place [*Makom*]: On Cultural History and on the Self-Conscripted Anthropology of Israel" (in Hebrew). *Alpaiim: A Multi-Disciplinary Publication for Contemorary Thought and Literature* 6: 57–68.

———. 1994a. "Merchants of Fear" (in Hebrew). *Musaf Haaretz* (24 June): 50–52.

———. 1994b. "Is Being a Part of the Nation a Necessary Condition For Historical Perversion?" (in Hebrew). *Haaretz* (23 December): 86.

———. 1994c. "On the Terrible Sins of the Critical Sociologists" (in Hebrew). *Devar HaShavua* (1 April):16–17.

———. 1995a. "Academic History Caught in the Cross-Fire: The Case of Israeli-Jewish Historiography." *History and Memory* 7, 1 (Spring/Summer): 41–65.

———. 1995b. "Civil Religion Versus National Religion" (in Hebrew). *Haaretz* (23 September): 14.

———. 1997. "History Here, Now" (in Hebrew). Pp. 257–274 in *Between Vision and Revision,* ed. Yehiam Weitz. Jerusalem: Merkaz Zalman Shazar.

———, ed. 1989. *The Israeli State and Society: Boundaries and Frontiers.* Albany, N.Y.: SUNY Press.

Kimmerling, Baruch, and Joel Migdal, eds. 1993. *Palestinians: The Making of a People.* New York: The Free Press.

Krausz, Ernest, ed. 1985. *Politics and Society in Israel.* New Brunswick, N.J.: Transaction Publishers.

Kurzweil, Barukh. 1971. "The Nature and Origins of the Young Hebrews Movement" in *Modern Hebrew Literature: Continuity or Revolution* (in Hebrew). *Schocken,* 270–300.

Kyle, Keith, and Joel Peters, eds. 1994. *Whither Israel: The Domestic Challenges.* New York: Tauris.

Laclau, Ernesto. 1986. "Class Interpellations and Democratic Interpellations." Pp. 27–33 in *Politics and Ideology,* eds. James Donald and Stuart Hall. Milton Keynes, England: Open University Press.

———, ed. 1994. *The Making of Political Identities.* London: Verso.

Laclau, Ernesto, and Chantal Mouffe. 1985. *Hegemony & Socialist Strategy.* London: Verso.

———. 1990. "Postmarxism without Apologies." Pp. 97–134 in *New Reflections on the Revolution of Our Time,* ed. Ernesto Laclau. London: Verso.

Landers, Yisrael. 1994. "The Sin that We Committed in Establishing the State" (in Hebrew). *Davar HaShavua* (18 March): 8–9.

Laqueur, Walter. 1973. *A History of Zionism.* New York: Holt, Rinehart & Winston.

Laqueur, Walter, and Barry Rubin, eds. 1984. *The Israel–Arab Reader.* New York: Penguin Books.

Lavie, Smadar, and Ted Swedenburg, eds. 1996. *Displacement, Diaspora, and Geographies of Identity.* Durham, N.C.: Duke University Press.

Leor, Yizhak. 1995. *Narratives with No Natives [Anu Kotvim Otakh Moledet]* (in Hebrew). Tel Aviv: HaKibbutz HaMeuhad.

Levine, Eitan, ed. 1983. *Diaspora: Exile, and the Jewish Condition.* New York: Jason Aaronson.

Lissak, Moshe. 1996. "Critical Sociology and Establishment Sociology in the Israeli Academic Community: Ideological Struggles or Academic Discourse?" *Israel Studies* 1, 1 (Spring): 247–294.

Lissak, Moshe, and Dan Horowitz. 1989. *Trouble in Utopia: The Overburdened Polity of Israel.* Albany, N.Y.: SUNY Press.

Lotan, Yael. 1986. "To Rejoice and Not to Mourn" (in Hebrew). *Mooznayim* 60, 3 (September): 28–30.

Lovejoy, Arthur O. 1965. *The Great Chain of Being. The History of an Idea.* New York: Harper & Row.

Lubin, Orly. 1990. "A Poetics of Evasion in the Spring of 1982: Amos Oz's *In The Land of Israel*" (in Hebrew). *Siman Keriah* 21 (September): 152–162.

———. 1995. "Trifles from Nehama's Kitchen: An Alternative Nationalism in Devora Baron's Novel *The Exiles*" (in Hebrew). *Theory and Criticism* 7 (Winter): 159–176.

Lustick, Ian S. 1980. *Arabs in the Jewish State: Israel's Control of a National Minority.* Austin: University of Texas Press.

———. 1988. *For the Land and the Lord: Jewish Fundamentalism in Israel.* New York: Council on Foreign Relations.

Luz, Ehud. 1988. *Parallels Meet: Religion and Nationalism in the Early Zionist Movement.* Philadelphia: Jewish Publication Society of America.

Lyotard, Jean François. 1984. *The Postmodern Condition: A Report on Knowledge.* Minneapolis: University of Minnesota Press.

———. 1988. *The Differend: Phrases in Dispute.* Minneapolis: University of Minnesota Press.

———. 1992. *The Postmodern Explained.* Afterword by Wlad Godzich. Minneapolis: University of Minnesota Press.

Macdonell, Diane. 1986. *Theories of Discourse.* Oxford: Blackwell.

Machover, Moshe, and Mario Offenberg. 1978. "Zionism & Its Scarecrows." *Khamsin* 6: 33–55.

Margalit, Dan. 1995. "Zionism, Postzionism, and Antizionism (A Symposium)" (in Hebrew). *Haaretz* (15 October): 4b–5b.

Massey, Doreen. 1994a. *Space, Place, and Gender.* Minneapolis: University of Minnesota Press.

———. 1994b. "Double Articulation: A Place in the World." Pp. 110–21 in *Displacements,* ed. A. Bammer. Indianapolis: Indiana University Press.

Massumi, Brian. 1992. *A User's Guide to Capitalism & Schizophrenia: Deviations from Deleuze & Guattari.* Cambridge: MIT Press.

Matalon, Ronit. 1995. *The One Facing Us* (in Hebrew). Tel Aviv: Am Oved.

———. 1998. *The One Facing Us.* New York: Metropolitan Books, Henry Holt and Company.

McClintock, Ann. 1995. *Imperial Leather: Race, Gender and Sexuality in the Colonial Context.* New York: Routledge.

———. 1996. "'No Longer in Future Heaven': Nationalism, Gender, and Race." Pp. 260–84 in *Becoming National,* ed. G. Eley & R. Suny. Oxford: Oxford University Press.

McClintock, Ann, Aamir Mufti, and Ella Shohat, eds. 1997. *Dangerous Liaisons:*

Gender, Nation, and Postcolonial Perspectives. Minneapolis: University of Minnesota Press.

Megged, Aaron. 1994a. "The Israeli Instinct for Self-Destruction" (in Hebrew). *Musaf Haaretz* (10 June): 27–29.

———. 1994b. "The Truth Will Sprout from the Land" (in Hebrew). *Musaf Haaretz* (24 June): 54.

Mehlman, Yossi. 1992. *The New Israelis: An Intimate Portrait of a Changing People*. New York: Birch Lane Press.

Mendes-Flohr, Paul, and Yehuda Reinharz, eds. 1995. *The Jew in the Modern World: A Documentary History*. 2d ed. Oxford: Oxford University Press.

Michman, Dan, ed. 1997. *Post-Zionism and the Holocaust: The Role of the Holocaust in the Public Debate on Postzionism in Israel*. Jerusalem: Bar Ilan University (Research AIDS Series 8).

Mikhael, Sami. 1986. "The Arabesques of Zionism: Notes on the Debate between A. B. Yehoshua and Anton Shammas" (in Hebrew). *Mooznayim* 160, 1–2 (July/August): 10–17.

Mitchell, Timothy. 1988. *Colonizing Egypt*. Cambridge: Cambridge University Press.

Moore-Gilbert, Bart. 1997. *Postcolonial Theory: Contexts, Practices, Politics*. London and New York: Verso.

Morris, Benny. 1987. *The Birth of the Palestinian Refugee Problem*. Cambridge: Cambridge University Press.

———. 1988. "The New Historiography: Israel Confronts Its Past." *Tikkun* 4 (November/December): 19–23, 99–102.

———. 1990. "The Eel and History: A Reply to Shabtai Teveth." *Tikkun* 5, 1 (March/April): 19–22, 79–86.

———. 1991. "The Origins of the Palestinian Refugee Problem." Pp. 42–56 in *New Perspectves on Israeli History: The Early Years of the State*, ed. L. J. Silberstein. New York: New York University Press.

———. 1994a. *1948 and After: Israel and The Palestinians*. Oxford: Oxford University Press.

———. 1994b. "Objective History" (in Hebrew). *Musaf Haaretz* (1 July): 40.

———. 1994c. "They Lied to Us, They Concealed, They Covered Up, Interview with Rami Tal" (in Hebrew). *Yediot Aharonot* (16 December): 29–30.

Morson, Gary, and Caryl Emerson. 1990. *Mikhael Bakhtin: Creation of a Prosaics*. Standford, Calif.: Stanford University Press.

Myers, David. 1995. *Re-Inventing the Jewish Past: European Jewish Intellectuals and the Zionist Return to History*. New York: Oxford University Press.

Nicholson, Linda, and S. Seidman, eds. 1995. *Social Postmodernism: Beyond Identity Politics*. Cambridge: Cambridge University Press.

Novick, Peter. 1988. *That Noble Dream: The "Objectivity Question" and the American Historical Profession*. Cambridge: Cambridge University Press.

Ofrat, Gideon. 1998. *One Hundred Years of Art in Israel*. Boulder, Colo.: Westview Press.

Ophir, Adi. 1992. "Introduction" (in Hebrew). *Theory and Criticism* 2 (Summer): 3–5.

————. 1994. "Introduction" (in Hebrew). *Theory and Criticism* 5 (Fall): 3.

————. 1996. "Introduction" (in Hebrew). *Theory and Criticism* 8 (Winter): 3–4.

Oppenheimer, Yohai. 1994. "The Great Right to Say No: Udan, Zach and Laor in a Political Context" (in Hebrew). *Alpayim* 10: 238–59.

Orian, Yehudit. 1986. "Anton Shammas, Israeli" (in Hebrew). *Yediot Aharonot 7 Yamim* (23 January): 26.

Orr, Akiva. 1994. *Israel: Politics, Myths and Identity Crises*. Boulder, Colo.: Pluto Press.

Oz, Amos. 1979. *Under This Blazing Light* (in Hebrew). Tel Aviv: Sifriat Poalim.

————. 1984. *In the Land of Israel*. New York: Vintage Books/Random House.

————. 1989. *The Slopes of Lebanon*. Translated by Maurie Goldberg-Bartura. New York: Harcourt, Brace, Jovanovich.

————. 1995. *Under This Blazing Light: Essays*. Translated by Nicholas de Lange. Cambridge: Cambridge University Press.

Pappe, Ilan. 1992. *The Making of the Arab–Israeli Conflict: 1947–1951*. London: I. B. Tauris.

————. 1993a. "Redemption from Judeocentrism" (in Hebrew). *Haaretz* (14 May): 8b.

————. 1993b. "There Is No History, Only Historians. Interview with Yona Hadari-Ramage" (in Hebrew). *Yediot Aharonot: Musaf LeShabat* (8 August): 31.

————. 1993c. "Haifa, Oxford, and Return" (in Hebrew). Pp. 436–460 in *Thinking It Over: Conflicts In Israeli Public Thought,* ed. Yona Hadari-Ramage. Efal: Yad Tabenkin.

————. 1993d. "The New History of the 1948 War" (in Hebrew). *Theory and Criticism* 3 (Winter): 99–114.

————. 1994a. "The Influence of Zionist Ideology on Israeli Historiography" (in Hebrew). *Davar* (15 May): 20.

————. 1994b. "A Lesson in the New History" (in Hebrew). *Musaf Haaretz* (24 June): 53–54.

————, ed. 1995a. *Jewish–Arab Relations in Mandatory Palestine: A New Approach to the Historical Research* (in Hebrew). Givat Havivah: Institute for Peace Studies.

————. 1995b. "The New History of Zionism: The Academic and Public Confrontation" (in Hebrew). *Kivvunim: A Journal of Zionism & Judaism* 8, 45 (June): 39–48.

————. 1995c. "Critique and Agenda: Post-Zionist Scholars in Israel." *History & Memory* 7, 1 (Spring/Summer): 66–90.

Pappe, Ilan, and Shlomo Swirski, eds. 1992. *The Intifada: An Inside View* (in Hebrew). Tel Aviv: Mefaresh.

Peled, Yoav. 1997a. *Cultural Autonomy and Class Struggle: The Development of The Bund's National Platform 1893–1903* (in Hebrew). Tel Aviv: The Hakibbutz Mameuhad.

————. 1997b. "The One Hundredth Year of the Bund" (in Hebrew). *Theory and Criticism* (Winter): 163–75.

Peled, Yoav, and Yagil Levi. 1993. "The Break that Never Was: Israeli Sociology Reflected through the Six Day War" (in Hebrew). *Theory and Criticism* 3: 115–28.

Pile, Steve, and Nigel Thrift, eds. 1995. *Mapping the Subject: Geographies of Cultural Transformation.* London: Routledge.

Piterberg, Gabi. 1995a. "The Nation and Its Reconteurs: Orientalism & Nationalist Historiography" (in Hebrew). *Theory and Criticism* 6 (Spring): 81–103.

———. 1995b. "The Stalinists: Nationalism, Totalitarianism and Paranoia: On the Israeli Inclination to Self-Destruction According to Aharon Megged" (in Hebrew). *Musaf HaAratz* (17 June): 44.

Porat, Dina. 1990. *The Blue and Yellow Stars of David: The Zionist Leadership in Palestine and the Holocaust, 1939–1945.* Cambridge, Mass.: Harvard University Press.

Porat, Yehoshua. 1994. "Response to Kimmerling" (in Hebrew). *Haaretz* 6.

Pred, Allan. 1997. "Hypermodernity, Identity, and the Montage Flow." Pp. 117–40 in *Space & Social Theory,* eds. J. Benko & U. Strohmayer. Oxford: Blackwell.

Rabinowitz, Dani. 1993. "Oriental Nostalgia: The Transformation of Palestinians to Israeli Arabs" (in Hebrew). *Theory and Criticism* 4 (Fall): 141–51.

Ram, Uri, ed. 1993. *Israeli Society: Critical Perspectives* (in Hebrew). Tel Aviv: Breirot.

——— .1994a. "Postzionist Ideology" (in Hebrew). *Haaretz* (8 April): 9b.

———. 1994b. "The Postzionism Debate: Five Points of Clarification" (in Hebrew). *Haaretz* (8 July): 24.

———. 1995a. *The Changing Agenda of Israeli Sociology: Theory, Ideology, and Identity.* Albany, N.Y.: SUNY Press.

———. 1995b. "The Voice of Israel and Other Voices" (in Hebrew). *Davar* (3 March): 20.

———. 1995c. "Zionist Historiography and the Invention of Modern Jewish Nationhood: The Case of Ben Zion Dinur." *History and Memory* 7, 1 (Spring/Summer): 91–124.

———. 1996. "Between Neozionism and Postzionism" (in Hebrew). *Gesher* 42: 132.

Raz-Krakotzkin, Amnon. 1993. "Exile in the Midst of Sovereignty: A Critique of 'Shelilat HaGalut' in Israeli Culture" (in Hebrew). *Theory and Criticism* 4 (Fall): 23–55.

———. 1994. "Exile in the Midst of Sovereignty: A Critique of 'Shelilat HaGalut' in Israeli Culture II" (in Hebrew). *Theory and Criticism* 5 (Fall): 113–132.

———. 1996. *The Representation of Galut: Zionist Historiography and Medieval Jewry* (in Hebrew). Ph.D Dissertation. Tel Aviv University.

———. 1997. "Historical Consciousness and Historical Responsibility" (in Hebrew). Pp. 97–134 in *Between Vision and Revision,* ed. Y. Weitz. Jerusalem.

Reinharz, Yehuda, and Anita Shapira, eds. 1996. *Essential Papers on Zionism.* New York: New York University Press.

Revel, Jacques, and Lynn Hunt, eds. 1995. *Histories: French Constructions of the Past.* New York: New Press.

Rose, Nikolas. 1996. "Identity, Genealogy, History." Pp. 128–50 in *Questions of Cultural Identity,* ed. S. Hall. Thousand Oaks, Calif.: Sage.

Rouhanna, Nadim N. 1997. *Palestinian Citizens in an Ethnic Jewish State: Identities in Conflict.* New Haven, Conn.: Yale University Press.

Rubinstein, Amnon. 1995. "The Perversion of Zionism" (in Hebrew). *Haaretz* 12 (September 12): 1b.

Said, Edward. 1983. *The World, The Text, and the Critic.* Cambridge, Mass.: Harvard University Press.

———. 1989. *Orientalism.* New York: Vintage Books.

———. 1993. *Culture and Imperialism.* New York: Alfred A. Knopf.

Savir, Uri. 1998. *The Process: 1,100 Days That Changed The Middle East.* New York: Random House.

Schmemann, Serge. 1998. "Half Century for Israelis: Many Voices in One Land." *New York Times* (6 April): 55–59, 74–78.

Schnell, Izhak. 1997. "The Emergence of an 'Urban' Life Style in the Center of Tel Aviv" (in Hebrew). Pp. 41–59 in *Mehkarei Tel Aviv-Yaffo: (Social Processes and Communal Politics),* ed. Dan Nehmias and Gila Menahem. Tel Aviv: Ramo.

Schnell, Izhak, and Iris Graicer. 1994. "Rejuvenation of Population in Tel Aviv Inner City." *The Geographical Journal* 160, 2 (July): 185–97.

———. 1996. "The Revitalization of Tel Aviv's Inner City." *Israel Affairs* 31 (Autumn): 104–27.

Schwartz, Yigal. 1993. "Israeli Fiction Prose? The Post Era" (in Hebrew). *Efes Shtaim* 3 (Winter): 7–15.

Schweid, Eliezer. 1994. "Zionism in a Postzionist Era" (in Hebrew). *Davar* (24 June): 21.

———. 1995. "The Essence and Background of Postzionism" (in Hebrew). *Gesher* 131 (Summer): 18–26.

———. 1998. "Beyond All That—Modernism, Zionism, Judaism." *Israel Studies* 1, 1 (Spring): 224–46.

Scott, Joan. 1992. "Experience." Pp. 22–40 in *Feminists Theorize the Political,* ed. Judith Butler and Joan Wallach Scott. New York: Routledge.

Segev, Tom. 1984. *1949: The First Israelis* (in Hebrew). Jerusalem: Domino Press.

———. 1986. *1949: The First Israelis.* New York: The Free Press.

———. 1993. *The Seventh Million: The Israelis and the Holocaust.* New York: Hill and Wang.

———. 1994. "The New Historians: Why Are They Angry?" (in Hebrew). *Haaretz* (16 September): 88.

Seidman, Steven, ed. 1994. *The Postmodern Turn: New Perspectives on Social Theory.* Cambridge: Cambridge University Press.

Seidman, Steven, and David Wagner, eds. 1992 *Postmodernism & Social Theory.* Cambridge, Mass.: Blackwell.

Shafir, Gershon. 1989. *Land, Labor and the Origins of the Israeli–Palestinian Conflict, 1882–1914.* Cambridge: Cambridge University Press.

———. 1996a. *Land, Labor and the origins of the Israeli–Palestinian Conflict, 1882–1914.* 2d ed. Cambridge: Cambridge University Press.

———. 1996b. "Israeli Society: A Counterview." *Israel Studies* 1, 2 (Fall): 189–213.

Shaked, Gershon. 1991. "Light and Shadow: Unity and Multiplicity" (in Hebrew). *Alpayim* 4: 113–39.

Shalev, Michael. 1992. *Labour and the Political Economy of Israel.* New York: Oxford.

———. 1996. "Time for Theory: Critical Notes on Lissak and Sternhell." *Israel Studies* 1, 2 (Fall): 170–88.

Shammas, Anton. 1980. "Under A Tree and Under A Roof: A Diary" (in Hebrew). *Iton 77* 20, 43 (March/April): 10–11. English version Shammas 1983a.

———. 1981. "The Wide Margins of Consolation" (in Hebrew). *Iton 77* (January/February): 27–44.

———. 1983a. "Diary." Pp. 29–44 in *Every Sixth Israeli,* ed. Alouph Har Even. Jerusalem: Van Leer Jerusalem Foundation.

———. 1983b. "A Black Stone on Herzl's Grave" (in Hebrew). *Iton 77* 40, 41:34.

———. 1985a. "The Meeting That Was, the Meeting That Will Not Be" (in Hebrew). *Mooznayim* 29, 3 (September): 30–32.

———. 1985b. "The Jewish New Year" (in Hebrew). *Kol Hair* (13 September): 17.

———. 1986a. *Arabesques* (in Hebrew). Tel Aviv: Am Oved.

———. 1986b. "The Guilt of the Babushka" (in Hebrew). *Politika* 5/6 (February/March): 44–45.

———. 1986c. "Interview with Naami Aviv" (in Hebrew). *Kol Hair* (4 April): 36–38.

———. 1986d. "My Battle with the Windmills of Men of the Spirit (Intellectuals)" (in Hebrew). *Mooznayim* 3: 26–27.

———. 1987a. "The Occupation According to Grossman" (in Hebrew). *Koteret Rashit* 232 (13 May): 54.

———. 1987b. "Kitsch 22: Or the Boundary of Culture" (in Hebrew). *Iton 77,* 84–85 (January–February): 24–26.

———. 1987c. "We? Who Is We?" (in Hebrew). *Politika* 17 (October): 26–27.

———. 1988a. *Arabesques: A Novel.* Translated by Vivian Eden. New York: Harper & Row.

———. 1988b. "A Stone's Throw." *New York Review of Books* (31 March): 9–10.

———. 1988c. "The Morning After." *New York Review of Books* (29 September): 47–51.

———. 1989a. "Your Worst Nightmare." *Jewish Frontier* 56, 4 (July/August): 8–10.

———. 1989b. "At Half-Mast" (in Hebrew). *Politika* 29 (September): 22–25.

———. 1991. "At Half Mast—Myths, Symbols, and Rituals of an Emerging State: A Personal Testimony of an 'Israeli Arab.'" Pp. 216–24 in *New Perspectives in Israeli History: The Early Years of the State,* ed. Laurence J. Silberstein. New York: New York University Press.

———. 1993. "The Art of Forgetting." *New York Times Magazine* (26 December): 32–33.

———. 1995a. "Palestinians in Israel: You Ain't Seen Nothin' Yet." *Journal of the International Institute* (Fall): 24–26.

———. 1995b. "The Morning After: Palestians, Israelis" (in Hebrew). Pp. 19–31 in *HaPolitika HaAravit Beyisrael,* ed. E. Rekhes and T. Yagnes. Tel Aviv: Dayan Center/Tel Aviv University.

———. 1996. "Autocartography: The Case of Palestine." Pp. 466–76 in *Geography of Identity,* ed. P. Yeager. Ann Arbor: University of Michigan Press.

Shapira, Anita. 1992. *Land & Power: The Zionist Resort to Force, 1881–1948.* Oxford: Oxford University Press.

———. 1994. "No Subject Is Taboo for a Historian (Interview with Rami Tal)" (in Hebrew). *Yediot Aharonot* (23 December): 30.

————. 1995. "Politics and Collective Memory: The Debate Over 'New Historians' in Israel." *History and Memory* 7, 1 (Spring/Summer): 9–40.

Shapira, Avraham, ed. 1970. *The Seventh Day: Soldiers Talk about the Six Day War.* New York: Charles Scribner's Sons.

Shapiro, Michael, ed. 1984a. *Language and Politics.* New York: New York University Press.

————. 1984b. "Literary Production as a Politicizing Practice." Pp. 215–53 in *Language and Politics,* ed. M. Shapiro. New York: New York University Press.

————. 1992. *Reading the Postmodern Polity: Political Theory as Textual Practice.* Minneapolis: University of Minnesota Press.

Shapiro, Raphael. 1978. "Zionism and Its Oriental Subjects, Part I. The Oriental Jews in Zionism's Dialectical Contradictions." *Khamsin* 5, 16: 5–26.

Shapiro, Yonathan. 1985. "Political Sociology in Israel: A Critical View." Pp. 6–16 in *Politics and Society in Israel,* ed. Ernest Krausz. New Brunswick, N.J.: Transaction Publishers.

Sharoni, Simona. 1995. *Gender and the Israeli–Palestinian Conflict.* Syracuse, N.Y.: Syracuse University Press.

Shavit, Yaacov. 1984. *From Hebrew to Canaanite* (in Hebrew). Jerusalem: Domino Press.

————. 1987. *The New Hebrew Nation: A Study in Israeli Heresy and Fantasy.* London: Frank Cass.

Sheffer, Gabriel. 1996. "From Israeli Hegemony to Diaspora Autonomy" (in Hebrew). *Gesher* 42, 132: 81–87.

Sheleg, Yair. 1995. "Zionism: The Battle over the Write/Righting" (in Hebrew). *Kol Hair* (6 October): 57–71.

Shimoni, Gideon. 1995. *The Zionist Ideology.* Hanover, N.H.: Brandeis University Press.

Shinhav, Yehuda, and Gideon Kunda. 1992. "The Fertile Western Imagination: How Israel's Ethnic Problem Is Represented" (in Hebrew). *Theory and Criticism* 2 (Summer): 140–41.

Shiran, Vicki. 1993. "Feminist Identity vs. Oriental Identity." Pp. 303–11 in *Calling the Equality Bluff,* ed. M. Safir and G. Swirski. New York: Teachers College Press, Columbia University.

Shlaim, Avi. 1988. *Collusion Across the Jordan.* New York: Columbia University Press.

Shmemann, Serge. 1988. "Half Century for Israelis: Many Voices in One Land." *New York Times* (6 April) A1: 12–13.

Shohat, Ella. 1988. "Sephardim in Israel: Zionism from the Standpoint of Its Jewish Victims." *Social Text* 19-20: 1–34.

————. 1989. *Israeli Cinema: East/West and the Politics of Representation.* Austin: University of Texas Press.

————. 1992. Notes on the Postcolonial. *Social Text* 31/32: 99–113.

Shohat, Urit. 1995. "Who Is a Postzionist?" (in Hebrew). *Haaretz* (25 August): 1b.

Silberman, Neil Asher. 1993. *A Prophet from Amongst You: The Life of Yigal Yadin.* Reading, Mass.: Addison-Wesley.

Silberman, Neil Asher, and David Small, eds. 1997. *The Archaeology of Israel: Constructing the Past, Interpreting the Present.* Sheffield, England: Sheffield Academic Press.

Silberstein, Laurence J. 1989. *Martin Buber's Social and Religious Thought: Alienation and the Quest for Meaning*. New York: New York University Press.
————, ed. 1991. *New Perspectives in Israeli History: The Early Years of the State*. New York: New York University Press.
————. 1994. "Others Without and Others Within: Rethinking Jewish Identity and Culture." Pp. 1–34 in *The Other in Jewish Thought and History: Constructions of Jewish Culture and Identity*, ed. L. Silberstein and R. Cohn. New York: New York University Press.
————. 1995. "Cultural Criticism, Ideology, and the Interpretation of Zionism: Toward a Post-Zionist Discourse." Pp. 325–60 in *Postmodern Interpretations of Judaism: Deconstructive and Constructive Approaches*, ed. Steven Kepnes. New York: New York University Press.
————. 1996. "Review of Uri Ram, *Changing Agenda of Israeli Sociology*." *Israel Bulletin Studies* 12, 2 (Fall): 22–24.
————. 1997. "Toward a Postzionist Discourse." Pp. 95–101 in *Judaism since Gender*, ed. Miriam Peskowitz and Laura Levitt. New York: Routledge.
Silberstein, Laurence, and Robert Cohn, eds. 1994. *The Other in Jewish Thought and History: Constructions of Jewish Culture and Identity*. New York: New York University Press.
Simon, Akiba Ernst. 1965. "Buber or Ben Gurion" (in Hebrew). *Ner* 9–10: 3–8.
Simons, John. 1995. "Feminist Coalition in Border Areas" (in Hebrew). *Theory and Criticism* 7 (Winter): 20–29.
Smart, Barry. 1992. *Modern Conditions. Postmodern Controversies*. London: Routledge.
————. 1993. *Postmodernity*. London: Routledge.
Smith, Anthony. 1986. *The Ethnic Origins of Nations*. Oxford: Blackwell Publishers.
————. 1991. *National Identity*. Reno: University of Nevada Press.
————. 1992. "The Question of Jewish Identity in a New Jewry: America since the Second World War." *Studies in Contemporary Jewry* 8: 219–33.
Smooha, Sammy. 1992. *Arabs and Jews in Israel*. 2 vol. Boulder, Colo.: Westview.
————. 1993a. "Jewish Ethnicity in Israel." Pp. 161–76 in *Whither Israel? The Domestic Challenge*, ed. K. Kyle and J. Peters.
————. 1993b. "Class, Ethnic, and National Cleavages." Pp. 309–42 in *Israeli Democracy Under Stress* (An Israel Democratic Institute Policy Study), ed. Larry Diamond and Ehud Sprinzak. Boulder, Colo.: Lynne Rienner Publishers.
Soja, Edward. 1996. *Thirdspace: Journey to Los Angeles and Other Real-and-Imagined Places*. Cambridge: Blackwell.
Somekh, Sasson. 1996. "Bridge of Creativity: On the Death of Emile Habiby" (in Hebrew). *Haaretz* (10 May): 10.
Spivak, Gayatri Chakravorty. 1990. *The Post-Colonial Critic*. Edited by S. Harasym. New York: Routledge.
Sprinzak, Ehud. 1991. *The Ascendance of Israel's Radical Right*. New York: Oxford.
Sternhell, Zeev. *The Founding Myths of Israel*. Princeton, N.J.: Princeton University Press.
Sturken, Marita. 1997. *Tangled Memories: The Vietnam War, the Aids Epidemic, and the Politics of Remembering*. Berkeley & Los Angeles: University of California Press.

Swirski, Shlomo. 1989. *Israel: The Oriental Majority.* London: Zed Books.

Terdiman, Richard. 1985. *Discourse/Counter-Discourse: The Theory and Practice of Symbolic Resistance in 19th Century France.* Ithaca, N.Y.: Cornell University Press.

———.1993. *Present and Past: Modernity & The Memory Crisis.* Ithica, N.Y.: Cornell University Press.

Teveth, Shabtai. 1989a. "The New Historians" (in Hebrew). *Haaretz* (7 April): 56.

———. 1989b. "The New Historians" (in Hebrew). *Haaretz* (14 April): 76.

———. 1989c. "The New Historians" (in Hebrew). *Haaretz* (21 April): 56.

———. 1989d. "Charging Israel with Original Sin." *Commentary* (September): 24–33.

Thrift, Nigel. 1997. "The Still Point." Pp. 124–51 in *Geographies of Resistance*, ed. Steve Pile and Michael Keith. New York: Routledge.

Trachtenberg, Graciella. 1998. "The East and Israeli Society" (in Hebrew). Pp. 33–45 in *To The East: Orientalism in the Arts in Israel.* Jerusalem: The Israel Museum.

Troen, Ilan S., and Noah Lucas, eds. 1995. *Israel: The First Decade of Independence.* Albany, N.Y.: SUNY Press.

Trouillot, Michel-Rolph. 1995. *Silencing the Past: Power and the Production of History.* Boston: Beacon Press.

Tsahor, Zeev. 1994. "Colonialist or Colonizer" (in Hebrew). *Haaretz* (22 December).

Turner, Graeme. 1990. *British Cultural Studies: An Introduction.* New York: Routledge.

VanTeefelen, Toni. 1981. "Tragic Heroes and Victims in Zionist Ideology." *Khamsin* 9: 117–135.

Veyne, Paul. 1997. "Foucault Revolutionizes History." Pp. 146–82 in *Foucault & His Interlocutors,* ed. and introduced by Arnold I. Davidson. Chicago: University of Chicago Press.

Vital, David. 1975. *The Origins of Zionism.* Oxford: Clarendon Press.

———. 1988. *Zionism: The Formative Years.* Oxford: Clarendon Press.

Weimann, Gabriel. 1995. "Zapping in the Holyland: Coping with Multi-channel T.V. in Israel." *Journal of Communication* 45: 97–103.

———. 1996. "Cable Comes to the Holy Land: The Impact of Cable T.V. on Israeli Viewers." *Journal of Broadcasting & Electronic Media* 40: 243–57.

Weitz, Yehiam, ed. 1997. *Between Vision and Revision: One Hundred Years of Zionist Historiography* (in Hebrew). Jerusalem: Merkaz Zalman Shazar.

White, Hayden. 1973. *Metahistory: The Historical Imagination in Nineteenth-Century Europe.* Baltimore: Johns Hopkins University Press.

———. 1978. *Tropics of Discourse: Essays in Cultural Criticism.* Baltimore: Johns Hopkins University Press.

———. 1987. *The Content of the Form: Narrative Discourse & Historical Representation.* Baltimore: Johns Hopkins University Press.

Williams, Patrick, and Laura Chrisman, eds. 1994. *Colonial Discourse & Post-Colonial Theory: A Reader.* New York: Columbia University Press.

Williams, Raymond. 1977. *Marxism and Literature.* Oxford: Oxford University Press.

Wittig, Monique. 1983. "The Point of View: Universal or Particular?" *Feminist Issues,* (2): 63–69.

Woocher, Jonathan. 1986. *Sacred Survival: The Civil Religion of American Jews*. Indianapolis: Indiana University Press.

Yeager, Patricia, ed. 1996. *The Geography of Identity*. Ann Arbor: University of Michigan Press.

Yehoshua, A. B. 1985. "The Guilt of the Left" (An Interview with Yaron London) (in Hebrew). *Politika* 4 (Novermber–December): 8–13.

———. 1986. "An Answer to Anton" (in Hebrew). *Hair* (31 January): 22–23.

———. 1995. "Israeli Identity in a Time of Peace: Prospects and Perils." *Tikkun* 10, 6 (November/December): 34–40, 94.

Yehoshua, B. Z., and Aaron Kedar, eds. 1978. *Zionist Ideology and Politics* (in Hebrew). Jerusalem: Zalmar Shazar Center.

Yizhaki, Yedidyah. 1993. "A Thousand Nights in Hof Akhziv" (in Hebrew). *Iton 77* 165 (October): 12–13, 50.

Young, Iris. 1992. "Five Faces of Oppression." Pp. 174–95 in *Rethinking Power*, ed. T. E. Waternburg. Albany: SUNY Press.

Young, Robert. 1990. *White Mythologies: Writing History and the West*. New York: Routledge.

———. 1995. *Colonial Desire: Hybridity in Theory, Culture, Race*. New York: Routledge.

Yovel, Yirmiyahu. 1994. "Response to Ilan Pappe's Article on New Historians" (in Hebrew). *Musaf Haaretz* 7/8: 6.

Zakim, Eric. 1998. "Palimpsests of National Identity: Israeli Culture and the End of the American Century." *Shofar* 16, 2 (Winter): 48–69.

Zalmona, Yigal. 1998. "To the East: To the East? The East in Israeli Art" (in Hebrew). Pp. ix–xv, 47–93 in *To the East: Orientalism in the Arts in Israel*. Jerusalem: The Israel Museum.

Zamir, Hamutal. 1995. "Love of the Homeland and the Discourse of the Deaf: One Poem of Esther Raab's and Its Masculine Reception" (in Hebrew). *Theory on Criticism* 7 (Winter): 125–145.

Zerubavel, Yael. 1995. *Recovered Roots: Collective Memory and the Making of Israeli National Tradition*. Chicago: University of Chicago Press.

Zipperstein, Steven J. 1993. *Elusive Prophet: Ahad Haam and the Origins of Zionism*. Berkeley: University of California Press.